C000246275

Because Your People Matter

a playbook for managers,
entrepreneurs and leaders

John Berry and Sue Berry
TimelessTime Ltd
www.timelesstime.co.uk

Grosvenor House
Publishing Limited

This book is published by
Grosvenor House Publishing Ltd
Link House, 140 The Broadway,
Tolworth, Surrey KT6 7HT
www.grosvenorhousepublishing.co.uk

A ClP record for this book
is available from the British Library

ISBN 978-1-80381-355-4
eBook ISBN 978-1-80381-356-1

Table of Contents

PREFACE TO THE THIRD EDITION.. xix

PREFACE TO THE SECOND EDITION xxiii

FIGURES... xxix

REFLECTIONS... xxxiii

1   ORGANISING PEOPLE... 1

    1.1   INCEPTION 1

        1.1.1   About management 1
        1.1.2   Going into management.. 2
        1.1.3   The firm... 3
        1.1.4   The manager 3
        1.1.5   Why firms succeed.. 3
        1.1.6   The focus.. 3

    1.2   THE BASICS OF A FIRM 4

        1.2.1   Money in and money out.. 5
        1.2.2   Consumables.. 5
        1.2.3   Technology.. 5
        1.2.4   People 6
        1.2.5   Managers 6
        1.2.6   Evolving the firm... 6
        1.2.7   Desirable outcomes... 6

    1.3   DEFINING MANAGEMENT.. 7

        1.3.1   Manager as commander 8
        1.3.2   Manager as leader.. 8
        1.3.3   Manager as entrepreneur and businessperson 8
        1.3.4   Alternatives to management.. 9

    1.4   DIFFERING ROLES 9

        1.4.1   Shareholder... 9
        1.4.2   Director and Managing Director... 9
        1.4.3   Supplier.. 10
        1.4.4   Employee/worker... 10
        1.4.5   Role confusion.. 11
        1.4.6   Managers, employees, and suppliers..................................... 11

    1.5   BASIC BUSINESS TYPES AND STRUCTURES 11

        1.5.1   Issues in managing real firms 12
        1.5.2   Nuclear firm... 12
        1.5.3   Dispersed firm... 12
        1.5.4   Distributed firm... 13

1.6   EXTENDING BUSINESS TO THE INTERNATIONAL...................................... 13
       1.6.1   Exporting 14
       1.6.2   Using foreign workers.. 14
       1.6.3   Issues in extending to the international 14

1.7   BUILDING STRATEGY 14
       1.7.1   Simple strategy.. 15
       1.7.2   Five ws and an h 15
       1.7.3   Strategy and the balanced scorecard................................. 15
       1.7.4   Acting on strategy 16
       1.7.5   People and strategy 16

1.8   A SYSTEM THAT DOES SOMETHING 17
       1.8.1   Introducing systems modelling 17
       1.8.2   'As is' and 'to be' models 18
       1.8.3   Concepts as technology and people.................................... 19

1.9   MONEY AS THE CENTRAL MEASURE 19
       1.9.1   The profit motive 19
       1.9.2   Pay... 20
       1.9.3   Pensions... 20
       1.9.4   Benefits.. 20
       1.9.5   Training as investment 20
       1.9.6   Taxes 21

1.10   INSTRUCTING PEOPLE TO DO WORK 21
       1.10.1   Issuing instruction 21
       1.10.2   Work instruction documents... 21
       1.10.3   Expected behaviour.. 22
       1.10.4   Procedures versus training 22

1.11   COMMON MISTAKES THAT MANAGERS MAKE 23
       1.11.1   Avoiding getting close.. 23
       1.11.2   Not learning the trade.. 24
       1.11.3   Not delegating.. 24
       1.11.4   Trusting but not verifying... 24
       1.11.5   Dithering.. 25

1.12   DOING MANAGEMENT 25
       1.12.1   Interventions 26
       1.12.2   Evolution.. 27
       1.12.3   Mutations... 27
       1.12.4   Searching for excellence.. 28

1.13   CHAPTER SUMMARY 28

2   LEADING PEOPLE 31

2.1   INTRODUCTION TO LEADERSHIP 31
       2.1.1   Defining leadership.. 31
       2.1.2   Great leaders 31
       2.1.3   Are leaders born or bread? 32
       2.1.4   Core idea – influencing.. 32

2.2   THE LANGUAGE OF LEADERSHIP 33

     2.2.1   *Leader* 33
     2.2.2   *Follower* 33
     2.2.3   *Leadership* 33
     2.2.4   *Team/group* 33
     2.2.5   *Intervention* 34
     2.2.6   *Outcome* 34

2.3   THE NATURE OF LEADERSHIP 34

     2.3.1   *The leader's influence on motivation* 34
     2.3.2   *The leader's influence on jobs* 35
     2.3.3   *The leader's influence on outcomes* 35
     2.3.4   *Leadership and technology* 36
     2.3.5   *Nature of contracts* 37
     2.3.6   *Necessary self-efficacy* 37

2.4   LEADERSHIP THEORY 38

     2.4.1   *The dyadic theory of leadership* 38
     2.4.2   *Roadblock removal* 38
     2.4.3   *Goal illumination* 39
     2.4.4   *Empowerment and delegation* 39
     2.4.5   *Participation* 39

2.5   LEADERSHIP IN PRACTICE 40

     2.5.1   *Doing leadership* 40
     2.5.2   *Trying something new* 41
     2.5.3   *Priming the pump* 42

2.6   LEADERSHIP APPROACHES 42

     2.6.1   *Professional leadership* 42
     2.6.2   *Procedural leadership* 43
     2.6.3   *Transformational leadership* 43
     2.6.4   *Transactional leadership* 44
     2.6.5   *Contingent leadership* 44
     2.6.6   *Leadership and culture* 45

2.7   LEADERSHIP STYLES 45

     2.7.1   *Directive* 46
     2.7.2   *Non-directive* 46
     2.7.3   *Laissez faire* 46
     2.7.4   *Deciding which style to use* 47

2.8   ALTERNATIVES TO LEADERSHIP 47

     2.8.1   *Distributed leadership* 47
     2.8.2   *Self-managed teams* 48

2.9   LEADERSHIP AND MANAGEMENT 49

     2.9.1   *The leader in context* 49
     2.9.2   *Reporting structures and numbers* 49
     2.9.3   *Functional and domain leadership* 50

2.9.4   Making leadership work 51
2.9.5   Effective team building 51
2.9.6   Leading virtual teams 51
2.9.7   Where managers fail at leadership 52
        2.9.7.1   Leader too detached 52
        2.9.7.2   Leader too close 52
        2.9.7.3   Leader not adjusting to online working 52

2.10 LEADER-MANAGER DEVELOPMENT 53
2.10.1 The need for technical competence 53
2.10.2 Personality of a leader 54
2.10.3 Intelligence of a leader 55
2.10.4 Developing leaders 55

2.11 CHAPTER SUMMARY 55

3   GAINING SERVICES 57

3.1   WORKING RELATIONSHIPS 57
3.1.1   Self-employed 57
3.1.2   Workers 58
        3.1.2.1   Casual workers 58
        3.1.2.2   Agency workers 58
        3.1.2.3   Freelance workers 58
        3.1.2.4   Seasonal workers 58
3.1.3   Employees 59
        3.1.3.1   Fixed term contract 59
        3.1.3.2   Permanent contract 59
        3.1.3.3   Zero-hours contract 59
3.1.4   Determining a person's employment status 59
3.1.5   The duck test 61
        3.1.5.1   Mutuality of obligation 61
        3.1.5.2   Control 61
        3.1.5.3   Personal service 61
        3.1.5.4   Other considerations 61

3.2   DETERMINING WHO'S NEEDED 62
3.2.1   Modelling the firm and its people 62
3.2.2   Defining who's needed 64
3.2.3   The recruitment and selection life cycle 64

3.3   SOURCING PEOPLE 66
3.3.1   Agencies 66
3.3.2   Online recruitment 67
3.3.3   Headhunting 67
3.3.4   Apprentices and graduates 68
3.3.5   Other sources and strategies 68

3.4   CHARACTERISING PEOPLE..68
    3.4.1   Intelligence *68*
    3.4.2   Personality..*69*
    3.4.3   Competencies..*70*
    3.4.4   Behaviours, attitudes, beliefs and values............................*71*
    3.4.5   Preferences..*71*
    3.4.6   Employee self-efficacy..*72*
    3.4.7   Growth needs strength *72*

3.5   INTERVIEWING AND SELECTION...73
    3.5.1   Intelligence tests *73*
    3.5.2   Personality profile..*73*
    3.5.3   Work sample tests...*74*
    3.5.4   Interviews...*74*
    3.5.5   Planning and doing interviews *74*
    3.5.6   Interviewing and testing in lockdown *75*
    3.5.7   Making decisions about people...*76*
    3.5.8   Pre-employment screening...*76*
    3.5.9   Issues in testing...*76*
    3.5.10 Mixing internal and external recruitment...........................*77*

3.6   MAKING JOB OFFERS 77
    3.6.1   Discussing offers by telephone *78*
    3.6.2   Negotiating the deal..*78*
    3.6.3   Confirming the offer...*79*

3.7   OTHER ISSUES IN RECRUITMENT AND SELECTION...............................80
    3.7.1   Overcoming roadblocks in recruitment..............................*80*
    3.7.2   Compromise and trade-offs...*80*
    3.7.3   Ensuring candidates take up posts.....................................*80*
    3.7.4   Inducting new staff...*81*
    3.7.5   Assessing the effectiveness of recruitment and selection....................*81*

3.8   RETAINING STAFF 81
    3.8.1   Why employees quit *81*
    3.8.2   Retaining staff..*82*

3.9   RECRUITING VOLUNTEERS 83
    3.9.1   Why volunteers volunteer...*83*
    3.9.2   Retaining volunteers *85*

3.10 CHAPTER SUMMARY 86

4   STARTING OPERATIONS **89**

4.1   PEOPLE AND WORK 89
    4.1.1   What work is *89*
    4.1.2   Work and contracts *90*
    4.1.3   The theory of the firm...*90*
    4.1.4   Differing employee types *91*
    4.1.5   Practical implications of the theory...................................*92*

      4.1.6   Systematising the firm *93*
      4.1.7   Building a company system *93*
  4.2   INSTRUCTING PEOPLE TO DO WORK 94
      4.2.1   The role of the manager *94*
      4.2.2   The employee-employer relationship *94*
      4.2.3   The supplier-firm relationship *95*
      4.2.4   Breaking work into parts *95*
      4.2.5   Training versus processes *96*
      4.2.6   Instructing employees and suppliers *97*
  4.3   PEOPLE AND TECHNOLOGY 98
      4.3.1   Capability and competitive advantage *98*
      4.3.2   Defining technology by its function *98*
      4.3.3   Defining people by their competencies *99*
      4.3.4   Balancing people and technology *99*
      4.3.5   Codifying knowledge in technology *99*
      4.3.6   Implementing change through technology *100*
      4.3.7   The impact of technology on people *100*
  4.4   PEOPLE AND QUALITY 101
      4.4.1   Defining quality *101*
      4.4.2   On what does quality depend? *101*
      4.4.3   Designing quality in to work *101*
      4.4.4   The role of peers *102*
      4.4.5   Teambuilding and cohesion through quality *102*
  4.5   PATTERNS OF WORK ORGANISATION 103
      4.5.1   Temporal nature of work *103*
      4.5.2   Spatial nature of work *104*
      4.5.3   Achieving manager control *104*
  4.6   WORKING FROM HOME 105
      4.6.1   The new office *105*
      4.6.2   Core concept *105*
      4.6.3   Space and physical arrangement *105*
      4.6.4   Contracts, time, and money *106*
      4.6.5   Management *106*
      4.6.6   Confidentiality *106*
      4.6.7   Permissions *106*
      4.6.8   Future trends *107*
  4.7   BRAND BUILDING 108
      4.7.1   Determining how you want to look *108*
      4.7.2   Identifying touch points *108*
  4.8   INNOVATING TO STAY AHEAD 109
      4.8.1   Implementing innovation practice *110*
      4.8.2   Structuring for innovation *110*
      4.8.3   Formal innovation *110*
      4.8.4   Innovation climate *110*

4.9   SUSTAINING BUSINESS 111
     4.9.1   Strategy and sustainability...112
     4.9.2   Identifying assets...113
     4.9.3   Assessing threats 113
     4.9.4   Determining risks...113
     4.9.5   Implementing controls 113
     4.9.6   Auditing...114

4.10   CHAPTER SUMMARY 114

5   MANAGING PEOPLE...117

5.1   INTRODUCING 117

5.2   PERFORMANCE...117
     5.2.1   Feedback-driven management...117
     5.2.2   Performance dependencies...118
     5.2.3   Personal characteristics 120
     5.2.4   Focus on outcomes...120
     5.2.5   Specifying outcomes in job descriptions..120
     5.2.6   Specifying outcomes in objectives..120

5.3   JOB DESIGN...121
     5.3.1   Jobs in firms...121
     5.3.2   What people look for in a job..122
     5.3.3   What makes a satisfying job...122
     5.3.4   Job crafting..123

5.4   COMMITMENT...123
     5.4.1   What is commitment?..123
     5.4.2   Why commitment is important 124
     5.4.3   Determinants of commitment..124
     5.4.4   Practical things to get commitment 124
     5.4.5   Crass management breaks commitment...125

5.5   MOTIVATION 125
     5.5.1   What is motivation? 125
     5.5.2   About motives and motivators...126
     5.5.3   About motivators and demotivators..126
     5.5.4   Managing unmotivated employees..127

5.6   ENGAGEMENT 128
     5.6.1   What is engagement? 128
     5.6.2   How engagement fits in the performance model....................................128
     5.6.3   Why engagement is important...129
     5.6.4   Practical things to do to get engagement...129
     5.6.5   Assessing engagement..129

5.7   CULTURE 130
     5.7.1   What is culture? 130
     5.7.2   Culture and the trading firm 130
     5.7.3   Assessing national culture 130

  5.7.4   Expressing organisational culture *131*
  5.7.5   Managing culture *131*

  5.8   EMOTIONS 132

  5.8.1   Understanding emotions *132*
  5.8.2   How emotions work *133*
  5.8.3   The laws of emotion *133*
  5.8.4   Managing emotions *134*

  5.9   POWER 134

  5.9.1   Defining power *134*
  5.9.2   Exploiting power *134*
  5.9.3   Forms of power *135*
  5.9.4   Power dominance *135*
  5.9.5   S-power benefits *135*
  5.9.6   Turning from the Dark Side *136*

  5.10 GROUPS 136

  5.10.1 About teams and groups *136*
  5.10.2 Forming groups for work *137*
  5.10.3 Basic ideas about people in groups *137*
  5.10.4 Employees as cooperative colleagues *138*

  5.11 BIAS 138

  5.11.1 Defining bias *139*
  5.11.2 Countering bias *139*
  5.11.3 Examples of bias *140*
  5.11.4 Typical manager bias *141*
  5.11.5 Prejudice *142*
  5.11.6 Equality *142*
  5.11.7 Gender inequality *143*

  5.12 CHAPTER SUMMARY 144

6   SETTING OBJECTIVES... 147

  6.1   INTRODUCTION 147

  6.2   CONCEPT OF PERFORMANCE IMPROVEMENT 148

  6.2.1   Basic ideas about performance appraisal *148*
  6.2.2   Maintaining performance *149*
  6.2.3   Growing performance *150*
  6.2.4   Measurement and metrics of performance *150*
  6.2.5   Role of the manager in performance improvement *151*

  6.3   OBJECTIVES, MOTIVATION, AND PERFORMANCE 151

  6.3.1   Basics of motivation *151*
  6.3.2   About people and objectives *152*
  6.3.3   About money and motivation *153*

  6.4   SETTING OBJECTIVES 153

  6.4.1   About objectives and people *154*
  6.4.2   Role of objectives in business *154*

	6.4.3	Setting organisational objectives	155
	6.4.4	Setting group objectives	156
	6.4.5	Setting personal objectives	156
	6.4.6	Involving employees in setting objectives	157

6.5   DEFINING PERFORMANCE 157

| | 6.5.1 | Performance dependencies | 157 |
| | 6.5.2 | Performance in an evolving environment | 158 |

6.6   APPRAISING PERFORMANCE 158

	6.6.1	The use of rating	158
	6.6.2	Rating performance	158
	6.6.3	Doing rating	159
	6.6.4	Multi-rater systems	160

6.7   APPRAISAL AND PERSONAL DEVELOPMENT 161

| | 6.7.1 | The right person in the right job | 161 |

6.8   SETTING OBJECTIVES AND DOING PERFORMANCE APPRAISAL 162

	6.8.1	Objectives and appraisal meetings	163
	6.8.2	Process pitfalls	164
	6.8.3	Power in performance appraisal	165
	6.8.4	Dos and don'ts of objectives	166
	6.8.5	Evolving the process	167

6.9   CHAPTER SUMMARY 168

7   MANAGING RELATIONS 171

7.1   THE EMPLOYER-EMPLOYEE RELATIONSHIP 171

	7.1.1	Economic and psychological relationships	171
	7.1.2	Understanding emotions and disputes	172
	7.1.3	Acting to defuse conflict	173

7.2   THE CENTRAL ROLE OF THE MANAGER 173

	7.2.1	Defining discipline and grievance	173
	7.2.2	Discipline and grievance day to day	174
	7.2.3	When relations turn sour	174
	7.2.4	The manager as prime actor	174
	7.2.5	Understanding the perspectives of the parties	175

7.3   SETTING THE EMPLOYMENT FOUNDATION 175

	7.3.1	Legal basis of the relationship	175
	7.3.2	Economic and psychological contracts	176
	7.3.3	Role of the staff handbook	176
	7.3.4	Role of policies and procedures	177
	7.3.5	Changing the foundations	177

7.4   MANAGING DISCIPLINE AND PERFORMANCE 177

	7.4.1	Won't do versus can't do	178
	7.4.2	The behaviour expected	178
	7.4.3	The capability expected	178
	7.4.4	Formal and informal management	179

7.4.5   Using the various policies and procedures 179
7.4.6   Role of investigations 180
7.4.7   Disciplinary and performance processes 180
7.4.8   Making decisions and handing down sanctions 181
7.4.9   Escalation in disciplinary management 181
7.4.10 The appeals process 182

7.5   MANAGING GRIEVANCES 182
7.5.1   Why grievances arise 182
7.5.2   Basic grievance process 182
7.5.3   The role of investigations 182
7.5.4   Grievance meetings 183
7.5.5   Making decisions and appeals 183
7.5.6   When grievance leads to tribunal 183

7.6   MANAGING BULLYING AND HARASSMENT 183
7.6.1   Definitions of bullying and harassment 183
7.6.2   How attitudes have changed 184
7.6.3   Using relevant procedures 184
7.6.4   Investigating bullying and harassment 185
7.6.5   Endemic cultures of bullying 185

7.7   THE ROLE OF MEDIATION 185
7.7.1   Defining mediation 185
7.7.2   The role of the manager 186
7.7.3   Selecting mediators 186
7.7.4   The process of mediation 186
7.7.5   If mediation fails 186

7.8   PRACTICAL DISCIPLINARY AND GRIEVANCE TOOLS 187
7.8.1   Suspension 187
7.8.2   Investigations 187
7.8.3   Processes in context 188
7.8.4   Practical sanctions 189

7.9   WHAT TO EXPECT FROM A TRIBUNAL 189
7.9.1   Early conciliation 189
7.9.2   The tribunal process 190
7.9.3   Attempts to resolve before the tribunal decision 190
7.9.4   Completing documents for the tribunal hearing 190
7.9.5   Judicial review 190
7.9.6   Preparing managers 190
7.9.7   Appointing counsel 191
7.9.8   Possible outcomes 191
7.9.9   Ranges of settlements 191

7.10   CHAPTER SUMMARY 191

8   DEVELOPING PEOPLE 193
8.1   THE LOGIC OF STAFF DEVELOPMENT 193
8.1.1   Development decisions 193
8.1.2   Capability and required outcomes 194

8.1.3	*Can't do versus won't do*	*194*
8.1.4	*Business case for developing employees*	*195*
	8.1.4.1 Developing to stand still	195
	8.1.4.2 Developing to grow	195
	8.1.4.3 Developing as an employee benefit	195
	8.1.4.4 Developing to exploit opportunity	195
8.1.5	*Development benefits*	*196*

8.2 THE LANGUAGE OF DEVELOPMENT 196

8.2.1	*Development driving performance improvement*	*196*
8.2.2	*Performance*	*197*
8.2.3	*Excellence*	*197*
8.2.4	*Competency*	*197*
8.2.5	*Behaviour*	*197*
8.2.6	*Experience*	*198*
8.2.7	*Intervention*	*198*
8.2.8	*Training transfer*	*198*

8.3 THE COMPETENCIES AND BEHAVIOURS NEEDED 198

8.3.1	*Using strategy as driver*	*198*
8.3.2	*Constructing jobs from the concept model*	*199*
8.3.3	*Institutional and organisational standards*	*199*
8.3.4	*Determining what development is needed*	*200*
8.3.5	*Standardised method for determining need*	*200*
8.3.6	*Defining the necessary mastery*	*200*

8.4 MATCHING THE NEEDS OF CAREER AND JOB 201

8.4.1	*The notion of employee careers*	*201*
8.4.2	*Today's careers*	*201*
8.4.3	*Conflict between needs and wants*	*202*
8.4.4	*So, who develops the people?*	*202*
8.4.5	*Attitude by worker type*	*202*
8.4.6	*Supporting career changes within the firm*	*204*

8.5 THE DEVELOPMENT PROCESS 205

8.5.1	*Progress from need to satisfaction*	*205*
8.5.2	*Building personal competency frameworks*	*205*
8.5.3	*Building organisation-wide competency frameworks*	*206*
8.5.4	*The continuum of development*	*207*

8.6 THE CONCEPT OF TALENT MANAGEMENT 207

8.6.1	*Who and what is talent?*	*207*
8.6.2	*The talent management process*	*207*
8.6.3	*Centralised talent management*	*208*

8.7 PRACTICAL DEVELOPMENT INTERVENTIONS 209

8.7.1	*Self-directed learning*	*209*
8.7.2	*Effective instruction*	*209*
8.7.3	*Computer-based training*	*210*
8.7.4	*Simulated work*	*210*
8.7.5	*Traditional classroom training*	*210*

   8.7.6 One-on-one interventions *210*

   8.7.7 Evolved opportunities *211*

 8.8 GETTING GOOD AT DEVELOPMENT *211*

   8.8.1 Overarching approach and method *211*

   8.8.2 Measuring successful development *212*

   8.8.3 Optimising training transfer *213*

 8.9 CHAPTER SUMMARY *214*

9 MANAGING WELLBEING *217*

 9.1 WELLBEING *217*

   9.1.1 Defining wellbeing *217*

   9.1.2 Why people work *218*

   9.1.3 Basic human needs and the link to wellbeing *218*

   9.1.4 Role of the manager in wellbeing *218*

   9.1.5 Resilience and coping *219*

 9.2 POOR WELLBEING *219*

   9.2.1 Genetics, childhood, and wellbeing *219*

   9.2.2 Events, environment, and wellbeing *220*

   9.2.3 Job conditions *221*

   9.2.4 Job security and change *221*

 9.3 MEASURING WELLBEING *222*

   9.3.1 Hedonic wellbeing *223*

   9.3.2 Eudaimonic wellbeing *223*

   9.3.3 Using a scorecard to manage wellbeing *223*

 9.4 STRESS *224*

   9.4.1 Workloads, pressures and performance *224*

   9.4.2 HSE model of management effectiveness *225*

   9.4.3 Practical action to manage stress *226*

 9.5 BURNOUT *227*

   9.5.1 When the machine crashes *227*

   9.5.2 Front line versus defence *227*

 9.6 ABSENCE *228*

   9.6.1 The nature of absence *228*

   9.6.2 Absence management approach *229*

   9.6.3 Spotting trends *229*

   9.6.4 Comparing absences *229*

   9.6.5 Practical absence management *230*

   9.6.6 Managing long term absence *230*

 9.7 INTOXICANTS *230*

   9.7.1 Tobacco *230*

   9.7.2 Drugs or alcohol *231*

   9.7.3 Managing drugs or alcohol at work *231*

9.8   BENEFITS AS MITIGATIONS...231
        9.8.1   Wellbeing-related benefits...232
        9.8.2   Commitment-building benefits...................................232
        9.8.3   Engagement-building benefits....................................232
9.9   FLEXIBILITY AND THE WORKHOME 233
        9.9.1   History...233
        9.9.2   Pressures...233
        9.9.3   Workhomes..234
9.10   HEALTH AND SAFETY 234
        9.10.1 Risk in work activities..235
        9.10.2 Nature of accidents and incidents............................235
        9.10.3 Integrated management process................................236
        9.10.4 Safe patterns of work...237
        9.10.5 Leading a safe working environment.........................238
9.11   CHAPTER SUMMARY 239

10 PAYING PEOPLE...241
10.1   THE IDEA OF A WAGE 241
        10.1.1 A brief history of pay...241
        10.1.2 Pay and contracts 242
        10.1.3 Paying employees, workers and suppliers..................242
        10.1.4 Concepts of fairness...242
        10.1.5 Who gets paid what and why 243
        10.1.6 Pay differences..244
        10.1.7 The way people think about pay...............................244
10.2   PAY AND THE LAW 245
        10.2.1 Pay and contract terms and conditions 245
        10.2.2 Discrimination..245
        10.2.3 Minimum wage..246
        10.2.4 Employee rights 246
10.3   STATUTORY PAYMENTS, DEDUCTIONS AND TAX...................246
        10.3.1 Social security...246
        10.3.2 Income tax..246
        10.3.3 Pensions...247
        10.3.4 Benefits in kind..247
        10.3.5 SMP, SAP, SPP and SSP..247
10.4   BASICS OF PAY SYSTEMS...247
        10.4.1 Idea of a labour market..248
        10.4.2 Pay policy 248
        10.4.3 Spot pay systems 248
        10.4.4 Banded pay systems 249
        10.4.5 Lifecycle of pay systems...251

        10.4.6 Performance-based pay *251*
        10.4.7 Giving employees a share *252*
   10.5 SIZING JOBS AND SETTING PAY *252*
        10.5.1 What gives a job a value? *253*
        10.5.2 Formal job evaluation *253*
               10.5.2.1 Job ranking *253*
               10.5.2.2 Pairwise comparison *253*
               10.5.2.3 Job classification *254*
               10.5.2.4 Rate factor *254*
               10.5.2.5 Points factor *255*
        10.5.3 What makes a big job *256*
   10.6 PAY IRREGULARITIES *256*
        10.6.1 Pay by age and experience *256*
        10.6.2 Managing scarcity *256*
        10.6.3 Managing anomalies *257*
        10.6.4 Negotiating pay *257*
        10.6.5 Bias and discrimination in pay *257*
        10.6.6 Directors' pay *258*
        10.6.7 Pay transparency *258*
        10.6.8 Managing an international workforce *258*
        10.6.9 Cost of living and corresponding salaries *259*
   10.7 COMPANY SICK PAY *260*
        10.7.1 Background *260*
        10.7.2 Typical absence curve *261*
        10.7.3 About income protection insurance *262*
   10.8 THE BENEFIT OF BENEFITS *263*
        10.8.1 Why give benefits? *263*
               10.8.1.1 Removal expenses *263*
               10.8.1.2 Cars and vans *264*
               10.8.1.3 Private medical cover *264*
               10.8.1.4 Income protection and sickness *264*
               10.8.1.5 Private pensions *264*
               10.8.1.6 Other assorted benefits *264*
   10.9 IDEA OF TOTAL REWARD *265*
        10.9.1 Concept of total reward *265*
        10.9.2 Attempting links to motivation *265*
        10.9.3 Aligning reward to the business *265*
        10.9.4 Idiosyncratic employment deals *266*
   10.10 CHAPTER SUMMARY *266*

11 **MAKING CHANGE** *269*
   11.1 INTRODUCING CHANGE *269*
        11.1.1 Change as strategy *269*
        11.1.2 Defining the required outcome *270*

11.1.3 Change as reaction to events 271
11.1.4 Pressure for sustainability 271
11.1.5 Role of productivity... 271
11.1.6 OD as the central change management tool................... 272
11.1.7 Variables in change... 274
11.1.8 Arguments against a planned approach............................ 274

11.2 UNDERSTANDING CHANGE.. 275
11.2.1 The concept of change 275
11.2.2 A dynamic model of change 275
11.2.3 A static force-field model 276
11.2.4 Change is like the wind... 277
11.2.5 A systems model of change... 277

11.3 DETERMINING WHAT TO CHANGE... 278
11.3.1 Forecasting with Delphi 279
11.3.2 The role of modelling in change... 279
11.3.3 Change examples 282
11.3.3.1 Reacting to a changing market 282
11.3.3.2 Implementing growth 283

11.4 ISSUES IN CHANGE 284
11.4.1 Overcoming inertia.. 285
11.4.2 Winning the mandate for change 285
11.4.3 Winning people over for change 285

11.5 THE EFFECT OF TIME 286
11.5.1 Effect of experience on outcomes...................................... 286
11.5.2 Trends in change 287
11.5.3 Forms of change plans.. 288

11.6 PRACTICAL CHANGE... 289
11.6.1 Changing people.. 289
11.6.2 Change and contracts.. 290
11.6.3 Changing technology... 291

11.7 THE PROCESS OF CHANGE... 292
11.7.1 Change in tangible systems... 292
11.7.2 Change in messy systems 293
11.7.3 Leading change.. 294
11.7.4 Using change agents.. 294

11.8 TRANSFER AS THE ULTIMATE CHANGE.. 295

11.9 WHAT GIVES A FIRM A VALUE? 295
11.9.1 Ability to sustain profits 295
11.9.2 Capability 296
11.9.3 Markets, products, and people.. 296

11.10 CHAPTER SUMMARY 297

12   BECOMING A MANAGER... *299*

    12.1   STARTING FROM IGNORANCE *299*

    12.2   BECOMING AN EXPERT 300

    12.3   LEVELS OF MANAGER COMPETENCE 302

    12.4   DEFINING MANAGEMENT COMPETENCE 302

    12.5   EXCELLING AT THE LITTLE THINGS 305

    12.6   SCIENTIFIC METHOD AS CENTRAL COMPETENCY............................ 307

    12.7   THE NOTION OF PERFORMANCE IN MANAGEMENT 308

    12.8   THE NEED FOR OUTCOMES 310

    12.9   GETTING THE SENSE THAT YOU'RE AN EXPERT............................... 311

    12.10 WORKING IN A MANAGEMENT TEAM 312

    12.11 PASSING ON YOUR ART 314

    12.12 THE MANAGING DIRECTOR 314

    12.13 AUTHOR'S STORIES.. 315
            12.13.1 Sue Berry... 315
            12.13.2 John Berry.. 316

    12.14 CHAPTER SUMMARY.. 317

BIBLIOGRAPHY 319

INDEX... **324**

Preface to the Third Edition

The first edition of *Because Your People Matter* was published in early 2019. The second edition followed in August 2020. Since then, much has happened. In business and employment, the World is arguably a very different place. This third edition covers the skills and knowledge necessary to understand and act in response to the many new pressures on managers.

The Covid pandemic struck in early 2020, with the first national lockdown in March. Wellbeing took centre stage, focussed on NHS and care sector staff, teachers, and a raft of 'essential workers' like couriers and supermarket drivers. Everyone watching social media and the press suddenly understood who earned what, with what risk, and for what effort expended. Of course, there was nothing completely new in what we saw (public sectors had been underfunded for years and we'd always known that certain 'gig' jobs were dire) – but the pandemic highlighted existing strains. As we exit the panic stage and now 'learn to live with Covid', those strains play out in stressed employee relations. The public now knows much of the management jargon like 'redundancies' and 'gig economy' through repetition daily, and they understand the variables of productivity and some of the sensitivities in supply.

As Covid subsided, at least for the time being, what emerged was a significant shift in employee thinking. Around 50% of employees had worked from home at the height of the pandemic, enjoying the experience, reducing commuting costs and recovering up to six hours a day of wasted personal time. Possibly as a result, many employees questioned what working life had been about pre-Covid. Many re-assessed what they wanted from work in the future. Post Covid, managers found that employees were quitting in significant numbers. In the USA the phenomenon of mass quitting became known as the Great Resignation. In response, we've discussed here why employees quit and what managers can do to engender commitment and secure a reasonable length of employee tenure.

Even if employees didn't quit, they did reassess both sides of the psychological contract. Many employers re-assessed their side of the deal and offered flexible working, with many introducing mixed regimes of home working and in-office attendance. Many senior managers, though, mandated that employees return. In April 2022, it was widely reported that Government Ministers had demanded that civil servants must all return. In summary, some firms changed toward flexibility while others did not. This shift from rigidity to flexibility for some continues, and more firms than ever are expanding their thinking by experimenting with a four-day week. Flexible working has now become a clear differentiator between firms in attracting staff.

As authors, we are agnostic about what managers should do about home working and the four-day week. We argue that managers must investigate what their firm needs and, in consultation with employees, reach a decision. In this third edition, we cover the issue of working from home in some detail, highlighting not just the potential advantages, but the significant difficulties that it may bring. It's for managers to balance the arguments and do what's right.

Before, during and after Covid, the number of job vacancies rose in the UK. In March 2022, there were 1,247,000 job vacancies. That's up by 462,000 on pre-Covid times. It's exacerbated by the UK's not-so-great-but-still-significant resignation, led by professionals like doctors and teachers retiring early. By anyone's assessment, that's a huge increase in jobs, made starker by the parallel reported figure of 1,296,000 jobless workers. At the time of writing, there are more job vacancies than job seekers and many firms report a simple inability to fill vacancies. One of the main explanations for the imbalance and problem is that the job seekers lack the skills and knowledge to do the jobs that are available. This suggests that the country has not re-skilled its workforce considering technology change, placing the onus for re-skilling on managers. This makes our chapter on developing people very relevant.

Covid highlighted huge inequities between employees. Some were paid full or at least near-full salary by their employers during absence when testing positive for the virus – they were paid what's termed Company Sick Pay (CSP). Others had to rely on Statutory Sick Pay of less that £100 a week. This highlighted that in the earlier editions we had not adequately described Company Sick Pay as part of employee conditions. That's corrected now and we suggest a model that managers might adopt to offer CSP while not inflicting too high a burden on the P&L.

In the period since we published the second edition, there have been many reports of managers behaving badly. Perhaps the most absurd action was taken by the MD of P&O Ferries. He dismissed about 800 employees, reaching settlement agreements with all but one to avoid tribunal claims. Those settlement agreements are reported to have cost P&O Ferries £36.5m. In his business case for the action, he cited the need to halve the salary budget. This could only be achieved, he said, by dismissing the UK employees and bringing on Indian workers to crew his ferries, engaged through an agency in Mumbai. We cover the detail of how this is possible in the sections about employing foreign workers and about dismissing employees by reason of redundancy. It seems likely that P&O will suffer the reputational fallout from this for some time to come.

This notion that managers seem to be behaving badly – or at least don't know how to behave – prompted us to write a chapter on how to become a manager. As managers who have benefitted from extensive training and development, we naturally advocate formal skills and knowledge acquisition along with experience. Our new chapter covers the arguments in favour of learning management and the methods by which managers can advance from trainee to expert. We maintain that management is the overarching competence in business – in the end, all who accept great business aims must manage people well. It's time that those who style themselves as entrepreneurs and leaders accepted that simple idea. Management is non-obvious and must be learned.

Part of that learning includes understanding and overcoming some of the many problems that occur through bias in management decision-making. Bias is a huge subject, and we cover it in seven new sections spanning definition of bias, examples of bias (and specifically manager bias), prejudice, and equality including gender equality. We then suggest a management approach.

In the period since the second edition, we have sensed that managers have moved away from their employees – physically and metaphorically. In managing remote employees, management has certainly become more complex, and it seems managers are becoming disinclined to engage. We evidence this in the development of new staff roles to which management is sub-contracted. The most obtuse example is the role of Chief

Happiness Officer. When we had responsibility for departments and whole firms, we readily accepted the obligation to secure employee wellbeing. As we argue in many sections of this third edition, management is a contact sport. Obligations like wellbeing can't be sub-contracted. We're saddened too that some of the management institutions have supported such evolution.

As a counter to this increased complexity, we again emphasise our two central models – the feed forward model and the feedback model. We continue to emphasise the idea that managers must intervene in their employees' working lives to maintain performance, improve outcomes, and make change. In the end, with tools like the feed-forward and feedback models, managers can gain expertise, become competent, and intervene with confidence in the variables needed to drive their firms forward.

Recently, we learned that in response to falling organisational performance, the London Ambulance Service was recruiting volunteers to attend the lowest category call-out. This, it hoped, would free-up ambulances to relieve those tied up at hospital accident and emergency departments and aid performance recovery. Again, we are agnostic about this. If that's what's needed, then it's perhaps a valid management response. But it has prompted us to write sections on finding, engaging and motivating volunteers – whether in organisations who predominately engage volunteers, or in those where a few volunteers augment many employees. We have many years of experience with the UK's largest youth organisation as volunteers and have completed many consulting assignments in the voluntary sector. We write from positions of experience and theoretical understanding and hopefully this brings some benefit to managers in the third sector.

Finally, we urge managers to be prepared; to be ready to exploit opportunity. We again suggest that opportunity favours the prepared firm. Between Brexit, Coronavirus, the war in Ukraine, and now a hard, right-wing government, there's significant turmoil in industries and markets. Technology too continues its relentless grind as investors fund innovation and invention in pursuit of profit, with daily stories of how machines running automation and AI 'stole' employees' jobs. It's difficult for any manager today to avoid change through technology but technology can be embraced, and jobs enhanced as a result. It just takes planning. We illustrate how managers might think about technology and how it can be applied in pursuit of competitive advantage. The whole management environment is evolving, and managers must embrace change and develop their firms – even if it's not clear where that development is headed.

In conclusion, we believe that in this edition we've covered most of the manager's lot. Until, of course, things change, and we find need for a fourth edition. For now, we commend our work to you.

John Berry and Sue Berry
TimelessTime Ltd
www.timelesstime.co.uk
October 2022

Preface to the Second Edition

The UK has a productivity issue. That's not disputed – it's the one thing that business leaders and politicians agree on! Both France and Germany are more productive than the UK, with each employee generating £53 (€60/$65) per hour worked as against the UK's £42 (€47/$52).

We assert that there are three main reasons for this. First, there's the short-term approach of UK investors, leading to poor investment in the technology used in firms. Compounding that, there's the reluctance of boards to invest in their people. Second, there's a poor attitude in the workforce towards personal learning, with people prioritising material over intellectual wealth. And third, there's the poor quality of management in firms and other organisations.

Arguably, this trend towards a poorer quality of management has come about because government and others have promoted entrepreneurship over management, thereby creating a Kardashian effect. As examples, we now have the job title 'serial entrepreneur' and the very special 'Entrepreneurs' Relief' tax allowance: everyone marvels at entrepreneurs and dreams of being one. The term 'entrepreneur' is typically defined as a person who starts an enterprise, taking financial risk in the hope of returning a profit. Personal characteristics for entrepreneurs abound in definitions: foresight, drive, ambition, self-motivation, flexibility, and passion. There's never a mention about being good at motivating people. And there's never a mention about managing people to make things happen.

Having many entrepreneurs in the UK is fine, but there's more to success than just starting firms.

Likewise, those in charge of businesses often style themselves 'leader'. Definitions of leadership coalesce around translating vision into reality, but few definitions get to the nub – it's that leaders must work close-up with people. Followers must feel that closeness, even if it is mediated though others. The result is that leadership teaching today espouses the need for vision, and charisma, along with the need to be authentic. Leadership gurus now talk of ethics and moral standards, stating the importance of the leader as role model. All are distal qualities – where followers view the leader from afar. Generally, both the metaphorical and physical gap between leader and follower is widening in organisations, and the strength of influence and resulting leadership effectiveness is therefore weakening.

And what then, of the term, 'manager'?

Well, that's a sad story. Managers are considered the administrators, though some definitions do include the idea of conducting the business. At least that suggests closer contact with followers in the 'orchestra'.

In *Because Your People Matter*, we don't differentiate between entrepreneurship, leadership, and management. For us, the manager is the generic term for the person who accepts responsibility for the success of the firm or other organisation or venture. They may, or may not, not be the owner or shareholder – but they will certainly be the owner's agent. Given that responsibility, they will necessarily be entrepreneur, leader, and manager in equal measure.

The information age in which we now live has allowed management thinking to be democratised. Anyone can now be a management guru and sell their brand of management science or pseudo-science. Simultaneously, the economy has evolved: large firms have diminished, and small firms have started up. Mirroring the rise of the entrepreneur, small is now beautiful. In the 80s and 90s, large firms ran mandatory in-house management development programmes for those taking on entrepreneurial, managerial or leadership positions. Many more managers now run their own show, unattached to any big organisation and hence there are now many more managers unattached to a learning infrastructure. Those new managers have no obligation to train.

Today, a new industry of gurus supplies this market of new managers with coaching, mentoring, training, and consulting services. As organisational behaviour professor Jeffrey Pfeffer notes, management development has become 'entertrainment'. The focus is on slogans and feel-good, rather than on learning how to assess evidence and apply management science.

And the data supports this shift away from management training to snake oil sales. Recent UK Government research suggests that as few as 20% of all managers are qualified for the job they do. As a society, we've now accepted that while we expect a doctor to be qualified, we don't place the same demands on a manager.

So, in short, UK firms desperately need to improve their productivity, and productivity depends on the quality of management in those firms. Yet managers, whether describing themselves as entrepreneur, leader, or plain old administrator, are disinclined to get trained.

If ever, now is a good time to introduce management science to those who run UK firms. And that is what we aim to do in the eleven chapters of *Because Your People Matter*.

In the period from about 1985 to 2012, we were managers, running departments in multi-nationals, large firms and quangos and running small-to-medium-sized-enterprises. We took management responsibility. We were the owners' agents as managers. We were C-suite executives. With others, we started some of those firms, taking financial stakes in their success. And we led organisations, developing, and implementing strategy. From 2012 to date, we've been consultants, helping managers to excel.

We were fortunate. Sue started her career with Ciba-Geigy and benefitted from its management training schemes. John started with Philips and was sent on a raft of mandatory local and international courses. In those days, management training was not optional. All managers in those firms were trained. And since then, we've enthusiastically embraced continuous personal development to ensure that as entrepreneurs, leaders and managers, our skills and knowledge remained at the forefront of management science.

Now, let's turn to this book.

Because Your People Matter was first published in January 2019. Chapter 11, entitled *Making Change to the Business*, was always a bit of a weird addition – after all, the whole book was about change. From comments received and our own use, however, we've found Chapter 11 in the first edition to be a bit light for managers seeking global approaches to change and seeking methods of determining the nature of problems. The result is this second edition with a strengthened last chapter.

Because Your People Matter is specifically written for the manager – the person who accepts the responsibility for the flourishing of their firm. As we've written, we've held in our minds us as department heads and company managers. We've designed the content by asking, "What is it that we needed to be able to do, to know and to understand when we were managing teams of people?"

We believe that understanding is key. Understanding trumps 'best practice'. Each manager will develop their own style, tools, models, and approaches. Each will build their own best practice. That's as it should be because management is context specific. Managing soldiers in the battlespace is very different from managing operatives on a production line. So, in *Because Your People Matter*, we aim to give knowledge in order that you build understanding.

We've called it a playbook. That's not to say that it's a prescriptive 'how to' to be applied verbatim. You will need to interpret what we say and apply it to your own environment, and the opportunity to reflect throughout the book will help you. Understanding takes effort, but it leads to appropriate application. Blind application, following best practice without understanding, is foolish and risky.

People-management is dyadic. There are two players – you, as manager, and your employee. Of course, there are a host of others, but they are third parties. They represent noise around the two of you. You and your employee are, for that moment when it matters, in a bubble. As a result of that close relationship, management is a 'contact sport'. And if you're not prepared to get up close and personal, don't sign up to manage people – leave that to others who are happy to get emotionally involved. Leave it to others who like working with and getting the best from people.

We are both positivists and as a result *Because Your People Matter* is written from the positivist perspective. Positivism embraces the idea that the manager can and should intervene in an employee's life to make things happen. Of course, we recognise the other paradigms of psychology that challenge positivism. But as positivists, we seek to explain what happens when a manager intervenes by exploring dependencies and causal relationships between constituent variables. The job someone does, for example, is one of their primary motivators. And without motivation, there's no performance. But just because someone can perform does not mean that the desired outcomes will be achieved. There are many mediators and moderators in the many relationships between variables. In this structure of inputs, outputs, mediators, and moderators, we follow the approach of the natural sciences.

We respect those who adopt the other paradigms: interpretivists who aim to understand the meaning behind management and the dyadic relationship; critics who retort, "Ah yes, but things are not that simple…there are other explanations to be discovered"; and realists who like to remain grounded in what's observed without speculation. For us, positivism matters because that lens, over all others, encourages the application of management science by managers and shifts it from academia to application in real firms.

You'll find that we like diagrams. John trained and worked for many years as an engineer and engineering manager. He learned systems theory and now has the desire to express himself using pictures, symbols, and lines. He also learned to work in the conceptual domain – engineering designs start with ideas and move through modelling to emerge as reality. As with engineering, one must generalise the work of academics in management science to understand new management situations. One must be able to apply concepts from research to managers' practical problems and opportunities. Diagrams allow causality and influence to be simply captured. We recognise psychologists' and other social scientists' reluctance to suggest that one thing 'causes' another. We accept that there are often too many variables, and relationships are often moderate and even weak but unfortunately, unless managers can work with causality and influence, management science will never be useful.

As with engineering, there are two central models. There's the feed-forward model suggesting that if the manager does this, that will happen. And there's the feedback model that allows the manager to sense outcomes and change inputs and other variables in search of optimum result. In all modelling we accept that there are huge numbers of variables and many, many unknowns. Management is not simple, and much can go wrong. And as with all systems, the manager must sense what's happening and act on one or more of those variables to control outcomes. Sensing is perhaps the manager's most important competency.

Since both the central models and some of the central ideas are common to several chapters, you will find themes repeated throughout the book. We do this to avoid you having to refer to previous chapters, thereby making reading easier. This repetition also means that each chapter stands alone.

We must emphasise that we favour models over theory. Theory is built by researchers who come, by way of analysis, to establish relationships between variables or to infer meaning from situations. An example would be the needs theory of motivation that suggests that employees will strive until their specific needs are achieved. We acknowledge such theory but prefer to encapsulate this with other theories to provide a useful model.

We recognise that this book would contain nothing but unsupported exhortation if it were not for the thousands of academics in management science who, over the past 100 years or so, have reported on their work. And yet, this work is not enough. Academia is replete with islands of ideas. Without apology we provide bridges between such islands. We build continents. We link numerous theories and empirical evidence from researchers such as Hackman and Oldham, Kehr, Bandura and Motowidlo to yield what we consider to be models which managers can use day to day. To maintain flow and readability, we don't individually reference each academic and their work but instead provide a general reading list that has influenced us. Our models are therefore based on sound science from our multiple studies at Masters level in technology, economics, sociology, psychology and law and from decades of reference to quality texts and academic papers.

Now, we also acknowledge that we all live in an Internet-connected world with copious sharing and reference to material on the World Wide Web. It's universally acknowledged that what's on the Web and what you hear on social media is unlikely to be of quality, and yet most managers will treat what they find as Gospel. We urge managers to read *Because Your People Matter* before browsing. Treat this book as a starting point for your Web search – use it as a source of keywords and phrases as input, and as a source of models by which you might evaluate the myth and pseudo-science that you'll find online. In the end though, we want *Because Your People Matter* to be used, bookmarked, scribbled over, and added to as your management learning progresses.

Right now, only a few managers are trained in management science, but we hope that by using this book, you'll come to regard yourself as one of those few and that the few will grow to the many. We hope that the term 'accidental manager', as someone thrust into management without preparation, will not apply to you.

All authors adopt a position for their arguments. Ours is simple. You, as manager, have accepted responsibility for the actions of others. In *Because Your People Matter,* we're batting for you, but we do expect you to respond by treating well those for whom you are responsible. Expect a lot from them, but, equally, invest in them.

And finally, just as this Second Edition was heading for the publishers to be typeset, the Coronavirus pandemic struck. As the World economies tanked, there was much discussion suggesting that employment and management would change forever.

Indeed, there will be changes, but the basics will still be there. The manager will still be the person accepting responsibility for the success of the firm. And people will be hired as employees to do work. Nothing that we've written here changes. People matter and managers must get good at working with them.

John Berry and Sue Berry
TimelessTime Ltd
www.timelesstime.co.uk
August 2020

Figures

Figure 1-1: The firm at the highest level of abstraction 4
Figure 1-2: The manager's sphere of influence.. 7
Figure 1-3: Activity model for workers and employees... 11
Figure 1-4: Three basic structures of the firm 13
Figure 1-5: The balanced scorecard 16
Figure 1-6: Simple example of systems modelling.. 18
Figure 1-7: Document-based communications system 22
Figure 1-8: The manager's lot, graphically, showing local maxima 26
Figure 1-9: The 7-S model describing a firm 27
Figure 2-1: The leader's influence on motivation 34
Figure 2-2: The leader's influence on jobs.. 35
Figure 2-3: The link from job to outcomes 36
Figure 2-4: In search of performance using a feedback loop 41
Figure 2-5: Leadership is not only top-down... 48
Figure 2-6: The rule of eights.. 50
Figure 2-7: Typical personality profile of a leader 54
Figure 3-1: Determining employment status... 60
Figure 3-2: Systems model with roles and jobs added... 62
Figure 3-3: Organisation chart with manpower plan 63
Figure 3-4: The recruitment and selection life cycle... 65
Figure 3-5: The Big 5 personality traits 69
Figure 3-6: Holland's RIASEC Preferences 72
Figure 3-7: The lifecycle of volunteer recruitment 84
Figure 3-8: Mechanisms in intention-to-quit and quitting 86
Figure 4-1: The trading firm.. 89
Figure 4-2: The evolution of the firm 92
Figure 4-3: Example basic company as a system... 93
Figure 4-4: Example WBS for a consulting project... 96
Figure 4-5: Balance between competence and technology for a given capability 98
Figure 4-6: Touch points for manufactured goods 109
Figure 4-7: Typical culture likely to foster innovation...111
Figure 4-8: Sustainability defined through threats and controls 112
Figure 5-1: Feedback control loop model of management 117
Figure 5-2: A comprehensive model of employee performance 118
Figure 5-3: Model of the firm showing roles 122
Figure 5-4: Motivation as the result of job, leadership, and culture.................................... 126
Figure 5-5: Engagement and the performance model 128
Figure 5-6: Organisational culture model 131
Figure 5-7: Emotion - linking event to behaviour.. 132
Figure 5-8: The 20 categories of bias... 141

Figure 5-9: The definition of gender pay gap.. 143
Figure 6-1: Variance of performance across employees of a firm.................... 147
Figure 6-2: Basic idea of performance maintenance....................................... 149
Figure 6-3: Sales funnel model 155
Figure 6-4: The balanced scorecard at the level of the firm 156
Figure 6-5: Task and contextual performance and their moderators............... 159
Figure 6-6: Objective setting and performance appraisal summarised 162
Figure 7-1: The iceberg metaphor for the manager-employee relationship 172
Figure 7-2: Primary Statutes Applying to the Employment Relationship......... 176
Figure 8-1: The flow from job to performance and outcomes.......................... 196
Figure 8-2: Example competencies and behaviours... 199
Figure 8-3: Bartram's Great 8 competencies 200
Figure 8-4: Characterising employees by value and uniqueness 203
Figure 8-5: Managerial thought process of development................................. 205
Figure 8-6: Example organisation-wide competency framework 206
Figure 8-7: The four-box model of talent management 208
Figure 8-8: Hierarchy of expectation 212
Figure 8-9: Ways of assessing the benefit of interventions 213
Figure 9-1: The Big 5 personality scales... 220
Figure 9-2: Describing an employee's wellbeing.. 222
Figure 9-3: Example wellbeing scorecard... 224
Figure 9-4: The peak performance zone 225
Figure 9-5: The HSE management standards model.. 226
Figure 9-6: Conceptual model of motivation and burnout.............................. 227
Figure 9-7: Typical absence profile for a firm 228
Figure 9-8: Integrated health and safety management process 236
Figure 10-1: Pay of different employee groups 243
Figure 10-2: The spot salary system - salaries plotted against value 249
Figure 10-3: An example banded salary system.. 250
Figure 10-4: Typical pay distribution within a band 251
Figure 10-5: Pairwise comparison matrix.. 254
Figure 10-6: Rate factor method of job evaluation 255
Figure 10-7: Relative salaries across Europe 259
Figure 10-8: Typical Absence Curve.. 261
Figure 10-9: Possible CSP Solution 262
Figure 11-1: "Cheshire puss! Would you tell me please...".............................. 270
Figure 11-2: The HR system 272
Figure 11-3: The OD system 273
Figure 11-4: Dynamic model of change.. 276
Figure 11-5: The firm as a system 278
Figure 11-6: Systems model of a firm 281
Figure 11-7: Possible internal and external perspectives as foci for models.... 281
Figure 11-8: Example systems modelling of concepts..................................... 283
Figure 11-9: Experience curves.. 287
Figure 11-10: An integrated hard systems methodology................................. 292
Figure 11-11: The soft-systems methodology for messy scenarios 293
Figure 12-1: The route to expert 301

Figure 12-2: Typical manager task competencies 303
Figure 12-3: Manager contextual competencies 305
Figure 12-4: Management primitives 306
Figure 12-5: Normative Processes 307
Figure 12-6: The feed-forward model applied to a group managed by a manager 309
Figure 12-7: Feedback model applied to a group 309
Figure 12-8: The Kepner-Tregoe approach to decision making 311
Figure 12-9: A typical management team 313

Reflections

Reflection 1-1 You, your firm, and your employees.. 4
Reflection 1-2 Desirable outcomes 7
Reflection 1-3 Management alternatives.. 9
Reflection 1-4 About the structure of your firm 13
Reflection 1-5 About your firm's strategy... 17
Reflection 1-6 About instructing employees in your firm.................................... 23
Reflection 1-7 Avoiding the common management mistakes 25
Reflection 2-1 You as a leader.. 33
Reflection 2-2 About high leadership self-efficacy 38
Reflection 2-3 Relationships 40
Reflection 2-4 Assessing performance... 42
Reflection 2-5 Leadership approaches 45
Reflection 2-6 Alternatives to leadership 48
Reflection 3-1 About the people you want to hire.. 73
Reflection 3-2 About your second selection interview 77
Reflection 3-3 About your offer 79
Reflection 3-4 About how you will now recruit and select 81
Reflection 4-1 About your firm's system model 94
Reflection 4-2 About instructing your employees.. 97
Reflection 4-3 About interchangeability of technology and competence 100
Reflection 4-4 About how you will achieve quality.. 102
Reflection 4-5 About your firm and innovation 111
Reflection 4-6 About sustainability.. 114
Reflection 5-1 About performance... 121
Reflection 5-2 About job design.. 123
Reflection 5-3 About commitment.. 125
Reflection 5-4 About motivation.. 127
Reflection 5-5 About engagement of your people.. 129
Reflection 5-6 About culture... 132
Reflection 5-7 About power 136
Reflection 6-1 About setting objectives 151
Reflection 6-2 About your people and their orientation.................................... 153
Reflection 6-3 The right person in the right job 162
Reflection 7-1 About formal and informal procedures 175
Reflection 8-1 About your attitude to staff development 204
Reflection 8-2 About your talent management... 209
Reflection 9-1 About wellbeing 224
Reflection 9-2 About stress 226
Reflection 9-3 About benefits and wellbeing 232
Reflection 10-1 About your salary policy, structure, and system...................... 252

Reflection 10-2 About benefits.. 265
Reflection 11-1 About systems and forces in change...................................... 278
Reflection 11-2 About sub-systems and multiple perspectives in change....... 282
Reflection 11-3 On modelling change.. 284
Reflection 11-4 About issues in change 286
Reflection 11-5 About making change happen 295
Reflection 12-1 Your primitives and normative methods................................ 307
Reflection 12-2 Your management journey.. 316

1

Organising People

1.1 Inception

This book centres on a perfectly normal person who puts themselves forward as 'manager' of a firm. In the context here, a manager is someone who sits between the shareholders and other stakeholders and the employees who work in the firm. Put simply, the manager makes the firm work. Without someone in that position, doing what the manager does in working with the employees, the firm would fail.

This book explains how the manager should work with their employees.

1.1.1 *About management*

Management is an amalgam of many disciplines. At its core is psychology: the science of people and their behaviour. Psychology describes behaviour stemming from both conscious and unconscious thought, and those thoughts are driven by personal and group feelings, attitudes, beliefs, and values.

All managers are psychologists. Each must continually strive to understand the thoughts of the people who work for them and consider what action they might take to influence those thoughts towards their point of view. Ultimately, managers want the people who work for them to behave in a particular way and to realise a particular work outcome.

How people behave is further influenced by their personality, intelligence, knowledge, skills, experiences, preferences, resilience, relationships, motives, and their physical and mental health. Since these personal characteristics are dependent entirely on the holder, the manager must therefore get the right person in the right job in the first place, and then manage them well. Management therefore begins at the firm's inception and continues daily thereafter, hiring people, motivating them, and dismissing them if things don't work out.

In thinking about management, there are four approaches, and we described these in the Preface. As noted, we favour positivism. Positivism suggests that the manager can infer some causal relationship between an intervention that they might make in a person's life, and their subsequent behaviour, performance, and personal outcome. There are many unknowns and many environmental and personal issues that might interfere in the relationship between variables, but nonetheless, without intervention, there is no management. And without management, there's no firm.

Management is therefore first and foremost about intervention.

Managers must also understand other disciplines - primarily law, economics, and politics – because those disciplines provide opportunity and constrain those interventions.

Management is therefore a complex science. It's a practice done by the person who puts themselves forward for the role. It's also a topic of study at universities with maybe 50,000 academics worldwide sharing research on topics from employee selection to wellbeing to employee commitment. There's much published about how to do it, and like science in general, society is understanding management better as time passes and new research is published.

Management applies across all organisations from the entrepreneur with a couple of employees and a few suppliers, to multi-nationals with thousands of managers and hundreds of thousands of employees and other workers. Many commentators focus their attentions at the multi-national end – or at least they assume that the manager to whom they talk is employing many. They assume that there are many layers of management and dedicated HR and OD professionals. We don't make that assumption. Our approaches and methods apply whatever the organisation size, but we focus more on the SME – the small to medium sized firm with between 10 and 250 employees.

Overall, management is about outcomes – and about interventions to realise specific, considered, and desired outcomes.

Finally, management is a practice comprising many techniques, approaches, and tools. It's something that should work. It should be able to be done well by managers, but mostly it's something that's done badly. That would be okay if each manager was cocooned within an excellent support framework – but they're not. For the most part, managers are alone. The HR and OD and other support services available to managers from trainers, coaches, mentors, and consultants that might augment the manager's competencies are woeful. And way too few would-be managers put themselves into training schemes.

So, there's work to be done by everyone who would manage. This book is a start.

1.1.2 *Going into management*

Many people, termed 'accidental managers', enter management without training and often without deliberate thought. Most who put themselves forward for management do so for one reason only – because they have a thirst for power. That power comes in two forms.

Personalised power or 'P-power' is the need to set and meet personal goals. Those high in P-power have a need to feed their own egos. They focus on the "I" and see that they are in competition with others in a zero-sum game in which they aim to win while others lose. Those high in P-power are the 'alphas'. For them, success breeds success and an even greater need for personal enhancement to fuel that power. For them, success is the growing fiefdom, the enlarged sphere of domination and the bigger "I".

Socialised power or 'S-power', on the other hand, is the need to derive power through others and for others. It's the desire to use power for the wider benefit. Those high in S-power tend to put the needs of their organisation above their own personal needs – something that is well established as a fundamental need of a good manager.

There's a balance in each person. Some people are dominant in P-power. Research has found that those high in P-power do drive huge change – but often the resulting organisation does not enjoy on-going stability.

Others are dominant in S-power. Those managers would build a coalition, a consensus for action, rather than giving an executive order.

This balance between S-power and P-power is not a measure of competitiveness, though. Whilst women are typically higher in S-power than P-power, they are just as competitive as men. People can be both highly competitive and dominant in S-power. It's just that in the S-power case, winning is done with others rather than over others.

So, everyone has both P and S. How each person behaves as a manager depends on which type is dominant.

1.1.3   *The firm*

We refer throughout to 'the firm'. We accept that this title has baggage – and describes many forms of entity - so let's be clear. The firm in this context is any legal, trading entity of any form that employs, or intends to employ people. It may be a commercial firm, in business to make a profit, and the profit motive is pervasive in this book. But the management activities we describe are substantially common in not-for-profits and governmental organisations and for this reason we discuss multiple 'outcomes' rather than singular 'profit' as the result of business activity.

We are agnostic about the form of firm. It could be a single entity in one place. Or it could be dispersed across a country or across the world. It's simply an organisation employing people that does something in pursuit of some aim.

1.1.4   *The manager*

Whilst we focus on the manager as a single person responsible for making the firm work, we acknowledge that the manager will be aided by a 'senior team' – a group of individuals who, together, provide all the personal characteristics, competencies and behaviours needed.

In micro firms, there is often only one manager. As the firm grows, the manager delegates more and more of their responsibilities until it's not one manager but many.

For simplicity, and to retain focus, we still refer to 'the manager' even if they delegate to others.

We therefore write for the most senior of senior managers, the first among equals, the managing director or chief executive officer. Equally, we write for all who manage others.

1.1.5   *Why firms succeed*

If there was a single reason why firms succeed, there would likely be a single set of actions needed and management would be simple. But there is no single reason and management is complex.

Summarising though, firms usually succeed because the manager is successful in motivating the employees to do what they want. Motivation is the central theme, supported by a host of other activities and devices that describe the environment in which that motivation takes place.

1.1.6   *The focus*

Since success comes from the ability of the manager to work with the employees, we refer throughout to the manager, the employees, and the firm (as a collective of manager and employees). And we leave the reader to reflect on the nuances that inevitably exist in specific cases. Those reflections are highlighted in each section. Here's the first.

Reflection 1-1: You, your firm, and your employees

Considering your firm, identify who your various stakeholders are –
a stakeholder is anyone who has interest in the firm's success.
Consider who put the money up to create the firm and what they,
as shareholders, expect from you and the firm. Any finally, think
through what the employees want.

1.2 The basics of a firm

One of the necessary skills a manager must have is the ability to abstract – to draw back
from the issue and understand its impact at the highest level. As a manager, if you don't
master this skill early, you'll be quickly mired in detail. Figure 1-1 shows a simplified or
abstracted model of the firm that helps in this understanding.

The firm can be considered simply as a process machine with inputs on the left that are
processed by the machine (the firm) to yield outputs or outcomes on the right.

Inputs are consumed. Money is significant, but it's an enabler, not an input. Investors
put money up. That money buys technology and enables people to be hired. Those people
then give their effort. That technology is put to work and gives function. And if the right
people are hired, the right technology is acquired and the manager engenders the right
culture within the machine, innovation will result. Innovation drives improvement in the
process of creating desirable outcomes.

Enablers enter the machine from the top. Controls enter from the bottom. Enablers
and controls are not inputs – they are not consumed by the machine but modify the
machine's behaviour. Enablers are things like the market in which the firm choses to trade.
Controls are things like government regulation with which the firm must comply.

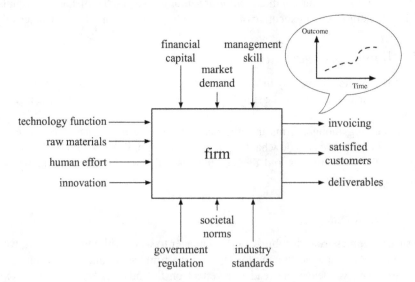

Figure 1-1: The firm at the highest level of abstraction

We've shown here the outputs or outcomes as invoicing, satisfied customers, and deliverables. As manager, you will want to track those outcomes.

Abstraction allows the manager to think about the firm in simple terms and to ask important questions about those inputs, enablers, controls, and outcomes to drive the firm's performance.

Your firm will have unique inputs, outcomes, enablers, and controls determined by your strategy. And it follows that if you change the inputs for a given firm, you'll change the outcomes. And of course, if you change the nature of the firm as a processing machine, but keep the same inputs, you'll again change the outcomes. This idea of changing the various mechanisms – changing the inputs, enablers and controls and changing the firm itself – to get a desirable outcome from the machine - is the essence of management. This theme will occur time and again as we present the various concepts in the coming chapters.

1.2.1   *Money in and money out*

Investors put money into a firm and become shareholders. Since there is no certainty that the outcome that they realise will be the outcome they want, they take a risk. Investment is, by definition, a payment today in the hope of a greater payback tomorrow. It's a hope that could be dashed if the firm fails. But conversely, it's a hope that could be rewarded handsomely as the firm grows and pays dividends to those shareholders as the years go by.

The flow of money in and out of the firm is a critical measure of the firm's health. If the 'machine' is effective in its markets, turnover will rise. If profits are realised, those surpluses are used as working capital to pay people for their effort and to buy more technology. And if the machine is ineffective, shareholders may have to invest more to avoid the firm running out of cash.

Since tax is just a levy on operations, we deliberately omit taxation from our model.

1.2.2   *Consumables*

Consumables are the raw material that goes to produce the goods or provide the services. They are purchased from suppliers and are a cost to the firm. On the one hand they might be like the coffee beans in a coffee shop – consumables literally input to the machine. On the other hand, they might be cars in a motor dealership – bought from the manufacturer and sold on with other added value services to realise the output of a satisfied customer now able to drive for pleasure and work. Consumables are acted upon by the machine and turned into products and services or other outcomes.

1.2.3   *Technology*

People and technology together form a capability – an ability for the person to do something; to do the processing. People can do little without technology. Technology itself is an enabler but as soon as it starts work, it becomes an input through its function. Technology is, for example, the laptop computer used to create the manuscript for this book. Or it's the coffee machine used by the barista in the coffee shop to create a cup of skinny latte.

Technology affords workers capability and the balance between human competence and technology function in achieving that capability is, and will always be, the subject of much management debate.

1.2.4   *People*

People bring their competencies to the firm. It's what they can do with a given technology that makes them valuable and worth paying a wage. Given the right conditions, people behave in a certain way. Hopefully that's how the manager wants them to behave and hopefully this behaviour realises the desired outcomes and their effort is effective.

So, at the highest level of abstraction, people are described by competencies and behaviours. Whilst this might seem a bit heartless, this abstraction to the lowest common denominator of human existence allows the manager to use the model in Figure 1-1 to determine change – if the manager changes those human characteristics, those competencies and behaviours, the outcomes will change.

People are more complex than this simple description suggests, and this complexity gives rise to the need for managers to understand how to manage people to maximise human effectiveness through motivation. It also gives rise to the need for this book, and we deal with motivation at length in the coming chapters.

1.2.5   *Managers*

You, as manager, are the change agent – the conductor of the orchestra of variables. You can change any of the variables – the inputs, enablers, controls, and the nature of the process machine - to change the outcomes. You sense the outcomes output from the machine. You act on each variable, and you look at what happens. If what you had hoped for doesn't happen, you do something else until you find the right combination of inputs, enablers, controls, and machine to give what you want.

In this much, you have complete control over the firm's destiny.

1.2.6   *Evolving the firm*

In the early days of a firm, the founder is often the only person working in the machine. Typically, as the markets demand more and the production from the machine rises, the founder finds that demand exceeds their capability to supply, and they need to invest in people and technology. The first management action to increase the capability is typically to sub-contract some of the work to others. The chair-maker will, for example, sub-contract production of chair legs. The garage mechanic will buy in ready-reconditioned engines.

As time passes and demand grows, the founder may find that sub-contracting is inefficient, costing more than the bought items cost to make in-house. And so, the founder will hire some people to make the items, and some others to manage that activity. Ultimately most firms are a mix of in-house production and sub-contractor supplied parts. Evolution of the machine continues as the firm grows.

1.2.7   *Desirable outcomes*

The most obvious outcomes for a commercial firm trading with customers in a market are turnover and profit. But this is seldom all that the manager monitors at the output of the machine. Typically, firms must operate efficiently and so the manager will monitor productivity – the amount produced by the machine for given inputs. Similarly, they'll monitor quality and safety because often such parameters are key to turnover and profit.

Those outcomes will vary with time. Often, for example, firms see seasonal demand and turnover stalls and profits plummet during holiday periods. And some firms will grow turnover and turn a profit within months of start-up whereas others will take several years. The online supermarket Ocado traded for over 10 years before reporting a profit – its strategic aim was to build its machine – its technology and people - ready for sale, rather than returning short-term dividends to the original founders.

Your desirable business outcomes will be unique. As part of your strategy-building, you must determine what they are to complete the high-level model of your firm.

Reflection 1-2: Desirable outcomes

Think through the inputs, enablers and controls that impinge upon your firm. Think through the outcomes that you seek. Then think through the links between each of the inputs, enablers and controls and those outcomes. What sort of firm, or machine, do you need to process those inputs to outputs? How might your model change with time?

1.3   Defining management

Management is many things to many people. Some consider the term 'management' to describe a pedestrian activity of administration. This definition stems from the days when firms had many layers of managers. It stems too from the military where a commander had an adjutant – a left hand man, someone who did the books and administered affairs while the commander did the real business of delivering outcomes.

Whatever management is, it needs definition before you can get on with the job – and before you can talk with your peers about something you all understand.

The manager's sphere of influence is ubiquitous. At an employee level, the manager's job spans from influencing the job they do, through the technology they use to the outcomes they produce. Figure 1-2 below describes this graphically.

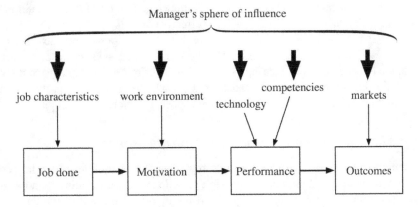

Figure 1-2: The manager's sphere of influence

Management is the exertion of influence over all aspects of the firm to achieve the desired outcomes. Here, we're interested in managing people and so we can re-define the manager's job as having influence over:

- the jobs done;
- the jobholders who do those jobs;
- the work environment, in turn driving jobholder motivation as they do the job;
- jobholder performance considering their competencies; and
- the technology jobholders use to achieve the desired outcomes given the markets in which the firm trades.

1.3.1   Manager as commander

The first role that the manager must adopt is that of commander. Someone must think about the strategy and then do everything necessary to cause jobs to get done, performance to be achieved and outcomes realised. In this sense the manager is commander – metaphorically, in complete command of the ship.

As we shall learn later in this book, there are ways of making this happen, but the truth is that the manager elects themselves commander. They have agreed to take total responsibility for the firm and hence are in command of success or failure. They may choose not to ram home the point every day. They might delegate parts of that responsibility. But in the end the buck stops with the manager.

It's that acceptance of responsibility that differentiates the manager from others.

1.3.2   Manager as leader

Leadership is a narrow sub-set of management. Management has influence over all aspects of the firm. Leadership, strictly, is the influence over each employee's motivation. Since it's a significant issue in firms, we cover leadership in more depth in Chapter 2.

Leaders can adopt directive and non-directive styles. A directive style is useful when the leader needs to take control, ignore what others think and tell people what to do. Sometimes things must be done and a directive style is essential, but it should be used sparingly. A non-directive style is where the leader discusses the issues with the employee and the employee elects to do what's needed as if they had thought of it. It's a subtler style and takes more time in execution but it is more effective overall.

Leaders can adopt a host of different approaches. A professional approach, leading by example, is valid when leading professionals like teachers and lawyers. In a transactional approach, the leader engages in exchange with the employee to get the employee to do what's needed. And using a transformational leadership approach, the leader sets out the vision and gets 'buy-in' from those needed to make the vision happen. But more on those approaches later.

1.3.3   Manager as entrepreneur and businessperson

Today, entrepreneurs are revered. But an entrepreneur is simply someone who realises that, with a given firm and market, it's possible to sell something for more than it costs to produce. The firm therefore makes a margin. If the margin is more than the costs of the operation, profit will be made.

In a sense, the entrepreneur is the commercial element of management – the sales department of the firm. A firm without an entrepreneur will fail. It would be a great machine without a purpose. Conversely, an entrepreneur without competence in management will have good ideas but no ability to realise them.

1.3.4   *Alternatives to management*

The truth is that the manager is commander, leader, and entrepreneur and a whole load more besides. But is there any alternative to management? Does someone always have to be manager, and can the firm get the right outcomes without such a determined person at the helm?

There is an academic research thread about alternatives to leadership and there is some evidence that leadership, as a moderator of motivation, need not necessarily be concentrated in one person. It can be distributed.

And certainly, an entrepreneur can have great ideas and buy and sell to generate profit – but they can never do that to a large scale. That takes management of technology and people working together in a firm.

So, we contend that there is no alternative to management.

Reflection 1-3: Management alternatives

Take a few minutes to consider the statement, "there is no alternative to management", and the description of management in Section 1.3.
Do you agree that there is no alternative to management?

1.4   Differing roles

It's important to recognise that people, including the manager, play multiple and sometimes conflicting roles in a firm. Initially, of course, the manager plays all roles. As others join the manager, these roles are adopted by others depending on the characteristics or role and attributes of the person.

There are four principal roles.

1.4.1   *Shareholder*

Someone or some group of investors puts up the money to start the firm. Each investor buys one or more shares in the firm and hence this person or group of people are referred to as shareholders.

Shareholders put up the financial stake but unless they become directors, they take little other direct interest in the management of the firm and are of little interest to us here.

1.4.2   *Director and Managing Director*

Typically, shareholders will enter into a shareholders' agreement that describes the powers that they have over the activities of the firm. Their power is applied by appointing a director to the board of directors to act on their behalf. Generally, they can appoint themselves. Usually, only shareholders with more than a certain number of shares get to appoint a director. Those directors appointed by shareholders will register at the UK Companies House.

In some countries, firms have two boards – a supervisory board and a management board. The supervisory board comprises shareholding directors while the management board members are appointed for their management and technical skills. In SMEs in the UK, one board typically does both supervision and management.

The board then elects one of its members as Managing Director (MD) and it delegates the board's power to the MD in return for reports on progress. Typically, the whole board would be involved in the development of strategy with each element of strategy forming a new objective for the MD.

1.4.3   *Supplier*

Suppliers are key players in the early evolution of the firm. Typically, the founder sub-contracts part of their activity to suppliers until the business grows to such a point when hiring staff becomes possible. Those suppliers are typically other small firms or sole-traders and are often referred to as contractors, associates, freelancers, or sub-contractors.

Suppliers should be under business-to-business contracts with the firm for the supply of services. Those contracts (and the relationship in general) should clearly show the supplier as a third party that supplies goods and services against a specification. Those suppliers must not come close and be able to be construed legally as employees. The firm and its suppliers are often considered to trade 'at arm's length', illustrating the separation between them. This separation should be maintained.

The distinction between workers/employees and suppliers is highlighted by this arm's length relationship.

1.4.4   *Employee/worker*

Every person associated with the firm should be under a contract. All people under a contract of service are workers. Some workers are employees. The distinction between workers and employees is complicated.

The distinction between suppliers (with a contract for supply of services) and those under contracts of service is an important one and one that the manager must think about and understand. If the manager gets the right contracts in place with the right people from the outset, significant future problems are avoided. We will cover this in more depth later.

The distinction between worker and employee is subtle. If you, as manager, gain the services of people through an intermediary such as a staffing agency, the people who work for you are workers. This is illustrated in Figure 1-3 where the intermediary invoices the firm, and the intermediary pays the worker a wage. Then the worker is an employee of the intermediary. If, instead, the firm pays the person a wage, they are employees of the firm.

This is a simple definition. It does get more complex, and we discuss this again later.

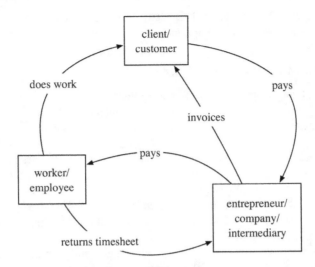

Figure 1-3: Activity model for workers and employees

1.4.5   *Role confusion*

Firms often confuse roles and titles.

Board members may also be members of the management team and attract the title 'director'. This is a valid title if they are indeed registered as directors at Companies House. And sometimes the MD appoints employees as 'directors' as a title suggesting high rank.

Many firms steal terms from the USA and call their MD the Chief Executive Officer (CEO). Then those directors representing shareholders, or indeed employees appointed to high-sounding positions, are termed the 'C-suite' with titles like the Chief Finance Officer (CFO) and the Chief Operating Officer (COO).

Managers should take care when giving people titles. An inappropriate or misleading title can unintentionally imply superior responsibility and the right to commit the firm.

1.4.6   *Managers, employees, and suppliers*

For the rest of this book, those who exert influence over all aspects of the firm to achieve the desired outcomes are termed 'managers' or 'the manager'. Those who do the manager's bidding are termed 'employees'. Those who augment the firm's capabilities by supplying services are termed 'suppliers'. There are only those three categories of person supporting the firm and throughout this book we strive to acknowledge the differences between them.

1.5   Basic business types and structures

Fundamentally, the type and structure of the firm will greatly influence the nature of the machine possible and the outcomes available (as illustrated in Figure 1-1). Today, there is huge interest in unusual types and structures in an effort on the part of managers to minimise costs. Typically, if a firm can avoid having premises, or can have a very small headquarters, this is highly attractive. This section discusses some of the options and some of the issues that arise through those options.

1.5.1 Issues in managing real firms

People are social beings. Employees need one another for their existence, and, to a greater or lesser degree, they actively seek out contact with others. It's common for employees to say that one of the big things they get out of work is the social interaction, the camaraderie. Typically, employees socialise with other employees in and out of the work setting. And managers structure the firm in a particular way and this structure enables a particular social interaction.

Firms work because employees cooperate with one another. And firms work because managers are able, through social interaction, enabled by the firm's structure, to influence their employees towards their point of view. This is one of the definitions of management – and specifically of leadership.

So, managers must create the right environment and a major element of that environment is the firm's structure. If the structure constrains interaction, the machine will not function optimally, and the manager will not achieve their desired outcomes.

Figure 1-4 shows three typical structures of small firms. EE are the employees and Mgr, the manager. In one case there is more than one manager.

1.5.2 Nuclear firm

The first and most obvious structure is that of the nuclear firm. Manager and employees are co-located. Here the manager will find it relatively simple to make their influence felt. The manager will see each employee daily and hence monitor work output and will command and facilitate. Here, calling a meeting is simple and issues can be dealt with immediately. And the proximity of all players enables trust to be built easily between them.

1.5.3 Dispersed firm

Soon after the manager has formed the nuclear firm, evolution typically demands recruitment of employees physically dispersed from the firm. Sometimes this will be to give the firm access to new product markets or sometimes it will be to access other labour markets. Certainly, small firms have significant problems overcoming the perception that they are volatile and as a result, employees are disinclined to move house to join them. Having staff dispersed is a common solution with employees traveling to the headquarters for varying lengths of time.

This also describes the firm that makes use of the services of external others where the staff comprises a mix of employees and suppliers.

Here the manager must make distinct efforts to exert their influence. Meetings must be set, and electronic means used to enable communications. Trust becomes more dependent on action and timescales will be strained as interaction potentially becomes less frequent.

Following the Covid pandemic, and subsequent return to work, many firms found themselves questioning previous rigidity. Firms that previously insisted that the only way for them was nuclear have acknowledged employee wishes for flexibility. Hybrid structures are now often being trialled with employees working in the headquarters on some days and at home on others.

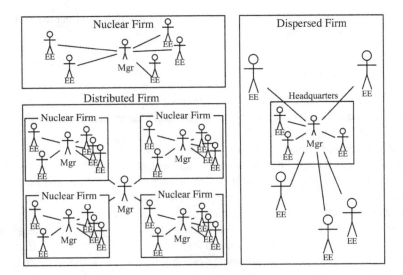

Figure 1-4: Three basic structures of the firm

Hybrid working is nothing new, but it may become more mainstream in years to come as firms realise it can work and allow significant benefits.

1.5.4   *Distributed firm*

Distributed firms come about as the nuclear firm finds need to open offices that are geographically separated from the headquarters. Here, typically, a manager runs each outpost with another more senior manager coordinating the inter-outpost activities.

Here the central manager must set up communications and inter-outpost interaction to achieve the desired outcomes. It is easy for each outpost to become an isolated nuclear firm, following its local manager, without harmonisation behind a common strategy.

Reflection 1-4: About the structure of your firm

Considering your firm, how do you see it evolving through the different structures? So how will you go about enabling frequent and fluid communication and interaction between you as manager and each employee, and between the employees?

1.6   Extending business to the international

Many firms serve their own locale. But many find that there's demand for their goods and services from further afield, and even internationally. And many will also find that there is value in extending the dispersed firm or distributed firm to include employees or suppliers located in other countries. This section discusses some of the issues in exporting and in contracting foreign employees – at least in so far as these activities affect the manager and their ability to manage people.

1.6.1   *Exporting*

Typically, selling goods and services abroad involves employees travelling to foreign lands to meet with would-be customers and clients. In a global, connected world, this is natural. But it does add another dimension to the firm.

Firstly, employees must be prepared to travel. This brings complexities. Employees must know that they have the firm's support abroad and specifically that they are supported financially. They must also know that they will be safe while travelling and experience no more risk than they would if living and working in the UK. Firms must deliberately organise themselves to export and to support employees abroad.

Secondly, employees must have the skills and knowledge to do business abroad. This necessity is extensive, spanning languages, culture, business practices, business law and local needs. We do have the advantage that English is the common language of the business world, but this tends to make us think that everyone thinks the way we do. Anyone intending doing business abroad must dump this assumption and be prepared to learn about other nations. Given that employees need new skills and knowledge, this must be part of employees' development plans.

1.6.2   *Using foreign workers*

Many managers will consider it advantageous to contract with people living abroad for the supply of services, either as employees or as suppliers. Employees pick up the employment legislation of the country in which they live and work, so for example someone living and working in Israel for a UK firm cannot enter an employment contract made under English law. They will naturally be employed under Israeli law, albeit with no local employer – and you'll instantly see the possible complexities that this brings.

There are two popular methods of gaining the services of foreign worker. The first method is to open a branch office in the worker's country. This is an extension of the UK firm in the country, registered locally. The employee is employed under the laws of their country. The second method is for the worker to become a supplier, forming themselves as a sole trader. The authorities in many countries permit this. In this case, they are employed locally in their own enterprise which enters a business-to-business contract with the firm.

Engaging the services of foreign workers is complex and we discuss it some more later.

1.6.3   *Issues in extending to the international*

Extending business to the international adds significant complexity, though the benefits can be considerable. Our advice is simple: get additional help from specialists.

1.7   Building strategy

Strategy is the set of guiding principles that give reason for the activities of the firm. Strategy exists at every level and with every manager. No manager is without strategy – it's just that often the strategy is formed by assumptions, biases and hunches and is in the manager's head rather than written down.

A firm's strategy should be considered, debated between interested parties, and written. But there's no prescriptive form that a strategy should take. You may find the following ideas helpful in formatting your strategy. We also cover some of the tools that will be useful in developing strategy in the sections below.

1.7.1   Simple strategy

At its simplest, strategy is a purpose that guides everyone in the firm in their everyday work and decision-making. This purpose guides managers and employees toward some eventual improved state. Strategy should address a customer or client problem. Here's a neat way, from Richard Rumelt, to state a firm's strategy: *Because A has a problem with B, we reckon that if we do C to D, we'll achieve outcome E.*

Here's an example of a simple strategy for some kids wanting to earn pocket money: Because the old folk in the houses at the end of the road (A) have problems cutting their lawns (B), we reckon that if we buy a lawn mower (C) and find where we can dump the cuttings (C) and then knock on the old folks' doors (C/D) to offer our lawn cutting services (C), we'll earn £50 a week between us (E).

The problem (A/B) is stated from the customer's or client's perspective. C and D tell us the offering to the market and E tells us the outcome expected.

1.7.2   Five ws and an h

Another way of expressing strategy is to use the headings of who, what, why, where, when and how, often called 'five ws and an h'. It's the same sort of thing as the A, B, C, D and E above.

The kids example above first defines 'why' the kids are going into business – because they reckon they can make money from the old folks' problem by offering them a service. Sometimes managers are less blunt than simply expressing the idea of making money – but in a commercial firm everything boils down to that. 'Who' then defines the company needed, 'what', the products and services to be offered, 'where', the geography, 'when' the time plan for the project and 'how', the values of the firm and more detail on the plan.

1.7.3   Strategy and the balanced scorecard

Whilst the strategy statement above is neat and complete, it's seldom enough to describe all that the firm will do to meet the manager's desired outcomes. It's not enough to guide the firm from inception to eventual sale or another endpoint.

In 1996, two academics/consultants, Robert Kaplan, and David Norton, developed the Balanced Scorecard. The idea behind the Balanced Scorecard is that, for a given strategy statement there are four domains on which managers should focus. These concern finances, customers, processes, and people. The people domain centres on employee development. This is shown as a grid in Figure 1-5.

The idea is to follow on from the simple method in 1.7.1 above by saying 'if that's the financial objective (E), as the desired outcome, then here are the customers, processes and people actions that will be needed to achieve that'.

strategy statement			
financial	objectives	measures	achievements
customers	objectives	measures	achievements
processes	objectives	measures	achievements
development	objectives	measures	achievements

Figure 1-5: The balanced scorecard

The customer objective is akin to C and the processes, to D. The people in need of development are of course the kids – who would have to go and learn how to cut grass! The other boxes in the grid give space to record the measures of the objectives – how you'll know, for each objective, when you've got there – and chart the achievements through time.

We could go on. Once a basic strategy is in place, it can be elaborated. Elaboration might use a balanced scorecard to define a complete statement of what is to be done and what outcomes are expected. Then it's just a matter of doing it.

1.7.4   *Acting on strategy*

Strategy gives the firm reason for its existence. It's a set of guiding principles that the manager believes will enable them to achieve those attractive outcomes and that will sustain this state over a chosen period.

The manager should consult widely in developing the strategy – with the board, employees, and customers. But it's not a straight-jacket. And the strategy should remain under constant review, changing considering changes in the market and in the competitive and regulatory environment.

Some managers value flexibility over what they argue is the straight-jacket of strategy. They insist that their firm's future lies in nimbleness, being able to grasp opportunity. That itself is a strategy. We would argue that it's a shallow strategy since the ability to grasp opportunity is predicated upon being prepared. And as the hyenas quipped sarcastically when Scar sang 'Be Prepared' in Disney's The Lion King, "Yeah, we'll be prepared…. For what?" Being prepared itself demands financial, customer, process and development plans and actions.

But most of all, strategy should guide managers and employees, day to day, in their activities. It's the mechanism by which the manager delegates.

1.7.5   *People and strategy*

Without strategy – those guiding principles – all management action is difficult. If shareholders and their directors can't say what they want from a business, the managing director can't make plans, assess progress and report if they have succeeded. And yet it's surprising how few firms have a sound strategy that is communicated across the managers and employees.

Strategy influences the jobs employees do, their motivation, the leadership that managers provide, employee performance and ultimately those desirable outcomes. Strategy must pervade the firm. Without it, the manager is 'failing to plan' and hence 'planning to fail'.

Reflection 1-5: About your firm's strategy

Take a few minutes to develop the sentence involving A, B, C, D and E for your firm. Then expand it and build the relevant objectives in a balanced scorecard. Develop multiple objectives and measures. How will you communicate your strategy? Do you think it will be well accepted? And is it realisable?

1.8 A system that does something

Above, we described the firm as a machine. It's time now to expand that simple model to see each of the machine's component parts. Of course, we can't see all the parts because many don't exist right now.

To expand the simple model to something more complex so that we can start developing plans, we need a more elaborate model. For this we need to consider the machine in its context as a system.

A system is a set of components, connected for some purpose. The purpose is defined in the strategy. This can be expanded to give a fuller definition stating that:

- The system is an assembly of components - each comprising human competence and technology function - connected in an organised way - a process - that will achieve those desirable outcomes.
- Each component is affected by being in the system – even if only because it participates in the system - and the behaviour of the system is changed if any component leaves or fails to perform as intended.
- The assembly of components, the system, has been identified as being of particular interest to some people – the shareholders, but also to all stakeholders including employees and customers/clients who benefit from its existence.

There are many approaches to elaborating the model. The most useful here is a method of analysis and synthesis developed by the authors from systems dynamics, an approach to looking at organisations developed initially by Jay W Forrester of MIT's Sloan School of Management. We call the method 'systems modelling'.

1.8.1 *Introducing systems modelling*

Systems modelling first requires the manager to identify the concepts of the firm. A concept is an idea – it may be something physical, it may be a process, or it may be something conceptual. Either way, as a component, each concept is essential to making the system work as we defined it above.

The system is a complete firm in its context of market and industry. Systems modelling can be best illustrated by example. In Figure 1-6, each label is a concept – like profit or order intake. The network of connected concepts is the system. It can be as complex or as simple as the person creating it wants it to be. The level of detail is determined by the purpose to which the model is to be put. The arrows indicate dependence or influence – so in this example, profit leads to investment, or in reverse, investment is caused by profit. Of course, causality is difficult in a firm because there are so many variables.

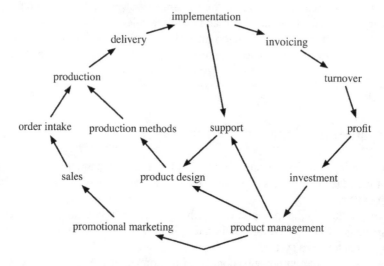

Figure 1-6: Simple example of systems modelling

Each concept elaborates the 'what' of the simple strategy. Each is defined by an element of the four domains of the balanced scorecard. Production, for example, will be defined financially, in terms of customer/client satisfaction, in terms of process and in terms of people and their developmental needs.

Once the concept model is built, it can be reviewed for its accuracy, completeness, and overall ability to achieve the desirable outcomes, were such a firm to be created.

1.8.2 'As is' and 'to be' models

Change is depicted by the difference between what the firm is today and what it might be tomorrow. Strategy is all about envisioning some improved state that the manager will make happen. The balanced scorecard is all about describing what's needed to bridge the gap.

Systems models can be built depicting those two states. If the change is small, and the differences are to occur with the same systems model, they can be described by focussing within a function. An example might be moving product design in-house. Many changes in a growing business will require fundamental changes to the systems model, perhaps introducing product design for the first time or ditching implementation by designing products that are delivered straight to the customer.

1.8.3 *Concepts as technology and people*

The important point about modelling the firm is that each concept comprises people and technology. Some concepts may be completed mostly by technology, working with minimum input from employees. Others will be completed mainly by people, working with minimal technology. As manager, you must determine what these concepts are. You must determine what technology function and what employee competencies and behaviours are needed for success.

1.9 Money as the central measure

As the saying goes, 'money makes the world go round'. We can fight the thought that all that matters is money, but we can't ever disagree that it is the universal common denominator in business. Even in charities and not-for-profit organisations, money is the universal measure to value their efforts, measuring each charity's impact.

Of course, just because money is the universal measure does not mean it is the most important, nor even the most used within the firm. As organisational psychologists and human resource specialists, we'd argue that it's people that matter most.

Starting with profit, the following section discusses the most significant financial metrics in many firms.

1.9.1 *The profit motive*

Profit is the surplus available from the firm once all the operating costs and cost of goods sold have been deducted from the sales value.

As the Emperor said to Darth Vader in Star Wars Episode V, when talking about Luke Skywaker, "the force is strong with him". And so it is with most managers – they aim to make profit by maximising sales and controlling costs and that underlying drive is strong and unrelenting.

That's not to suggest that there's anything wrong with profit. Far from it. Profit enables many things, like employment of more people, payment of bonuses as reward for success and the sponsoring of employees' personal development. And of course, it enables payment of dividend, as a return on their investment, to those shareholders who, at their own risk, put up the money to start the firm in the first place.

Because profit enables so much, that drive for profit must be respected.

There are two 'types' of profit – normal profit and super-normal profit. We say that a firm makes normal profit when it realises earnings before interest, tax, depreciation, and amortisation (EBITDA) of about 10% - the return that an investor might expect to earn if the money was invested instead in the stock markets. A firm makes super-normal profit if the firm realises more than normal profit.

Some firms make colossal profit – up to say 50%. Super-normal profit depends a lot on the products and services sold and the market in which the firm trades. Realising super-normal profit normally indicates that the firm has a unique idea that is highly valued by customers, enabling it to charge a premium for its goods and services.

'Normal' is normal for a reason and that's where most firms operate.

1.9.2 *Pay*

People surrender their personal freedoms in return for a regular wage or salary. They agree to be told what to do by the manager and become what is legally termed an employee because the manager, as agent for the shareholders and directors, gives the employee earnings security.

Pay is an important point that pervades the whole manager-employee relationship and it differentiates employees and suppliers. A supplier is a free man (or woman). An employee is a wage slave. And at least in free societies, both have made their choice willingly.

Pay is determined in a negotiation between employee and manager, tempered by the labour market and the market price for the job. Pay is contentious. Paying more does not make employees work harder, but inadequate pay and unfair pay decisions are responsible for much disquiet in firms. It is the single most significant factor in why employees decide to quit.

1.9.3 *Pensions*

The cost of keeping the elderly is rising. To reduce the burden on the State, the payment of an amount linked to a percentage of an employee's salary must now be made to a private pension for them. This amounts to a few percent of each employee's salary.

Pensions are however part of the manager's ability to differentiate their firm from others and attract and retain good employees. And some occupations and parts of the labour market have established norms where firms pay anything up to 20% of salary into private pensions. Some demand that the employee matches the firm's payment.

You, as manager, will need to decide on your attitude towards pensions.

1.9.4 *Benefits*

Like pensions, benefits have established normative levels for occupations and specific parts of the labour market. It's typical now for the firm to fund a growing range of benefits such as private medical treatment, long term illness insurance, gym membership and even cycle purchase.

While many managers are inclined to consider benefits as a cost and a necessary evil, benefits must also work for the firm. For example, private medical insurance reduces long-term sickness absence and gym membership increase the overall employee wellbeing. When considering benefits, we recommend that managers focus on those that will be popular with employees but those that also bring tangible benefit to the firm.

1.9.5 *Training as investment*

Under strategy and the balanced scorecard, the people contribution was headed 'development' indicating the ability to achieve financial objectives through the training and development of people. Development and training differ. Training is the formal change in competencies and behaviours through planned learning. Development is everything else that drives change through people taking up new roles and responsibilities.

Training and development ensure that the firm stays ahead of its competitors.

Many managers think of training as a cost. This is a short-sighted view. Training (and development) is an investment. The manager pays out today in the hope of a return on their investment tomorrow. There are various norms quoted for training and development, but it would not be unreasonable for managers to pay 10% of their sales value to train and re-train their employees.

We discuss training and development in more depth later in this book.

In terms of return on investment, the payback must be assessed considering the counterfactual – what would have happened if employees had not been trained; if they'd not been encouraged to develop by taking on new roles and responsibilities. And that's often difficult to quantify.

1.9.6 *Taxes*

And finally, there are taxes. Firms must behave as the Government's tax collector, taxing income from employees at source. Suppliers, of course, are responsible for their own tax payments and are paid gross sums.

1.10 Instructing people to do work

Communicating in English is ambiguous. And that is true even when the manager does communicate effectively. Instructing people to do work, and communicating how the work is to be done, is one of the biggest problems in firms. Good communication centres on clarity of information and confirmation that the instruction has been received and understood and will be acted on.

As we outlined above, people start their relationship with the firm as suppliers, trading at arm's length. As the firm grows, those suppliers, metaphorically, come indoors and join the firm as employees. In so doing they surrender their rights in return for a wage and allow the manager to instruct them in what to do.

But what is it that the manager can tell the employee to do and how might this be done?

1.10.1 *Issuing instruction*

The simplest form of instruction is the verbal order – 'please do this'. In instructing an employee, the manager must take care that what they ask is lawful, decent, socially acceptable and within the employee's competencies. Provided that the instruction is within the scope of what the employee signed up to do, the manager can pretty much expect their instruction to be complied with to the best of the employee's ability.

1.10.2 *Work instruction documents*

Most firms develop beyond the manager issuing verbal instructions throughout the day. Most move to a document-based operating system. Figure 1-7 illustrates the sort of approach.

Typically, the manager, as agent for the shareholders and directors and hence the firm, enters a contract with a client. This is usually done by making an offer (perhaps in a quotation). The customer accepts the offer by placing an order. There may be a written contract, but whether verbal or written, an agreement for supply will be made.

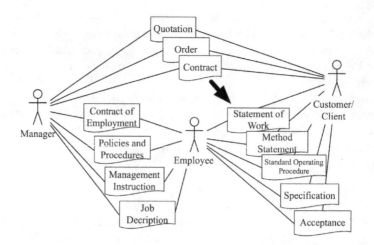

Figure 1-7: Document-based communications system

Someone in the firm must then translate the contract into something actionable by the employee – shown by the dark arrow in Figure 1-7. Often this is done through documents like a statement of work, method statement or standard operating procedure. These centre on a common understanding of a specification. In a building firm, these might be replaced by drawings showing the building to be constructed. In a café, there might not be any documents, but instruction might be given through on-the-job training with the manager translating the specification for the employee. One way or another the manager must communicate what's needed.

1.10.3   *Expected behaviour*

As we noted, the employee has entered an employment contract with the firm. Universally, the employee is considered weak and the manager, as employer, powerful. The result is that much of this contract is now set in statute. Nonetheless, there is a contract under which the manager can expect their instruction to be heeded.

The employee has an important job. They must work to gain the customer's acceptance that the specification has been complied with. If they can't or won't do that, the contract can't be determined and a breach of contract between customer and firm will result – even if that only means the return of the goods for a refund.

The expected behaviour is set down in documents like the policies and procedures of the firm and the employee's job description.

If the employee's behaviour is not as expected, there are grievance and disciplinary procedures built into the employment contract and described in the policies and procedures. So, the employee is instructed to carry out the work as set out in the instructions.

1.10.4   *Procedures versus training*

It's often expected that the manager will develop their system as a set of procedures. As we noted above, those procedures would be carried out in part by technology and in part by the employee demonstrating their competencies and behaviours.

But there is a natural trade-off between written processes or procedures describing what's to be done and employee training. The degree to which one or other dominates depends much on the job. Examples of procedures abound – even surgeons talk of procedures. Airline pilots have procedures and it's only when conditions become extreme that they revert to what they learned in training.

The balance between procedures and training has a lot to do with employee job satisfaction. Certainly, the more a person uses their training, the more satisfied they will likely be.

Reflection 1-6: About instructing employees in your firm

Considering your firm, how will you instruct your employees
to do what you need them to? Will you lean towards written
procedures or towards training? What role will your employees
have in securing customer/client acceptance of the goods or
services that you deliver? Remember that it is they
who normally interface with the customer.

1.11   Common mistakes that managers make

We've talked a lot about training but unfortunately less that 20% of all managers in the UK have been trained to do the management job. The result is that they make a lot of mistakes. And it's worth highlighting some of these mistakes here.

1.11.1   *Avoiding getting close*

Many advisors say that managers should work 'on the firm' and not 'in the firm'. By this they mean that the firm should be a project, starting with inception and ending with sale or another endgame. And they argue that to do this, the manager must retain an objectivity that getting stuck in, doing the work, does not permit. The result is that many managers stay back, detached, avoiding getting close to their employees.

One good example of detachment behaviour is the manager of the 8-man personal training firm. She ceased her own work as a personal trainer and now spends her day on spreadsheets, marketing, and networking. She rarely sees her trainers working and seldom interfaces with her customers.

Another is the MD of a 100-man surveying firm who is still a major fee earner, returning a ratio of billable-hours-to-total-hours-worked of 85%. He simply has no time to get involved and spends his days out of the office on expert witness work!

By being detached, albeit in very different ways, these managers have lost touch with their employees, with the work done and with the customers and clients. They risk losing their businesses.

All managers must stay involved, with just the right detachment to enable objectivity, while influencing their followers. 'Working on the firm, not in it' should be a metaphor for objectivity – and not practiced literally.

1.11.2   *Not learning the trade*

Managers must be expert in the trade of the business and be expert managers.

In the UK, we are happy to let our businesses be managed by accountants, 'professional managers' and others who have little or no competence in the business. This was brought into stark relief in the National Health Service in the 1990s and 2000s where departments were headed by 'managers' with no clinical abilities. The result was caricatured in TV serials like the BBC's Casualty where ignorant managers were pitched against hero clinicians. Slowly, this is being corrected as nurse-managers are taking over wards and surgeons are becoming hospital CEOs.

Fundamentally, the manager must understand the firm, its processes, and its customers and clients. They must be very good generalists in all technical aspects of the work. Then they must train as managers.

It's interesting that in Germany, the country with the highest productivity in Europe, managing directors are generally technical specialists who have retrained for their new role. In Germany, promoting a management generalist or accountant to MD is anathema.

1.11.3   *Not delegating*

A sole trader does everything there is to do in a firm. They are alone. As soon as an employee is hired, the sole-trader becomes manager and must delegate.

Delegating is not just getting someone else to do the menial bits of the work that the manager is well rid of. It's the passing to a trusted colleague of complete work packages for which that colleague takes responsibility. With responsibility comes the freedom to act to secure success. Managers must never micro-manage – delegating but interfering incessantly to direct the work.

Now, that said, all delegation must be within the employee's scope of work defined in their job description. Of course, all job descriptions should also include that all-encompassing phrase that 'the job holder may also be asked to do other things from time to time within their competencies'. So, delegation can be wide – but only within the employee's competencies.

Many managers pass over menial work but retain control of success (or failure). The result is that employee motivation is less than it could be.

Similarly, many managers think they delegate – but they don't monitor progress. With delegation comes a strict set of conditions. The employee should have the freedom to act – but only if they report progress and seek help if needed.

Delegation is to be learned by the manager.

1.11.4   *Trusting but not verifying*

Trust, but verify is a Russian proverb, used by US President Ronald Regan when talking about nuclear disarmament. It became the motto of the US Defense Threat Reduction Agency.

Trust, but verify should likewise be the manager's motto when delegating work of any kind to any employee or group of employees. In the end, the buck stops with the manager, so the manager must verify that the work is progressing to schedule and the costs are under control and as predicted.

But many employees will tell a promising story. It is for the manager to trust the employees but take such steps that might be needed to confirm the stories that they're told – without overtly letting the employee know that they are checking, thereby breaching that trust.

Many managers pass over work and projects and are then very disappointed when things drift, and costs escalate. They trust, blindly. Remember that you, as manager, know a lot more than your employees about the business. Delegation is about motivating and hence you must delegate. But you must always delegate under control.

1.11.5   *Dithering*

Many of the decisions a manager must take are unpleasant. The manager must steel themselves to tell an employee that they've done a poor job. Making someone redundant is challenging. And facing up to an employee who is aggressive or loud may involve heightened personal threat. The result is that many managers fail to act at all in those and similar cases or fail to act immediately.

Generally, if action is deferred, if the manager dithers, the moment is lost and the effect of what's said and the action taken by the manager are diluted. In the case of feedback, it is only effective as a motivator if given moments after the event.

Reflection 1-7: Avoiding the common management mistakes

Take a few moments and identify any of these mistakes in your present
behaviour as a manager. What might you change now and how? Then,
thinking about some of the managers that you've known, identify
at least one example of each of these mistakes. Again, think about
how that manager might have behaved differently and what you think
the resulting outcome might have been.

1.12   Doing management

Management is not unidimensional. It's not about doing one thing that will result in one outcome like profit. There are multiple desired outcomes to be achieved and sustained simultaneously. A firm, for example, needs high quality, turnover and profit. And these can be achieved through the manager taking a huge combination of actions. Each action contributes to the end outcomes - or sometimes not! It's the interaction of these actions that realises the outcomes. This makes successful management hugely complex.

As a result of this complexity, it's no surprise that managers abandon any thought of theory and resort to bumbling along, doing whatever their gut tells them at any time.

The good news, though, is that all the action-outcome relationships obey laws. There are principles that can be learned.

But before exploring those laws throughout the rest of the book, let's look at the overview: what is it that the manager is trying to do?

1.12.1   *Interventions*

Fundamentally, management is the intervention by the manager into the working lives of the employees to persuade them to do things that they might not have done otherwise.

The manager must therefore get used to the idea of change – of continually sensing the outcomes, doing more of what's working, stopping doing what doesn't work and launching new interventions in search of greater things. This is shown graphically below in Figure 1-8.

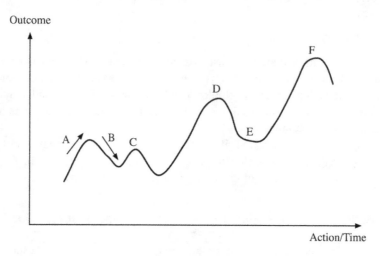

Figure 1-8: The manager's lot, graphically, showing local maxima

Taking an action that starts improvement in outcome up the slope at A is good – it's an action in the right direction. It might be something like introducing performance appraisals. People become more focused and committed because they welcome the interest shown in them by their manager. So, the manager then deepens the appraisal action by linking each person's performance rating to their pay. That drives outcomes down the slope B (you'll learn more about why this is, later in the book).

The manager can then either re-trace their steps back to A or introduce some evolved bonus system that partially corrects for the previously misguided intervention. This then leads to the local maximum C.

While resting, rejoicing at C, the manager might consider that there's more to be had and so they launch a new initiative, such as a re-structure. Let's speculate that this results in hugely improved responsibility for all, resulting in improved motivation. The result is arrival, with heightened outcomes, at point D. The question for the manager is whether there's more to be had by striving for F (if only they could see what F is), or whether by upsetting what's now been achieved, the firm will come crashing down to the local minimum at E.

Now, this is us playing in two dimensions. It's a model – a way of visualising the effects in a complex world. In truth, the figure, with its local minima and maxima, is in multiple dimensions. It's presented here to illustrate the lot of the manager – as someone who is continually intervening in search of greater things. Sometimes what they do has a good result, and sometimes the variables will conspire to reduce the outcome.

But the manager can never rest, since the environment around the firm is changing too, and evolution is fundamental.

1.12.2 *Evolution*

Management of a firm can be likened to the evolution of a species. The continual injection of management energy by the manager in the fashion depicted above results in what might be termed the firm's DNA. A firm's DNA can be described at a high level using the McKinsey 7-S model first postulated by Tom Peters and Robert Waterman in the 1982 book *In Search of Excellence*. They worked at the time for the McKinsey consulting firm. This model is shown in Figure 1-9.

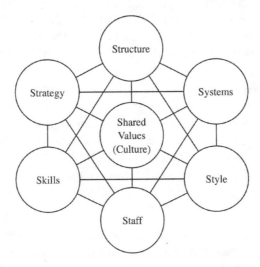

Figure 1-9: The 7-S model describing a firm

In the McKinsey 7-S model, every aspect of the firm can be categorised under one of seven headings. Conveniently, each category begins with the letter 's'. In simple terms, the manager could write a sentence describing each 's' and that would give a pretty good description of the firm's 'DNA'.

Taking the analogy a little further, the firm adjusts itself – its skills, staff, style, strategy, structure, systems and culture – to meet the needs of its stakeholders within its chosen environment. If there's a match between firm and environment, the 'organism' of the firm succeeds. If not, like Darwinian natural selection, that combination of DNA fails.

But the environment is changing and it's the manager's never-ending job to adjust the firm's DNA to optimise the match.

1.12.3 *Mutations*

Like evolution, no-one knows if the present version of the organism, the firm, is the best that there could be. The evolution described in Figure 1-8 could progress without any step change in outcomes. Perhaps the manager and the shareholders, in search of profit, will be satisfied, and perhaps not.

Sometimes, managers can create a hugely changed DNA for the firm, which, they believe from various modelling activities, will give a step change in outcomes. We might liken this to a mutation in Darwinian evolution.

If the mutation is better suited to the environment, and more of the desired outcomes result, this version of the firm can be kept. Evolution then progresses as before with the manager making more incremental change to improve key performance indicators such as turnover, profit, quality, and safety.

1.12.4   *Searching for excellence*

Peters and Waterman's book was well titled. It perfectly describes the manager's lot – to use their competencies to search for optimised outcomes that might be described for their firm as the state of excellence. Of course, like nirvana and other desirable but un-reachable states, excellence is never really achieved, but hopefully at least normal if not super-normal profits can be sustained over a long period.

1.13   Chapter Summary

Chapter 1 is an overview, setting the scene for the eleven chapters that follow.

We define the manager of a firm as the person who takes responsibility for the actions of their employees in the pursuit of agreed goals. The manager differs from other, perhaps more glamorous titles like 'entrepreneur' and 'leader'. The 'entrepreneur' and 'leader' are simply management roles – generally, managers must be entrepreneurs and must lead. That distinction of manager as the person who elects to take responsibility, is crucial to the firm's success.

Some might say that accepting responsibility is all that's needed – because the skills and knowledge of management can then be learned on the job. There's some truth in that.

The manager is responsible for the creation and running of the firm. The firm converts inputs to outputs using processes. This idea of treating a firm as a system allows the complexity of the firm to be abstracted and hence simplified. Simplification without loss aids understanding. The system can be measured for its ability to produce key performance metrics like turnover and profit and to do so with effectiveness metrics like productivity.

Since the manager creates the processes within the system, they can adjust those processes to optimise the desired outcomes. This gives rise to the central manager activity – intervention. The manager intervenes if they want change. The manager has an ever-growing intervention repertoire. It's then a question of choosing the right intervention to effect the right change.

Employees work in the system of the firm with technology. The duality of employees and technology gives the firm its capability. In intervening, the manager can elect to adjust the employees and their competencies and behaviours or can adjust the technology.

In the beginning, firms start with an entrepreneur with a good idea. The entrepreneur produces goods and services for supply to their customer. There are then two key steps in the firm's growth – the first when the entrepreneur sub-contracts to others to supply goods and services and the second when the entrepreneur hires some employees to serve in producing the goods and services. Both enable growth. This distinction between supplier and employee is important and many managers confuse the two. In this book we drive a clear wedge between the two and focus on employees.

As the firm grows and hires more employees, its structure becomes ever-more important. Humans are social beings and employees work together in social groups. This interaction aids the firm in achieving its goals but is also the source of much of the manager's worry.

The firm's goals are defined in its strategy. A strategy is a statement of what the manager and the employees will do to meet the goals. We define simple ideas about how to state a firm's strategy.

Having said that systemising the firm will simplify, the manager does need to elaborate to characterise the system components – its employees and its technology. We describe a method of concept modelling taken from the field of systems dynamics. Using concept modelling, we describe how the firm can be described, and hence built.

Management is about change and hence change can be managed by modelling what is, and what will be. The difference between the present and intended states is the motivation for action.

Following our declared positivist approach, we describe in this chapter how it is that the manager sets up their system, setting it running to achieve its aims, and we describe how the manager intervenes. Positivism is about establishing the dependencies between the variables – the links from employee competencies and behaviours to business outcomes. We portray the manager as an incessant intervener, knowing the links and adjusting to achieve the desired goals.

Chapter 1 is an overview. In the following eleven chapters, we discuss how such interventions on the human resource of the firm are made to best effect. In those eleven, we discuss a mix of management theory stemming from the science of psychology, the professions of the law and economics and from a modicum of politics too.

Few managers are trained. Few managers get management right so there's much to be learned. We hope that you read on and enjoy the learning experience.

2

Leading People

2.1 Introduction to leadership

To lead, managers must do stuff. Outcomes require action. Managers as leaders do what they do by personal intervention. This chapter sets out the theoretical underpinning that managers need to know to understand leadership. The chapter also presents the key practical interventions.

2.1.1 Defining leadership

Leadership is the act of persuading or influencing followers to do what the leader wants.

On the one extreme, a despotic leader persuades thought coercion. At the other extreme is perhaps laissez-faire (or 'don't care') leadership, so apparently lacking in leadership interaction and activity that it's questionable as to whether it's leadership at all. Reality for most managers is somewhere in the middle.

By way of example, a manager seeking increased profit might convene a conference of their sales staff at which delegates discuss the various future pricing strategies. The outcome of this conference might be a new price structure and a resulting improvement in profit. In another example, a manager might take a direct lead in accompanying sales staff on customer visits to improve their selling skills by direct intervention. The outcome this time might be a better quotation-to-order conversion rate and thus more sales. Both might lead to the same business outcome of increased profit. As examples, they show that different interventions with different approaches can achieve the same aim.

These examples show the importance of the behaviour of the leader and the approach taken in the persuasive act. Behaviour and approach must be appropriate for the desired outcome.

Intervention demands conscious decisions by the leader: decisions about the desired outcome, approaches, initiatives, actions, and behaviours. As the situation changes, the approaches, initiatives, actions, and behaviours may change to ensure that the desired outcomes are reached. Leadership is a highly dynamic, adaptive activity.

2.1.2 Great leaders

Looking at those people who society considers 'great leaders' certainly gives plenty of examples. Whether a new leader should follow their example is a different issue. But how do we decide who gets into the 'great leaders' club?

Is it the leaders who apparently had huge following? Jesus Christ and Mohammed both headed worldwide religions and had huge followings. Their approach was often moral, laying down the behaviours expected from the followers in return for a place in heaven.

Or is it the leaders who caused their followers to achieve momentous things – those who persuaded their followers to change destiny, for better or for worse? Hitler fits this latter category, energising Germany to arise but doing so through evil.

Perhaps it's better to look to explorers who did one-off feats of leadership like Ernest Shackleton. The plight of Shackleton and his men was hopeless, but he galvanised his followers to cross the ice of Antarctica. His leadership interventions saved his followers from near-certain death.

We could go on. History from antiquity to present day is replete with tales of venerated leaders. The important point is that those leaders had followers. And leaders achieve things through their followers that, apparently, without leadership, might not be achieved.

2.1.3   *Are leaders born or bread?*

Leader selection has been under discussion for decades. In the First World War the British military selected their officers (and hence their wartime military leaders) from the upper classes of society. By the Second World War, the American military was selecting its leaders by elaborate psychometric tests assessing both personality and intelligence.

Research suggested that it took a particular personality to make an officer – but this only suggested that if the personality was right, leadership could then be learned. The right personality did not make the leader, but it made leadership possible. Personality is part inherited and part developed. And intelligence enabled leadership learning. So, leaders are part 'born' to the job and part 'bred' into the job. If they have the right personal characteristics, including personality and intelligence, then they must go to leadership school.

In large firms and government, most leaders are appointed to a role because someone in authority in the firm thought that they had what it would take and had already learned or could learn the trade of leadership. In small firms, leaders seldom go on to learn the trade of leadership and are often what is termed 'accidental leaders'- with obvious parallels to 'accidental managers'.

2.1.4   *Core idea – influencing*

So, what happens when a leader intervenes and injects a bit of 'leadership'? The answer is that if the leadership is appropriate, the outcome is improved. Here's a simple example of this.

Consider that you want to get fit. Imagine a personal trainer working with you in the gym. You're doing some exercise and coping OK but you're weakening rep by rep as you get towards the end of the activity. Imagine the personal trainer shouting at you, "good technique, good effort, last 20 seconds, give it everything!"

Most people will be buoyed up by the encouragement. Most will modify their behaviour to improve the quality of the exercise and the speed of the reps. Ultimately, this encouragement will improve your fitness – particularly if repeated and sustained. This simple example of encouragement by a personal trainer shows the power of a leadership intervention.

Not all leaders get things right. Just as it is possible to intervene and change for the better, so it is possible to intervene for the worse. Crass, ill-timed, and inappropriate leadership intervention can quickly destroy the leader-follower relationship.

The job of the leader in a firm is to intervene whenever necessary in a follower's life to achieve improved outcomes. The leader uses the relationship between them and their follower to change follower behaviour. Giving encouragement is just one of a host of leadership tactics.

Reflection 2-1: You as a leader

Thinking about you as a leader, list the various leadership interventions that you have done in the past few weeks. Note with them your aims, expressed or otherwise, and whether those aims were met.

2.2 The language of leadership

Leadership has its jargon. It's important that managers understand this jargon. Those unfamiliar with leadership tend also to confuse terms.

The following shows a common vocabulary of leadership, carefully defining each term to mean the same as that used by a broad consensus of leadership writers and academics.

2.2.1 *Leader*

The leader is the individual appointed (or who choses) to influence others to carry out, or change the way they carry out, a particular task. Those others are identified as followers.

2.2.2 *Follower*

A follower is a person who chooses for some reason to be persuaded by a leader to do that leader's bidding or to change what they do in favour of what's wanted by the leader.

2.2.3 *Leadership*

Leadership is the presence of persuasion by a leader on a follower. The follower then takes action that they would not otherwise take without the persuasion.

2.2.4 *Team/group*

Often leaders lead teams. A team is a group of people, each of whom builds a dyadic or one-to-one relationship with a leader. People may be members of many teams each with a different leader. Teams and their leaders may have different membership and aims. We comment later about the distinction between teams and groups.

2.2.5   *Intervention*

An intervention is a single act done by a leader on a follower to influence that follower to change their behaviour towards that wanted by the leader. Leadership is simply intervention after intervention. The presence of interventions is therefore an indication of the presence of leadership in a group.

2.2.6   *Outcome*

An outcome is some result stemming from the efforts of many followers. Typically, this will be an improvement in some valued key performance indicator such as turnover, profit, productivity, quality or safety.

2.3   The nature of leadership

To be able to lead, managers must be able to understand the systems of leadership.

Unfortunately, we can't physically touch the leadership scenario, with its leaders and followers doing the leading and being led. It's abstract; it's conceptual, in the minds of the participants. But we can treat it as a black box, or series of black boxes describing the various concepts. Black boxes are systems and system elements that are closed to us. We can only determine what they do by observing the effect that the systems have on the participants using and experiencing them.

One can understand what's inside these black boxes by inference. The systems and models and how the various concepts interact can be described.

2.3.1   *The leader's influence on motivation*

Systems can be thought of as having an input, an output, and a process. Complex systems are just a plethora of discrete input-process-output units. There are obvious parallels with the input-process-output models discussed in Chapter 1.

Motivation is an example of a conceptual system associated with leadership. Motivation is the in-person cognitive process that get us going, directs our energy toward a particular project, dictates how much energy we put into a particular activity and for how long, and stops us and makes us change activities.

If leadership is to be effective, a leader must influence a follower's motivation. This can be shown as the simple model in Figure 2-1.

Figure 2-1: The leader's influence on motivation

Conceptually, if the leader can do something positive to influence the follower's motivation, good things will happen. The follower will do what the leader wants. They'll put more effort in, perhaps for longer, or they'll stop doing what they are doing now and do instead what the leader wants. Overall, more of the desired output will be realised for a given input.

This is the simplest model of leadership. It describes leadership as dyadic or binary – involving two people, the leader, and the follower.

2.3.2   The leader's influence on jobs

In the work setting, the job done hugely influences motivation. The job done comprises five characteristics; variety, identity, significance, autonomy and feedback.

If each is in line with the person's implicit (non-conscious) motives, or their explicit (conscious) motives, motivation will be enhanced. This idea is shown in the extended model in Figure 2-2. The manager as leader has, of course, every opportunity to modify the job characteristics to enable motivation. A job holder doing a job with high variety is likely to be more motivated than someone with a monotonous job; that job characteristic will better tap the job holder's motives with greater resulting effect.

The same applies to the other characteristics. It's in the manager's interests therefore to design the job to trigger job holder motives.

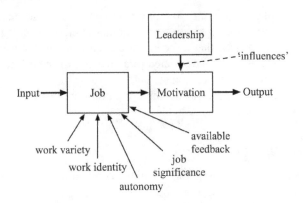

Figure 2-2: The leader's influence on jobs

2.3.3   The leader's influence on outcomes

The model developed so far is incomplete. The outcome from motivation is a motivated person. That outcome itself is useless. It needs to be turned into more practical, usable concepts that ultimately yield business outcomes like growth, profit, quality, and safety.

The first step in linking motivation to outcomes is the system of behaviour. Motivation influences behaviour. It's not all that acts to cause behaviour, but for the purposes of explaining leadership, the simplification is useful.

Behaviour then creates personal performance. Performance is itself a complex concept and will be dealt with elsewhere in this book. For now, it's enough to take it at face value, using its everyday meaning of doing stuff that the leader needs done.

Personal performance yields personal outcomes. And those personal outcomes aggregate to yield business outcomes. The idea is shown in Figure 2-3.

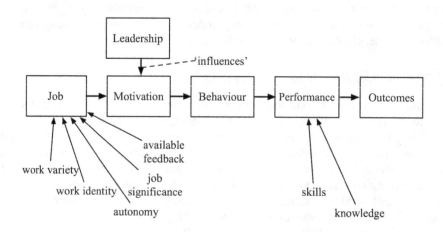

Figure 2-3: The link from job to outcomes

This model is remarkably intuitive, fitting common sense understanding of the way people contribute in a firm. It is also supported in organisational psychology research.

So, the idea of leadership is that if the leader can influence a follower's motivation, a change in behaviour results. That's translated to a change in performance which yields a change, ultimately, in the business outcomes.

Simplifying it further, good leadership, resulting in positive changes, enables improved business outcomes.

2.3.4 *Leadership and technology*

In today's connected world, computers mediate communications between people in the workplace. Studies show that around 50% of a manager's time is spent with their subordinates and 50% of their emails are between them and their subordinates. And many employees and managers work from home or other remote site. Remote working is set to increase. As a result, this balance between face-to-face and computer-mediated communications will only swing to reduce future personal contact between leader and followers.

So, leadership is enabled, and in some senses hampered, by electronic communications in today's workplace and its effects will be exacerbated in years to come.

Communication between humans is part expressed – verbal or written – and part non-verbal, transmitted and received in gestures and postures. Some commentators put the latter at 80% of meaningful communication.

This means that a leader's ability to influence is, potentially, reduced by physical displacement between them and their followers and constrained by the function of the communications medium. Today, workers use a host of different communications media – from short text or WhatsApp messages through video Skype or Zoom calls to face-to-face meetings. It means that to be effective, a leader must consider, case by case, what the best medium is to achieve the right level of influence to realise the desired outcome. It means that leaders must stop and think before routinely sending an email. For every proposed action, they must ask themselves if they should pick up the phone, or if they should go to their follower's desk or arrange an online call or if they should take a plane, train, or car to meet with their follower.

Leadership will fail if influence is constrained by the communications medium.

2.3.5   *Nature of contracts*

The relationship between manager and worker is shifting. Of the 32 million workers in the UK, only about three quarters are employees of a firm or the government. The other quarter are self-employed and under a supplier contract of one sort or other. This shift towards self-employment or freelancing is set to increase.

This shift suggests that most managers will gather round them a mix of employees, workers, and suppliers. And the expectations of each worker type are very different.

As a result, the leader's ability to create followership in these two worker types differs. Employees expect their manager to invest in them for the long term. Suppliers take a much shorter-term view – they could have their contract terminated tomorrow. Theirs is more an economic relationship – an exchange of labour for money - whereby the manager and contractor respect one another but understand it's not a leader-follower relationship.

The nature of the contractual foundation that underpins the leadership relationship fundamentally enables or constrains the leadership possible.

2.3.6   *Necessary self-efficacy*

Leadership self-efficacy is the leader's beliefs about their competence in leadership. Leadership self-efficacy is their belief that they can produce the necessary levels of personal performance to influence their followers and that those followers will in turn do what's wanted.

Put simply, if the manager has high leadership self-efficacy, they are likely to actively engage with their followers and with the tools of leadership. They will see the leadership challenges as opportunities. They will likely go on to encourage and influence their followers to achieve great things by trying and adjusting their leadership activities.

If a manager has low leadership self-efficacy, they will be full of self-doubt that their leadership efforts will have the necessary influence to achieve the required outcome. If they have low leadership self-efficacy, the manager will not enjoy successful leadership interventions

Undoubtedly, the best way to build a sense of leadership efficacy is through mastery of the science of leadership followed by experience of leadership resulting in both successful and unsuccessful outcomes. As with most development, success builds self-efficacy while failure allows reflection. Ultimately it helps if the leader overcomes obstacles to give eventual success from potential failure.

Reflection 2-2: About high leadership self-efficacy

High leadership self-efficacy is essential for leadership success. Thinking
about some of the interventions that you identified, can you make the
links for each all the way from modified behaviours on the part of
your followers to realise improved business outcomes?

2.4   Leadership theory

Theory is generally the domain of academics. The work they do to understand phenomena
and explain phenomena with theories does eventually filter down to the management
coalface. But typically, it takes decades for managers to adopt theory in their day-to-day
behaviours. Managers do need to embrace theory and to reduce the time from emergence of
new thinking to employed practice.

2.4.1   *The dyadic theory of leadership*

Under the dyadic theory of leadership, the leader and follower are said to have a one-to-one
relationship in which the leader can influence the follower. Under the dyadic theory, the
manager as leader is also able to design the environment that the follower will enjoy such
that the influence and motivation are maximised, and the required changes take place.

The dyadic theory also supports the various tactics like roadblock removal and goal
illumination (discussed further later). It is simple for a manager to understand how they
should behave – leadership in that case is not about standing up at 'town hall' meetings
espousing vision, but rather about being in the trenches getting close to the followers. The
dyadic theory also supports leadership from within the group, with every person capable of
influencing every other. Leadership is never just top-down.

2.4.2   *Roadblock removal*

Often the leader is in a superior position within the organisation. Often the leader will have
a more extensive social network and will be able to reach out to colleague managers for
assistance.

Followers often find difficulty in completing projects. Their motivation is sapped by
colleagues who perhaps should contribute and support but don't. Often that refusal to assist
stems from organisational policies and politics.

Leaders can use their superior positions to influence peers and other followers to gain
the assistance needed. They can remove the roadblocks.

Applying this to the leadership model (Figure 2-3), the intervention by the leader
recovers the follower's motivation. It perhaps allows enhanced motivation, allowing the
follower to re-make the link between the job and their behaviour.

This tactic can be assessed for its effect by counting the instances and size of the
roadblock removal in each instance and the effects these interventions had. It has a
particular place in transformational and professional approaches (2.6).

2.4.3   Goal illumination

Remarkably, people are eager to strive for the completion of goals. Humans are wired that way. Working towards goals is a source of motivation.

Research shows that the more a leader illuminates an agreed goal and the associated path towards that goal, the greater the result in a follower's behaviour and performance. It's neatly summed up in the common adage that says, 'when up to your backside in alligators, it's difficult to remember that the original aim was to drain the swamp'. The leader can continually remind the follower(s) of the aim to drain the swamp. And it follows that, all other things being equal, if the behaviour and performance rise, it's more likely that the goal will be achieved.

This relies on the leader having a very clear view of the goals and that they have agreed the goals with the followers. It also relies on the leader having the technical skills and knowledge to identify the path which, if followed, will lead to a positive outcome. Goal illumination tactic, often referred to as the path-goal theory, has useful application in the professional leadership approach (2.6.1).

2.4.4   Empowerment and delegation

The degree to which an individual is empowered in their work influences their motivation. Empowerment stems from the delegation to the employee of many of the important decisions about how work is done. This in turn taps intrinsic motives, heightening the meaningfulness derived from the work. Meaningfulness in what we do is a fundamental human need, and we are all motivated to strive to satisfy needs.

Managers must determine what can and can't be delegated and hence where in the various activities the follower can be empowered. Delegation requires that that the leader takes risks. The follower feels increase in self-worth by knowing the risks that the leader has taken to allow them self-determination.

Delegation can be relatively risk free within procedural leadership where processes provide a wrapper within which followers can be empowered. And delegation is expected by followers under professional leadership where empowerment is just part of the job.

2.4.5   Participation

Participation has two aspects. The first is the effects on followers of leaders 'in the trenches working with the troops'. This allows the leader to show that they are authentic and to practice impression management. The second aspect is to allow decision sharing.

Authentic leadership is a whole subject on its own, posing the question 'how authentic should a leader be'? It poses the sub-question about who or what the leader should be authentic to. Generally, though, it's essential for the leader to demonstrate their commitment to the cause or goal that everyone is working to. Impression management is the idea that there is benefit in the follower building a generally favourable impression of the leader. Impressions are managed by the leader by saying and doing things that the followers admire. Once followers admire the leader, other tactics become easier.

There are many benefits of decision sharing. Decision quality is often increased (since innovation coming from collective work methods can be embedded in decision making) and, once made, decisions are often more readily accepted by the followers. Follower development can also be built into the decision processes, thereby increasing follower skill and knowledge.

Participation requires that the leader is technically competent. Participation is found to positively influence follower motivation. Participative tactics are particularly relevant in transactional leadership (2.6.4) because participation allows exchange of services. Impression management is relevant in transformational leadership (2.6.3).

Reflection 2-3: Relationships

Reflect on the various dyadic relationships that exist in your leadership scenarios. Think through the various objectives that you have and how you have flowed those objectives down to personal goals for your followers. Think through where you could develop further goals for each follower and how you will work with them to ensure the goals are achieved.

2.5   Leadership in Practice

If managers are to understand and practice good leadership, they need tools. If leadership development is to be anything other than a few exhortations proclaiming that "a good manager should…", managers must have ways of working which enable good leadership. The most important tools centre on the use of feedback to continually modify action in pursuit of improvement in outcome.

2.5.1   Doing leadership

No manager knows exactly what to do and when to do it to effect positive influence on the performance of a follower. Every scenario is different. There is therefore no 'best practice'. There is no rule book. There is no look-up table of effects and corresponding actions.

To 'do' leadership, we must look to other areas of science such as human learning. Humans learn by using the concept of feedback. We sense outcomes for given actions and we store away what works and what doesn't work. The basic idea is shown in Figure 2-4.

Using this model, the leader compares some idea that they have about what they'd consider as an acceptable reference performance from the follower with actual performance occurring now. In the conceptual model shown, this is done in the device labelled the comparator.

In practice this comparison is done in the leader's mind in their cognitive processes.

If the actual and reference performances are equal, the follower is performing to expectations and hence there is no feedback, or at least nothing that triggers leadership action. If the actual performance is below the reference performance, the feedback creates a need for change. The leader must then take some leadership action.

After leadership action, the comparison is then repeated. If the leadership action worked, the actual performance rises. If it worked well enough, the loop is once again balanced, and the leadership action can stop. An example might be the use of goal illumination. Reminding followers of some agreed goal might be enough to spur them on and recover performance.

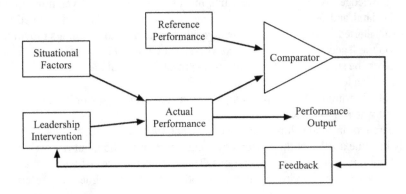

Figure 2-4: In search of performance using a feedback loop

In reality of course, the system depicted is completely dynamic. First the comparison suggests that intervention is needed. The manager intervenes. Performance rises. Leadership intervention drops. Performance drops and intervention is needed again.

Intervention is incessant. Ideas about reference performances change. And of course, situational factors – things outside the leadership system - act to thwart the leader's best efforts.

2.5.2   *Trying something new*

Feedback, as depicted above, suggests that all that a leader need do is find some intervention that works and apply the feedback model to it. If the actual performance drops, the leader need simply do more of the same to effect correction.

All leadership occurs in a shifting environment. Just because one thing worked yesterday doesn't mean it will work again today. In the above example, there's the suggestion that goal illumination might be enough to recover loop balance. It may be that this is insufficient – no amount of goal illumination works. A complete change of tactic may be needed.

This is a common scenario in science. In evolution, progress stalls and the species will not reach optimum fitness for survival if breeding continues without introduction of new strains in the genome. In evolution, mutations occur. Sometimes these are successful and are fitter than previous and thrive. Others are less fit and perish.

The idea in leadership learning is similar. The leader needs to experiment with new interventions. Sometimes these will be better than that previous. Other times, the intervention will be a dismal failure and the leader will move on. The leader learns what works and what doesn't work in their environment.

And just as in other areas of science where optimums are sought, false summits will be found – interventions will seem to work, until, that is, the leader tries something completely different and greater performance results.

2.5.3 *Priming the pump*

If this sounds a bit hit and miss, it's not. Scientists know well that there's 'no knowledge without knowledge'. All systems of learning must start somewhere. Even modern thinking about 'big data' and learning machines using Bayesian methods needs something with which to get started. There must be some algorithm or method to get things moving.

So too the leader needs to start somewhere. They must start by using an intervention that will likely be successful. It might not be the most successful method possible, but it's a start from which learning occurs.

It's called 'priming the pump'. Pumps, by way of an analogy, won't draw water unless there is first water in the tubes.

Researchers in leadership have given us that start point. Such a start point is not perfectly in context. It's not the leader's own algorithm or method, but research has shown that there are typographies of interventions. There are catalogues of tactics that are more likely to work in one environment than another. Such catalogues are referred to as approaches.

Leaders must first adopt an approach as a point of departure for their leadership learning. They must choose the approach likely to give the greatest positive influence on followers' motivation.

Reflection 2-4: Assessing performance

Objectively assessing performance is difficult. Take a few minutes to think about individual accountabilities in several jobs. Write down how you'll measure performance in each. Are your methods objective?

2.6   Leadership approaches

An approach is like a disposition, deliberately adopted for the long term and not changed to suit immediate urgencies. Approaches are catalogues of discrete interventions. The approach adopted is chosen by considering what will work for that leader and their followers, goals, and environment.

An approach is a point of departure for modification and optimisation of leadership interventions. The following gives an initial compendium.

2.6.1 *Professional leadership*

There are many who embark on a career and see their employer and its various leaders as vehicles supporting that career, rather than to support lifestyle and family. Such individuals generally have high growth needs. More than most, their career taps their intrinsic motives. So long as the quality of experiences is in tune with their expectations, they'll take suggestion for new projects, they'll strive for goals developed within the project and they'll work hard to succeed.

Provided that the experiences they get from work satisfy their needs for growth, they'll be happy and motivated.

One could be mistaken for assuming that leadership has no place in helping such a 'professional' to be further motivated. From this description, they seem to be motivated enough, just from engaging with their career. But just like everyone else, motivation is what gets them going and causes them to choose what to do, how much effort to expend and when to stop. Arguably such people need more leadership to have them do what the firm needs them to do rather than just doing what they fancy.

Such 'professionals' don't respond much to charisma or transaction. They likely consider themselves peers of the leader. It's unlikely that the leader can give them much that they haven't got already just from doing what they do. So, leaders must take a different approach.

Professional leadership demands that the leader is also a professional of the same discipline – or that at least they have significant technical skills that the follower will value. When adopting this approach, the leader uses opportunities brought by the work to engage directly with the follower. Examples include peer review of work, walk throughs of project methods and direct assistance overcoming project complexity.

These activities give the professional leader scope to influence the follower towards their point of view and hence influence the follower's motivation. That influencing comes from the follower's respect for the leader's superior technical knowledge or the quality of argument made in favour of their points of view.

2.6.2   *Procedural leadership*

Firms thrive because work is largely repetitive. Each action is part of a process of linked actions that does something. Even original work like academic research is highly procedural. And arguably, the more we can fit work to processes, the more efficient we'll be at doing the work. People generally make processes of repetitive actions. We're all wired to do that.

Procedural leadership exploits this human need for structure. In this approach, the leader organises the work into processes such that it can be done efficiently. Followers are motivated to expend effort on the various tasks because the processes tap their need for achievement in turn leading to meaningfulness. Explicit motives can also be tapped by bringing in reward for compliance and success.

All leadership embraces the procedural approach but on its own, procedural leadership fits well in businesses such as hospitality and retail. In these environments, making procedures of work helps workers achieve. The leadership task centres on reinforcing and rewarding adherence to the procedure.

2.6.3   *Transformational leadership*

Transformational leadership has at its heart an identification of the needs of followers and the marrying of the needs of the task or project with those follower needs. The leader's aim is to successfully satisfy both.

Follower needs are typically characterised in three headings: existence, association, and achievement. The transformational leader harnesses the power that comes from being the manager able to satisfy those needs in their followers.

To tap this power, the leader might develop a clear and appealing vision of success that they desire in a project. This can then be extended to suggest that all those followers who are part of this success will enjoy needs satisfaction – promotion, heightened self-worth and being associated with the winning team.

All that's needed then is for the transformational leader to develop the vision and how they see it being achieved. The leader must then communicate the messages through symbolic speeches and actions.

Of course, the danger here is that it's all jam tomorrow and transformational leaders will need to build follower confidence by highlighting success along the way.

2.6.4   *Transactional leadership*

The essence of transactional leadership is that the leader and follower exchange things of value. The leader wants to influence the follower to change activities, put more effort in or the like. The follower needs something from the leader such as perhaps flexibility in hours or duties. If the leader gives that flexibility, this obligates the follower to respond in kind.

Transactional leadership makes use of social exchange theory. Social exchange theory proposes that people naturally exchange things of value throughout their lives. Even a smile can be exchanged, and certainly the leader's attention is a valuable commodity ripe for use in gaining some change in motivation.

There are myriad services that might be exchanged. There are practical things like flexibility and developmental opportunities. And there are less-tangible services like friendship and admiration. Keep in mind though that social exchange is not the same as simple economic exchange, such as the award of promotion and a bigger salary. Social exchange is subtler and, as such, more powerful in influencing motivation and behaviour.

It's worth also noting that the more exchange there is between leader and follower, the greater the trust there will be between them. Trust cements the transactional relationship.

A transactional leadership approach is one characterised by exchange and the leader must build a library of possible exchange services and commodities. Transactional leadership is marked by the frequency of exchange and the value of the services and commodities exchanged.

2.6.5   *Contingent leadership*

Reality is that the leadership approach adopted will likely end up a mix of several approaches. One will be dominant – those leading professionals will likely turn mainly to the professional approach, whilst those attempting major change in an organisation might adopt a transformational approach. Even where transactional leadership is chosen initially, elements of the other three approaches will be found to work and added to the mix. This idea of mixing and matching is referred to as contingent leadership – the approach is contingent on the context and is no one thing or other. Interventions are taken from all available approaches.

It's also important to emphasise that the approach or mix of approaches adopted will change with time. The new manager will need to adopt one approach when appointed and another as their relationship with those that they lead evolves.

In selecting an approach, the manager must be highly adaptive.

2.6.6   *Leadership and culture*

There are many definitions of culture. One useful definition suggests that it's the sum of the learned behaviour of a group of people that, though social transmission, becomes tradition. It becomes 'the way we do things around here'. The people share a common skill, knowledge, values, attitudes, beliefs, and motives. So, culture is visible through the behaviour of each team or group.

Previously, we have argued that leadership is the influence that a leader has on a follower because of their dyadic relationship. The leader behaves in a certain way to exert the influence to achieve the outcomes they need. And a follower reacts to a leader's interventions with behaviour. They modify their values, attitudes, and beliefs in response to the leader's actions. Leaders therefore affect culture.

Culture also exists without leadership. The team or group exhibits a culture built from the sum of all social transmissions from their home lives and across the organisation.

So, we can see that culture comes about, in part, through the efforts of a leader, in part by the sum of the collective responses to that leader's actions and in part from all other cultural influences. Culture therefore depends on the leadership approach chosen, the leadership styles used day by day and the various interventions experienced by the team or group. The leader influences culture but they do not direct it.

Culture is difficult to express in an organisation without a model. One well regarded model is that by Bob Waisfisz, based on the work of Geert Hofstede. Under this model, the manager can greatly influence certain of the indices such as creating an open culture (as opposed to one that is secretive) by interventions like holding 'town hall' meetings when detailed financial and other information is made public. Even in day-to-day interventions, the manager can adopt an informing style. Likewise, the manager can drive an easy-going culture (as opposed to a strict, conforming culture), transmitting expectations across the whole workforce about required easy-going behaviour.

Reflection 2-5: Leadership approaches

Reflect on what leadership approach might be best for your organisation. If this is not the approach you are using, consider what you might need to do to change your approach. If this is the approach you are using, what approaches might yield useful interventions for addition to your repertoire?

2.7   Leadership styles

Style is like a mood. It is adopted and changed to suit the moment in which the leader finds themselves and the immediate issue that needs addressing in the leader-follower relationship.

There are only three styles: directive, non-directive, and laissez-faire.

2.7.1   *Directive*

The directive style is synonymous with telling the follower what's wanted. Sometimes there's enough time to discuss with followers, ask for suggestions and have the group come to a decision. In other situations, followers need to be given an order for them to do something the leader wants. In this latter case, the leader would be said to use a directive style.

Historically we'd identify the directive style with the military order, given perhaps by a sergeant, often loudly.

Typically, the directive style requires the leader to have the power, the authority, to give the order. In the military this comes from a hierarchical command structure and a norm of obedience from followers, both supported by a strict disciplinary code such as that laid down in Queen's Regulations. In a firm, it can only come from appointment of the leader over the followers. Followers generally dislike being told what to do and therefore the directive style should be used sparingly and reserved for management situations where a 'tell' method will succeed better than others.

2.7.2   *Non-directive*

Back in 1966 The Boy Scout Association (now The Scouts) published its Chief Scout's Advanced Party Report to create the Venture Scout section for boys (and later girls) between the ages of 16 and 20. Any parent bringing up young people of this age range knows the difficulties of balancing direction with a lighter touch leadership. Such leadership must permit the young people to explore, discuss and make decisions whilst still under influence of the leader's hidden hand.

Those conceiving the Venture Scout section back then got it right. The predominant leadership style to be used was non-directive and Venture Scout Leaders were trained to adopt this style. The aim behind the non-directive style is that the leader knows what is wanted but is disinclined to declare their hand. The leader prefers instead to create discussion such that the required outcome is reached by consensus within the follower group. The followers – the Venture Scouts in this case – would go on to achieve great things in the belief that they did the directing.

The mental energy needed in adopting a non-directive style as the predominant style is huge. The leader training and competence needed is also huge because the leader must not only see what's needed, but engineer situations that facilitate a desired, acceptable, or appropriate outcome.

Non-directive leadership is the predominant style in management within firms. Whilst staff are remunerated and enter an employment contract, staff volunteer to come to work. No worker wants to be told what to do.

2.7.3   *Laissez faire*

Laissez-faire leadership describes a state where the appointed leader is disinclined to take any part in motivating the group to perform. Translated from French, laissez-faire literally means 'leave (it) be' or, in other words, do nothing.

This leadership style can be appropriate when the task is well defined by rules or where a leadership intervention would not change the outcome. It can also be effective when group cohesion is more important than a particular outcome. Group cohesion can be enhanced by letting the group have a free hand in its direction.

Laissez-faire and non-directive leadership are often confused. The difference is in the hidden hand of the leader. Under non-directive leadership, the hidden hand is strong but not apparent. In a laissez-faire style, it's non-existent.

A movement promoting long-term laissez-faire or leaderless leadership exists and companies have toyed with it. It has had some support in the technology and software industries but it's unclear how such apparently leaderless companies fair in the long term beyond the fun of the initial experiment.

2.7.4   *Deciding which style to use*

Leadership style is like a mood. And mood changes depending on the situation. Leaders must learn to use one style or other depending on the situation at that moment. Once used, the leader must continually evaluate how effective that style is and decide if a change of style might be more effective.

As we note, leadership is a highly dynamic activity.

2.8   Alternatives to leadership

We do need to take care that we don't simply assume that leadership, as we've described it above, is the only management tool in the toolkit. Many scenarios are served by well by alternatives.

2.8.1   *Distributed leadership*

Distributed leadership is as it sounds – there is no one leader, rather, leadership is distributed to each member of the 'follower' group.

In organisations, some teams train so frequently together and with such emotional and technical intensity that they learn to read one another's needs. They react to those needs automatically. The whole group behaves as one. Examples include a well-trained football team, a Special Forces patrol, or a fishing boat crew.

By way of analogy, anyone viewing murmuration of starlings will understand the idea. Starlings dance in the sky and many researchers have speculated on the reason. One possible reason is that predators such as peregrine falcons find it hard to target one bird in the middle of a flock of thousands. They gather over their roosting site and perform their aerial acrobatics before they roost for the night. In essence the starlings work together to behave as one – there is no leader, and the leadership of the flock is distributed.

Distributed leadership is useful when the team members are peers – but this is seldom so in a company. Generally, in a company, there's a hierarchy and there's the idea of abstraction, with senior managers developing strategies for junior members to operationalise.

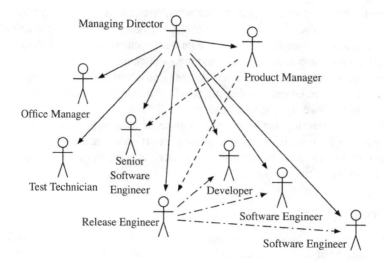

Figure 2-5: Leadership is not only top-down

2.8.2 *Self-managed teams*

Self-managed teams is an interesting idea that some firms experiment with.

Unlike distributed leadership, where the team knows the needs of the members and acts as one, self-managed teams require each member to take the lead of the whole activity when they are the most competent. The accountant would take the lead when it's about accounting, the salesperson would lead when it's sales, and so on. In principle, it is perhaps utopia, and hence of course it's an interesting notion for attracting employees to work in the business. Until, that is, there's disagreement. And most leadership must operate in conditions of ambiguity and across disciplines. Most leadership requires managers to give coherent visons and manage those disagreements.

Self-management is often referred to as democratic leadership: each team member has an equal opportunity to lead, and their leadership has equal weight.

This type of leadership takes the structure in Figure 2-5 to the limit, removing the managing director and linking each member in a many-to-many, or even all-to-all, matrix. To be effective, self-managed teams require each member to be highly competent, both technically and in leadership itself. And since democracy takes time, self-managed teams are inefficient. For these reasons, it's seldom a practical form found in organisations.

Reflection 2-6: Alternatives to leadership

Considering your organisation, and other organisations with which
you are familiar (including voluntary and social organisations).
Reflect on whether in any, the alternatives to leadership would give
better outcomes than the approach to leadership presently adopted
by their leaders.

2.9   Leadership and management

2.9.1   *The leader in context*

Organisations today comprise managers managing workers organised in some structure. The structures are manifold, though two popular styles prevail – the hierarchy and the matrix. The hierarchy is a top-down one-to-many arrangement whereas the matrix is a top-down and side-in few-to-many structure. These are structures that likely reflect how leadership works in those firms.

2.9.2   *Reporting structures and numbers*

It's clear from discussions so far that there are two players, the leader, and the follower. They are in a relationship - a dyadic or binary relationship. A firm is just a plurality of dyadic relationships that link leaders with their followers.

Describing the leader-follower relationship as 'dyadic' implies that the leader must have a close relationship with each follower.

In a small firm of say 20 people, that's simple to imagine. As the firm gets bigger, others must deputise for the leader. The leader must work by communicating their relationship through others. So how does this work?

Take a familiar organisational structure. The most basic fighting unit in an army, the section, comprises eight men commanded by a corporal. And eight army sections make a company of sixty-four men commanded by a captain. A lieutenant-colonel then commands eight companies of 512 men. The exact numbers differ army by army and regiment by regiment, but the form has persisted, even as far back in history as the Romans. It's the 'rule of eights'.

There are some very good reasons for this time-tested structure both in the military and in business. Primarily it's because the leader can monitor and influence the activities of eight subordinates whilst still doing productive work themselves. Ultimately the lieutenant-colonel commands around 500 people because that's the largest number that a human can 'know', albeit not closely.

Typically, therefore, a small firm MD will think about appointing a manager when the number of employees in the firm exceeds eight. A firm of 24 staff might therefore have two or three managers lead by the MD. In this case the MD may double as a manager leading eight as well as leading the managers, themselves leading eight. Those managers are proxies for the organisation leader and are themselves leaders and followers. This idea is shown in Figure 2-6.

As with the military, this 'rule of eights' is not hard and fast and depends on context. It could be eight or it could be 30. Eight is, however, a good overall starting point before looking at specifics.

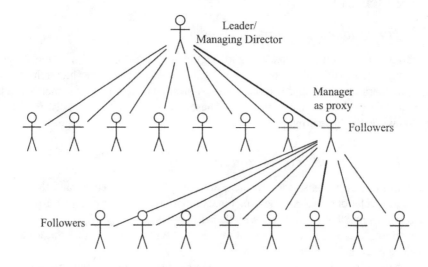

Figure 2-6: The rule of eights

As the MD employs managers to whom they delegate, their direct involvement evolves to be the leader of strategy, policy, and change. With 512 staff, for example, they work day-to-day in dyadic relationships with their eight senior managers, leading, training, mentoring and coaching them. Those eight senior managers work day-to-day in dyadic relationships with their eight junior managers and so on.

In larger organisations, where senior management have only weak relationships with junior followers, leadership takes on a different form, but the dyadic relationship persists with the relationship brokered through intermediaries.

2.9.3 *Functional and domain leadership*

Whilst it's general to assume that the leader is the commander, put in place by higher authority, leadership itself exists across the firm with each employee leading each other employee, at least to some extent.

An example of this matrix of leadership is the product manager or product owner. They are responsible for product success but often they have no executive power – they are not at the top of the tree. Such individuals will often exploit a professional approach, exuding technical and domain competence. Others want to follow them to be part of their success.

Arguably, senior managers want their whole team to be leaders, for if they each lead in their own specialism, the resulting integration is highly valuable.

Another example is of so-called matrix management. One manager may be responsible for a follower's functional performance while another is responsible for their pastoral development. The functional manager may be in another country, liaising online, while the pastoral manager is local, working daily with the follower. Despite adding complexity, matrix management is popular.

2.9.4   *Making leadership work*

Leaders start by having a set of plans and initiatives with which to engage with their followers. Plans and initiatives coupled with the environment of the business and the characteristics of the followers give the context of leadership in which the leader must act.

That context will likely suggest a leadership approach. The leader must spend time to understand the context, adjusting the approach to fit as the context and the leader's understanding shifts.

Once the approach is mature and the plans and initiatives are in place, it's time to start the leadership machine.

At the heart of the machine is the desired performance from the group or firm. Performance takes effort to quantify. The leader must have a clear idea of the performance that they expect from each follower. Generally, this flows from a corporate objective setting activity that culminates in personal objectives for all.

Given plans and initiatives and the required performance, the leader starts work. If performance is achieved, no leadership intervention is needed. But if it's felt that the machine will fail to achieve performance without intervention, the leader must act. And so, the machine grinds on with a combination of sensing, assessment of performance and outcomes and intervention after intervention until it's time to refresh organisational aims. Then the machine resets and it all begins again.

2.9.5   *Effective team building*

There's much published about team building and we won't repeat that here. It is however worth illustrating how team building might work such that leadership, as we've defined it here, will be effective.

The essence of team building is to set up a group where each group member brings personal characteristics to the group to contribute to a team capability. That done, the leader must build a dyadic relationship with each team member and encourage dyadic relationships between the team members when needed.

This is shown diagrammatically in Figure 2-5 above for a small software engineering company. Here the primary influences shown are the managing director, the product manager, and the release engineer. The direction of influence is in the direction of the arrow from influencer to influenced, leader to follower. Others take the lead in their own specialism from time to time. A diagram showing all leadership in the firm would be complex.

2.9.6   *Leading virtual teams*

Virtual teams, participating over Zoom or another of the many online meeting platforms, are now commonplace. Managers and staff are often dispersed geographically. And so, leadership is made more complex. But that's not to say it's impossible – or even difficult.

The essence of leadership is the manager's ability to influence the employee's motivation and that can be done just as well by electronic means. It does however mean that the manager as leader must be more deliberate in setting up plans and initiatives and reviews of performance. Accidental meetings by the water cooler are rare and it needs deliberate action to replace those with the electronic equivalent. This point is significant.

Many managers worry that the very employee worldview – the attitudes, values, beliefs, and expectations about the firm - that they have worked hard to establish through face-to-face interaction will be decimated by remote, home, or virtual working. Worldviews underpin leadership.

Managers should remember that online communities are highly effective in creating a worldview – one only need look at areas like terrorism, political extremism, and sexual preferences to see how large groups bond under shared belief. So, one should not think that what happens online is in any way less effective than the power of face-to-face office-based interactions. Online is just different.

We note above that trust is central to leadership. Leaders of virtual teams must build that trust through actions, engaging in exchange to build the feeling in followers that the leader will do what they say they will.

In summary, leadership of virtual teams requires managers as leaders to think more about how their leadership will work to achieve the outcomes. They'll need to put more energy in to the machine and be more deliberate in choice of approach and style.

2.9.7   Where managers fail at leadership

Management requires action. So, managers must not dither or delay. Leadership requires a delicate balance. The leader must influence with compassion and understanding to achieve the required outcomes.

Here are three common mistakes leaders make.

2.9.7.1   Leader too detached
Many coaches and other advisors suggest that managers should work 'on the company, not in the company'. This is often interpreted as a need for managers to detach themselves from their teams. The benefit of detachment is objectivity. The dis-benefit is that the manager ceases to have the necessary understanding and the ability to influence – they cease to be able to lead.

Being a leader requires engagement and the required objectivity is a state of mind rather than any idea of distance between them and their followers.

2.9.7.2   Leader too close
Effective leadership requires the ability to influence followers. Influencing requires proximity – getting close and personal. But this proximity must not extent to emotional involvement such that the manager shies away from difficult and emotion laden decisions.

Managers should recall that emotions obey laws and learn an appropriate repertoire of emotional responses to allow closeness without loss of objectivity.

2.9.7.3   Leader not adjusting to online working
Leaders must acknowledge the inevitable weaknesses of online remote, home, or virtual working.

Non-verbal cues are substantially absent in remote leadership. Information projected from all parties is substantially targeted; some would say, curated. It's what individuals want to convey to others in the group. Unless designed in to the medium, no-one just chats online. Unless the medium facilitates it, incidental information exchange is missing.

There's no overheard discussion, no dialogue that triggers thoughts, and no conveyed expected behaviours like dress.

Managers must select the online communications channels carefully to include appropriate information exchange.

2.10   Leader-manager development

The reality is that few firms select managers to be leaders and few firms develop managers to lead once appointed. These two points alone lead to generally poor leadership in firms. Most leaders are 'accidental' – they are appointed because they were at the right place at the right time. As a result, the strength of followership in organisations is low and few staff believe they work for a great firm with great leaders. Most, as a result, report that they are substantially uncommitted to their employer and only weakly engaged with their job.

It's not a good picture, and it gets worse.

Firms don't appoint managers for their excellence at leadership. Most boards are enamoured with the Alpha Wolf; the narcissist who uses coercion and bullying to get their way. Television programmes like The Apprentice and Dragons Den don't help. Boards tend to be happier placing their trust in someone who is hugely self-confident, forceful, and clear about their direction. A person who was empathic and accommodating of others would do less well in interview for a senior post – and yet they would likely be a better leader.

Many studies have also shown that women make better leaders than men, and yet few women make it to senior positions. Setting aside that women often take time out for child-rearing (and hence slip in seniority), boards are less likely to appoint a woman. The reason is that women are considered less likely to exhibit Alpha tendencies. This disinclination to select women suggests generally flawed leadership selection processes.

If businesses are to enjoy greater long-term success, they must look to the long term. This means selecting those who will excel at leadership. And it means developing leaders once appointed. Optimum selection and development are rooted in scientific methods rather than myth and bias. Until science takes over in leadership, the UK's firms are generally unlikely to take a leading position in the world stage.

So, how does one select and develop leaders?

2.10.1   *The need for technical competence*

We've discussed above that the essence of leadership is a dyadic relationship between leader and follower. We've noted that under some models, the leader manages the impressions that the follower has of them and that it's useful if the follower admires the leader. We've also noted that under other models, the leader is useful to the follower, intervening for the better in the follower's life. All this leadership is difficult – even impossible – if the leader is not technically competent in the business in which the leader and follower have a shared interest.

Of course, we need to define technical competence.

For a manager, or any team member for that matter, to lead, they need to have competence. It could be that in a group of engineers, the marketing manager leads in marketing. They have technical competence in that domain. Likewise, in finance, operations and all the other disciplines.

There must be a sufficiency of competence. It's not necessary for the leader to be an expert. It's just enough that they have high competence in the full breadth of their domain.

All leaders should be technically competent and engage in continuous professional development in their chosen career and domain.

Later, we discuss how managers become managers, and within this we include further discussion about the manager as leader.

2.10.2   *Personality of a leader*

Leader personality is important. If certain personality extremes are evident, it's likely that the leader will struggle to influence their followers. Here are some examples.

Leadership requires that leaders interact with followers to exert influence. For leadership success in this case, leaders must be extroversive. Extroversive people like, and seek out, social interaction. Someone who is more introversive, preferring their own company, is likely to do less well.

Similarly, a leader who is highly anxious is likely to transmit this to their followers. And a leader who is not open to new ideas will naturally use 'tell' tactics, potentially preventing adoption of other useful leadership approaches and styles.

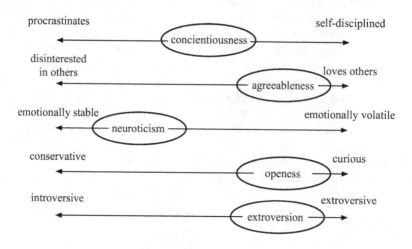

Figure 2-7: Typical personality profile of a leader

There is therefore a personality for every approach and style. Figure 2-7 illustrates the idea with an indication of a generic leader personality profile. In this case our leader should exhibit mid-range contentiousness, towards the high end of agreeableness (with a tendency to think about people, rather than themselves), towards the lower end of anxiety and towards the upper end of both openness to new ideas and extroversion.

This idea that there is a link between personality and likely success as a leader suggests that leaders should be selected for their personality.

2.10.3   *Intelligence of a leader*

Leadership is about making argument that persuades followers to do the leader's bidding. Making forceful argument needs high verbal, numerical and abstract reasoning ability. Those three forms of reasoning make up what psychologists call general mental ability – intelligence to the lay person. There's no denying that leaders need to be intelligent.

General mental ability can be determined by administering a test on leadership candidates. Intelligence can be selected for in future leaders.

2.10.4   *Developing leaders*

Given the right personality and intelligence, leadership can be learned. We've illustrated here the skills and knowledge needed. Since leadership involves working with people, it's difficult to learn anything other than the models in the classroom and from books.

By far the best way to learn leadership is on the job, supported by appropriate study. But learning is helped by having a mentor, themselves an accomplished leader, who helps interpret feedback. We discuss ideas about how managers become managers in Chapter 12.

2.11   Chapter Summary

Throughout our discussion on leadership, we assume that leadership is a management role. Many authors assume that leadership is what the MD does while others manager. We do not agree. Leadership is a role that all managers must embrace.

Leadership can be thought of on two planes: first, as a one-to-one, or dyadic, relationship that the manager must build between themselves and each employee; and second, a one-to-many relationship requiring the manager to exhort their expectations on the group or firm.

The dyadic plane is easier to understand and significantly simpler to make work. We recommend that managers start their leadership there. Dyadic leadership is the foundation of all. Once dyadic relationships are in place, one-to-many, or leader-to-group, exhorting activities can be added.

In effective leadership, the leader intervenes in their follower's lives to persuade them to do what the leader wants. Without leadership intervention, the followers would do something else. There are many ways for the leader to achieve this. At one extreme is coercion. Coercion would be of limited effect in the environment of a firm where employees voluntarily enter an employment contract and can leave at a whim. Toward the other extreme is a host of leadership approaches and we detail these.

Professional leadership requires that the leader is a peer of their followers and a master of their trade. The followers respect the leader and, as a result, agree to be persuaded.

Procedural leadership recognises that firms have procedures. It's how they do what they do. The procedural leader's job is to build procedure. Procedural leadership embraces reward for compliance with those procedures.

Transformational leadership requires the leader to espouse vision of some future 'promised land'. The followers will be persuaded because they believe that they will benefit from rewards when the 'promised land' is reached.

And transactional leadership exploits exchange theory where the leader and follower exchange valuable assets – the leader wants the follower to do as they say while the follower wants flexibility, personal development, or even new experiences.

Leaders are often accidental – they are the person in the frame at a particular point in time and are automatically (or accidentally) appointed. They may or may not go on to be an effective leader. On the one hand leaders are 'born' to the job – they have the right innate personal characteristics like personality and intelligence. On the other they are 'bred' to the job – given the right personal characteristics, they can learn the trade. As we intimate elsewhere, reading this book is a good start.

We list several failings in leaders, mostly associated with the flawed assumption by many in leadership positions that leadership is obvious.

Leadership requires leaders to get close to their followers such that they can use various leadership tactics to influence them. We outline two such tactics: roadblock removal and goal illumination.

The leader's job does not end once the followers agree to do what's wanted. The leader must engage with feedback – they must sense the desired outcomes and determine if those are met. If not, the leader must intervene again and again until their desired goal is met. We discuss the use of feedback in this chapter and in others because it is so hugely important in management.

And finally, we refer to online leadership. Before the Covid pandemic, a small but significant number of people worked day-to-day online. Following the drive to work from home, this has now increased, and we comment that managers must adjust to lead in this new environment. It can yield good benefits.

Leadership is a never-ending machine in which the leader sets goals, selects leadership interventions, acts, monitors success and repeats – forever.

3

Gaining Services

In Chapter 1 we introduced the concept that all people involved in a firm should be under contract. In this chapter we explore the various types of relationship in more detail. We'll then look at how you, as manager, should find, recruit, select and ensure that the best people join and remain with your firm.

3.1   Working relationships

The relationship between the firm and the person providing their effort is termed 'employment status'. In the UK there are three types of working relationship – self-employed, worker and employee. This definition determines the rights that the person has. It's a very grey area with confusion between the three in managers, and in government.

Firms engage with workers in different ways throughout their lifecycle. Typically, an entrepreneur will start a firm. When the firm grows to a point where the entrepreneur can no longer do the work themselves, they will contract out work to suppliers. This gets the work done but avoids having to hire an employee. That state will sustain until the entrepreneur realises that it costs more to manage lots of external contracts. At that point the entrepreneur becomes manager and hires employees. All firms are a mix of suppliers, workers, and employees, each under a unique contract.

Here we discuss the three worker types and their contracts with the firm.

3.1.1   Self-employed

Whilst being self-employed is recognised as an employment status, there is no legal definition and no single description of how a self-employed person operates. A self-employed person typically runs their own business, and they are responsible for the success of that business. They invoice their customers and may do work for more than one customer in any period. Self-employed people are often referred to as associates, freelancers, contractors, sub-contractors or suppliers.

Broadly, from the firm's perspective, contracting with someone who is self-employed is the same as having a business-to-business relationship with a firm. The person doing the work is effectively employed in that firm. Some self-employed people operate as sole traders, taking personal liability for their enterprise. Others form a limited liability company – a personal services company - through which they trade.

When working with the self-employed it is important to have a business-to-business contract in place emphasising the arm's length nature of the relationship and setting out the terms and conditions of the arrangement. You wouldn't purchase, or rent, plant without a contract with the supplier. Using the services of self-employed suppliers is no different.

Business-to-business agreements are contracts 'for services'. The manager has, of course, no obligation to pay employee benefits such as holiday pay or sick pay, but there is an obligation to protect the self-employed under health and safety law when they are on a firm's premises.

3.1.2   Workers

A worker may be self-employed. They may be able to sub-contract the work they do. But generally, the worker will be expected to undertake the work themselves, and usually they will be subject to a contract of employment.

A worker is afforded some employment rights by law. For example, a worker must not be treated less favourably than a similar employee. This includes the right, if they work part-time, to not to be treated less favourably than a full-time employee. A worker is entitled to minimum wage, holiday pay and has protection against unlawful discrimination. There are several categories of worker as discussed below.

3.1.2.1   Casual workers
Casual workers are used to manage peaks in the work of a firm. For example, fruit farmers will engage workers to pick apples and strawberries. Firms providing staff for events, such as pop festivals, will also make use of casual workers. Such workers provide a flexible work-force supplying a service as demanded by the firm's customers.

3.1.2.2   Agency workers
An agency worker has a contract with an agency, normally a recruitment or staffing agency. The agency then supplies the worker to a firm as employer for whom the agency worker temporarily works. Under these circumstances the worker is controlled by the employer whilst they are on assignment. But they are paid and employed by the agency. Some agency workers are paid full time, even when they have no assignment. Others are only paid if the agency can place them with an employer.

3.1.2.3   Freelance workers
Freelance workers are self-employed workers who choose who they will work for, and when they will work. They have no allegiance to the firm that they are providing services for. In the UK such workers might also be referred to as contractors – and significantly, we refer to them throughout this book as suppliers. There is a grey area surrounding the appointment of contractors and freelancers. Under certain circumstances they may be construed as employees.

3.1.2.4   Seasonal workers
Seasonal workers are very similar to casual workers, but they are employed at specific times of the year to cope with demand. For example, fruit pickers in summer or sales assistants employed in stores to cover the Christmas period. The employment status of a seasonal worker will be determined by the relationship they have with the firm. This was discussed further in 3.1.1.

3.1.3   *Employees*

Employees have more rights that workers. All the rights covering workers also cover employees. Employees work under a contract of employment – a contract 'of service' - often referred to as the 'terms and conditions of employment'. As well as the rights discussed above, an employee has the right to a written statement of employment, an itemised payslip, family friendly leave (for example, maternity and paternity leave), the right to request flexible working and the right not to be discriminated against. The development of contracts of employment is dealt with in detail in Chapter 7.

There are three types of employment contract.

3.1.3.1   *Fixed term contract*
A fixed-term contract describes a contract that ends on a specified date. Such contracts are often used to provide temporary cover for employees who are away from work for a period, for example on maternity leave, adoption leave and long-term sickness absence. Fixed-term contracts can also be used to employ employees on specific projects and to manage seasonal peaks of work.

Whilst there is a defined end to the contract, the person must still be dismissed fairly by following the firm's dismissal process. This is discussed further in Chapter 7.

3.1.3.2   *Permanent contract*
When an employee is given an employment contract, it is normally open-ended or 'permanent'. It can, however, be ended for specific reasons and timescales as laid down in statute or in the contract of employment. Statute will always take precedent when dismissing.

3.1.3.3   *Zero-hours contract*
Those under zero-hours contracts have a contract with the employer but the employer is not obliged to provide work. Likewise, the worker is not obliged to accept any work offered. It is another form of casual agreement reached by employer and worker. This type of contract has come under fire recently since it is often considered as unfair to workers.

However, many workers are happy with this type of relationship since it can fit well around childcare and university studies. For the employer it provides a pool of people who are known to them, and whom they can approach when there is a work to be done.

Those employed on zero hours contracts will have the same statutory rights as employees.

3.1.4   *Determining a person's employment status*

While you, as a manager representing the firm, can contract a person to undertake work and issue paperwork that attempts to set the employment status, it is an employment tribunal, court or Government tax authority that will decide finally and conclusively what the legal relationship is.

Figure 3-1 gives guidance on this complex area by indicating important criteria that go to define the relationship.

Tribunals will consider the contractual terms but more importantly, they will look at the reality of the relationship between the person and the firm.

Criteria	Employment type		
	Self-employed	Worker	Employee
Has responsibility for the success or failure of the business.	yes	no	no
Decides how, when and where they work.	yes	no	no
Can hire other people to do the work for them.	yes	sometimes	no
Can work for several customers at one time.	yes	no	no
Provides most of the equipment to undertake work.	yes	no	no
Is paid against an invoice.	yes	no	no
Is entitled to statutory minimum wages.	no	yes	yes
Is entitled to holiday pay.	no	yes	yes
Is protected under health & safety legislation.	yes	yes	yes
Is protected against unlawful discrimination.	no	yes	yes
Has the right to comparable treatment to similar full-time workers.	no	yes	yes
Has the right to maternity, paternity and adoption leave.	no	no	yes
Has the right to statutory redundancy pay.	no	no	yes
Has the way the work is done controlled by the firm.	no	sometimes	yes

Figure 3-1: Determining employment status

Figure 3-1 documents the key criteria which assist in defining the employment status of a person. Note that all employees are workers, but not all workers are employees, and we use the term 'worker' in other chapters to describe anyone doing work for a firm.

Some workers are employed through what's termed an 'intermediary'. An employment intermediary is a firm that arranges for a worker to do work for another firm and intervenes in the payments between the two. The intermediary attracts the responsibilities of an employer. Employment agencies, for example, supply farms with workers for fruit picking and they would employ those workers. They would bill the farms for the total effort and then pay the pickers.

Some industries have long histories of using casual labour. In those cases, firms often comprise a small cadre of key staff with a huge list of casual workers that the firm calls on when it wins a contract. The construction industry is one example in which firms tried to avoid becoming the employer, with its associated tax gathering obligations. Prior to introduction of the Construction Industry Scheme (CIS) in 1972, for example, tax avoidance in construction was rife. The UK Government set up the scheme to demand that deductions must be made by the firm on behalf of the tax authorities in lieu of tax, leaving the worker to adjust the final tax paid through their annual tax return.

The 'gig-economy' is a recently coined phrase used to identify industries in which people are contracted on an ad-hoc basis to provide a service. Self-employed and freelance workers employed as Deliveroo riders, Hermes drivers and Uber drivers are high profile examples. Each delivery or fare is a separate 'gig' for which the worker is paid a few Pounds. The worker waits around throughout the day to be called forward to work. They are paid for the 'gig' and stand down afterwards, returning to the pool of available workers.

This arrangement has historical parallels with 'piece work' – where the worker is paid for the piece of work or the piece-part they produce. Recent tribunal cases have judged people engaged in this way as workers, attracting associated rights.

3.1.5   *The duck test*

The employment relationship is never clearly defined, and managers must get used to making decisions about employment in an environment of ambiguity.

The duck test is a form of popular abductive reasoning that allows managers to make inference based on what they see – the duck test goes like this: "if it looks like a duck, swims like a duck, and quacks like a duck, then it probably is a duck."

The duck test is useful for managers to infer employment status of any person engaged by them. Whilst it is for a tribunal or the tax authorities to ultimately confirm the status of a person, managers need to strive to ensure that the correct contracts are entered, the correct taxes (if any) are deducted, and the appropriate reporting is done.

There are three key tests that tribunals and tax authorities will apply when determining the employment relationship.

3.1.5.1   *Mutuality of obligation*
Under mutuality, there is a duty on the employer to provide work and pay for it, and there is a reciprocal duty on the worker to turn up and to complete the work. A self-employed person would not be under the same obligation.

3.1.5.2   *Control*
Under control, a tribunal would seek to understand whether the employer has control over the work done and how and where the person does do it. Whilst the person may have some discretion, working under a job description would be, for example, a clear indication of employer control. Further examples of control would be the requirement for a worker to request holiday before it is taken and if the worker must advise their employer if they are ill and unable to attend work.

3.1.5.3   *Personal service*
Under personal service, only a named person can provide the service. An employee will have no right to send someone else in their place. However, a self-employed worker will have no such obligation and may choose whom they send.

3.1.5.4   *Other considerations*
Self-employed workers tend to provide their own equipment. This can range from laptops and mobile phones to other tools of the trade. Employees are normally provided with the tools they need to do their work.

Self-employed workers are also likely to work for more than one firm at the same time. They may have several contracts in play, with different firms. They will decide how and when they undertake the work. They will invoice each firm for sums for specified deliverables. The means of how and when invoicing occurs should be including in a business-to-business agreement.

Whist employees can be appointed on fixed-term contracts, most are employed indefinitely. A self-employed worker will undertake a piece of work for a defined duration. In some cases, this will be a few hours, and in other cases may be for a few months. The timescale will be determined by project requirements.

Reflection 3-1: About employment relationships

Using the criteria above, consider what type of people who work in or for your firm. Think about whether you have the correct documentation in place to adequately determine and manage each type of relationship.

3.2 Determining who's needed

3.2.1 *Modelling the firm and its people*

It's important to ensure that the right people are working in the firm. That might sound daft, but reality is that many firms employ people because that's the way it's always been or because it's a norm in the industry.

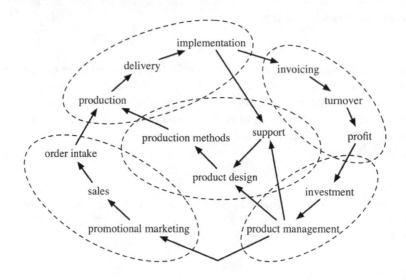

Figure 3-2: Systems model with roles and jobs added

We need some definitions first. A job describes the total activity of an employee whilst at work. Jobs comprise several roles. Example roles for an accountant might be to assemble the trial balance; to develop the profit and loss account and the balance sheet; and to prepare the necessary returns to the various authorities – three roles. Typically, the roles are developed from the principal accountabilities or responsibilities and are expressed in the job description. In a small firm, employees will have many roles. As the firm grows, employees will likely specialise and the number of roles per job will reduce. Typically, for a well-specialised firm, each job will comprise five or six roles.

Managers must determine the roles needed to achieve the desired business outcomes. How jobs are built is for the manager to determine and this will be a key determinant in successful recruitment and ultimately in achieving competitive advantage through differentiation and efficiency.

In many cases recruitment happens because someone has left. There is little thought about how the role fits into the organisation or if it is required. This leads to people being appointed to non-roles.

Figure 3-2 illustrates concepts as described in Chapter 1. Now, the concept model can be modified to break out specific roles in each function. From that, jobs can be built. These are described in Figure 3-2 by the roles contained within the dashed lozenges. In the diagram, product design is joined with support and production methods. A larger firm might separate the three. Similarly, the three commercial areas of promotional marketing, sales and order intake are joined. The model, the functions, how functions yield roles, how roles are joined in jobs and ultimately how many job holders there are for each job will be different for every firm and every manager.

The concept model with its functions, roles and jobs can now be assembled into an organisation chart and manpower plan. The business plan will illustrate a wage bill that the manager will argue can be supported. This represents the effort needed to enable the turnover. The example in Figure 3-3 shows the number of full-time heads needed. In this example, there are 15 full time equivalent heads (FTE).

In this example, the manager might employ themselves and nine full time and ten part time staff to provide the required effort in the right jobs and roles.

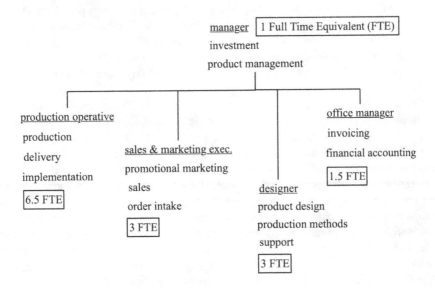

Figure 3-3: Organisation chart with manpower plan

3.2.2   Defining who's needed

The people working in an organisation, whether as managers, employees or workers are defined by their job description. At this stage in building the argument about who is needed there are four key parts to the job description: the job purpose, the job scope and dimensions, the principal accountabilities or responsibilities and the work context.

The job purpose defines why the job exists and why the organisation chart, the concept model and the firm would fall apart without it.

The job scope and dimensions set out the size of the job and its influence. Here we'd expect dimensions like budget responsibility, headcount reports, geographic reach, and market accountability.

The principal accountabilities or responsibilities are best defined very specifically using the form "do something, to something, to achieve a result". An example might be, 'Design software solutions for clients which are compliant with agreed requirements and budget'. These statements should derive directly from the concept model described in Chapter 1 and again in Figure 3-2.

The work context might set out where the job is based and the job holder's primary contacts.

Once the job description has been developed for each job, a person specification can be developed by asking 'what personal characteristics are necessary to excel in each activity and role? The development of the necessary personal characteristics is described in 3.2.

3.2.3   The recruitment and selection life cycle

Once the job description and person specification are available, recruitment can start. Every firm will recruit in a different way. There is no prescriptive 'best practice'. There are however elements to the process that are key to success. If these elements are not given due care and attention, the recruitment process will not be as effective as it might. The seven steps of our process are shown in Figure 3-4.

This process is somewhat more scientific and considerably more robust than that done by most firms.

Above we've described the job with a job description. This is stage 1 shown in the diagram and the primary input to the next stage is the job roles. Below we show how these job roles are developed to characterise the person needed – in essence asking, "what sort of person will do well in these roles?". We would typically advise that at that point some prototyping should be done to interact with the labour market. As we outline elsewhere, we would expect that the people needed would be characterised by attributes like their competencies, behaviours, intelligence, personality, experience, and values. The thinking at this stage is deep and would typically need the support of an organisational psychologist, or someone with similar training, to be done right. The key output from stage 2 is the search criteria. The search criteria are defined in practical terms and describe the characteristics that the search agent will look for and advertise for – attributes like experience in a particular field, or likely qualifications. The search criteria are not selection criteria.

The search criteria feed into the prototyping stage 3. In stage 3, the search agent has a look in the labour market to see if what's wanted exists at the sorts of salary expected. Many firms launch full scale search activities, only to fail because what they asked for was not available. Prototyping allows change to be made following learning from some skirmishing in the labour market. What's done here will depend on the job and the industry, but the aim is to be sure that once a full search project starts, it will be successful.

Search begins once the manager and search agent agree that it's likely to be successful.

The search activity, stage 4, is described at length below and we discuss the merits of the various sources of candidates that might be used. As we indicate, the outputs at this stage are candidates and associated metadata gleaned by telephone interviews.

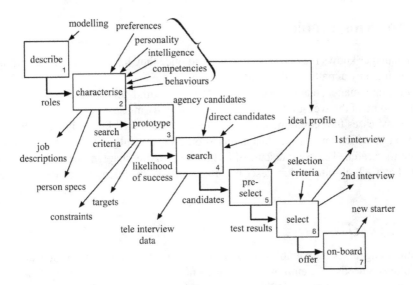

Figure 3-4: The recruitment and selection life cycle

Once candidates are identified, we recommend a two-stage activity where candidates are 'pre-selected' using light psychometric and work sample tests. If they pass that stage (stage 5), the main selection (stage 6) can begin with its two-step interview or perhaps assessment centre. An assessment centre is simply where all candidates are invited to interview at the same time and the tests and interviews are administered and marked all in one day. Assessment centres offer no improvement in quality over discrete interviews but are liked by some managers because of their efficiency.

Decisions at both stages are made using the selection criteria developed in stage 2. The selection criteria are developed from the profile of the ideal jobholder, effectively asking, 'does this candidate have the right characteristics to do well?' As we note above, selection criteria are specific characteristics developed from the person specification. If a candidate is deemed to meet the selection criteria, they are a viable candidate to whom an offer might be made. Selection criteria should only be relaxed by returning to stage 1 to adjust the job and repeating the steps.

There are many viable versions of stages 5 and 6. Generally, we prefer the first interview to be informed by the preselect tests and to be a light-weight discussion aiming to convince the candidate that the firm is great and that they'd do well in the job. Some managers (particularly when faced with huge numbers of applicants) will design an application portal and candidates will need to pass pre-selection before progressing to first interview.

Generally, second interview is the 'big one'. It's there that the candidate will face full a psychometric assessment, exhaustive work sample tests and scenario interviewing. Second interview testing asks, 'can this candidate do the job?' Second interview testing should have high predictive validity and be objective. We discuss these points further below.

Then it's on to offer and managing the on-boarding process, stage 7, to make sure the chosen candidates join.

3.3   Sourcing people

Once a manager knows the person they want and once they have a process for finding and selecting, it's only a matter of doing it!

There are many sources that can be tapped to find job candidates. This section considers some of the well-established methods currently in use.

In most cases the requirements of the role are determined by the job description and the person specification. These documents should be carefully crafted as they form the basis for the search. These are discussed further later in this chapter. For now, let's assume that we have a high-quality job description and person specification (JDPS) that defines who's needed.

3.3.1   *Agencies*

Recruitment agencies help employers by trying to match individuals on their database to the employer's needs. The employer states their needs to the agency via the job description and the person specification (JDPS). The agency then searches its databases of candidates using keywords such as 'accountant', 'senior product specialist' or the like, using the search criteria developed from the JDPS. It's important that the keywords follow from the selection criteria.

There are many problems with the agency approach. It's far from a perfect system.

Firstly, agencies are typically paid on success. They will typically only be about 30% successful and hence successful placements of candidates with client firms must pay for the 70% of cases where they work on the task but fail to get their candidate accepted.

From the firm's perspective, the 'no-win, no-fee' model is logically very interesting. Managers can launch search tasks without need for funding and can even use these tasks to learn about the labour market in their domain. A little analysis by the manager would, of course, reveal that they are paying significantly more than the cost of the effort – in fact about three times the cost. But whilst it's a poor model, it's the way the industry has evolved, and no-one seems minded to upset the norm.

Agency search is typically invoiced at anything from 10 to 30% of the appointee's first year remuneration. In many cases the total reward package, including benefits, is used to determine fees. Agencies will normally negotiate their fees.

Secondly, agencies tend to supply quantity over quality. The agent will not generally be an experienced manager with a detailed understanding of what makes a candidate suitable for a given role. Whilst some agencies specialise, this generally does not mean greater understanding of the psychology of performance and hence of what makes a good employee in a particular case. It's important that the work done to develop the job description, person specification and search criteria are used in the search, and not some other interpretation of need.

The agency will then submit potential candidates who meet the search criteria. This could be quite a number as the agency works to maximise the chance of getting its candidate accepted. The manager must be prepared to do much of the down-selecting work themselves and to compare the candidates against the search criteria.

Thirdly, agencies have natural problems matching candidates to search criteria and JDPS characteristics if the person is not already in the industry – if the keywords don't match. This means that transferrable skills are often missed – a candidate with good numerical skills and an eye for detail might make a good accountant, but would likely be missed by an agency. Whether transferable skills are interesting depends, of course, on the manager's appetite for training candidates over hiring people with existing competencies and behaviours.

Agencies may also operate a jobs board themselves or subscribe to a jobs board. Jobs boards are Web sites on which agencies advertise their clients' vacancies. There are about ten general jobs boards in the UK and a host of others that are industry specific. The main aim of the jobs boards is to attract candidates that the agency can then retain on its own database. Once registered with an agency, the job seeker's CV can then be harvested later. Here, the more job seekers on the database, the greater the likelihood of a later placement.

Privacy regulations have recently complicated the agencies' activities. Any job seeker will need to have consented to the agency keeping their details. Privacy also precludes the established practice of sending out CVs to employers without the job-seeker's permission to be the first to land a CV on a hiring manager's desk (or email inbox).

Generalising, agencies are good at filling lower level, simply defined commodity jobs and less good at finding candidates with specialist skills and knowledge.

3.3.2   Online recruitment

Just as the agency can advertise on a jobs board, so can the manager. And many managers choose to advertise directly in relevant online sites. A good example is the IET site 'E&T Jobs' for engineers and technologists. These sites typically cost a few hundred Pounds per month to advertise a job and they provide a basic back-end portal to manage candidate CVs and the application process.

3.3.3   Headhunting

Agencies and adverts target those who are looking for a job. Headhunting targets everyone and seeks out the best person for the job, even if they are apparently happy with their present job and employer.

Traditionally, headhunting was done by a person with good knowledge about a particular industry and who was particularly well connected with managers and employees across that industry. Upon being given a headhunting task, the head-hunter would place telephone call after telephone call. Each call was a stepping stone to the next three or four calls as the head-hunter expanded their net in search of candidates.

Today, the telephone has been replaced by LinkedIn. LinkedIn allows the head-hunter to find candidates that meet the keywords from the search criteria and JDPS. And of course, everyone on LinkedIn has opted in to being contacted, thereby avoiding a breach of privacy regulations.

Many professionals are registered on LinkedIn and hence headhunting using LinkedIn is ideal for professional jobs. Searching and calling candidates typically takes anything from 50 to 200 man-hours from initial skirmish to first interviews and, unlike agency search, jobs are costed by head-hunters for the effort expended.

3.3.4   *Apprentices and graduates*

Many medium sized firms now encourage applications from recent graduates. Many often run their own apprenticeship schemes. Both are excellent ways of hiring good people, but of course, training staff takes time. Typically, it takes two years post-graduation for graduates, while apprentices are typically ready to work effectively at the end of their apprenticeship. Typically graduates and apprentices do jobs of different complexity and size.

3.3.5   *Other sources and strategies*

Few jobs are advertised today in paper media.

Some lower-level jobs for trades and semi-skilled and unskilled labour can be usefully advertised through Jobcentre Plus, the UK government-funded employment agency. Jobcentre Plus provides resources to enable jobseekers to find work through Jobpoints (touch-screen computer terminals), Jobseeker Direct (telephone service) and the Jobcentre Plus website.

Many firms offer bonuses if staff can recommend a friend. This is a cheap source of new staff since many employees know others in the same profession.

Traditionally, firms would launch a search activity ending in a job offer and appointment. Today, however, many firms embrace continuous search, interviewing, offering, and appointing whenever a good candidate comes their way.

3.4   Characterising people

When considering the sort of person needed to excel in a job, managers need to be rational and objective.

There are around 20 discrete criteria which, if present in the right form, define a person and predict their performance and their ability to excel in a particular environment. Below we discuss the seven most important.

3.4.1   *Intelligence*

Of all criteria, the most accurate predictor of a person's ability to perform in a job is their intelligence. Put simply, bright people generally do best. So, if the manager could test for just one criterion, they should use intelligence.

Intelligence is a person's ability to reason. There are three types of reasoning that matter: numerical reasoning, verbal reasoning and abstract reasoning. Numerical reasoning is the ability to use numbers. Verbal reasoning is the ability to use language. And abstract reasoning is the ability to use concepts and ideas. Verbal and numerical reasoning are learned and hence are part of what's called crystallised intelligence. Abstract reasoning is termed fluid or innate intelligence and this comes from parents. Intelligence is talked of with reference to a reference group – for example, 'above average in numerical reasoning when compared to a reference group of accountants'.

Jobs need different types and amounts of intelligence. Someone doing a routine job that is well defined perhaps needs numerical and verbal reasoning, but the job holder can be lower than average in abstract reasoning. Conversely, a research scientist might need to be high in abstract and numerical reasoning but can be lower in verbal reasoning. The intelligence of the job holder needs to match the required intelligence to do well in the job.

Intelligence is assessed by administering an intelligence or mental ability test. Intelligence can also be inferred from performance in specific job-related tests. And managers sometimes use proxies for intelligence such as results in GCSEs and A Levels (National 1-5s, Highers/Advanced Highers and Baccalaureate in Scotland) and class of degree and ranking of university attended. Such qualifications are often included in search criteria since they are tangible and can be searched for.

3.4.2   *Personality*

Personality is the set of habits, cognitive processes and emotional thought held by a person that predict how they will behave. Personality is part inherited and part built during upbringing and early years experiences. There's much myth surrounding personality and methods of assessment.

The most respected assessment of personality is that described by the Big 5 personality traits. The Big 5 has a fifty-year pedigree from research by thousands of academics publishing thousands of peer-reviewed papers and books. The Big 5 approach to personality description suggests that everyone's personality lies between two extremes on each of five scales. The Big 5 scales are shown in Figure 3-5. As with intelligence, a job holder must have a personality that assists in carrying out their job.

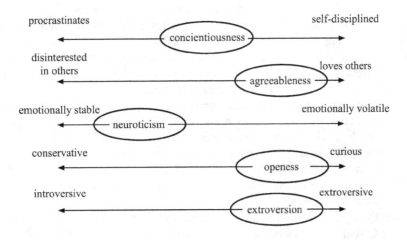

Figure 3-5: The Big 5 personality traits

As an example of the fit between personality needed and that held, salespeople typically need to be outgoing, seeking to build relationships with others. This would typically place the personality needed on the right on the introversive-extroversive scale. The opposite, introversive, would lie on the left and would describe someone who is happier working on their own.

There is no right personality – just a personality that fits the needs of a particular job – though the conscientiousness trait on the right, describing someone who is self-disciplined, is generally desirable for getting work done and hence is desirable in most jobs.

Personality is assessed using a personality inventory – many paired questions that together tease out where the test subject sits on each of the personality scales. A personality test typically takes 45 minutes to complete using a personal computer online to a hosting site. There are several well-respected inventories including 16PF, 15FQ+ and NEO-PI. Their results generalise well across age, gender, and culture and, broadly, those taking such tests would agree that the results do represent their personality as they see it.

Managers should proceed with due cynicism when buying personality assessments. Generally, you get what you pay for. If there's no need for qualifications to administer and analyse personality tests, and, if it's on the Web and free, it's likely useless and misleading.

As with intelligence, an optimum personality profile can be built and the manager should search and select using those attributes as criteria. We note the use of this as an ideal profile below.

3.4.3   Competencies

A competency is the ability to do something to a required standard. An example might be 'to make presentations of the technology to prospective industrial clients in German, leaving the prospects with a positive view of the solution'. The competency should be measurable and hence not some woolly statement or sentiment.

An employee's overall competence comprises many competencies. And typically, each job would likely require something like 40 primary competencies.

As we note in Chapter 4, the firm's capability (to achieve the required outcomes) is given by its staff competencies and technology functions.

A competency is a mash of a person's skills and knowledge. Without skill, someone with knowledge can't perform and without knowledge, someone with skill doesn't know what to do. Both go hand in hand to give their competency.

As we illustrate in Chapter 8, each competency is held at a defined level spanning typically four grades: trainee, supervised practitioner, practitioner and expert. It's typical for an employee to have some competencies falling in each grade. Most jobs need some mastery, but to expect high grades in every competency would demand huge and unnecessary investment. For most jobs, it would also result in jobholders being over-qualified. So typically, employees will be trainees in some competencies. Everyone has areas of required development.

Typically, a group of people, such as paramedics and ambulance technicians attending emergencies, would possess a range of complementary competencies. They will be paired according to the competencies needed in any shift. Pairs with specific expertise might be identified by their vehicle callsign such that the appropriate vehicle (technology) and competencies are dispatched to any incident.

Broadly there's also correlation between competence and salary for a given industry, job and technology used. The manager must develop a manpower plan setting out jobs, roles, grades, and competencies considering the supervision available, the technology used and the budgeted salaries.

3.4.4   *Behaviours, attitudes, beliefs and values*

Behaviours are actions that people habitually do, like being courteous and friendly, having good attendance and punctuality, accepting responsibility and being proactive. Managers must consider what behaviours are necessary for the job.

Attitudes are often confused with personality, beliefs, and values, and even with competencies and behaviours. An attitude is how a person thinks and feels about situations and environments. Attitudes influence the way a person behaves day to day. Attitudes can be changed.

Richard Branson famously suggested that managers should 'hire attitudes and train skills'. He was asserting that attitudes were predispositions in a person. Attitudes are a function of the environment in which a person works. The employee will develop an attitude towards their manager, an attitude towards colleagues and an attitude towards the job they do. Their attitude will depend much on how they are treated and hence 'attitude' is not a stable personal characteristic that's useful in defining the sort of person wanted for a particular job. Attitudes depend on a person's personality, values, and beliefs and on their experience, preferences, self-efficacy and growth needs strength.

Beliefs are things that people hold dear – that they feel are, or should be, subjective norms. A person may believe, for example, that management should always treat employees with respect. Beliefs are socially constructed and built from experiences during childhood.

Values are desirable end states that people admire and aim to uphold, such as justice, loyalty, and honesty. Values are influenced by beliefs. Many managers place candidate values foremost in desirable characteristics. They want to be sure that candidate values are in congruence with those of the firm as represented by managers and existing employees.

Unfortunately, 'values' are complex to assess and beyond the scope of a conventional manager-led interview. As we note below, however, it can be useful to define desirable values and watch out for any evidence of breach of values when discussing past experiences with candidates.

3.4.5   *Preferences*

Each person has preferences. Those preferences tend to determine the sorts of activities in which they will likely expend energy. The most popular method of specifying preferences is that used in the world of career consulting from John Holland's 1950s work resulting in the hexagon shown in Figure 3-6.

Just as in intelligence and personality, managers should be particularly interested in talking to candidates who have a preference profile that best matches that characterising the job. A good example might be the job of quality auditor (shown by the dotted lines in Figure 3-6). We might expect the job holder to be quite realistic (R) in their preferences, highly investigative (I), not at all artistic (A), quite social (S), not particularly enterprising (E) and highly interested in conventional (C) activities.

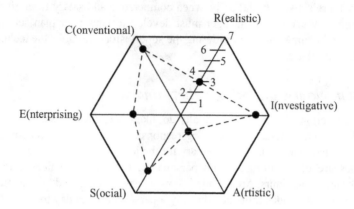

Figure 3-6: Holland's RIASEC Preferences

Conceptually, this comparison between the attributes of a job and the preferences of a person gives rise to the idea of person-environment fit (P-E fit). Research shows that a person with high P-E fit is likely to enjoy higher commitment, engagement, and job satisfaction.

Holland's preferences are scored out of seven. Preferences are assessed using a preference inventory – a questionnaire with around 50 questions.

3.4.6 Employee self-efficacy

Self-efficacy is a person's perceived beliefs about their capabilities to produce the required performance when needed. Self-efficacy influences how people feel, think, and behave.

People with high self-efficacy tend to approach problems as opportunities to master their trade, rather than as something to be avoided and at which they'll likely fail.

Clearly managers will want to hire people with high self-efficacy in important job activities.

3.4.7 Growth needs strength

People can be split into those who tend to have growth mind-sets and those who tend to have achievement mind-sets. Like personality, a person's mindset will lie on a greyscale between the two extremes. Managers need to decide which is more desirable for a particular job – toward growth or toward achievement. And the strength of the need for growth in a person can be measured in a term called 'growth needs strength' (GNS).

GNS is one aspect of a person's intrinsic motives. It's the strength of the person's need for personal fulfilment, learning and development. GNS is socially constructed – formed in a person's upbringing, adolescence, and adulthood in the environment in which they work. If GNS is high, the right job will have the capacity to motivate. If GNS is low, this will block the motivating potential of the job. High GNS is desirable in many professional jobs, but achievement might be more important in others.

3.5 Interviewing and selection

Once the person needed has been characterised (as outlined in 3.4), all that remains is to undertake such interviewing and testing as needed to confirm that the candidate proposed from the search stage has those characteristics.

Unfortunately, selection is not a perfect science. The quality measure of a selection tool such as testing, or interviewing is termed its predictive validity. The higher the predictive validity, the stronger the relationship between performance in the tool during interview and selection, and performance on the job once in post. Predictive validity is a metric that lies between 0 and 1. A predictive validity score of near zero indicates that a test says little about how well a candidate will perform on the job. Conversely, a predictive validity score of over 0.3 would suggest that this test is useful in predicting job performance.

Not all selection tools have high predictive validity and no one tool has a high enough coefficient to be used on its own. To maximise the overall predictive validity, several tools must be used together. Predictive validity adds marginally, with the first tool contributing the most and others adding incrementally. The best predictive validity available is about 0.65, achieved by using four tools. As with other correlation coefficients throughout science, such a figure would be described as illustrating a moderate to strong relationship – in other words, the tools used in that case do predict performance on the job.

The four tools that we recommend are described below. We don't consider any other tools worthwhile.

3.5.1 *Intelligence tests*

Intelligence or general mental ability tests assess numerical, verbal and abstract reasoning. They typically comprise around 15 questions on each reasoning type. Candidates are given a set time to complete the tests so that they are under some pressure when responding. The assessment is given as the percentage of questions attempted and the percentage of those answered correctly.

Typically, the final answer is a score out of ten and this is related to a reference group so a candidate might, for example, perform above average when compared with a reference group of several thousand graduates.

General mental ability tests typically have a predictive validity of around 0.51.

3.5.2 *Personality profile*

As we note in 3.4.2, the primary use of a personality test or inventory is to determine a candidate's personality and compare that with the personality considered necessary to excel in the job.

Each of the Big 5 has a predictive validity but the figure depends on the role. For example, a research scientist would need to have a high openness to new ideas and hence high openness in a test would predict good performance in a research job. It's impossible therefore to generalise on predictive validity overall.

That said, conscientiousness is a common requirement for most jobs. A personality profile scoring high in conscientiousness (towards the self-disciplined end of the scale) predicts high performance in the job with a predictive validity of around 0.35.

3.5.3   Work sample tests

Literally, work sample tests are tests of samples of the work. Take a carpet fitter. It would be impossible to ask each candidate for a carpet fitter job to fit a whole carpet or vinyl. But it would be possible to construct a mini-room measuring about two metres square and to ask each candidate to fit a carpet in one half, vinyl in the other and a threshold rod between. Each candidate can be asked to describe the key points as they work. Each candidate can be observed and scored against a pre-agreed scale. It's a sample of reality.

If constructed to be a good representation of the work, work sample tests typically have a predictive validity of around 0.50.

3.5.4   Interviews

Interviews vary. Broadly there are two types – structured and unstructured.

Unstructured interviews are not specifically tailored to the role and ask general questions.

The key facet of the structured interview is that it is pre-scored and makes use of selection criteria developed beforehand from the key attributes sought in the candidates. Structured interviews are designed for the job in hand, so there are no boilerplate questions - you won't find structured interview questions on the Web. There's no, "Tell me what you'd like to be doing in five years' time" or, "Tell me the accomplishment about which you are most proud". Such generic questions don't tell the interviewer anything about how the candidate will perform in the job. They don't contribute to predictive validity.

Interview questions in a structured interview flow from the competencies and behaviours that will enable performance.

In building the job from accountabilities to necessary competencies and behaviours, the hiring manager will learn that they need a person with particular attributes. They may, for example, need someone who thinks in a structured fashion. Structured thinking would, in this case, be one of many criteria. In a structured interview the manager would build a question that, if answered particularly well, would show a candidate's competency in structured thinking. A good answer, illustrating high structured thinking would score highly. The opposite, chaotic thinking, would score low.

Unstructured interviews typically have a predictive validity of around 0.30 whereas structured interviews have a significantly higher coefficient of around 0.50.

Structured interviews are job-specific and take time to plan and pre-score.

3.5.5   Planning and doing interviews

Most managers think they can interview. Many even believe that they are good at it. And yet precious few have been trained and fewer still understand the true role of interviewing and testing in ensuring fairness and quality.

The task is simple enough. Given several candidates for a job, the manager must select one to whom they'll make an offer.

Fairness demands that the decision that the manager makes must be based only on the candidates' relative abilities. Fairness is a legal requirement. It also makes complete business sense. Managers generally, are becoming more educated about the dangers of bias and there's much been written on the business benefits of diversity. After all, who would want to make a hiring decision based on who they like or who their 'gut' suggests will perform. Objective selection using testing and a structured interview helps secure fairness.

It takes quite some time to administer the tests and the interview we describe above. We would typically recommend that candidates are asked to attend two interviews. In the first, the firm sells the job and aims to have the candidate leave with a good honest picture of what it's like to work in the firm. At that point, if the first interview is done well, the candidate will want the job and be happy to proceed to selection. The second is the selection testing and interview.

We believe that 60 minutes is needed for the first interview and anything up to 150 minutes for the second, with perhaps the intelligence and personality tests completed online at home after the first interview. Test scores can then be available for the second interview.

3.5.6 *Interviewing and testing in lockdown*

Many firms needed to hire staff during the Covid lockdown in 2020 and 2021. This meant interviewing online and having new starters work from home. It's useful to speculate about how successful recruitment and selection was for those firms and employees, and hence how firms might go about recruitment and selection if such constraints are placed on firms again.

It's important to recognise that the process and methods described above still apply, as does the use of tools that are of high predictive validity. What is different of course is that the interview will lack many of the non-verbal cues normally available in a face-to-face meeting. So, what does this mean for the hiring manager?

Arguably, online tests and interviews are likely to be lower in bias than those conducted face to face, simply because interviewers can concentrate on the evidence produced, without getting side-tracked. Bias can be defined as an inclination or prejudice in favour of, or against, a person and much of the bias incurred in an interview scenario occurs when the interviewer can see, hear, and even smell the whole person sitting before them. Online, all parties focus more on the task and hence on the evidence from the tests and questions. That's not to say that bias is eradicated: hiring managers can still see and listen to the candidate. And different issues like the candidate's ability to get online and present themselves with their technology come to the fore.

Tests and interviews aim to provide hiring managers with evidence about the candidate's ability to do the job. Provided that suitable tests and interviews can be designed, the online scenario can be as good as, if not better than, the conventional face-to-face meeting. This depends on test and interview relevance. Practical tests like driving and cooking will still need practical test and interview equivalents for the lock-down environment.

3.5.7   Making decisions about people

All managers would want to make as good a decision as possible. A 'good' decision is one where, subsequently, there proves to be a link between the evidence from the selection tools used and the performance of a candidate once they're in the job.

Each manager participating in interviews should score the results from the various assessments independently. To avoid bias, scores should be aggregated and a strict 'first past the post' system used to determine who gets hired. Only discuss the candidates if there's a tie.

3.5.8   Pre-employment screening

Managers would often like to know if the person they intend to hire would at some stage in the future be a threat to the firm. Managers may therefore be keen to vet candidates before they employ them.

Vetting is defined in the Collins English Dictionary as "making prior examination and critical appraisal of a person". It's checking facts that the hiring manager is provided with by the candidate in support of their job application.

Managers are entitled to ask questions during the hiring process about anything that materially affects a candidate's ability to do the job. Under the Equality Act 2010, they may not ask anything that departs from this before making an offer – that would be unfair.

Once an offer has been made, it can be subject to health screening, references and satisfactory searches of public information and criminal records. But even here, the searches and enquiries will need to be proportionate and relevant, and conclusions reached fairly and reasonably. Just because a candidate has a criminal record, for example, does not automatically exclude them from employment.

We recommend the following basic checks:

- Proof of identity and address corroborating that the person is who they say they are.
- Proof of nationality and right to work in the UK.
- Proof of claims such as qualifications, experience, and past employment.

References should always be sought but only to corroborate information (they have a relatively low predicative validity of 0.26).

3.5.9   Issues in testing

The important point about all this testing and interviewing is that it must tell the interviewing manager if the candidate before them can likely do the job. It must be objective, proportionate, and relevant. It must be free of bias. In discussing some of the issues with such testing, we assume that this rule will be applied.

That's a big ask. Here are some of the main issues in applying testing.

First, we assume that the managers assessing the candidates have themselves the competencies needed to score the tests. Metaphorically, we assume that the carpet fitter managers in our discussion about work sample tests can tell when a carpet gets fitted well. Likewise, in our other example, we assume that the hospital managers can judge when a clinician before them will meet the requirements. If the managers have put together a poor set of tests with low predictive validity, or if they are unable to score candidates despite high test quality, the whole testing and assessment structure falls. Managers must be able to interpret test results – describing a candidate as extroversive, for example, does not mean that they will be gregarious. Managers must be trained to test, assess, and interview.

Second, testing is not perfect. It's very good. But it's not perfect. Some aptitude testing, for example, can score candidates from different parts of the World slightly differently when compared with British candidates. Some candidates are scored slightly more favourably. Some are scored slightly less so. Psychologists are unclear about why this might occur. There are several theories spanning differences in worldwide genetics, social upbringing, mindsets, and education. To counter the chance of bias in the tests themselves, we recommend that tests are designed to be correlative. Two or more tests should be used to assess a competency and the results compared.

Third, managers must look for reasons why candidates might score low. For example, a candidate who is dyslexic might score low simply because they take longer to read test material. The test might truly reflect the job requirement – someone who takes too long to assimilate information would perhaps not be good in the job. Or it might be something that has simply been added to the requirement subconsciously. The rule requiring objectivity, proportionality, and relevance must be applied fastidiously, and managers should always be awake to the possibility that candidates have undeclared disabilities which may mask their competencies and behaviours. Quality must be designed into selection and our model in Figure 3-4 embraces this concept.

3.5.10 *Mixing internal and external recruitment*

Managers often open vacancies simultaneously to both internal and external candidates.

Simply, consider internals first, in isolation. If there are no internals good enough, then, and only then, should the manager seek external applicants. Don't mix internal and external recruitment. To do so risks decimating staff commitment.

Reflection 3-2: About your second selection interview

Considering a job vacancy with which you are familiar, assemble a
second-interview plan based on the above guidance. You will need
first to assemble some competencies and behaviours that you will use
to build work sample tests and interview questions with which
to assess the candidates.

3.6 Making job offers

Landing the 'catch' is possibly more complex and just as time consuming as finding and interviewing candidates. Here are some clear 'dos' and some equally clear 'don'ts' to help success.

3.6.1 *Discussing offers by telephone*

We recommend treating the whole recruitment and selection activity as a series of business meetings. Imagine that you as manager are trying to sell your firm's goods and services to a client (the candidate). And, of course, the converse is true too – the candidate is trying to sell themselves to you. All interactions are therefore between two professionals who are trying to see if it would be right for them to do business together.

Firstly, there's no need to discuss money until discussing an offer. Asking crass questions like, 'What salary are you expecting?' or worse still, 'How much do you earn in your current job?' taint all discussions. You'd not do that when selling. Selling starts by establishing if the product the seller has meets the buyer's needs.

You should do your homework to find out roughly what each candidate is earning. And you should benchmark your intended salary with the labour market for that job and think through what will constitute a competitive salary and benefits. Candidates can therefore proceed on the assumption that you'll not insult them with a derisory offer, and you can proceed on the assumption that your offer will be competitive.

We discuss pay and benefits in Chapter 10.

Secondly, you should discuss the offer personally. Do that by telephone. That way, you can sense the reaction and prepare yourself for any negotiation. There is something very gratifying for a candidate to be called by their future boss and hence a personal call is much more likely to be successful. And even if the initial reaction is not favourable, the scene is set for discussion, and you can open with some questions about what it would take to have the candidate join you.

Discussing offers in person also grows knowledge about the labour market and about your firm's place in it.

Any offer made by telephone is legally binding so you will not at this point 'make' an offer. You will be discussing the content of the offer and asking for feedback from the candidate. Managers must always make offers conditional and the conditions will be set out in the formal offer sent to confirm discussions.

3.6.2 *Negotiating the deal*

Most managers are faced with a negotiation. In the late 80s and 90s, managers could perhaps assume that they had the upper hand – that candidates would automatically be overjoyed at being made an offer. Today, the power is more equal, and candidates will negotiate.

Generation Y – those born in the 80s and 90s – expect a fair salary, so the salary benchmarking activity is key to successful negotiation. But Gen Y candidates often value non-financial elements of the offer over the raw salary.

What matters often is the working conditions. Gen Y values flexible working – flexibility rather than flexi-time. They want to be treated with respect. They'll put in the effort, but they'll want there to be trust between manager and employee. You may have to relax rigid attendance hours, allowing some time working from home to accommodate the candidate's home life and travel arrangements.

Likewise, Gen Y values personal development and the quality of the work. They expect to be given responsibility quickly. The days of expecting an accountant to spend many years in audit are gone. They want progress. You will need to prepare for questions like, 'What's the firm's attitude to personal development, because I'd like to do a Masters sometime soon?' and 'when will I make Senior Consultant, because I'll be getting married and will want to apply for a mortgage?' These questions are not about the financial offer, but about the candidate's future with you. They are setting the foundations of the psychological contract. Reneging subsequently on anything said at this point, simply to land the catch, will destroy trust later.

Managers need to think through the offer and possible negotiating positions carefully and research typical salaries and benefits in the labour market to understand possible candidate negotiating positions.

Salaries, benefits, and conditions enjoyed by existing staff will also be strained if new employees are made unique offers to land them. Anomalies will need to be resolved – and not by simply red-circling the new arrival.

3.6.3   Confirming the offer

On receipt of a verbal indication that an offer will be made, most candidates will want some time to think.

During discussions in first and second interviews, and in subsequent telephone discussions, it's always good to ask if the candidate would be minded to accept if made a suitable offer. Unless manager and candidate haven't been honest, there should now be no surprises when the offer is finally made. When telephoning to discuss the offer, ask if the candidate would be minded to accept on receipt of a formal offer. That's enough at this stage.

On following up with a written offer, managers need to understand that they are likely one of several opportunities being pursued by the candidate and what happens now will probably tip the balance in favour of, or against, the firm's offer.

The manager must now close the deal by assembling a package of documents. The aim is to 'wow' the candidate – but not with a high salary. We recommend that this package comprises a letter of offer setting out the salary and benefits and a contract of employment. The package should also include any supporting information such as the staff handbook, supporting policies and publicity material supporting the manager's claims about how good the firm is to work for.

All offers should be conditional upon receipt of satisfactory references and on success in relevant checks such as the ability to work in the UK, security clearance, employability vetting and health assessments as appropriate. All offers should be open for acceptance for a finite time, such as four weeks, after which the offer will be automatically withdrawn.

Reflection 3-3: About your offer

Considering a job with which you are familiar, think through the details
of an offer that you would make to a candidate. Would it 'wow' you?
Would you be impressed and minded to accept, and why? And if not,
what do you believe you will need to do to make the offer a 'killer'
that no one could turn down. Remember that it's not all about money.

3.7   Other issues in recruitment and selection

3.7.1   Overcoming roadblocks in recruitment

We'd like to think that recruitment and selection is a process that starts with a need for a new employee and ends with that new employee in the firm's employment after a sensible period elapsed, such as three months. We'd like to think that the process outlined in Figure 3-4 is successfully run every time. This is seldom the case. Often the process is disrupted by the firm. At other times it may fail simply because there were no candidates that were predicted to perform satisfactorily in the job – with or without compromise.

Lately in the UK, it's become evident that there's a skills shortage. Attempts to find and hire good candidates in industries like information technology and medicine will often fail.

In this case, the firm needs to revise its whole hiring and retention strategies. It becomes even more important to keep hold of existing employees and to develop them to take up enlarged jobs in the future. This then moves the problem to the lower skill end where, perhaps, the skills shortage is less acute.

Running the process shown in Figure 3-4 from time to time involves opening a window for applications for a short timeframe. The shorter the timeframe, the fewer the number of applicants. Managers should consider adopting a continuous recruitment approach where the firm lets it be known that it always has vacancies and is continuously interviewing – and the window is always open. Whenever a high-competence individual is discovered, an offer is made. This demands of course that the firm has the cash flow to support this. It may also require adjustment to the JDPS against which the recruitment and selection process relies.

3.7.2   Compromise and trade-offs

While we advocate a simple system of scoring and a first-past-the-post decision, we also acknowledge that sometimes there's no-one who meets all the requirements and compromise is needed.

In this case, managers should not just abandon all the scoring and return to gut feel. Ideally, hiring managers should return to the job modelling and see if there are parts of the job that can be omitted. Alternatively, we suggest that managers go back to the job description and look again at the person specification. We suggest asking which person-characteristics are essential and which are desirable, and could, for example, be trained for if absent. This may in turn suggest changes to what the job is to achieve though the accountabilities or responsibilities.

The manager can then return to the scoring with a revised requirement. Scoring can be amended, and the first-past-the-post re-assessed.

In essence, compromise should be done with eyes wide open, and reduced job outcomes identified and accepted.

3.7.3   Ensuring candidates take up posts

Even once a contract has been signed and returned, there's no certainty that the new employee will join on the agreed day. The fishing analogy is strong here. It's like playing a big fish with a light line – one tug and it's gone.

The manager must keep the recruit on the line by inviting them to important company days, like monthly briefings. Most likely they won't come, but you will be showing that you have high regard for them. Keep them involved by sending out briefing notes. Try to find ways by which they might become more closely involved too, such as writing Web material in their specialist subject or proof-reading documents like sales proposals. You want them to feel wanted, and in any case, the more involved they are before they join, the less effort you'll have to put in when they turn up.

3.7.4   *Inducting new staff*

No new employees ever come ready to perform. They are typically not aware of how the firm works and how they can best fit in to be able to perform. To overcome this, new staff should be inducted – after all, it's in the manager's interest to ensure that the new hire succeeds. A written programme of activities should be developed.

How this is done is for the manager, but we'd recommend that most new employees will need between 10 and 100 hours of induction depending on the job and organisation complexity.

3.7.5   *Assessing the effectiveness of recruitment and selection*

A structured process overall allows the manager to determine how many good hires they make and to generally improve their hiring quality over time by amending the selection activities considering experience.

Recruitment and selection comprise a closed loop system that relies on feedback to improve.

Reflection 3-4: About how you will now recruit and select

Now think through your whole recruitment and selection process and determine where you need to improve. Determine things that you can do now to benefit from a quick win, and others where you would like to do further research before concluding the change you need to make.

3.8   Retaining staff

It's typically much more costly to hire a replacement for a member of staff than it is to retain and work with them. It rarely makes sense to be in any way enthusiastic about staff leaving. Managers therefore need to understand why employees might want to leave and develop appropriate retention strategies.

3.8.1   *Why employees quit*

Employees don't just wake up one day and decide they want to leave. It takes time, and significant negative management action to drive someone away. Conversely, it takes significant personal energy on the part of the employee to plan a move. There are two stages in quitting. First, the employee develops an intention to quit (ITQ). Then they take quitting action by finding another job. Each stage might last years – and some employees may harbour intention-to-quit thoughts for many years without acting.

There are two things that keep an employee with a firm – commitment to the firm, and engagement with the job. An employee can be committed to the firm but not engaged with their job. We note elsewhere that engagement is a special case, built through a sense of career that culminates in high motivation and outcomes.

An employee can therefore be committed (with a low ITQ), but with either low or high engagement. ITQ may be accompanied by withdrawal behaviour, but often the manager will never know the employee's real thoughts.

Employees are driven to quit by two interacting forces. Under the first, the employee may consider that whilst they are committed to the firm, their job no longer satisfies their needs. And under the second, the employee may build an overall negative view of the firm and their manager. In this latter case, the job may be fine, but the employee becomes sick of the environment in which the job exists. Generally quitting comes from some mix of the two.

If we assume that the manager has successfully hired the right person to the right job, ITQ typically arises because something has changed. It's perhaps because of a change in what the psychologist Frederick Herzberg called hygiene factors – for example, obstructive company policies, poor job quality and bad manager support. In effect these hygiene factors are the inverse of everything that a manager should be doing to motivate their people and achieve optimum performance. We discuss these variables in later chapters.

Degraded hygiene factors typically come from organisation change – for example, take overs, department amalgamations, new managers with new ideas and transfers to other jobs. Pay can play a part. Usually though, it's some pay injustice that's the trigger. Sometimes though, a slow degradation of real wages and a corresponding increase in workload causes a growing ITQ until eventually some tolerance threshold is reached.

Some staff turnover could, arguably, be healthy. Some staff turnover may be inevitable as the firm evolves. But when an employee leaves and cites a list of hygiene factors as the reason, that's never good since their colleagues will likely follow.

Managers of small organisations will have to work hard to build ever-enlarged opportunities to retain staff with high growth needs strength and desire to further their career. The manager, in this case, must accept and rejoice in the ability to retain staff for five or six years, and enable their progression and subsequent departure when the time comes.

3.8.2 *Retaining staff*

It would be too easy to say simply that you retain staff by doing all the things discussed elsewhere to gain commitment and engagement. So, can we provide further guidance and perhaps summarise?

There's one word that says it all, one facet of the employer-employee relationship that, if present, enables all – and that's respect. Managers must respect the employees who work for them. And from that, employees will come to respect their managers. Google gives a meaning of respect as, 'due regard for the feelings, wishes, or rights of others'.

Considered simply, the mineworkers of the northeast of England in the early 1900s are an interesting exemplar. The miner's job was horrid, dirty, and dangerous. But the miner could plan a family and have a good life. They were given a free house, free coal and a modest but not low wage, so compared to others around them, they could hold their heads up and be proud of their lot. From that grew a community of music, gala, and church and sons followed their fathers down the mines for generations. Viewed through an anthropological lens focussed on the era, miners had everything needed to bolster their respect for, and commitment to their managers.

Of course, the mineworker's lot was not all harmony. Huge battles ensued over the years between miners and employers over safety, productivity, and wages, illustrating that respect must be worked on constantly.

Intention to quit will rise if respect is diminished. Respect is earned through action. Respect is earned over a long period and destroyed in an instant through crass management.

Today, employees don't stay with firms forever, with their sons and daughters joining the firm. The average tenure varies with age, ranging from five years for younger employees to seven years for older employees with families. Managers should plan with this in mind and rejoice if they can gain that sort of dedicated service. Even if the manager does everything right and commitment is high, even if the sense of career is strong and with that there's strong engagement, employees will always want, and need, a change.

3.9   Recruiting Volunteers

So far, we've assumed that everyone involved with an organisation is a paid employee. In real life, that's often not so. In for-profit firms, managers sometimes offer what amounts to a volunteer opportunity to a young person by way of internship or period of work experience. The person gives their time and energy and the firm, through the work, builds the young person's skills, knowledge, and self-confidence.

And of course, there are also many not-for-profit organisations that secure the services of volunteers. In some there are a few paid managers, and a host of volunteers. In some, the employees run activities like fundraising and provide a core infrastructure while volunteers deliver services on the ground to the organisation's beneficiaries. The balance between employees and volunteers varies to suit the organisational need.

Many managers consider that recruiting and managing volunteers is very special – as if somehow the absence of paid remuneration fundamentally changes the person doing the work. Of course, there are differences, but the basic ideas are the same. We cover recruitment and management of volunteers here and in other chapters where relevant.

3.9.1   *Why volunteers volunteer*

Getting enough volunteers with the right skill set is a huge problem for organisations reliant on volunteers. Managers of volunteers must continually engage in recruitment. But how does the manager of volunteers succeed in getting 'the right people in the right jobs, always'.

Here's a simple three-step model that is useful in understanding the problem, and its solution.

Like chicken and egg, it's difficult to know where to start. From the organisation's perspective it's with opinion. Would-be volunteers must have a good opinion of the organisation. Building an opinion in potential volunteers is a long-term ongoing activity. But for the would-be volunteer, everything starts with the trigger.

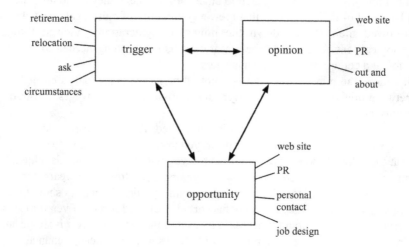

Figure 3-7: The lifecycle of volunteer recruitment

Everyone follows a life stages trajectory from youth to retirement. Along the way, individuals evolve. In their early teens they are too busy at school to be concerned with causes.

In early adulthood, they build opinion about causes and it's then that many decide to volunteer. They learn, for example, about global warming, are aghast and moved to act – and they volunteer as activists.

In their 30s and 40s, they become settled in careers and have children. At this stage, they see atrocities, like homelessness and migration, and are moved to volunteer. Or as parents, they hear that the local youth club is going to fold, and they volunteer as parent leaders – at least for as long as their kids are members.

And in middle-age and into retirement, they relocate or reduce work commitment or stop working altogether, and hence have time on their hands.

In every case, something triggers action. In every case, something moves the person to volunteer. The trigger will be different at each life stage. But for the organisation, knowing that people might be out there experiencing a trigger event is no good unless the managers in those organisations are ready with active marketing.

Being ready starts many years before.

Before the trigger means anything, the potential volunteer must have a positive opinion about the organisation's cause. This means engaging with all the usual marketing tools like web site, PR and face to face events. Those events must be designed to ensure that when the potential volunteer experiences the organisation, they come away with the sub-conscious idea that it would be a cause to which they might give time.

Targeting the right demographic is essential here if marketing effort is to be successful. This involves knowing the profile of the typical volunteer for that cause.

But trigger and opinion are no good unless the potential volunteer can perceive how they might contribute, and how they might benefit. Remember that with opinion, they are minded. With trigger, they might act in the organisation's favour. But there's nothing certain that the organisation would be the beneficiary when the time comes. The would-be volunteer must perceive a role for themselves.

Opinion marketing is about laying out how worthy the cause is. Opportunity marketing is different. Opportunity marketing shows anyone who might enquire, what they might do, and what a difference they might make. Remember the reasons why people volunteer in the first place: to satisfy their affiliation, growth, and significance needs. Opportunity marketing shows would-be volunteers how, subliminally, those needs would be met.

Again, the traditional marketing tools are used, but this time, the aim is to say, "This could be you". The organisation web site might run a series of testimonials. The Tomorrow's Engineers website is a brilliant example of this. The jobs are not all voluntary, but their Real Jobs page sets out a host of possibilities. A good example of a volunteer-inspiring video is on the Tomorrow's Engineers Volunteers page. A reference to Tomorrow's Engineers is given in the Bibliography.

And ultimately, of course, it must be clear that for good volunteer candidates, the organisation can design a role around the person. All charities and other organisations offering volunteering must engage with job design. Someone who has the right opinion and is 'triggered' must not be turned away just because there's no suitable role right now.

Recruiting volunteers is a long-term activity. Positive opinion must be created in potential volunteers. As they come closer to trigger points in their career journey, they must be given tangible information showing how they could contribute to real jobs.

Then, on experiencing their trigger, they must know where to go to start discussions about their next volunteer engagement. When the trigger comes, the volunteer must turn away from hobbies and interests that would otherwise consume their time toward volunteering. They must turn specifically towards the organisation and its volunteer roles. Ideally, they should be known by the organisation, and can then be asked in person to commit.

3.9.2   *Retaining volunteers*

Like their salaried colleagues, volunteers give their labour because their needs are satisfied. The rewards for volunteering that come from those needs are manifold, and arguably unique to the individual.

So, being simplistic, a volunteer will remain in post so long as they get what they need from the job, and they'll quit when those needs are no longer being met. Like their salaried colleagues, they will also be sensitive to negative hygiene factors like feelings of injustice and poor manager relationships. Arguably volunteers will be hyper-sensitive and negative hygiene factors will result in decisive and quick departure – after all, they have nothing to lose if their needs are already lost.

In the first instance then, managers of volunteers need to understand why people volunteer, and understand the needs that must be satisfied. The model in Figure 3-8 shows the mechanisms.

Everything starts with the manager setting up a meaningful job for the volunteer to do. If there were no effects external to the person, intention to quit would be low. They'd be happy in a great job and that would be the end of the matter. We discuss this in the sections above and there are clear parallels with the start point for salaried employees. But of course, the volunteer works in an environment and is managed.

If the support provided by the manager of the volunteers is strong, and there are no significant negative hygiene factors like poor colleague relations, perceived injustice and incessant change, the intention to quit will be low.

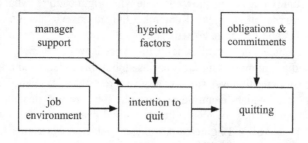

Figure 3-8: Mechanisms in intention-to-quit and quitting

Like the salaried colleague, intention to quit does not mean quitting. There's a significant energy needed to make the move to resign. The volunteer doesn't rely on the firm for their financial welfare so perhaps they don't need to stay. Likewise, they've not signed an agreement that says they'll stay. Perhaps though there's a significant moral commitment – perhaps if they leave, the group they run, the path they lay or the shop they serve in will be materially and perhaps catastrophically impacted. In such cases, they'll perhaps announce they're going, but stay until a replacement is found.

So, on the one hand, volunteers can quit in an instant, and on the other, there are often moral obligations arising from their beliefs about the organisation and its causes that block or delay departure. Often organisations with poor management and bad hygiene are stopped from collapse by such obligations widely held.

This discussion shows the apparent simplicity of how to retain volunteers. Give them a good job that meets their needs in an organisation about which they have positive beliefs, manage them well and take care over hygiene factors. But they may still leave. Externalities may still dictate that they move on. But at least the manager of volunteers will have done everything possible to retain them for a few years.

3.10   Chapter Summary

Gaining the services of people starts with the manager thinking about what those services are and how they might be procured. In the UK we have very muddled regulations that determine worker status – employee, worker, or supplier. In fact, it's impossible for the manager to determine the status of their workers with certainty. In the end, only a government agency like the HMRC or an employment tribunal or court can do this. And simply, that's not fair on the manager.

But be that as it may, the manager must reason what that status should be – what it is that they want – and then set up the right structure. Then, probably, the right status will follow.

We highlight that there are three ways a manager can engage with a person, to have then do work on behalf of the firm. The first is our focus here – the employee. Employees are under contracts of service. And they enjoy the strongest worker rights. The second is the other end of the spectrum – the supplier. The supplier is a separate entity, a self-employed person or a person employed in their own limited liability company, trading at arms' length with the firm, under a contract for services. They don't get regular pay. They get paid for deliverables. And the third is the worker – almost an employee, but not quite.

Managers get those states confused. The confusion comes in part because many employees or workers want to be a supplier, because they can charge more and enjoy reduced tax. That beneficial tax state is diminishing, to the point now that the benefit is almost indiscernible. The confusion also comes from an over-enthusiasm on the part of managers to avoid employing people, choosing instead to call them associates or contractors. Remember the 'duck test'. If it gets paid regularly like an employee, turns up every day like an employee and gets told what to do like an employee, it is almost certainly an employee.

One day soon, HMRC are going to have a purge, catching all suppliers who are really employees. Watch out! It will be costly for both parties.

So, given that the intended status is 'employee', how does the manager get some of those and enter an appropriate employment contract with them?

Firstly, the manager must characterise the person needed. We describe how modelling can help here, illustrating the functions, roles, and jobs. The essential document is the job description. Once a quality job description is available, the person who will excel in the job can be defined and a person specification written.

Secondly, the manager must find the person defined by the person specification. That's done through search. There are three main search methods: recruitment agencies, advertising, and headhunting. Recruitment agencies use jobs boards to advertise. Headhunting has come on hugely and now typically uses LinkedIn. Now the manager can approach would-be candidates directly.

We propose a process with seven distinct activities from description of the roles to on-boarding the jobholder. Every firm should build such a process embracing appropriate science at each stage.

We recommend that firms abandon the idea of popping up to announce a vacancy, then trying to find someone in a few weeks. The chances of success are reduced by only searching when a vacancy arises. The window must be ever open, searching and selecting as soon as a good candidate comes along.

Then it's down to selection. Selection is a science. There are four tools in this science: intelligence (or general mental ability) tests, personality assessments, work sample tests and the structured (pre-scored) interview. Never dump the science. Always use selection instruments with high predictive validity and aim for the best predictive validity by using several tools together. We discuss psychometric assessment tools at length.

Whist we are clear about the essential use of high predictive-validity tools in running a high-quality process, we are also realistic. Psychometric assessment is an aid to decision making but no one tool should be used alone. Some candidates with cognitive disabilities will have problems taking some types of tests and may have to be given alternatives. Psychometric assessments like those reporting on intelligence and personality should allow managers to from an opinion and ask further questions. They should not incorporate a decision threshold.

We then discuss how to land the catch. The fishing metaphor is strong. Never assume that the candidate will fawn over the firm and be grateful of an offer. Work to land them.

Get close to them. Make the offer personally. And keep in touch until their bum is on your seat.

We also address compromise. Often managers will make compromise and select a less than ideal candidate at point of selection. We argue that this is wrong. We argue that compromise needs a return to the job description to change the accountabilities to better suit the chosen candidate. That in turn may need a return to the organisation modelling since some roles may have to be given to others.

Once in a firm and performing, all managers hope that this state sustains for a long time. We counter the popular myth that tenure is shortening to just one or two years, but we also discuss what managers must do to make sure employees stay with the firm for a reasonable time. Managers must ensure that employees quit for reasons external to the firm such as career change.

Finally, we note that some managers believe that recruiting and managing volunteers is a very special case. We argue that whilst it needs to be understood, the person volunteering is still human and has needs that they seek to satisfy in the job. The theories and models of commitment and engagement still apply. We propose a model to understand what the manager must do to find and engage the volunteer, and another model to understand how they might retain the volunteer once in post.

4

Starting Operations

4.1 People and work

4.1.1 *What work is*

In Chapter 1 we identified that the organisation could be likened to a machine. This machine takes in a mix of raw materials, technology and human effort that together outputs something useful by way of deliverables to a customer or other stakeholder. In return for these deliverables, the company invoices and receives payment.

In Chapter 1 we also introduced the idea of modelling, emphasising the need for the manager to be able to abstract their thinking to distinguish the big picture from the noise of the work itself. And we introduced an input-output model of a typical trading firm or company. This is shown again in Figure 4-1.

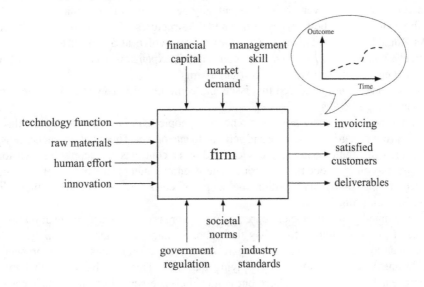

Figure 4-1: The trading firm

Operations is the term used to describe the various activities within the company that work together to convert inputs to outputs. As a function, Operations is often described by models – modelling is, after all, the only real way to describe the set of abstract concepts that define what goes on inside the machine. In such models, we might have owners (of the firm), managers (acting as agents for the owners), employees and suppliers. And such models can be elaborated to ever greater levels of detail as needed by managers to understand and analyse the work.

This chapter discusses how the firm works – how it's described, what holds it together and how it comes about that people do work to realise the desired outcomes.

4.1.2   *Work and contracts*

Typically, the relationship a firm has with its customers is through a contract of sale. The essence of this contract is that "we, the company, will supply you, the customer, goods and services under the following conditions". Other organisation types will likewise have contracts between the organisation and its customers or stakeholders – some may just be promises. But one way or another there's an upstream agreement or expectation of some sort.

The contract of sale in the trading firm is important because it triggers a chain of downstream requirements for other agreements. Importantly, this contract of sale spawns relationships and agreements between the firm and its employees and its suppliers and we discuss these in more depth below.

4.1.3   *The theory of the firm*

Why is it that the firm came about? Why did an entrepreneur, making and supplying goods and services to others, ever evolve to eventually become a multi-national concern? There is nothing God-given about this evolution and the structures of the company finally arrived at. As Ronald Coase questioned, why does a firm evolve at all in an economy? What, ultimately, controls its size? And what controls this expansion from an industry of many individual entrepreneurs to one of a few large firms?

Coase and others pondered this issue and came up with The Theory of the Firm. It goes something like this.

In the beginning there are entrepreneurs – people who have an idea and realise that they can produce a good or service and sell this to customers. These entrepreneurs sense the market price for their goods and services and enter contracts for supply with customers based on this market-determined price. These entrepreneurs are aware of the cost of production and supply, and, within the scope of costs and market price, they aim to maximise their profit.

As demand grows for the entrepreneur's good or service, the entrepreneur realises that they can't produce enough to satisfy their chosen market. To increase supply, the only option open to them is to contract out part of the production to another entrepreneur who is in business and specialises in supplying that part. This will be a part that the first entrepreneur is less able to produce but is nonetheless essential to satisfy their customer. The price charged by the contracted supplier is set by the market price for the part.

The first entrepreneur now has a supply chain and in cases of complex goods and services, this supply chain will comprise many supplier agreements. It will be a system of relationships with others, each comprising parts specifications, contracts, and prices.

Each supplier agreement takes effort to negotiate and manage. And as systems engineers know all too well, 'errors collect at boundaries'. In a complex system of sub-contracts, there are lots of boundaries. The entrepreneur must specify the parts and check their quality and function. The entrepreneur is responsible for the assembly of the parts. The quantities for supply by each supplier will be forecast and ordered by the first entrepreneur and unless carefully managed, will result in increased inventory as the parts are stored ready for use. Such a system of relationships takes some significant effort to organise.

Each supplier is in business for themselves and hence will have sales and marketing costs and will expect to realise a profit. They will include those costs and profit in calculating the price they would wish to charge.

The first entrepreneur will always be comparing the bought-in prices from their supply chain with the cost of producing each good or service in-house using raw materials. Of course, if they were to produce in-house, they would need to employ and pay an employee to do this.

At some stage, and for each entrepreneur and market, it becomes non-cost-effective to buy-in parts and the entrepreneur will switch to produce in-house.

The entrepreneur will also consider how, by employing someone to produce many different goods and services in-house, all previously the subject of discrete supplier agreements, they can further gain from internal flexibility. Internal flexibility will remove the need to forecast demand accurately and will allow the entrepreneur to cope with demand peaks and troughs by moving employees' production facilities internally.

As the entrepreneur grows, employing more and more workers, their internal costs will rise. Efficiencies initially apparent in bringing the production in-house will be overtaken by the inefficiencies of having tens, hundreds or even thousands of employees, all under one roof, all needing direction and management. Frederick Brooks summed up this phenomenon well in his book *The Mythical Man Month*. For every worker added to an endeavour, a growing additional management effort (and hence additional headcount or overhead) is needed just to make the endeavour successful.

So, the firm, as an entity comprising entrepreneur and employees, is created to escape the costs of an extensive entrepreneur-to-entrepreneur supply system. Ultimately, its size is limited by growing internal overhead costs.

Every part will have its own point of equilibrium. For some parts, internal production (and hence employment of workers) will be the best option. For other, perhaps more specialised parts, the balance will never swing in favour of in-house.

And so it is that all firms comprise entrepreneur(s), employees, and suppliers.

4.1.4   *Differing employee types*

Frank Knight's thesis from 1921 suggests a wonderful definition of the employee and employer.

"Employment is the system under which the confident and venturesome assume the risk for, or insure, the doubtful and timid by guaranteeing the latter specified income in return for an assignment in the actual results. With human nature as we know it, it would be impractical or very unusual for one man to guarantee to another a definite result without being given the power to direct his work. And on the other hand, the second party would not place himself under the direction of the first without such a guarantee (of wages). The result of this manifold specialisation of function is the enterprise and wage system of industry. Its existence in the world is the direct result of the fact of uncertainty."

Coase goes on to criticise this as overly simplistic, but it serves us well here to describe why it is that some remain as entrepreneurs while others become employees.

As the firm grows, the entrepreneur, as owner, will inevitably find that they cannot manage the employees on their own. The entrepreneur then typically employs a manager. A manager is an agent of the entrepreneur. Managers are generally also employees. In larger firms, the original entrepreneurs or owners sit on the Board of Directors, delegating to managers to run the firm. The concept of the evolving firm with its owners, directors, managers, employees, and suppliers is shown in Figure 4-2.

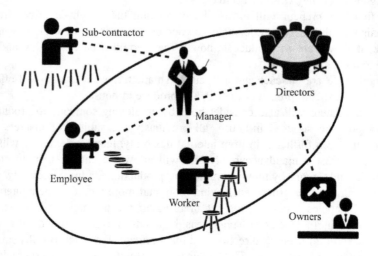

Figure 4-2: The evolution of the firm

4.1.5 *Practical implications of the theory*

Apart from being academically interesting, the Theory of the Firm is important for managers.

Their firm will need to acquire the right balance of products and services to satisfy its customers. Some of those goods and services will be produced and supplied using in-house employees with a set of skills and knowledge working with raw materials and using particular technologies. In cases where there is a cost benefit to be had, managers should not produce the goods and services in-house, but should set up supplier agreements and buy those in. In-house and bought-in goods and services will together yield the total goods and services needed for a composite solution.

The Theory of the Firm tells us that the manager must assess the relative merits of the source of its goods and services and must engage with what's termed the manager's 'make or buy decision'. Ultimately the firm's competitive advantage is achieved when all make or buy decisions are optimised with cost as the key criterion.

Practically, when a good or service costs more to buy than make, the manager should gear up to produce it locally. And of course, the converse should lead to the firm buying in the good or service. When making such evaluations it's important to consider all costs over an appropriate time.

And ultimately as the firm grows, the manager must continually re-assess the various costs and adjust the source of goods and services.

4.1.6   *Systematising the firm*

From the above discussion on how the firm comes about, there is suggestion of form, but we get no inkling of how the various contributors are ordered. Scientific theory tells us that order is not natural – quite the opposite, with disorder prevailing in firms without input of significant management effort. Managers are required by directors and owners to create order in search of certainty. Order comes about by shaping the organisations' activities to be predictable. For directors and owners, the unknown is very problematic and maybe even daunting.

The manager's job is therefore to systematise. If the system fails to return the outcomes wanted, it can, in an ordered fashion, be changed and evolved in search of optimum.

We discussed in Chapter 1 how the company can be thought of as a machine, as a system that does something. We also discussed how the company could be modelled at a high level of abstraction. To be able to build a system, we need detail. Operations is the defining of that detail such that the manager can construct the organisation to achieve the aims of the directors and owners.

Typically, the order that the manager creates is defined by processes defining sequences of events in the system, relationships between entities in the system, information flows and storage within the system and definition of the key human and machine players and how they use the system.

4.1.7   *Building a company system*

A company is a complex system. To synthesise the system and realise the necessary detail, we need now to break the system into discernible parts. There's no established approach to this, though norms have evolved. Figure 4-3 shows a system model for a simple company.

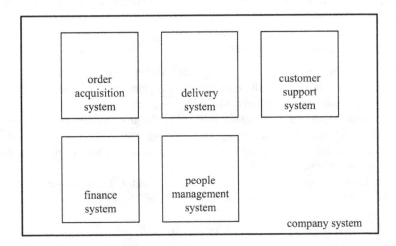

Figure 4-3: Example basic company as a system

This type of modelling, where the machine is deconstructed into component parts, is one of the most useful. There's no effort here to show inputs, outputs, flows or any other functional detail. System models simply show the boundaries, first of the company system itself and then between the sub-systems at the next level down. Anything outside the company is outside the system boundary.

In this simple company, orders are acquired, goods and services delivered, customers supported post-sale and finances and people managed. We could label these in a host of different ways. And there could be any number of them. It's for the manager to build the firm needed to meet their strategy.

Reflection 4-1: About your firm's system model

Thinking about your own firm, construct its system model. Take care
in determining what's inside the system boundary and what's
outside. For example, will you include suppliers inside the boundary?
Then lay out the various sub-systems. Do these naturally
suggest internal departments?

Then put your first effort aside. Re-make the system but try to use
different ideas this time to get a different outcome. What are
the advantages and disadvantages of each result?

4.2   Instructing people to do work

We know from above that the company comprises entrepreneurs, managers, employees, and suppliers. If synthesised in a particular way, using technology and consuming raw materials, the firm has the potential to produce the required deliverables. But unless something else happens, unless there's action, all will remain static. People must act for outcomes to be realised.

4.2.1   *The role of the manager*

In Chapter 1, we established that the manager and leader were one. Managers lead when they influence their followers' motivation. We also suggested that some regard management as a pedestrian, administrative activity, likened to the army adjutant.

The manager's job, like an adjutant, is to create the environment in which employees will do work. And that covers everything from buildings and vehicles to raw materials and methods of production. As we noted in Chapter 1, the entrepreneur as manager does this themselves in the early days, later delegating to others.

Simply leading – by motivating followers - won't cut it. The manager must now take direct action to build the environment and instruct the employees.

4.2.2   *The employee-employer relationship*

The employee and the firm enter an employment contract. In the UK, much of this is covered in statute and the contract is automatically entered as soon as the employee starts work. The essence of the employment contract is that the employee agrees to come under the firm's direction in return for a wage. The employment contract sets out the conditions of this contract of service.

As an agent of the firm, the manager can therefore tell the employee what to do day-to-day. But only in a simple firm would that be enough to create a functioning organisation. The manager must form those orders into operating policies and procedures that take the place of orders. In some designed environment, employees must be caused to do what's needed to satisfy the customer.

4.2.3   *The supplier-firm relationship*

The firm enters a contract of sale with its customers. In this, the firm undertakes to supply some good or undertake some service in return for payment. If the firm is trading in the consumer market, much of this contract too will be set out in statute. In the business-to-business market, there is less statutory customer protection and what's agreed must be expressed.

The work instructions from manager to employee must embody what has been agreed with the customer.

As we noted in Chapter 1, many firms start by contracting out work to suppliers. While the employee is bound to do what they're told, suppliers are free agents and need to agree what they'll do through a contract for services. The contract with a supplier is like the contract between firm and its customer – the two must agree the goods and services and payment.

Managers will place orders for goods and services on suppliers to meet some essential need within the firm's contract of sale.

Generally, what happens is for suppliers' goods and services to be delivered to employees for further work and aggregation with their own efforts before delivery to the firm's customer. Managers must therefore create instructions for both employees and suppliers.

4.2.4   *Breaking work into parts*

All managers in all firms must go through a deliberate action to take the contract of sale for goods and services and break it down into what must be done, what must be delivered and by when. There are many ways of doing this and a plethora of software applications to help.

Our favourite tool is the work breakdown structure or WBS.

All contracts for goods and services comprise smaller work packages. Those work packages aggregate to yield interim deliverables. Those interim deliverables aggregate to meet the obligations of the contract. Even a visit to the hairdressers might be broken into four work packages – agreeing scope and style; shampooing; cutting, drying, and styling; and acceptance and payment. And each can be broken down into even smaller packages. Whilst in this example, a temporal progression is assumed, there is no intention to produce a sequential time plan. It's purely an exercise in work breakdown.

The WBS example in Figure 4-4 shows what's needed. This contract has been broken into six major tasks. Each major task comprises between two and eight sub-tasks. Interim deliverables are shown as documents at the foot of each task.

The WBS approach allows the contract for delivery to be broken into sub-tasks, each with its own deliverables. In small firms, those sub-tasks might be arranged to be of a size that can be completed by one employee. In larger firms, further breakdown will be needed. Sub-tasks may be the responsibility of employees, or suppliers with an employee taking responsibility for aggregating all deliverables in a task.

There are myriad ways in which to construct a WBS and managers must find one that works for them and their business. Each sub-task can be defined completely, unambiguously and such that it fits with the others. Each can be elaborated to become an instruction given to an employee or supplier, which, with policies and procedures, defines all that is to be done.

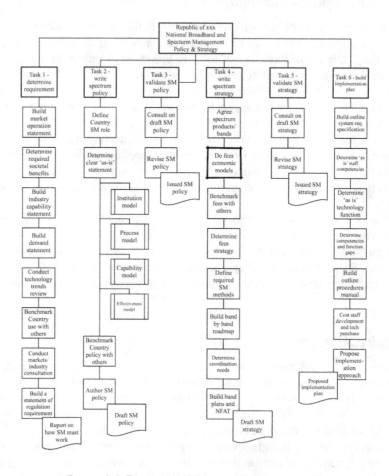

Figure 4-4: Example WBS for a consulting project

4.2.5 *Training versus processes*

No manager wants to spend their time detailing everything that is to be done. At some level of abstraction, the detailing must stop, and the manager must rely on the existing skills and knowledge – the competencies – of the employee.

Managers are therefore faced with determining the level of abstraction needed for their technology and employees. Take hairdressing, for example. The manager may dictate how the customer is to be greeted, how the stylist determines what is to be done, the standard catalogue of styles to be offered and the list of techniques for cutting that the salon wants to hold as its signature methods. At some point though, the manager must stop defining.

Take Figure 4-4 and the sub-task 'Do fees economic model' (under Task 4). This will be done by an economics consultant and is perhaps an extreme to illustrate the point. The consultant will propose various models, discuss with colleagues which are appropriate for the country involved and build the final models in MS Excel. None of this activity can be written down by the manager. It's just too complicated. The manager's role in this is to recruit a suitably qualified consultant in the first place and to ensure that they are suitably trained in the firm's methods.

For more routine work there is more of a trade-off. On the one hand the manager can write a process model that sets out exactly what the employee is to do. The employee is then directed (and controlled) to follow that. On the other, the manager can train the employee in what to do, and to direct and re-train as needed to achieve compliance.

4.2.6   *Instructing employees and suppliers*

The central document used to 'instruct' an employee in what they are to achieve in their job is the job description or JD. In the UK, the law states that the employee must be given a statement of their duties. Such a statement is wholly inadequate. Employees should have a comprehensive job description that defines between six and eight key accountabilities or responsibilities.

A responsibility is just that. It's not a duty, but something that the employee is responsible for achieving. It should be of the form 'do something, to something, to achieve a result'. In our hairdresser example, it might define that the scope, style, and price are to be agreed clearly with the customer. Two other responsibilities might define the core work while other responsibilities might set expectations for clearing up, taking payments, and engaging in continuing professional development in hair styling.

The JD is not an instruction on how to do a job. Operational policies and procedures do that. The JD is, however, the central document that instructs the jobholder to act.

Instructions to suppliers are different. Since the contract with the supplier is for delivery of goods and services, the instruction here must be in the form of an order and a specification.

Reflection 4-2: About instructing your employees

Considering the above, take a few minutes to write down how you will instruct your employees, including the documents that you will put in place. Take a current or past customer contract. Build a WBS for it. Find the right level of abstraction such that work packages feel well bounded and differentiated. Share this with a colleague and evolve it to be complete.

4.3   People and technology

Economists would argue that firms comprise people and financial capital. That's true, but, as well as funding the ordinary operations of the firm, that financial capital is used to purchase technology. For the discussion about work done, firms therefore comprise people and technology. Some, like consulting firms, are light on technology, perhaps only exploiting conventional information technology tools such as word processors and spreadsheets. The capability of others, like car manufacturing plants, comprises mainly technology, with some being described as 'lights out' environments where robots work, remotely monitored by a few high-skill employees.

At its simplest, people and technology together give the firm capability to do work.

4.3.1   *Capability and competitive advantage*

A firm's competitive advantage is its ability to sell more and to make more profit when compared to its competitors. It will sell more if its customers prefer its goods and services over those of the firm's competitors. The firm's competitive advantage is determined by its capability to supply what its customer's need.

The manager's role is to optimise the firm's capability, thereby maximising its competitive advantage.

The balance between the contribution made by technology and humans is in part determined by the norms of the industry and in part by the firm's strategy. Both are, to a greater or lesser extent, under the manager's control.

4.3.2   *Defining technology by its function*

We typically think of technology as artefacts. Technology is the smartphone, the motor car, the array of solar panels or the like. But it's only when technology interacts with or is used by humans, and specifically by human systems of work, that technology has any meaning. It's only when technology affords humans a capability that we get excited.

Technology gives humans the ability to do things that, without the technology, they would not be able to do.

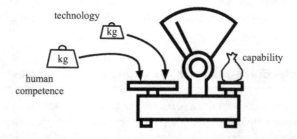

Figure 4-5: Balance between competence and technology for a given capability

Technology 'affords' a person a capability. An example of required capability might be, 'the user shall be able to compute the fuel efficiency of the car as the user drives along the road'. There's no hint here about how this might be done using technology. The technology could be an odometer and a fuel gauge. If the user has high competence, it's possible that they could use some mental arithmetic to divide distance by consumption. If they have medium competence, a personal calculator might also be useful. And if they have low competence, the machine may need an in-built computer and display to do the calculation and report the fuel efficiency in miles per gallon or kilometres per litre. In each case both technology function and human competence must be specified and in these examples the balance in each of the three differs.

Technology is specified by its function. In the above high human competence case, this function might read as 'the system shall report both distance travelled and fuel consumed'. In the low competence case, we'd need to add 'and make a calculation of distance divided by consumption and output this result to a display visible to the driver'. When the user competence is low, the technology function must be high for the same capability and vice versa. Technology must always be specified for a given (or assumed) human competence.

This idea of balance between competence and technology is shown in Figure 4-5.

4.3.3   *Defining people by their competencies*

Competence is the aggregation of all competencies held by an employee. An individual competency is the ability to do something, given a particular technology. The ability to do something with that technology yields a capability. Whether, of course, the employee does what's wanted with that technology, thereby turning the capability into an outcome, is not the issue here – it's the subject of later chapters where we add topics like motivation.

So, what gives the employee a competency, for a given technology? The answer lies in whether they have the right personal characteristics. The key personal characteristics that determine if a job can be done are intelligence, personality, skills, and knowledge. Whilst this is an over-simplification, it's adequate for now.

4.3.4   *Balancing people and technology*

This idea of balance shows the dilemma that all managers face. They must fix either technology or competence. If they hire people to do work – to give a capability – they must hire them with a particular technology in mind. And if they are about to specify new technology, they must have in mind a particular group of employees who will work with it.

Of course, norms of society, education and industry will dictate the personal characteristics and technology that will be developed with this in mind. Nonetheless, this balance or duality gives managers a mechanism for change and organisational development.

4.3.5   *Codifying knowledge in technology*

Information technology is a special case and exemplifies the idea of balance because it can store knowledge. Knowledge in this case can be information that can be retrieved, processes which can be run automatically, and algorithms that can compute answers using complex maths. The three together (information technology, knowledge, algorithms) are termed 'artificial intelligence'.

Artificial intelligence can be stored in the technology – knowledge can be codified in a machine. Artificial intelligence effectively balances all the personal characteristics of the employee – and not just their intelligence per se.

4.3.6   *Implementing change through technology*

The manager's options are illustrated by example. Consider a manager in the insurance business.

If a customer wants a quotation for insurance, they can call a broker. The broker will consult various paper journals and calculate a price. They will call the customer back and provide the quotation. Alternatively, the customer can go online, enter their details, and get a quotation on screen. The information involved is the same, but in the second scenario, technology has displaced the broker.

The choice of balance point between competence and technology is the manager's considering their firm's strategy. The firm's strategy operates, of course, considering the norms of the industry, regulations and other statutes, shareholder expectation and market need.

4.3.7   *The impact of technology on people*

The balance point between competence and technology is for the manager to select. Human competence can be changed, but only slowly. Technology can be changed in an instant (assuming, of course, that the desired technology function is presently available).

As innovation drives the development of more technology function in industry, so managers can reduce the required competence and simply purchase ever-increasing technology function. The result is the concern that people have that 'robots will steal our jobs'.

For a fixed capability, this would be true, but in search of competitive advantage, all managers seek ever-greater capability. Technology function and human competence can evolve together.

And finally, a note of caution. This model assumes that competence and technology are interchangeable; that technology can always replace competence and vice versa. There are many exceptions and limitations to this. Presently debates rage in both academia and the press; debates about just what can and can't be done with technology and what will, and will not, be able to be done in 10, 20 or more years' time.

Reflection 4-3: About interchangeability of technology and competence

---

To what extent has your firm 'computerised' – embraced technology to build greater capability? Remember that capability includes desirable outcomes like productivity, quality, and reduced cost as well as new goods and services for customers.

How do you see this changing over the coming few years? And what strategy will you adopt – one that maximises technology function or one that maximises the competence of the staff employed? What are the advantages and disadvantages for you of both?

4.4   People and quality

4.4.1   *Defining quality*

To the lay person, quality is often thought of as beauty. To an engineer, that beauty comes from compliance with a specification. That specification might be in their head, or dictated in standards, norms, or expectations. Software code can be beautiful by being parsimonious – giving the required function using the minimum of code while embracing highly effective algorithms. A bridge can exude quality, and like software, perhaps this too would be parsimonious – spanning the river using the minimum of materials whilst meeting load bearing, safety, and cost specifications.

In management, quality fundamentally involves the business doing what it says it will. If the customer and the firm agree that a supplied bottle of beer shall be of a particular taste, specific gravity and volume, and the supplied bottles conform, that's quality. If sometimes a there's a little less in the bottles, that would be a non-conformity. And we'd not expect the supplier to be entitled to open the supplied bottles and top up those falling short. That gives that idea that quality is also getting the specification right first time with zero defects.

Ultimately in business, the customer is king. So, only the customer can dictate what is and is not quality. Of course, if there's a contract involved, the customer and supplier would expect to agree on the meaning of quality – but ultimately the customer is the final arbiter. Quality is therefore meeting the customer's need, whether expressed individually or collectively as a market. If the goods and services are fit for the purpose that the customer has in mind, that's quality. And since there are many internal contracts between people and departments within a firm, the idea of 'customer' and quality extends to those too.

Overall, something is of quality if it complies with an agreed specification. But even the degree of agreement is open to interpretation. Customers have become more discerning and demanding in their interpretation and industry has continually improved compliance tolerances over the decades to suit. This leads also to the idea of quality as continuous improvement.

In the end, if a firm sets its price based on compliance with a specification, any non-conformity, met with a reaction of one form or other from its customer(s), will cost the firm. Poor quality costs money. Good quality wins customers and gives more certain outcomes.

4.4.2   *On what does quality depend?*

Quality is about the ability of the firm's systems to meet the specifications required by customer contracts.

By the arguments in the two sub-sections above, quality depends on the people and technology in those systems. The firm can only meet its agreed specifications with the right human competence and technology function. And achieving quality depends on having the right balance between the two. Conceivably therefore, improved quality comes from changing that balance, thereby improving human competence or technology function, or both.

4.4.3   *Designing quality in to work*

Historically, in manufacturing, quality was 'controlled in' to deliverables with quality controllers sitting at the end of the production lines inspecting products. Non-conforming product was rejected and re-worked. Managers soon realised that to avoid rework costs, specifications had to be met first time with both zero defect and zero rejects. To achieve this, quality had to be designed-in to work done.

There are many techniques that can be used, but the essence of designing quality in is to ensure that the work instruction is right – that if the work is done in this way, the specification of the delivered goods and services will be compliant and meet the customer need. Designing for quality demands effort up front in quality assurance rather than later in quality control. This work definition assumes a particular technology and employee competence.

4.4.4   The role of peers

There are several techniques that can be used to achieve quality in deliverables.

The first is to, metaphorically, walk through the processes, using the technology and the skills and knowledge available. Walking through allows issues to be uncovered and corrective action made to processes and technology and training intervention made where needed. Walk-throughs are generally done in a group and are led by the process or deliverable owner.

The second is to peer review work. Peer review allows colleagues who know about how to implement the deliverables to comment on present work to trap issues and ensure that all deliverables are compliant.

The third is audit of deliverables against their contracted specification. If audit is done on early-day deliverables, non-conformities can be trapped early in the deliverables process and corrective action taken.

The fourth is simple inspection. Colleagues can be asked to quickly inspect the deliverables using their own experience of the specification and process to trap errors before delivery.

All make use of peers in the firm. All have the common aim of ensuring compliance. All aim to adjust the methods, skills, knowledge, and technology to achieve quality outcomes for both firm and customer.

4.4.5   Teambuilding and cohesion through quality

Managers need to unite employees behind the firm's strategies. Quality improvement is often selected as one such strategy.

Managers can heighten both commitment and engagement by involving employees in quality management activities. By participating in audit, for example, those not directly involved in deliveries can become aware of adjunct areas of the business. Designers can learn the realities of installation, for example. And purchasing executives can experience first-hand the results of their cost cutting. In fact, the whole company can heighten understanding.

Using employees across the firm in quality assurance can have a huge unifying effect – but managers must allow the time for it. And they must fully support it.

Reflection 4-4: About how you will achieve quality

Determine the specifications for goods and services that you typically agree with your customers. Considering the ideas above, how do you propose to achieve quality deliverables every time?

4.5   Patterns of work organisation

Before the Enlightenment in the 1800s, UK workers toiled in the fields in an agrarian economy. During the Enlightenment and its industrial revolutions, workers came in from the fields to toil collectively as employees in factories. This sustained as the predominant form until the UK lost its manufacturing prowess around 1980 and developed a dominant service arm to the economy. Today, services account for about 80% of economic output.

When working in a factory, employees needed to be there together to cooperate. Services, on the other hand, can be worked on and delivered at almost any time and from almost anywhere with computer-mediated communications. Patterns of work and the necessary work organisation are now diverse.

4.5.1   *Temporal nature of work*

The UK still works to a normal business day of typically 09:00am to 5:00pm, giving 7.5 working hours a day from Monday to Friday. Probably something like 50% of employees work those hours.

But managers need flexibility. Most employees do offer to work outside of normal hours – either as paid overtime, or as a formal or informal flexi-time system where additional hours worked are recovered when convenient for both manager and employee. Reports indicate that UK employees work an average of 42 hours per week. This compares unfavourably with employees in other European countries, with Denmark working an average of 37 hours. Various studies suggest that productivity rises with lower hours so working longer does not always benefit the firm.

Some firms seek to increase their asset utilisation. There is, after all, no point in having expensive plant of any sort sitting idle from 5:00pm through to 09:00am the next morning. Night working in several shifts is highly attractive. Great care is needed when introducing night working. It takes a particular type of person who is prepared to disrupt their natural rhythms to work when they should be sleeping. There have been many studies illustrating the detrimental effects on the human body of shift work.

As discussed in Chapter 3, there are many types of employment contract, each adding a degree of flexibility for both employee and manager.

Zero-hours contracts allow the employee to be offered work ad hoc. The employee can refuse and can have similar arrangements with several firms, building a Protean career embracing flexibility and change. Careers researchers coined the term 'Protean' to describe a career that was made up of many different elements. Proteus, from which the term comes, was the Greek god of change.

Employment contracts can specify less than (or indeed more than) normal hours. And contracts can be for a fixed term.

'Annualised hours' is a further extreme case where the employee is contracted for, say, 1,650 hours per year. The understanding is that these hours are worked when demand for the firm's goods and services is greatest, perhaps during the summer. Generally, under annualised hours, pay is normalised to an equal monthly amount throughout the year.

And finally, we live in a global business environment. Many firms have foreign outposts, and many UK firms are outposts of foreign concerns. As a result, many employees, and particularly managers, find that they can be on conference calls early in the morning and late at night. Many live in what the sociologist Manuel Castells termed timeless time, where work time and private time merge.

Work has many temporal themes. It's for the manager to determine what their firm needs and what fits with the local labour market.

4.5.2 *Spatial nature of work*

As we note in Chapter 1, many firms are nuclear, with a headquarters and all employees assembling there to put in a 7.5 hour working day. But many are not.

Many firms require staff to travel. Some will travel within the UK to meetings with partners, suppliers, and customers. For others, that travel will be international. For some the duration of this 'posting' will be a day or so, whereas for others it may be months or even years. Whilst, often, travel is seen by employees as exciting, it does place obligations on managers for employee wellbeing and security. Travel is often linked to long working hours.

There are many reasons why firms will open branch offices or subsidiaries at some distance from the headquarters. Today, opening an office is easy, with many flexible working space providers across the UK and worldwide. Often labour is more available or cheaper in the provinces or in other countries. And for firms trading over wide areas, the need for long-distance travel is reduced by having representatives on the customer's doorstep.

And in the UK today, with perceived employment uncertainty, regional house price variations and difficulties re-mortgaging, few employees are prepared to relocate to be near a new employer. This, along with a desire on the part of firms to cut costs, has meant a rise in homeworking.

The idea that all staff will work from a central location is gone. Managers must decide their attitude to such new organisational forms and make plans and implement what works best.

4.5.3 *Achieving manager control*

A manager needs to be assured that an employee will perform, whenever and wherever they work. As other chapters will discuss, performance is a complex concept. It depends a lot on the characteristics of the job the employee does, their own motives and the leadership they experience.

In history, managers controlled their employees to achieve performance. Today, managers encourage employees to excel. Nonetheless, the manager's need for control gives rise to several guidance documents that set out the manager's expectations of performance.

The first, and the most useful is the job description. We discussed this in 4.2.6 above. This defines the responsibilities and accountabilities of the jobholder. We also discussed some of the ways of instructing employees in 4.2.4 and 4.2.5 above. Humans are also motivated by goals or objectives. Most people are encouraged by slightly stretching goals agreed between them and their manager. Documents should be used to express those goals.

Documents are nothing, however, without continuous interaction between employee and manager to review progress and to continue encouragement and effect leadership. Lack of interaction and review is a common failing in UK managers. Performance management is a continuous activity and not something invoked when performance is seen to degrade so far below expectations that formal processes are needed.

Using a systems-engineering analogy, intervention is needed as soon as the actual performance deviates from the reference or expected performance. We discuss this in Chapter 2 on leadership. The manager must therefore be continually comparing the two.

Whilst the world of work may have moved on from the factory, employees still need to be managed to ensure that they perform. Computer-mediated communications assist in this, allowing performance management whenever and wherever the employee is working.

4.6   Working from home

The Covid pandemic of 2020 coincided with a general disquiet, particularly within younger employees, about how work constrained and choked people. The result was an enthusiasm when the UK Government said, "work from home" . And the return post-Covid to the central workplace was slow and considered with many firms adopting a hybrid home/office work location model.

But few people are well organised to work from home. Modern homes are designed for living in. The assumption by the architects and builders is that those in the family who are economically active will spend most of their day commuting to a remote location to work. The others will be in school, playing, or relaxing. No modern home is a workhome, physically or legally.

4.6.1   *The new office*

Simply, if people are to work from home for some or all their time, their homes must be oriented toward that task. If firms and the government want people to work from home, both must assist in this. Here are a few of the issues to be discussed and concluded in re-orienting a firm, and some or all its employees, to work from home.

4.6.2   *Core concept*

In essence, the firm extends its workspace to the employee's home. That carries with it big responsibility for all.

For example, obligations in client and supplier contracts extend. Health and safety liability naturally extends. And employment law obligations naturally extend. Quality systems must be extended to sustain performance. Information security systems must be extended to maintain certification. Each must be considered fully and carefully.

4.6.3   *Space and physical arrangement*

There are as many forms of workhomes as there are job types. For example, there's the software engineer's coding 'loft' with its sit-stand desk, large portrait monitors, high power computers, and high-speed internet connection. There's the osteopath's consulting room with its easy parking, patient waiting area, consulting room with treatment bed, and exercise area and technology. And there's the administrator's simple station with its desk, comfortable chair, laptop, and display.

All must have toilet and kitchen facilities too.

Today, the UK health and safety and wellbeing recommendation is a minimum of 11 cubic metres per person. That's around 5 square metres of ground space in the home and is very small. We'd suggest a minimum of 7 square metres for an office worker with minimum needs. Those with specialist technology like an osteopath will need considerably more.

4.6.4   Contracts, time, and money

Typically, when an employee becomes a home worker, their contract will change to show the home as normal place of work. If the firm wants the employee to travel to the firm from time to time, it will then need to pay the employee expenses and allow time.

Of course, the firm's argument would be that the employee no longer need commute and that this is a saving that can offset other emerging employee costs such as occasional travel, heating, electricity, broadband, and facilities. There are also many issues about equity and fairness – particularly when mixing employment conditions across a workforce.

4.6.5   Management

Working from home demands that managers trust their employees. That in turn requires that employees reciprocate and earn that trust. Firms may need to re-define management and adopt the approaches and methods we advocate in this book. Central to that is clarity of role and expression in a job description of what's to be achieved. All will need objectives. All will need regular reviews. We describe management as a contact sport and that must never be forgotten, wherever work is done.

Employee wellbeing must be managed differently. The daily casual opportunity to see colleagues has diminished. Managers must make deliberate effort to go and see employees whether during their occasional in-work attendance or in the workhome.

4.6.6   Confidentiality

Firms must keep private all information they store and process. This is enabled though process and practice. Hence, if information storage and processing extend to the workhome, those processes and practices must apply there too.

There are two key tenets.

First, home working employees must only be able to access the information they need to do their job. Information processing systems should be partitioned by work group, work type or project. That way, any leak is of minimal use to a third party.

Second, the employee should, by design, keep work and home life separate. In the workspace, desk, computer, tools, and filing should be for work and should belong to the firm.

4.6.7   Permissions

In essence, by having an employee work from home, the firm extends its business activities from its premises to an employee's home. A small part of the employee's home is taken over by the firm for its benefit.

In asking the employee to work from home, the manager must understand that this may create problems for the employee. Working from home will likely be in breach of the employee's mortgage or tenancy agreement, and the permission of mortgagor or landlord will be needed. Since the employer shifts its location to the home, it must also advise its insurers, since the employee now bears the employer's risk in their house.

Areas of towns are set aside for specific use. These use classes are currently described in the Town and Country Planning (Use Classes) Order 1987. It's unusual for a zone to have dual use. If indeed a person is working from home - and, hence their property is in dual use - they would be due to pay both Business Rates and Council Tax.

Practically, it's likely that a home office would only attract business rates if it did not return to domestic use at the end of the day. A spare room doubling as bedroom and office would likely not be separately rateable. A converted garage with suspended ceilings, separate door and custom desking would likely be separately rateable because its purpose is fixed and obvious. There's more on this on the Valuation Office Agency site on GOV.UK.

For various reasons, most people working from home in the UK do so illegally - and simply keep quiet, keeping 'under the radar', hoping no-one will notice. There are no obvious fixes for these issues.

4.6.8   *Future trends*

Houses are just not built for home working and adaptation in space, services, heating, and the like will be needed if the trend towards home working employees and suppliers is to be sustained.

If reductions in carbon dioxide are to be achieved by governments, employees must travel less. Whilst the argument for a complete ban on commuting is strong, such an all-or-nothing approach negates worker need for affiliation and manager need for interaction. A compromise perhaps suggests a mixed work regime, working at home part of the week, but travelling to a shared workspace for the remainder.

Working from home, and working flexibly, requires the worker to be in communications and able to pass data just as if they were in the office or other workplace. But the UK is relatively poorly connected. Broadband (offering at least 30Mb/s in the downstream) or greater connectivity covers 96% of population. The Government's aim is to deliver an in-the-office equivalent gigabit-capability to 85% by 2025. Mobile networks could take up the slack to achieve 99% population coverage, but their evolution is pitifully slow. Connectivity is improving, but it has a way to go.

Presently, with employees travelling to a place of work, their homes are typically utilised for only 60% of the time. Likewise, firms occupy their premises for only 35%. If workplace and home become one, and the parties share the costs, building utilisation skyrockets and that's good. Firms can dispense with big corporate offices. The result is a space continually occupied and heated. Cost reduction is a big motivator in firms supporting this pressure.

For now, it's only one segment of the labour corps who benefit from the flexibility and working from home revolution. Perhaps, though, we will see a day when manufacturing employees will produce widgets on a home production line and dispatch direct to customers. Or perhaps it will be just too difficult for 'blue collar' staff to join their 'white collar' colleagues. For that, there will need to be significant workhome adoption and adaptation.

The drivers for change are there. But so are the difficulties. Time will tell if flexibility and home working take hold universally.

4.7   Brand building

Customers buy because the brand gives a promise of a desirable emotional experience. Brand is how the firm looks and feels to its customers. Customers experience a firm's brand at touch points where they encounter it – like the point of sale, when the customer meets the salesperson, or the point of use of the firm's products when the customer tries to enjoy benefit. Clearly, the firm can change the customer experience at those touch points and hence the firm is in command of its brand.

Brand is dependent on the people associated with the firm. People create the firm's capability (whether by their own efforts or by using technology or a mix of the two) and drive its quality. And whilst brand takes time to build, it can be destroyed in an instant.

4.7.1   *Determining how you want to look*

Frequently, managers determine that their brand looks tired and needs to be refreshed. They decide that some empathic words and artefacts like logo and web site are needed to express modern ideas. Strap lines are developed like 'the listening bank' – describing the Midland Bank around 1992 before its merger with HSBC.

Such a strap line that aims to depict brand values presumes that employees have (in the Midland example) the time to listen, the skills and knowledge to interpret what the customer is telling them and the motivation to act to improve the customer's utility of the firm's product or service.

If brand is about customer experience at touch points, that experience depends on the employees' competencies and behaviours. Brand building is therefore about building those competencies and behaviours at those customer touch points.

4.7.2   *Identifying touch points*

We might imagine that touch points are where customers and staff meet. Touch points extend to all points where the customer experiences the firm, its goods, and its services. This means that touch points are to be found right back in research and development (R&D) where products are developed.

Figure 4-6 shows the touch points for a product like an Apple laptop. Whilst R&D may not be visible to the customer, they experience this point during use and in the pride that use brings. Utility and pride stem from excellence in the R&D engineers. Many would argue that Apple succeeds because of its R&D.

Competencies and behaviours are key to brand and managers control those by hiring, managing, and developing the right people. Brand is much more than a few wacky artefacts.

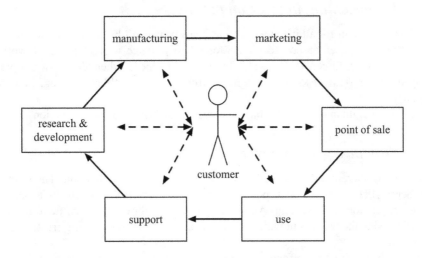

Figure 4-6: Touch points for manufactured goods

4.8   Innovating to stay ahead

There are many definitions of 'innovation'. Here's one developed by the UK Federation of Communications Services to judge one of its innovation awards that aims to cover most of the bases.

An innovation is a new or evolved method, process, idea, product, service, algorithm, or concept that is realised though a discernible process by a group of people to have a value and impact on the firm and its customers.

To be an innovation, the new or evolved method, process, idea, product, service, algorithm, or concept must be able to be applied at an economical cost and must satisfy a need. An innovation can solve a new need or problem in a new way, an existing need or problem in a new way, or just be a different application of old science.

To be an innovation, there must be an evident step between the new state and a previous old state.

Innovation involves deliberate application of information, imagination, and initiative in deriving greater or different values from resources. Innovation includes all processes by which new ideas are generated and converted into useful solutions.

And most importantly, innovation is a huge source of competitive advantage for firms.

We defined competitive advantage in Chapter 1 as the state where customers would prefer to buy from the firm than from its competitors and that the firm trades with lower costs, and hence higher margins that its competitors. Firms innovate to differentiate their products and services and to optimise their costs. All managers must encourage and manage innovation.

4.8.1   *Implementing innovation practice*

The primary problem for all managers is that innovation can't be driven. In the same way as the artist, composer or poet can't be forced to produce a great piece of work, an employee can't be forced to innovate. Innovation happens when the right people are employed on the right tasks in the right environment. If anything's wrong, innovation won't happen.

So, what's right and wrong? What encourages, and what blocks, innovation?

4.8.2   *Structuring for innovation*

Fundamentally there must be something to be done to enable innovation. There must be some identifiable tasks on which people work and on which they could investigate and explore options for improvement. And as the definition above suggests, there must be a group addressing the tasks. Innovation is a group activity – individuals are creative, groups are innovative.

Typically, the greater the focus, the greater the purpose, and hence the more likely that innovation will occur. There needs to be a modicum of time pressure – not too much or everyone ignores possibilities. But each person needs enough spare effort to go 'off-piste' from time to time to explore options. Each person needs to know that they can take a risk and explore. It's no good closing all options down and driving for specific outcomes.

4.8.3   *Formal innovation*

Many commentators confuse innovation and formal research and development. R&D is the business activity that aims to realise new products and services. Generally, it's well funded and, indeed, innovation may occur during formal R&D. But innovation is different. R&D is meant to produce new products. When innovation occurs from everyday business activities, managers rejoice because often it costs little and has significant impact on outcomes.

There are however approaches to planned innovation - not forced but enabled.

It's always possible to look for ideas in other unrelated businesses or industries. Here, employees involved scan activities and spot opportunities that can be ported from one environment to another.

Such discoveries come from the deliberate search for new knowledge. When staff undertake any form of advanced learning, the knowledge and skills acquired are often the catalyst for discovery. Continuous professional development (CPD) is a thriving environment for ideas.

Those ideas need to be encouraged and developed. But ideas are nothing unless they are considered, evaluated, and supported (or dumped). Formal innovation requires a process for ideas development, rejection, and adoption.

4.8.4   *Innovation climate*

All innovation needs the right culture – what some refer to as an innovation climate.

Figure 4-7 shows a typical culture or climate that fosters innovation. Here's a brief explanation describing the diagram for an innovative firm. Each phrase describes a position between extreme left and extreme right on the six horizontal bars. Innovation is a team game so there's no space for individual- or self-focus. All employees should be goal oriented. And ideas will be found in an externally driven firm – one that welcomes customer involvement. Whilst it doesn't do to be too easy going, a strict culture focusses on outcomes to the detriment of innovation. The culture should be between easy going and strict. And looking to local management for ideas strokes their egos while a professional focus casts a wide net. Employees should be professionally focussed. If employees know what's needed, because business performance is shared in an open culture, this helps develop the context for innovation. And finally, focussing on employees rather than the work alone helps them build the confidence needed to take those all-important risks.

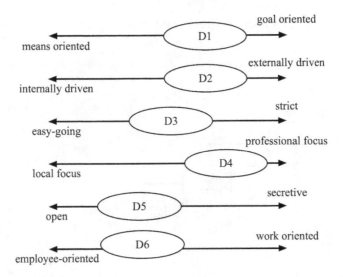

Figure 4-7: Typical culture likely to foster innovation

Building a culture is not a perfect science but with the wrong culture, innovation will not flourish. We discuss culture further in Chapter 5.

Reflection 4-5: About your firm and innovation

Using Figure 4-7, estimate your firm's culture. Highlight the differences and think through the changes that you might need to make to engender the right culture for innovation.

4.9   Sustaining business

Various commentators talk of sustainability as if it's about embracing 'green' environmental policies, saying how the firm will reduce its environmental impact. But such a definition is much, much too narrow. Sustainability is about managers setting out how they intend to maintain the firm in the long term, at, or about, its present activity level – or indeed after growth plans are implemented.

Sustainability is therefore simply defined: it's being in business tomorrow, despite all the threats upon the firm. Figure 4-8 shows a mental process for achieving sustainability. The diagram should be read as a process, stepping from left to right and we describe each step below.

There are typically about eight other general areas of business in which there are threats: environmental management, information security, privacy, quality, business continuity, health and safety, employee wellbeing and business risk. In addition, there are a plethora of other risks to be managed in specialist firms such as those operating in shipping, nuclear energy, and bio-medical research. Your firm will have its own threats and risks and you will need to run your own risk management process and develop your own specific controls.

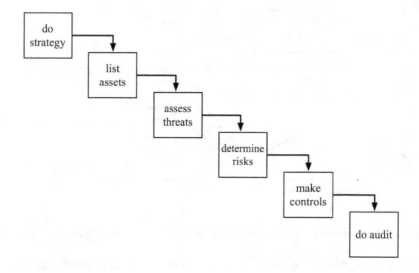

Figure 4-8: Sustainability defined through threats and controls

Here's how to consider the impact of the six activities that we set out in Figure 4.8 with their contribution to sustainability. The following describe the cascade from left to right.

4.9.1   *Strategy and sustainability*

Sustainability begins with strategy. The manager must provide the context and objectives for sustainability, defining the areas of operations to be protected and the implications for the business if untoward events occur. This stage should identify why sustainability is important and business activities affected if the business is not sustainable.

This is relatively easily done by using the strategy-building tools discussed in Chapter 1.

4.9.2   *Identifying assets*

Each firm has important assets which, if disrupted, will endanger operations. In information security, this will be information assets like knowledge bases and source code. In privacy, this will extend to CRM databases containing information on customers.

Before an asset can be protected from loss or failure, it must be identified by its nature, location, and content.

4.9.3   *Assessing threats*

All assets are under some threat or other. Before protection can be planned, those threats must be identified.

For a firm working in central London, relying on employees commuting to work, strikes by public transport workers can be a big threat. And where employees face relentless pressure to perform, stress can be a significant source of absenteeism from burnout.

Most threats involve people. Employees make errors. Sometimes they are coerced or induced to do things against the firm. Sometimes managers do crass things that affect employees. Suppliers will let managers down. Customers will delay payments. And sometimes employees just don't have the skills and knowledge to prevent mistakes.

4.9.4   *Determining risks*

Just because an asset might be under threat does not mean that there is a risk of disruption.

Risk is calculated by considering the chance of occurrence of the threat and its impact on the asset – and loss of business as a result. Managers will need to set a threshold of risk, above which they will act to control the threat, reducing the risk to some residual risk that they find acceptable.

No firm can reduce all risks to zero.

There are a host of approaches to risk assessment. We consider that describing all risks by their financial impact is one of the better approaches.

4.9.5   *Implementing controls*

Risks that are scored as significant must have controls developed to reduce the risk to an acceptable residual level. Insurance can then be taken out to cover that residual chance.

Controls might involve training and development of employees to improve skills and knowledge. Or they might involve introducing new processes such as peer review of work. In extreme cases, controls might involve replacing employee competence and behaviour with technology function, as described in 4.3.

Managers should also be aware of the risk in fostering a high-risk culture in pursuit of financial results, accepting all risk in search of progress. Indeed, some entrepreneurs espouse a blitzkrieg approach, crashing forward swiftly, ignoring the collateral and direct damage caused. Some live by the 'move fast and break things' mantra. Such an approach is never sustainable.

4.9.6 *Auditing*

Once controls are in place, the policies, practices, and procedures must run and inspection, walk-throughs, audit, and review used to show that controls are effective.

Reflection 4-6: About sustainability

Considering the principles outlined above, think through you firm's sustainability needs, assets to be protected, threats to those assets and risks considering chance and impact. What sort of controls do you see as necessary to reduce the risks to that which you would accept in each case?

4.10   Chapter Summary

A firm doesn't just work. Someone – the manager – must determine, in detail, what the firm is to do and how it's to do it. The firm, as a system and in turn as a series of processes involving people and technology, must be defined.

This definition starts with the contract that the firm has with its customers. The contract of sale sets out what's to be delivered. This contract, with its deliverables, can be expressed or implied. Either way, it's to be complied with.

The manager's job is then making order from chaos. They must shape the firm to be predictable. Predictability comes from determining the processes, and in determining the people and technology in each. We discussed that predictability and processes can't be guessed. Modelling is essential. There are several models that are particularly useful here – the concept model capturing the whole firm, the use case model showing who does what and the process engineering models using flow charting. We also illustrate the overarching systems model – the model of the systems (incorporating the processes) showing systems boundaries.

Modelling enables managers to set out what is, to exercise that, and to show what might be if changes are made. The 'as is' and the 'to be' are key statements in determining change.

But still, people must be told what to do in a firm. Even if they are expert professionals, consistency demands defined methods. It's the manager's job to instruct their people. We put forward the work breakdown structure (WBS) as the most significant tool to convey necessary activity. And we illustrate how even a hairdressing salon should make use of such thinking. The WBS conveys to the employees what the firm has agreed with its customer.

Of course, the WBS and other methods of work definition can't, and shouldn't, set out every detail. The employee's competencies and behaviours should give them the ability to interpret high level work definitions and to do what's needed. It's for the manager to determine the level of abstraction of such definitions. Too much detail threatens employee job satisfaction. Too little risks poor quality and misunderstandings.

We develop several definitions of quality but centre on the thought that quality is doing what is agreed with the customer – even if that agreement is tacit and the subject of societal norms. Quality also depends on technology function and the competencies and behaviours of the employees using the technology. We illustrate that managers can change the technology or change the competencies and behaviours of the employees to achieve the desired capability.

That leads us to the 'where' and the 'when' of processes and work done – and the definition of working hours and the spatial nature of the firm. All managers must recognise the modern trends of flexible working, timeless time, and distributed workforces.

This flexibility trend has been amplified by the Covid pandemic where as many as 45% of UK employees worked from home, with many enjoying huge improvement in work-life balance. We have characterised this idea of homeworking by describing what's needed. We define the location where work is done as the workhome. Critically, we point out that if working from home is to become a norm, dwelling design, government regulations and mortgage and rental contracts must change to facilitate workhomes for all.

The systems of the firm would be incomplete without discussion about innovation. Innovation is a badly understood and badly defined word and, to help managers, we develop a clear definition. This leads us to look at how managers can encourage innovation in their firms, and hence what organisational culture is needed for innovation to happen.

Finally, we ask what makes a firm sustainable – and sustainability is not about the firm's green credentials. Sustainability is the ability of the firm to still be in business, satisfying customers and employing people in the years to come. We present sustainability as the ability to counter threats to the business and we set out an approach involving identification of strategy, threat identification, risk assessment and the use of controls to sustain performance for the long term.

5
Managing People

5.1 Introducing

Few managers learn their trade in any formal sense. Most learn on the job, by trial and error, without engaging with the theories of management science. We aim to correct this absence of formal learning by providing here just enough theory to be useful, but not so much that managers dump the theory and return to dark side. We aim to provide theory as a means to learning itself.

Managers need to be able to understand what to do case by case. But inferring that what worked last time will work this time is fundamentally flawed. No manager can experience enough instances of each type of management situation to give them anything like the generalisations to apply when faced with a new event. But academics can.

Academics spend their lives 'experiencing' thousands of situations by postulating hypotheses and gathering evidence. And they develop theories that help managers understand what they should do. Models are another form of generalisation. Models embrace one or more theory. We use several academic theories here and have developed and set out a number of models. Managers should use these models day-by-day.

5.2 Performance

5.2.1 *Feedback-driven management*

Probably the most useful model for managers is the feedback control loop.

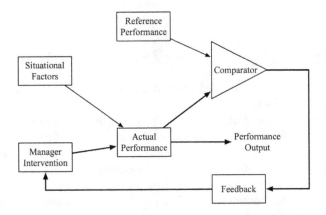

Figure 5-1: Feedback control loop model of management

The manager is constantly sensing performance given by their people. They have in mind a reference performance that they'd find acceptable. And they are constantly comparing the actual performance with the reference. If the performance falls below the reference performance, the manager will act by way of an intervention. The idea is shown in Figure 5-1. We used this same model in discussing leadership in Chapter 2.

5.2.2 *Performance dependencies*

In order to determine what to do about performance variance or non-conformity with the reference performance, the manager must know on what performance depends. It's in those dependencies that the manager is going to intervene. Performance is dependent upon many variables that must work together. There's a lot going on in a jobholder's life and it's the manager's job to ensure that the jobholder is committed, motivated, and engaged. In the direct feed-forward path we show that the person's job motivates them. That motivation causes behaviour which in turn causes performance. Performance causes outcomes. The model is shown in Figure 5-2. We used a simplified version of this model in Chapter 2 on leadership.

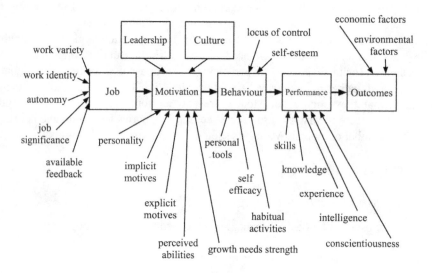

Figure 5-2: A comprehensive model of employee performance

The model shows the five feed-forward concepts of job, motivation, behaviour, performance, and outcomes.

Whether the job done motivates depends on whether the job gives the jobholder variety and whether the jobholder sees the job has having significance. Motivation also depends on whether the jobholder identifies with the work and is given the autonomy to get on and do the job as they see fit. And the job will motivate if the jobholder gets immediate feedback about how well they're doing. If these attributes are missing, motivation won't happen. The manager has control of these five job characteristics and can re-design the job as needed to improve job motivation.

Chapter 2 described how leadership influences motivation, and this is repeated in Figure 5-2. The culture in which the jobholder works enables or constrains their motivation and this too is shown in the figure.

Whilst the biggest motivation a person has comes from their job, they will only be motivated if the job itself is in congruence with their own personal implicit or internal motives. If they've always wanted to be a doctor, and they become one, it's likely that they'll be motivated. If they've always wanted to be a doctor, and now they are a bus driver, that incongruence will work against other positive influences on motivation.

Many managers try to tap the employee's explicit or external motives by offering bonuses and commission as incentives. Unfortunately, this is misplaced. Explicit motives are better tapped with things like recognition and promotion. Regardless of exactly what is used, tapping explicit motives is one area of influence available to the manager to enable motivation.

Personality also plays a big part in motivation. Someone who is extroversive is likely to be keen to interact with people at work. But if the work precludes that social interaction, they'll likely be demotivated. Likewise, someone who is naturally not open to new ideas will find it difficult to get excited when asked to be creative.

And finally, in considering motivation, if the jobholder does not feel that they can perform, they won't. Development to achieve the right level of mastery will be needed to change that opinion. But development will likely only work if the jobholder has a strong need for growth. If their need for growth is low, the manager had better tap other variables and maybe accept that, in this job and for this jobholder, the performance desired is just not going to be realised.

The link from job to motivation is not the whole story. People can be motivated, but somehow just not turn that motivation into performance. For performance, the person must exhibit necessary behaviours. And that depends on whether they have learned the necessary personal performance tools and habitual behaviours. For example, if we had never learned to concentrate on a task, this book would never have been written. Likewise, the jobholder needs self-efficacy – the knowledge that they can try, and that striving will lead to success. Managers might intervene to boost self-efficacy through persuasion, but such action will likely be of limited effect since this variable is substantially inherited and dependent on upbringing and early life experience.

Behaviour is also degraded if the employee feels that they are not in control of their own destiny. Those with an internal locus of control feel that they are in charge of what they do and hence they can perform. Those with an external locus of control feel that, regardless of what they do, they will not be allowed to perform. They feel that external factors will control their efforts. In a similar sense, self-esteem describes how an employee feels about themselves. Low self-esteem will thwart behaviour. Managers can help build self-esteem by giving employees good work experience and recognition.

As we noted above, if all other things are equal, the job done motivates and this motivation causes behaviour. But behaviour only realises performance if the jobholder has the wherewithal to do the job. They need skills and knowledge to be able to do what's needed. Experience builds confidence and the ability to know what performance looks like. And adequate intelligence (called general mental ability or 'g') helps the jobholder learn new tasks and apply difficult concepts like quality in work done.

Whilst we've discussed personality above as an influencer of motivation, one aspect, conscientiousness, also plays directly on performance. Conscientiousness is the trait that drives the jobholder to get stuck in and finish what they started. Conscientiousness is mostly inherited and learned in childhood and hence is substantially unchangeable.

5.2.3   *Personal characteristics*

It's clear here that some variables like leadership are under the manager's control. Others like employee intelligence are not.

The manager can influence variables like skills by implementing a personal development programme. Whether that is right to do depends much on the scale of the deficiency and the cost. And variables like work variety can be adjusted by re-designing the job.

Personality is fixed but differs person to person. Managers must, in the first place, select the jobholder for the right personal characteristics – for their ability to perform in the job. That done, they can then play with the variables that are under their control to make sure the employee does indeed perform.

5.2.4   *Focus on outcomes*

Ultimately, the manager is looking for outcomes – initially outcomes personal to the employee, and then, when all work is aggregated, outcomes for the firm. Outcomes for the firm are typically performance indicators like turnover, profit, productivity, quality, safety, and staff wellbeing.

Sometimes, despite individual performance, outcomes just don't happen. Sometimes economic factors preclude turning performance into outcomes – perhaps the market has just dried up and no matter what the salesperson does, they simply can't get orders. Likewise, sometimes, environmental factors like bureaucracy and budget constraints in the firm prevent outcomes.

Management is the continual adjustment of each employee situation spanning all the variables discussed above in pursuit of the desired outcomes.

5.2.5   *Specifying outcomes in job descriptions*

The job description is possibly the most important document that the manager has at their disposal in managing people. Managers must ensure that they define an outcome for each of the accountabilities or responsibilities in the job description. An example might be the development of a market to achieve sales values agreed from time to time. Another might be the obvious requirement to deliver projects on time and to budget.

Every accountability/responsibility should have an associated outcome as a measure.

5.2.6   *Specifying outcomes in objectives*

Accountabilities, complete with their outcome expectations, are generic. Sales targets will be agreed from time to time. Projects will be expected to be done to budget. But nowhere in the job description is the target number. Specific targets and the like are agreed as objectives throughout the year, and certainly annually or more frequently at the performance review. Specific targets will differ year by year.

Outcomes, as measures of performance, are fundamentally difficult to specify and even more difficult to measure.

Take setting and assessing objectives for a waiter. The obvious measure is takings from the tables served. But some tables will be more lucrative than others. So, the manager will need to be careful to divide out the tables equitably. Perhaps that's done, but then what happens if one waiter is busy? Does the other waiter say, 'Filling in for colleagues is not in my job description', and therefore reduce the overall restaurant service quality? This simple example can be chased to a very unsatisfactory conclusion where objectives lead to undesirable outcomes. Determining and assessing that all-important performance is complicated and we discuss it further in Chapter 6.

Reflection 5-1: About performance

Take a typical job with which you are very familiar. Develop one performance objective for this. Work back through the model in Figure 5-2 to determine the sort of personal characteristics you'll need the person to have to meet the objective. Look at each variable in turn and say whether you feel you have control of this and the degree to which you can vary it to influence performance. Finally, think about some of the sorts of development activities that you can implement to change variables that might, on first inspection, be fixed.

5.3   Job design

5.3.1   *Jobs in firms*

A job is a set of accountabilities that an employee has for achieving personal outcomes. If those personal outcomes, achieved by several employees, aggregate, the firm will achieve its desired corporate outcomes. An entrepreneur knows what it's like to wear many hats – developing exciting solutions to customer problems, promoting products and services, pitching for business, building the deliverables, implementing systems on site, supporting them as the customer uses them, chasing payments and paying suppliers. Simply, the smaller the firm, the more roles a jobholder takes on. As the firm grows, so the jobholders specialise, and the number of roles played reduces as the jobholders focus.

But the concept is still sound. A small number of roles aggregate to yield a job. Given the total number of roles across a firm, those roles can be constructed and re-constructed in various ways. Jobs can be designed and re-designed in pursuit of task variety, work identity, autonomy, job significance and available feedback. In a firm with twenty different jobs, there may be over a hundred roles, giving plenty scope to build the company as the manager wants.

There are many tools available to conduct job design but first, the manager must create a model of the firm. The concept model outlined in Chapter 1 is useful again here.

This model, Figure 5-3, shows the various roles. It's a very simple example and the model can be elaborated to illustrate the huge complexity of any firm and, with that, the huge numbers of roles amalgamating to several designed jobs.

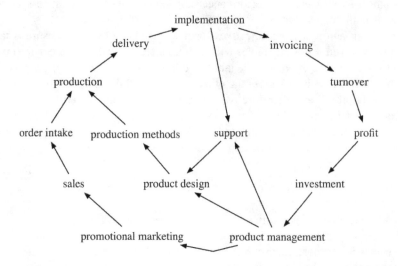

Figure 5-3: Model of the firm showing roles

As we noted in Chapter 1, first the manager must determine what's to be done. Then they must determine the necessary roles and then aggregate roles to jobs. It's a top-down approach.

5.3.2   *What people look for in a job*

It's maybe too simple to just reiterate that staff seek task variety, work identity, autonomy, job significance and available feedback because that's what will motivate them.

Typically, people look first to do challenging and interesting work. Then they seek a reasonable work-life balance. Many staff train for several years, with 50% of the United Kingdom population today attending university and others undertaking lengthy apprenticeships. It's no surprise therefore to learn that they expect to use what they've learned and to continue to be supported in their personal development as their career progresses. When they come into work, they also expect to be treated well and to be valued by their manager. And young people seek to do work of some value to society.

These expectations or requirements won't motivate but if absent, or their converse is present, they'll certainly demotivate, acting to destroy the psychological contract – the unwritten set of expectations held by both manager and employee.

5.3.3   *What makes a satisfying job*

Job satisfaction comes about first when a person does a job where the characteristics of the job and their needs are in harmony. This emphasises the obligation on the manager to select the person well for the job and we discuss how this should be done in Chapter 3.

Job satisfaction also occurs when an employee performs well against personal expectations and objectives, and they gain a feeling of meaningfulness from that. People work to build and achieve a sense of meaning in their lives.

Job satisfaction enhances engagement in that job in a reinforcing cycle. The more satisfied they are, the better they perform, so the more satisfied they become. Work engagement is discussed further in 5.6.

5.3.4   *Job crafting*

However good a manager is at job design, and no matter how closely supervised an employee is, they will always be able to be at least a little creative with exactly what work they do. In extreme cases, some employees have a job description that says one thing and in practice they do something else. This drift between what's written and what's done is termed job crafting – expressing how the job is 'crafted' over time by the jobholder, generally to their own benefit and to suit them.

Exactly how much job crafting occurs depends pretty much on the manager. If the manager takes no action when the job done evolves or drifts, it's likely to keep on evolving until it's as the jobholder wants. Whether or not that's a problem is for the manager to judge.

Reflection 5-2: About job design

Develop a concept model for your own firm following the format in Figure 5-3. Include all the main activities and concepts.

Now go over the model and circle the activities and concepts that you think should be grouped together in a job.

Once you've finished, repeat the exercise but group the functions and concepts differently. How different are the jobs now? In which version do you feel the jobs you designed will work best?

5.4   Commitment

5.4.1   *What is commitment?*

Commitment is the psychological state existing within an employee that causes them to attach to their organisation. Those committed make open or private promises to continue to provide their labour for the benefit of the organisation.

Several researchers have deconstructed commitment as a variable. Possibly the most useful idea is that commitment is formed of three factors: affective, continuance and normative commitment. Under affective commitment, an employee wants to stay. Under continuance commitment, they need to stay. And under normative commitment they are obliged to stay. Clearly, it's affective commitment that's the prize to be won.

Commitment is about wanting to be with a firm. It says nothing directly about enhanced motivation, behaviour, and job performance.

5.4.2   Why commitment is important

By attaching to and intending to stay with the firm, the employee makes other management intervention possible and this in turn influences performance. There is therefore an important indirect link between commitment to the firm and performance.

Commitment must first be won by the manager. Other things then follow.

5.4.3   Determinants of commitment

If the conditions of the contract of employment between employee and manager meet their needs, employees will commit. Those conditions are expressed in the written contract of employment and implied in the various promises and expectations that the employee comes to understand through various communications. Employee needs are often considered in three forms: attachment, subsistence and growth.

If the firm provides a great social environment and the employee likes their manager, the employee's need for attachment (to people) is satisfied and that's a good start.

Employees need to live adequately. And they'll commit to the firm if the terms of their employment allow them to pay the rent or mortgage, buy a car and keep their family in adequate comfort.

Employees also expect that their employer will sponsor their growth, either by offering them job opportunities or more formal development.

So, in essence, commitment is won through the human resource management practices in place in the firm and in use by the manager.

Employee behaviours illustrating commitment include willingness to do what's asked, good relationships with manager and colleagues, making the normal private financial and family commitments, not participating in job search and the willingness to accept personal development.

5.4.4   Practical things to get commitment

The start point in winning commitment is to ensure that the right employee is in the right job. Fundamentally the employee must want to be in the firm doing the job they do, rather than somewhere else, doing something else. Managers must first recruit and select the right person for each job. The aim should be to maximise the person-environment fit. We discuss recruitment and selection in Chapter 3.

Commitment is then built by the manager through their one-to-one relationship with the employee and the management actions that define that relationship. And in the end, if employee commitment does not ensue, despite the manager's best efforts, they might have to question whether they have the right person in the job.

Humans respond to the giving of valuable items. They respond with commitment. This doesn't mean that the manager should spend their day giving the employee gifts. It means that on occasion when the employee needs flexibility to solve a childcare problem, the manager should be flexible and grant time off. It means that when the employee seeks opportunity such as secondment to another group or permission to head up an improvement project, the manager should grant this. In granting these requests, the manager is showing the value that they place in the employee. The more the employee values the 'gift', the greater their commitment will be in return. Even the manager saying 'well done' is a gift.

This giving of things of value associated with the job and the receiving of commitment in return is effectively a modification to the implied element of the contract of employment. Each unique, private, and very special request-grant exchange builds employee commitment and the manager should signal to all employees that they are open to discuss such gifting.

5.4.5   *Crass management breaks commitment*

Commitment takes time to build and is destroyed in an instant.

Employee commitment is sustained through the continual meeting of needs of the employee by the manager. And both parties expect that this state will exist for the foreseeable future. So, anything that disrupts this status quo damages commitment.

Employees expect that they can plan their future and that of their family based on their present employment. Rumour of redundancies and other discord breaks the implied promise and hence decimates employee commitment. Clearly, managers must manage through times of change, and redundancies are one of many tools available. But how change is announced and managed is critically important.

Giving 'gifts' of value cannot occur every day or the value placed in them diminishes. So, commitment sustains through the expectation that valuable gifting will occur in the future. The employee is motivated to respond (with commitment) only through further expectations of future reward and the desire to sustain the relationship with their manager.

It's clear from this description that commitment is built slowly. It's based on multiple exchanges that build trust between manager and employee. Trust is delicate. Managers build trust by ensuring fair treatment of all their employees and by ensuring that procedural justice is always seen to be done. This places a huge obligation on the manager as controller of the relationship.

There are many examples of decisions that managers must get right. To avoid damaging commitment, managers must ensure that wages are awarded objectively to employees– we discuss pay in Chapter 10. Any promotion must be merit-based. Disciplinaries should be scrupulously fair and procedurally transparent – see Chapter 7. And those all-important gifts of flexibility and development must be different but balanced across all employees.

Reflection 5-3: About commitment

Thinking individually about some of your people, what needs do you perceive they have? And what are they asking for – and hence what can you give – to build their commitment? And how will you sense their commitment?

5.5   Motivation

5.5.1   *What is motivation?*

Motivation is the psychological process that gets employees going, keeps them going, and determines the direction and strength of the effort they apply. It's what causes them to stop and apply their energies elsewhere. It's often characterised by three dimensions: attention (or direction), effort and persistence.

Motivation can't be seen. Its presence can only be surmised by observing the resulting behaviours and performance.

Substantially, employees are motivated by the jobs they do and the context of these jobs. As Figure 5-4 illustrates, if there's motivation, there's likely to be behaviour. Given the right behaviour, performance is possible. Motivation, behaviour, and performance lead to desirable business outcomes like turnover and profit.

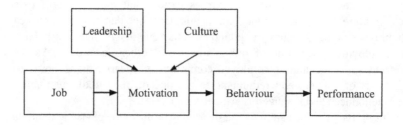

Figure 5-4: Motivation as the result of job, leadership, and culture

Motivation sits between the job a person does and the behaviour they exhibit, and it's influenced by leadership and the environment or culture in which the work is done.

Motivation drives choice – the employee can choose to allocate some or all their personal resources to any task. The manager's job is to create conditions such that the employee will choose to allocate the resources needed for the work in hand.

5.5.2 *About motives and motivators*

Often managers say that they want to hire 'motivated people'. Given that motivation is a function of job, leadership, and environment within the firm, this is a fundamentally misplaced aim. It's impossible to hire someone who is motivated, to a job they've yet to experience. Those managers likely want a person whose motives are in line with the job and firm.

Psychologists consider that there are two types of motive – intrinsic and extrinsic. Intrinsic motives can be thought of as personal drivers developed in early childhood that act on a person's unconscious mind. Extrinsic motives can be thought of as drivers constructed though interaction with others. Extrinsic motives evolve and change and act in a person's conscious mind. Motives practically manifest in the person as needs, values, orientations, preferences, attitudes and beliefs and we discuss these in Chapter 3.

5.5.3 *About motivators and demotivators*

Like leadership, the question the manager must ask is simple: *what do I have to do to influence the motivation of this employee?* The answer, other than making sure their job has high motivating potential and that the culture in the organisation is right, is to launch one or more interventions in search of the required performance. There are several theories associated with intervention that help managers understand what they might do.

Firstly, there's pay. Pay itself is not a motivator. Employees don't put in more effort in return for their normal pay. And any motivating effect of a pay rise soon wears off. Lack of pay and perceived lack of justice around pay decisions are demotivators.

Additional payment can be offered on condition of performance. The amount of money offered in return for achievement of outcomes must be considerable to reflect the low perceived chance of earning it given the large number of confounding factors. In deriving its motivational effect, employees will make an actuarial computation. Research suggests that the unfactored sum should be over 30% of normal pay to have any motivational effect.

Performance related pay is shunned by most managers because it encourages anti-social, isolationist behaviour. We deal more with this in Chapter 10.

Secondly, there are the needs theories. These hold that a need influences an employee's motivation until satisfied. The manager has the power to satisfy needs by directing work resources. Examples include the need for employees to hold power over colleagues, achieve great outcomes or be affiliated with certain work groups. The manager must identify the needs in each employee and set the conditions such that each employee will strive until their individual needs are satisfied. Needs are measured by their strength.

Thirdly there are a set of theories around goal setting. Since this is the single most useful area of theory, we dedicate Chapter 6 to this and its associated management practices.

5.5.4   *Managing unmotivated employees*

Managers lament employees who, from their perspective, won't get motivated.

Let's assume first that the employee is in a motivating job. Let's assume too that there are no downstream issues associated with their behaviour and performance which might be thwarting outcomes. Let's also assume that the employee experiences good leadership and works in a favourable culture. We're now focussing only on motivation and its independent variables.

Motivational variables come in two forms – those like explicit motives and growth needs strength that the manager can tap by intervening in the job environment, and those like personality and implicit motives that the manager can do little about. 'Perceived abilities' sits in both camps and can be strengthened with positive work experience.

Growth needs strength (GNS) is hugely significant. The strength of the need for personal growth varies person by person. Some people have high growth needs strength and others low. Generally, those with high GNS will be keen to grasp developmental opportunities and will be motivated by them. Those low in GNS will likely be motivated by opportunities for achievement and associated rewards. Managers need to assess employees' GNS and choose appropriate interventions.

And finally, managers need to recognise that there's often significant conflict between intrinsic and extrinsic motives with employees perhaps driven one way by needs (intrinsic motives) and the other way by norms (extrinsic motives). Employees overcome such conflict using what's termed 'volitional control' – perhaps overcoming subconscious feelings with rational thought.

Reflection 5-4: About motivation

Consider each of your staff in turn. Considering all that you've now read, what interventions will you launch to motivate each employee?

5.6   Engagement

5.6.1   *What is engagement?*

Engagement is sometimes referred to as 'super-motivation'. To use the dictionary definition of engagement and the metaphor of cogs, it's when an employee meshes completely with the job they do.

As a topic of academic study, engagement is relatively new, though managers have used the term commonly for many years. Engagement is conceptually confused with commitment and motivation. Here, we drive deliberate wedges between the three. Commitment comes about from the way an employee is treated by their firm and is described by their need or desire to work there. Commitment makes other management action possible. Motivation comes primarily from the job the employee does and leads to performance (see Figure 5-4). And engagement stems from performance-related learning and achievement and leads to high energy input, dedication, and absorption in the job.

There is a strict hierarchy from commitment through motivation to engagement. As such, some managers would argue that engagement – as super-motivation - is not always necessary. They would argue that managers need only achieve engagement for employees in jobs with high physical, cognitive and emotional demand.

5.6.2   *How engagement fits in the performance model*

Figure 5-5 illustrates how engagement comes about. Performance in the job causes increased learning and heightened feelings of achievement. Learning from performance and outcomes taps implicit motives which increases motivation and striving in a reinforcing loop.

Achievement of outcomes in turn taps explicit motives which further enhances motivation, again in a reinforcing loop.

Engagement is further enhanced by social interaction from, for example, membership of elite groups. And managers can positively influence here by arranging social support from themselves and work colleagues.

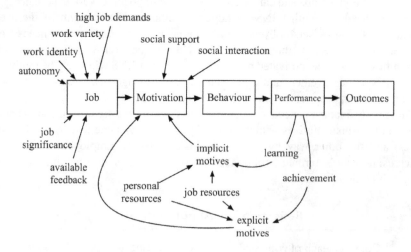

Figure 5-5: Engagement and the performance model

5.6.3   Why engagement is important

Managers generally agree that engagement is useful. It describes a striving for performance, contribution and inspiration and few managers would object to employees exhibiting such super-motivation. But many might ask whether engagement is needed in all employees, and if the benefits outweigh the costs in management time.

There are a few studies that illustrate a direct relationship between the state of engagement and performance, but most academics would argue that the link is subtler.

Studies have indicated moderate to strong positive relationships between work engagement and innovativeness, proactivity, initiative-taking, wellbeing, exhibiting discretionary behaviours, enthusiasm for work and a host of other beneficial outcomes for manager and employee.

Engagement has been shown to have application in balancing challenging work demand with ever improving personal and work-related resources. These stem from the continual learning and achievement that form the core of engagement. Engagement therefore works to counter stress and burnout (though in Chapter 10 we look at how engagement can itself result in burnout).

5.6.4   Practical things to do to get engagement

The argument so far indicates that engagement follows commitment and motivation. So, to move toward employee engagement, the manager's systems for building commitment and for motivating their staff must be effective.

The motivating potential of the employee's job must be high, since it is the job that is the source of super-motivation. Optimising job and jobholder start with getting the right person in the right job, and hence engagement starts at job design and places heavy onus on recruitment and selection. The competencies of the employee must match the demands of the job and there must be high person-environment fit. Fundamentally the jobholder must feel a huge attachment to what they do.

Finally, the values of the manager, firm and employee must all be in harmony.

5.6.5   Assessing engagement

There are two reasonably well-regarded inventories that assess engagement – the Gallup Q12 and the Utrecht Work Engagement Scale (UWES). The Gallup Q12 focuses on resources while the UWES seeks to assess vigour, dedication and absorption in the work.

Practically, managers can sense engagement through evidence of employee behaviours like initiative-taking, attention, questioning and positive emotions.

Reflection 5-5: About engagement of your people

Engagement is desirable, though perhaps difficult to sustain.
Of your employees, can you identify those who are routinely engaged with their work? Which employees do you wish were more engaged?
Are you prepared to put in the investment needed to foster engagement in those employees?

5.7   Culture

5.7.1   *What is culture?*

Culture can be summed up as the 'way we do things around here' – it's the undocumented but ever-present pressures that go to influence employees in their work. Employees and managers work within the work culture. Their behaviour is to a large extent determined and controlled by that culture and to some greater or lesser degree they influence the culture by their presence in it.

Since the manager has executive power, they can manipulate the culture by launching interventions. Employees will react to those interventions with modified behaviours, attitudes, beliefs, values, symbolism, behaviours, ideas, and other products of management action. Such changes go to influence employees and will influence managers in subsequent behaviour in a cyclical system that is ever changing. The 'way we do things' therefore evolves.

Each employee will also be immersed in other cultures such as that existing at home and in religious, political, and social groups. The cultural impact on each employee is therefore multi-faceted and the work culture is the result of pressures from many discrete cultures.

There are of course major threads. Whole firms can be directed through culture to be highly customer oriented. And others can become very conservative and staid. Commentators report daily on firms' cultural styles, holding some up as the 'new way' that all firms should be.

Cultures can also collide. Asking employees to take responsibility as individuals and to make personal decisions at work can collide with a home or societal pressure to share responsibility and decide collectively. The result is likely personal conflict and observed under-performance in the job.

So, work culture is complex, but it can be moulded over time to fit business objectives.

5.7.2   *Culture and the trading firm*

Firms trade. Some trade internationally. As a result of this trade, employees will experience the culture in their customers', suppliers', and partners' organisations. This will apply particularly to sales staff and those involved in product and service delivery who encounter customer, supplier, and partner staff. It will also apply to engineers, scientists and other professionals collaborating within an industry. Where those other organisations are in different countries, their national culture will have a significant impact on the interactions. The way employees in those other organisations 'do things' may be very different.

Culture is most significant in interactions when employees want to influence customer, supplier, and partner staff towards their point of view.

5.7.3   *Assessing national culture*

Probably the best national culture model today is that proposed by Geert Hofstede. The essence of Hofstede's model is that nations are defined by people and people have common characteristics that determine their behaviours, attitudes, beliefs, values, symbolism, and ideas. The result is 114 unique national cultures.

Hofstede's model has six 'dimensions' – power distance, individualism, masculinity, uncertainly avoidance, long term orientation and indulgence.

5.7.4 *Expressing organisational culture*

Hofstede has collaborated with others to build an organisational culture model, and this is illustrated in Figure 5-6.

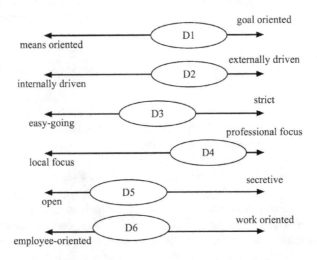

Figure 5-6: Organisational culture model

In this model, the dimensions have two poles – shown as labels right and left above. The position of the lozenges between the polar extremes marked with the dimensions D1-D6 is set for an organisation culture optimised for innovation. As the model shows, organisations can be described as 'means oriented' versus 'goal oriented', 'internally driven' versus 'externally (customer) driven' and so on.

This culture model can be used with its associated questionnaire to assess extant culture and make plans for initiatives to change to some more desirable culture.

5.7.5 *Managing culture*

To succeed in managing culture, a manager needs to build their cultural intelligence. There are three essentials.

The first essential is knowledge of culture, of how it manifests, and the beliefs, behaviours and traditions that can exist. The manager also needs a model for building and expressing their understanding of the culture in which they find themselves (such as that described in 5.7.4).

The second essential is a mindfulness of culture and an ability to 'tune in' to the surroundings and the firm. This starts with the basic acknowledgement that there is such a thing as culture, that culture in the firm is unique and that it is built from many parts. Sensing can be learned so long as the manager is open to that learning.

Finally, the manager needs to build a basket of interventions and the ability to choose an appropriate intervention to suit the culture in hand and the culture change desired.

Reflection 5-6: About culture

Using the model in 5.7.4, estimate the culture in your organisation. Is this as you would want it? Model the changes you might want by relocating the lozenges. What interventions might achieve this change?

5.8   Emotions

5.8.1   *Understanding emotions*

Emotions are responses to events that, unless regulated, cause behaviour. That behaviour could be desirable or undesirable. Managers must understand emotion to control it and use it as a tool to understand and influence employees.

The model in Figure 5-7 is taken from Frijda's Laws of Emotion. It's a process model illustrating in-person activities, read left to right. Firm lines show causality. Dashed lines show control.

And it works like this. An employee sees, hears, or feels some event. They appraise it. They think about it. The flow of thought enters their emotion centre. Emotions have three parts – action readiness, affect (that is, liking and disliking) and arousal. If the event arouses feeling and if that feeling is strong enough and the person is awake enough to act, they may exhibit a reaction – a behaviour.

Whether or not a reaction results also depends on the person's regulation processes.

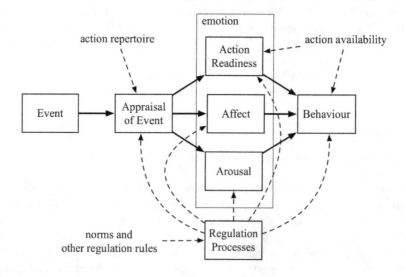

Figure 5-7: Emotion - linking event to behaviour

5.8.2   *How emotions work*

Emotions are perhaps best understood by example.

Let's consider the case where an employee gets angry and out of hand in a meeting. An event has obviously occurred about which the employee has concerns – they care about the topic; it matters to them. It could be that their reputation has been challenged or they could be victim to some injustice, or about to become a victim. The employee appraises the situation. They may become aroused, feel dislike and be ready for action. Whether they act depends much on their repertoire of possible actions and their ability to regulate their behaviour. That in turn depends on the employee's mood at the time of the event.

5.8.3   *The laws of emotion*

Frijda went on to describe a series of laws to aid understanding of how subjects would act once in the model.

His Law of Closure suggests that when the emotion process triggers, the employee exists within 'closed walls'. It may be difficult to have them put the event in any larger context to allow them to appraise it as less significant. In the example above, this instantly suggests that stopping the meeting might be a valid strategy. The employee (and the manager who will work with the employee) can move out of the meeting context to begin recovery.

The fact that the employee is already angry negates any action at the front end of the process. The Law of Situational Meaning and the Law of Concern will have already clicked in. The employee cares (about something of significant meaning) and a motive's been triggered! Some sensibility has been enflamed.

Humans react (and exhibit some emotional behaviour) when the difference between their normal state and aroused state becomes sufficiently great. This is governed by the Law of Comparative Feeling. But the employee has already reacted! They believe that the event is significant, and the Law of Comparative Reality suggests the event is real – even if it's a rumour or just imagined by the employee.

Now to action. The Law of Conservation of Emotional Momentum suggests that emotion will persist indefinitely unless counteracted by exposure to other events that permit extinction. So, to do nothing is not an option! The manager must act to create another event of significant meaning to replace the first.

We must believe that the employee is aware of what they are doing. The Law of Care of Consequence suggests that every emotional impulse elicits a secondary impulse that tends to modify the behaviour considering possible consequence. The employee will be concerned about what happens because they got angry and exhibited anti-social behaviour. It's eminently possible to change the behaviour through some new event, like an expression of empathy with the employee. Perhaps the first words from the manager, on getting the employee out of the meeting, should be "I understand how you feel".

Adding all these together, the manager must now create an event that permits the employee to suffer minimum emotional load and encourage the employee to view the situation in another way – one that allows maximum emotional gain. The manager must get the employee alone and suggest an alternative meaning to the events. The manager must break the closed walls of the event, allowing it to be interpreted in a bigger context.

The key thing is that the employee's regulation processes must be strengthened such that the meeting can resume without danger of repetition of the behaviour. Incorrect beliefs and assumptions must be corrected. And the employee must be encouraged to cope.

5.8.4 *Managing emotions*

Managers can learn to manage emotions in themselves and others – they can build their emotional intelligence. They can control extant behaviour and trigger new desired behaviours. There are three requirements for this.

First, the manager must understand the fundamental principles of emotions illustrated in 5.8.1 and 5.8.2. Second, the manager needs to practice mindfulness; the ability to pay attention in a reflective and creative way to emotional cues in situations encountered. Third, based on understanding and mindfulness, the manager must a build the necessary behavioral skills, and become competent in managing emotions across a wide range of situations. These skills involve choosing, where necessary, the appropriate event or counter-event to change the path or start a new path through the process. Doing this will realise a different or other more desirable behaviour.

5.9 Power

5.9.1 *Defining power*

In Chapter 16.1, we saw how the entrepreneur appoints an agent - a manager. The manager wields the entrepreneur's power to cause action in the firm.

Power over employees comes from the manager's ability to determine their welfare – satisfying their existence, affiliation and growth needs for the foreseeable future. Power allows the manager to persuade staff to do the manager's bidding – to order them, to make them do, particularly since they might otherwise do something else.

In becoming an employee, we noted that the supplier 'comes indoors' and submits to the will of the manager in return for a wage. It's a voluntary arrangement. It's an exchange – a contract that can be broken at an instant by either party. Power is therefore fragile - a delicate tool to be used with great care and precision.

In Chapter 2 we illustrated that leadership is a lot about facilitation – about setting goals and helping employees meet those goals. It's about coaching from a proximal position rather than commanding from a distance. Management is about taking responsibility for the actions of employees and guiding them to success rather than simply blaming them for failure. We saw also that a directive leadership style can be useful, but mostly, successful leaders use the subtler non-directive form.

5.9.2 *Exploiting power*

How that 'ordering' is done is all-important. Those who use social skills to 'work with' rather than 'boss around' enjoy greater success. For some, being a social manager comes naturally. For others it can be learned.

How managers exploit power has huge implications for companies; in manager selection, succession planning, and manager development and in the functioning of management teams. The way in which managers exploit power influences the culture of the organisation – itself an antecedent for higher-level concepts like the way the organisation learns, and the way staff innovate new ideas and products.

We hear much about the abuse of power in big organisations. But it's not just in big companies that issues arise in the way managers exploit power.

Managers are typically recruited for their psychological need for power. It's common for Boards to recruit the 'Alpha-wolf' – male or female. Somehow naturally, alphas like the idea of appointing other alphas to act in their stead. They feel that someone who will 'kick ass' is to be trusted whereas someone who will sympathetically work with other managers and staff is somehow a higher risk.

All who might excel as a manager typically have a high psychological need for power.

5.9.3 *Forms of power*

Research done over the past thirty years or so suggests that power has two discrete forms.

Personalised power or 'P-power' is the need to set and meet personal goals. Those high in P-power have a need to feed their own egos. They focus on the "I" and see that they are in competition with others in a zero-sum game in which they aim to win while others lose. Those high in P-power are the alphas. For them, success breeds success and an even greater need for personal enhancement to fuel that power. For them, success is the growing fiefdom, the enlarged sphere of domination and the bigger "I".

Socialised power or 'S-power', on the other hand, is the need to derive power through others and for others. It's the desire to use power for the wider benefit. Those high in S-power tend to put the needs of their organisation above their own personal needs – something that is well established as a fundamental need of a good manager.

Teachers and nurses tend to be high in S-power. They need to command – but not for themselves alone. And women generally tend to be S-power dominant.

5.9.4 *Power dominance*

There's a balance in each person. Some people are dominant in P-power. Research has found, for example, that those high in P-power do drive huge change – but often the resulting organisation does not enjoy on-going stability. National leaders high in P-power are also more likely to take their countries to war.

Others are dominant in S-power. That's not to say that this latter group would not take their countries to war. It's just that they'd build a coalition, a consensus for action, rather than giving an executive order.

This balance between S-power and P-power is not a measure of competitiveness, though. Whilst women are typically higher in S-power than P-power, they are just as competitive as men. People can be both highly competitive and dominant in S-power. It's just that in the S-power case, winning is done with others rather than over others.

So, everyone has both P and S. How each person behaves depends on which is dominant.

5.9.5 *S-power benefits*

Research over the years shows that the use of socialised power is related to effectiveness as a manager. Indeed, it also suggests the converse – that personalised-power managers have many undesirable characteristics. P-power managers are, for example, impulsive and, as one commentator noted, "not disciplined enough to be good institution builders".

So, for excellence in the management task, managers need to use socialised power. They need to be inclined to build alliances, networks, coalitions, or groups to get things done. In turn they need self-control. They must be able to inhibit personal ego, needs and desires in favour of the needs of the organisation.

5.9.6   Turning from the Dark Side

Arguably, the preference for S over P and the ability to use S-power effectively is a form of crystallised intelligence, learned throughout life. Firms developing young employees to exploit S-power would therefore be wise to start early and discourage use of personalised power when appraising and coaching.

Whether someone who is low in the personality trait of empathy and high in need for personalised power can ever shun the 'dark side' of power is a moot point. Certainly, being trained to see the values of S-power and learning the techniques of alliance, network, coalition, and team building is a start. Behaviour change will then need significant coaching to dump the narcissistic ways.

Reflection 5-7: About power

What form of power do you naturally use? Is that the right form for the environment? If you dominate in P-power, how might you exploit S-power to be more effective?

5.10   Groups

In Chapter 1, we discuss how a contract evolves from one between an entrepreneur and their suppliers to become one between a firm and its employees. It's for the manager to decide the best way to organise those employees. Groups naturally form in society to get things done and firms have likewise found that having employees work in groups is useful to facilitate the business endeavour. This section discusses how groups function.

When discussing groups, there's significant overlap with leadership and management discussed earlier in this chapter and in Chapter 2.

5.10.1   About teams and groups

Many managers talk synonymously about groups and teams. There's a huge difference in the manager and member energy needed to build and sustain each and so definitions are essential.

A team is a small, closely knit collection of individuals who train and perform together. The emphasis here is on training. A team likely trains more than it performs.

There are a host of examples of teams: a fire station 'watch', a football team, a Special Forces patrol. A team trains so hard together that they learn one another's characteristics, needs, preferences and personalities. They learn to second guess one another because, typically, they are involved in routine but high-intensity work. Each knows the next step in the process. Each is looking out for, protecting, and helping the team members. And team performance and outcomes reign supreme over personal performance or gain.

But the cost of building and maintaining a team is huge.

Most managers would agree that they don't need teams. They need functioning, effective, cooperative employees working in groups to provide mutual support. The emphasis here is on cooperation. Group members need to build mutual trust by being reliable colleagues. Each needs to be competent in their own job. And each needs to communicate well, express meaning and work through difficulties.

5.10.2   *Forming groups for work*

Unlike social groups that form to make society function, work groups have a very specific purpose, defined by the manager. A small firm will comprise a single group. Managers will divide super-groups into smaller groups and sub-groups as the firm grows.

There's a useful five-word sequence that describes a group lifecycle – forming, storming, norming, performing and disbanding. Storming describes the phase after formation when the group members sort out their issues and begin to develop the trust needed to become cooperative colleagues. Norming describes when they cease to be a plurality of individuals and gel to establish norms of behaviour in pursuit of common goals. After the initial shakedown, the group performs until a time when the manager has no further use for the group in its extant form and they disband it.

Most managers inherit ready-formed groups that are already well into the performing phase. Many groups will have problems caused by difficulties in their storming and norming phases. Many groups will be plagued by leavers and joiners interrupting group processes. And many managers will be struggling to sub-divide and re-form groups to meet new purposes. Group organisation in firms is dynamic.

There are four key requirements in building groups. Firstly, group members should be competent in their jobs. Secondly, members should be encouraged to cooperate rather than compete. Thirdly, members should stimulate one another such that their collective effort is greater than the sum of their individual efforts. And fourthly, the manager as group leader should deliberately orchestrate group outcomes by intervening in group activity.

5.10.3   *Basic ideas about people in groups*

To be a group, members must interact. Interaction ideally requires a face-to-face presence. This is simple when co-located and working the same hours, but difficult when group members work remotely, perhaps across time zones.

The value of the group is two-fold. Firstly, each member finds value in membership and is, in turn, influenced by the group towards group behaviour norms. Value for the member comes from the basic human desire to join, to not be left isolated. A group member will stay a member, physically and metaphorically, for as long as their affiliation needs are being met. Secondly, each member is supported technically and emotionally in their endeavours by other group members. It's for the manager therefore to appoint the right members and engineer the right behaviour norms through the introduction of useful work processes and periodic other interventions. The manager's aim here is to have group outcomes exceed the outcomes that would otherwise be realised by a plurality of individuals each with a dyadic relationship with the manager.

Inevitably members form opinions about one another. Members also form opinions about their own position in the group and they work to optimise that position. They engage in exchange and as a result grow to trust one another. The more they exchange and the greater the value of the objects of that exchange, the greater the value placed in the intra-group relationships.

Groups develop. They evolve. Relationships between group members change. Trust grows – and is sometimes broken. Change comes through pressure from the environment outside the group, from leavers and joiners and from manager interventions. Over time, those group behaviour norms form a group culture or climate, and each group becomes an identifiable entity simply because of its members and their interaction.

5.10.4   *Employees as cooperative colleagues*

To realise the benefits of groups, managers need group members to cooperate. Ultimately, they need group members to be reliable. When one member says they'll do something for another, that's a commitment and must happen or the group function is damaged and, with that, future group outcomes.

Managers can build members to be trusted colleagues by teaching the idea of a contract as an exchange. The intra-group process works like this. Where one member asks another for help, the requestor must set out what's needed and by when. The requestee has the right to negotiate. It may be that only half of the activity can be completed in the time. Or it may be that some other commitment that the requestee has already made to another member prevents accepting this new contract, and the request is impossible given current resources. In this latter case, perhaps the manager must be asked to adjudicate. Ultimately, the negotiation leads to a deal that is acceptable to both parties – a compromise. The requestor accepts because they need help and the requestee accepts because they expect to likewise need help in the future.

Each member has multiple contracts forming and maturing with every other member.

This inter-member contracting works for co-located members and is even more important when members are dislocated in time and space. Contracting works worldwide, mediated by electronic communications, to build trust in international project teams.

But here's the rub. As the requested activity proceeds, any risk to the contract must cause the two members to meet again. They must discuss how the integrity of the contract is to be maintained. It's no use waiting until the day of delivery to announce that what was agreed was impossible anyway!

5.11   Bias

Day to day management is not a perfect activity. Managers must learn to recognise that imperfection, using methods and tools to moderate the errors that would otherwise be inherent in their decisions. Often, those errors come from the manager's personal biases. Those biases are manifold, and we describe below how they manifest, and how they can, at least to some extent, be overcome.

5.11.1   *Defining bias*

All managers would hope that they make rational decisions. All would hope that they will conduct their day-to-day activities considering only assessments, ideas and plans that are developed because of critical thinking, duly supported by evidence.

The reality is a long way from this. Most managers make decisions using a mix of gut feel and repetition from experience, based on evidence from hearsay. The result is that managers' decisions are open to the effects of bias.

Bias is best explained by comparing real decision-making with ideal decision making. Ideal decision making would always return the same result for a given scenario, independent of the person making the decision. So, under ideal decision-making, a thousand managers randomly distributed across the globe, would all make the same decision, given the same scenario and information. Those managers would be a mix of women and men, young and old, white and non-white, engineers and sociologists, and all variants between and many more besides. They would be completely objective, making their decision using the same psychological processing engine considering evidence alone. Each decision-maker brings their different upbringing, education, and experience to the task, modified in turn by their identities, attitudes, beliefs and values. Their cognitive assessments would not all be the same. The result would be a thousand different decisions.

Some of those decisions might coalesce towards various normative forms. Culture might account for some of this. All managers in Japan, for example, might think similarly about a given scenario and make similar decisions. And all managers who had a UK public schooling might likewise have similar ideas, resulting in similar decisions. But there would be more differences than similarities. Bias is an idiosyncratic effect and must be understood, assessed, and countered personally.

Bias, or rather, being biased, is the termed we use to describe the fact that everyone interprets and processes information differently, and hence everyone comes to different conclusions about each scenario faced. In principle, bias doesn't matter. One could just conclude that the differing conclusions and outcomes are part of the so-called rich tapestry of life. But, it does matter because often the result of this flawed decision-making is that people get harmed.

As a result of bias, a manager might discriminate between a white person and a non-white person. The white person might get promotion, while the other person gets poor quality work. As a result of bias, employees might bully a gay man, to the point where he commits suicide. The likelihood and effect of hurtful outcomes varies.

Bias is a serious societal problem.

5.11.2   *Countering bias*

As we suggest, bias is individual, and hence it must be dealt with individually. No quick introduction of process or new technology will counter bias. It might be useful to recruit 'blind', ignoring names, genders, and ages on CVs, but in the end such tactics only mask the problem, rather than overcome it. No technology or process can root out bias. Indeed, potentially, the presence of technology to control bias itself introduces bias! Fundamentally, managers must change their worldview. They must unlearn their biased ways and learn to interpret and process data objectively. And that's hugely difficult.

Bias training, leading ultimately to objective decision-making, is best done in three-parts.

First, the manager must understand how bias works and the huge range of resulting effects from it. We discuss this and illustrate this scope below in a diagram. This understanding will take time to achieve, requiring significant reading and reflection. During this period, the manager must form a view about what objective decision-making is for them and how they will tell an objective decision from a biased one.

Second, the manager must practice mindfulness. They must stop themselves at the start of every possible decision and ask, 'how can I be objective about the data I'm presented with and the way that I'm going to process it'. And they must trap their own bias by writing down where they could go wrong, and the undesirable effects bias might cause.

Third, the manager must introduce criteria, process, and technology. Objective decision-making requires criteria. Criteria are principles or standards against which something can be judged. Criteria must be valid. Validity demands that each criterion helps predict a desirable business outcome, such as performance, quality, or safety. We might, for example, say that someone with high abstract reasoning will perform well in a scientific job, and we'd use abstract reasoning as one of our decision-making criteria in personnel selection and development. That claim is well supported by evidence from publicly available academic research. Whether an applicant is black or white, male or female, or gay or straight, is irrelevant when it comes to personal performance in that job. To introduce bias would corrupt the decision by introducing a non-valid criterion. In our example, it only matters that they have high abstract reasoning.

Managers must ask themselves every minute of every day what criteria they will use to make the decision before them. Managers must build libraries of criteria for every decision they might make – and it's here that process and technology help. There are many, many tools available. We discuss the various tools, processes, and technologies in other sections – indeed this entire book focusses on objective, evidence-based decision making, using valid criteria.

But in the end, all decisions will still be biased, even if only slightly. With personal development and the use of tools, however, the decisions will be less outlandish, less extreme, and more objective and managers and their staff will be more aware of the risks they run as a result of bias.

5.11.3   *Examples of bias*

The problem with bias and the countering of biases is that there are simply too many identifiable biases to remember. Benson and Manoogian have developed the Cognitive Bias Codex grouping over 200 biases into 20 categories, and in turn into four families. But even that doesn't help.

And in line with our biases as authors(!), we've simplified these to give Figure 5-8. To avoid information overload, this graphic sets out the biases in the 20 categories – describing the categories as an action acting on an object. As an example, we see the bias category, 'simplifying to make consumption easier', at the five o'clock position.

Under this example category, there are nine individually identifiable biases, like Zero Sum Bias. Under zero sum bias, a person would assume that for someone to gain, someone else must lose. The person's worldview expressed as a bias prevents them from accepting that both parties could gain (or lose) as a result of a decision. Each category covers between three and 21 discrete biases. Space precludes us describing all biases.

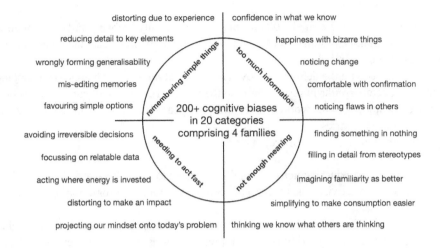

Figure 5-8: The 20 categories of bias

We give a reference to the Cognitive Bias Codex (in which all biases are described) in the Bibliography.

5.11.4   *Typical manager bias*

It's hugely difficult to select biases that might be typical of managers. We consider the following four to be useful as examples.

- Frequency Illusion: once an event is noticed, it seems to repeat. Once it's noticed that someone is off sick, they seem to be off sick again and again. They're not off sick often – it just seems that way.
- Confirmation Bias: managers tend to interpret what they see in a way that supports their prior belief. Having had a great female marketing manager in a previous company, for example, the belief is that no male will be as good in that role.
- Stereotyping: managers tend to bundle people into types and form generalised opinions based on superficial observation. The assumption is that because one engineer is judgemental (jumping quickly to conclusions), all engineers will be likewise.
- Primacy effect: people tend to remember things cited at the beginning of a list of items better than things lost in the middle. This applies to many written and verbal lists in documents like CVs and disciplinary investigation reports.

It is futile for a manager to try to remember all the forms of bias, and then to scan the list at every decision. As we note above, it's better to understand how to make a rational decision in the first place, based on suitable criteria and evidence. But it is important that all managers read about all 200 plus biases, to recognise the scope and depth of bias in their day to day lives, and its possible effects.

5.11.5   *Prejudice*

Above, we discussed bias as if all 200 plus biases were equally probably and of equal effect in each person. Simply, in some people, some biases are more prevalent than others. One of the most prevalent is prejudice.

Prejudice fits with the definition above and is one of the simpler biases to understand. Prejudice frequently results in serious harm to the victim. The degree of harm that has been suffered by employees and workers over the past years has resulted in statute against prejudice in most countries.

There are many examples of prejudice.

- Prejudice against women – not inviting women to team after-work drinks, making it a man's activity. The result in the company is perhaps promotion of males over females.
- Prejudice against non-white people – supporting and encouraging white employees but ignoring other employees such as those whose ethnicity stems from Africa, the Caribbean and Asia.
- Prejudice against people practicing the Jewish faith – perhaps vociferously claiming that the Holocaust did not happen, causing hurt feelings.

In the UK, prejudice has been so engrained, and so damaging to victims, that the UK Government passed the Equality Act 2010 and set up the Equality and Human Rights Commission (EHRC) to counter it.

5.11.6   *Equality*

As we've illustrated, cognitive bias is an esoteric, complex, and difficult human psychological problem. And of all, prejudice is possibly the most prevalent and damaging. Equality, or rather inequality, is its frequent outcome.

The EHRC commenced activities in 2007 and incorporated the activities of three extant organisations: the Commission for Racial Equality, the Disability Rights Commission, and the Equal Opportunities Commission.

The EHRC uses its "enforcement powers to protect people against serious and systemic abuses of their (equality) rights and to clarify equality and human rights law". It also has an informing and influencing role to aid compliance with standards.

The Equality Act (2010) identifies nine 'protected characteristics': age, disability, gender reassignment, marriage and civil partnership, pregnancy and maternity, race, region or belief, sex, and sexual orientation.

The Act then makes it an offence to discriminate against someone – to treat them less favourably than someone else – because of any of those characteristics. In employment, the aggrieved party has access to the Employment Tribunals system for remedy.

The question then for managers is whether the Government's introduction of a statute solves all issues where managers, or employees, might be prejudiced against others. This is unlikely and we recommend again that managers adopt the three-step approach outlined above comprising knowledge, awareness, and interventions. We recommend this as a general approach to make sure that the need for equality is satisfied.

5.11.7   *Gender inequality*

Gender (or sex, as the equality act calls it) has been the topic of prejudice for centuries. Simply, gender inequality is the social process by which men and women are treated differently. It has its roots in prejudice, but appears in many other biases such as stereotyping, belief bias, and illusory superiority. One significant inequality outcome is in pay, and we discuss this in Chapter 10. We continue the discussion here.

Gender inequality has its roots in society. There are many elements to the topic.

Science, technology, engineering, and mathematics (STEM) careers pay well. But those who might influence career choice, such as schools and parents, tend to persuade girls towards other careers such as health and social care. Those careers are less well paid. The result is a significant national gender pay gap. There is no biological reason why women are less able in high-paid STEM careers, nor is there any reason why girls find STEM subjects less interesting. It's simply that influencers don't consider it 'right' and that bias causes girls to drop STEM subjects in their early teens. Conversely, society tends to influence boys away from nursing, suggesting that it is insufficiently 'manly'. The result is a huge gender pay gap in hospitals where we find a very high number of women employed as nurses. The definition of gender pay gap is shown graphically in Figure 5-9.

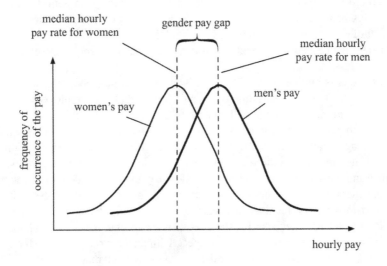

Figure 5-9: The definition of gender pay gap

But career choice is not the whole story. Gender inequality exists even when men and women join firms to do the same job. Managers are more often male and, in applying their prejudice and other biases, they favour male employees. As a result, there are many claims of discrimination in the work women are given and in their speed of promotion.

Couples seldom share child rearing duties equally - despite the existence now of shared parental leave. If they did, both would take equal time off and both would be held back equally from progressing in seniority and salary. Instead, it is very likely that the woman takes more time off – simply because culturally that has always been the way. As a result, child-rearing women slip in seniority when they eventually return to work.

Because child-rearing women shoulder the bulk of the child-rearing effort, they are also discriminated against because they are not able to put in the extra hours that are needed to progress. Women typically work their contracted hours, but men work 20% or even 30% more and that's highly valued by managers when considering promotion.

Significant research has shown the value of balance in numbers of men and women in work groups and the value generally of women in a workforce. Research shows that gender inequality is, for many reasons, bad for firms and managers should strive to overcome the biases that cause it. But it will take many years to correct. Managers can't hope to fix this societal problem overnight.

5.12   Chapter Summary

This chapter has dealt with what many would describe as 'people skills'. Unfortunately, often, people skills are learned on the job, forgetting, or ignoring the science behind the building and maintaining of relationships to secure employee performance. In this chapter we've introduced much of this theory in the hope that managers can mix theory and practice to build their own management competence.

Firstly, we describe a linear feed-forward model of employee performance that starts with the job the employee does. The job motivates and creates behaviour. Behaviour can, all other things being equal, cause performance and, of course, performance leads to the achievement of outcomes. If only it were that simple!

For performance using the feed-forward model, the manager must set up the right conditions.

But as systems engineers would say, this is management operating in 'open loop' configuration. The manager sets things up and hopes that the employees are suitably motivated, have the right tools and will then perform. But what if they don't?

We argue that the manager must make use of feedback. If performance is not achieved, an error message that there's something wrong must trigger corrective action by the manager. We then introduced the feedback control model. Here, the manager observes the performance and measures the outcomes realised. The manager then determines appropriate interventions that will recover the performance and achieve the outcomes desired.

The feed-forward and feedback models are fundamental to managing people.

Employees, in taking a job, seek task variety. They expect to make use of all that they've learned. And they expect to be treated with respect. Ultimately, work must give them purpose and meaning. The manager must therefore design the job with all that in mind.

If the work and the working conditions that the manager has organised are right, the employee will commit to the firm. Commitment is the first stop on a continuum from commitment through motivation to engagement. There are three types of commitment, two involve obligation while one involves affect. Managers should seek affective commitment in employees - emotional commitment in which the employee expresses desire to work for the firm. Affective commitment is for the manager to win.

If conditions are right, the job will cause the employee to be motivated.

And if the right conditions are in place to enable learning and achievement, super-motivation or engagement can ensue. We argue that super-motivation is not needed in all. But certainly, it's essential that key employees – those forming the kernel of the firm's capability – are engaged.

The feed-forward model is overly simplistic in assuming a cascade from job through motivation to behaviour and performance. It ignores the environment in which the job and jobholder exist. Part of that environment is the culture created by colleagues and managers – and in part by each employee's home life. We discuss the application of models for culture definition in the context of making change to culture, thereby influencing employee motivation.

Managers must learn to use emotions in their management lives. And we give a model that allows managers to understand and direct emotions.

We discuss also how power plays in the firm – how the manager gets their way. We note the existence of P-power and S-power, and we suggest that it's S-power that managers need in abundance.

Then we look at how groups form and contribute to getting things done. We suggest, perhaps controversially, that few firms need teams. All that's needed is cooperation between employees and hence the building of cooperative groups. Employees can learn to contract with one another, thereby becoming reliable colleagues. The extreme effort needed to create teams is unnecessary in all but a few instances.

And finally, we discussed the huge topic of bias. We suggest a general model for understanding. We then focused on one of the most common and damaging biases, prejudice. Prejudice results in inequality so much so that the UK Government has implemented statute – the Equality Act 2010 - to try to counter it. In the last sections we set out how one outcome of bias, the gender pay gap, is measured. Gender pay-gap reporting is now mandatory for larger firms. In closing, we make the statement that gender inequality is a societal problem.

In summary, management is about understanding the mechanisms – what, for a given employee, will cause performance. Once those variables are known, the manager can start the management 'engine' to sense outcomes and launch interventions to maintain performance to that needed. Using this model, management loses its myth and becomes a science that can be learned by all.

6

Setting Objectives

6.1 Introduction

The general topic of objective setting and subsequent performance appraisal is hugely complicated and mired in myth. In the latter half of the 20th century when most people worked for large firms, the annual round of objective setting and performance appraisal was commonplace. Then, generally, performance management was badly done. Managers assumed that by running a mechanistic process, performance would automatically come under control. But performance was, and is still, far too complex for that.

As large firms fragmented and smaller firms rose, many commentators claimed that objective setting and performance appraisal was no longer useful for what they described as a new age of management. And yet nothing has successfully replaced this old science.

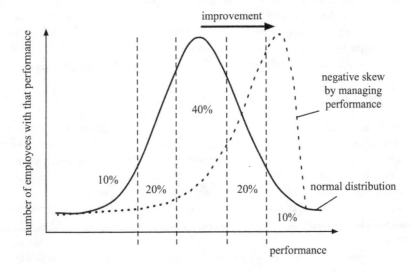

Figure 6-1: Variance of performance across employees of a firm

Most managers, when asked about their employee performance, will be happy with most of their employees (about 70%). Of their employees, some (and maybe up to 20%) will repeatedly perform well, and a small number (say, 10%) will be stars.

At the other end, managers will continually gripe about 30% whose performance is typically below par. And managers will teeter on dismissing the worst 10%. The result is the now-famous normal or bell-curve applied to performance and shown in Figure 6-1.

This spread of performance, however defined, and whatever the numbers, exists today in most firms. Some method of managing performance and improving it such that more employees move into the upper segments is therefore essential. Something is needed to produce a negative skew such that the performance of 98% or more of the employees is good.

This chapter is about the need for objective setting and performance appraisal, and how to go about it to bring performance under control and achieve this sort of improvement.

6.2   Concept of performance improvement

Several high-profile consulting firms have become infamous for culling employees who perform poorly and are judged to be in the bottom 10%. Their practices draw the issue of performance management into sharp focus.

Such extreme practice is understandable: performance is almost all that matters to a firm. Good performance enables a sustainable firm. All other things being equal, performance generates the cash to fund ordinary and developmental activities. Poor performance will almost certainly see the firm's demise. And so there must be some system for ensuring that all employees perform.

The culling example does however show one possible extreme approach to achieving acceptable performance across the workforce – hire people each year knowing that you'll not always get the people needed and continually cull the bottom 10% the following year. A kind of 'two steps forward, one step back' strategy. An approach of culling and hiring new is perhaps valid, but it's costly in every sense and certainly does not lead to a committed, motivated, engaged workforce. Simply, there must be better ways.

6.2.1   Basic ideas about performance appraisal

The simple idea behind objective setting and performance appraisal is that employees respond to objectives set in agreement with their manager. Done right, those objectives are motivating. As a result of mechanisms discussed in Chapter 5, the employee puts in more energy and the desired performance results. This performance is over and above any performance that would otherwise be achieved if no objectives were set.

We've seen in other chapters too that management then proceeds in a closed-loop fashion, with the manager sensing the performance and intervening to achieve the desired outcomes.

The complexity comes when we look at how objective setting and performance appraisal is to be done.

Performance management is made more complex by the fact that employees can be considered to exhibit one of two possible orientations – a growth orientation or an achievement orientation. These two mindsets determine what managers might achieve in objective setting and performance appraisal. Someone with a growth mindset will respond to growth activities. Someone with an achievement mindset will need other forms of objective.

This chapter also expands on our ideas in Chapter 2 where we expect the manager to measure the employee's performance to enable corrective action.

So objective setting and performance appraisal is about how the manager sets objectives for each employee, and then how they appraise and manage the resulting performance to have the firm achieve its goals.

6.2.2 *Maintaining performance*

All managers need to achieve a level of performance in each employee and then work to have the employee sustain that. This simple idea gives us the dual management activity of performance appraisal and performance management. Figure 6-2 shows the idea of performance day by day, event by event, project by project, to sustain acceptable performance.

Employee performance, however we measure it, will vary. Sometimes employees will excel, sometimes, they'll not do so well, but their manager hopes that all employees will perform within expected bounds. Figure 6-2 shows two employees. Employee 1 performs within expected bounds for most of the time. Employee 2 has many episodes of poor performance.

The first concept of performance appraisal, and ultimately, performance maintenance, is that each employee needs to be told how they're doing. Generally, feedback on performance should be given soon after performance events, and not left until some performance appraisal meeting months later. And then it's for the employee to internalise what's said and effect corrective action – if, of course, they are so motivated.

Unfortunately, there's little evidence that simply telling an employee they're performing poorly is enough on its own. There's also significant evidence to suggest that criticism alone is damaging and will degrade performance further. Performance management is complex.

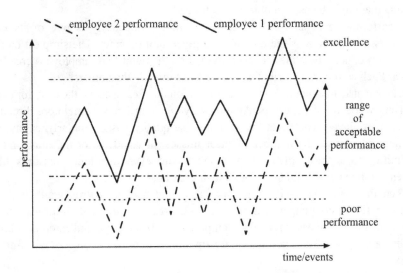

Figure 6-2: Basic idea of performance maintenance

Partly because of the two differing mindsets, and partly out of difficulty in setting objectives for those in routine jobs, there's a view that objective setting, and performance appraisal and management, applies only to 'white collar' jobs. The assumption is that because performance appraisal is a complex cognitive process, it is inappropriate for those outside professional and managerial groups. The argument is that staff who clean, service and sell need supervision day by day or even hour by hour and that development is not a major part of these jobs. We disagree. And there is nothing in the tools we describe here that precludes such application. It is for the manager to determine where and with whom they use the tools.

6.2.3   *Growing performance*

The thrust of the argument is that managers can intervene in their employees' working lives first to effect performance maintenance and then to effect performance improvement by setting and agreeing objectives. So, is this true? Is there a cause-and-effect relationship between setting and managing objectives and the performance exhibited?

The simple answer is, yes. Recent studies show that, if done right, the more objectives are set and managed, the greater the performance realised.

The caveat is, of course, that managers must get the process right. And to set and manage objectives to maintain performance is one thing, while doing so to improve performance is another. The latter has greater constraints and demands on the manager, and we will look at this later in this chapter.

6.2.4   *Measurement and metrics of performance*

Performance is a complex metric and will vary case by case and firm by firm. What matters to one manager is less significant to another. Let's look at some typical key performance indicators that might be used in objective setting.

If performance is all that matters in a firm, productivity is one of its primary antecedents. Productivity is the output for a given unit of input. The simplest method of calculating productivity is the turnover divided by the number of employees creating that turnover. Each employee contributes – some more directly than others.

Take a metric like quality. One definition of quality is as a cost – the cost, for example, of revising work to correct errors. Again, everyone contributes, some more directly than others and employees can be tasked to minimise quality costs. Similarly, safety, can be calculated, perhaps as the number of 'near misses' or accidents or the number of non-conformities to a safety plan when audited. And even nebulous measures like the involvement in external affairs can be made measurable.

Then there are financial metrics like sales and budget control, wellbeing, project delivery to time and budget, customer satisfaction, commitment of group members, engagement of employees with jobs, competencies, behaviours and internal affairs and communications. We could go on. All are ripe fields in which managers will find useful objectives.

The aim ultimately is to set objectives that become the focus of employees' attention and for the manager to hold them to account for a specific goal.

6.2.5   *Role of the manager in performance improvement*

The business of objective setting and performance appraisal was, historically, for some, a simple matter of setting objectives at the beginning of the year and then appraising the performance of the employee a year later. Put so simply, it's no surprise that the activity failed. With such a cycle, when the time comes for appraisal, life in the firm has moved on and many objectives are irrelevant.

Objective setting and performance appraisal begins when the manager determines strategy. Strategy leads to what the manager sees as necessary individual employee contribution. That contribution suggests gaps between what each employee is contributing today and what the manager would like them to contribute tomorrow. That leads to individual objectives.

Objectives must be both short-term and longer term. And once set and agreed, the manager must continually review progress with the employee. As we argue in Chapter 2 under leadership, the manager's job never ends, and they must intervene to help each employee achieve their objectives. Management is a closed loop, hands on activity.

Finally, to conclude these introductory sections, managers must remember the importance of the job description and person specification. The job description defines the broad responsibilities and accountabilities of the job. Objectives simply give the specifics of the goals within each. In principle, each objective should fit within at least one job description responsibility or accountability.

And the person specification defines the person who will excel in the role. In the end, if performance is not happening, and results from use of the feedback control loop suggest that it never will, the manager might have to admit that they've got the wrong person in the job. They might have to resort to culling.

Reflection 6-1: About setting objectives

Considering your firm's aims over the next year, identify the
six primary metrics that will need to be improved in order that
you achieve those aims. Considering your various employees,
what objectives might you be keen to discuss with each to achieve
this improvement?

6.3   Objectives, motivation, and performance

6.3.1   *Basics of motivation*

Motivation theory tells us that staff will want to perform well in their jobs if certain things are present in the workplace - if the work is interesting and of significance, if it involves variety, if the role played is relatively clear, if co-workers are supportive and if managers lead with consistency and integrity. Thus, individual performance comes from personal motivation and from the way the person is managed.

So, if the individual is personally motivated and is also motivated by manager action, conceivably high-performance will result. Systems thinking tells us that this is an open loop system; that is to say, we put personal motivation in, and performance comes out. For more than hope to prevail, the system must operate in closed loop form. We must appraise the performance of the individual and feed this back to them to effect continued performance improvement. Where the loop is effective and good performance is realised, continued feedback sustains the performance by the manager stroking and rewarding.

In Chapter 2 we saw that leadership is an intervention on a person's motivation. Tactics like roadblock removal and leader-manager exchange can be used by the manager to influence that motivation. We also saw that goal illumination was a form of influencing. Goal illumination relies on there being goals or objectives in place to focus the employee's efforts. The manager then encourages the employee to expend more energy towards those objectives, at the expense of other possible activities.

There is a clear link here between objectives and motivation, facilitated by the manager. Firstly, the manager must set the objectives and have the employee adopt them. Secondly, the manager must continually work with the employee to illuminate the goals and use the raft of other leadership tactics in the manager's repertoire to help the employee succeed. During the various meetings about the progress of goals, the manager can provide the necessary feedback and monitor progress.

By making this link between objectives and motivation, we've also shown objective setting and performance appraisal as just another of the many leadership tactics available to managers.

6.3.2   About people and objectives

Employees have one of two mindsets – growth orientation or achievement orientation. For objectives to work for all, the manager must work with learning goals and performance goals. In line with their mindsets, people are oriented towards one or other goal type.

A person who is learning goal oriented strives to improve their own performance by increasing their understanding of the world about them and about the tasks that form part of their job. They believe that they achieve through learning. They recognise that to progress they must seek genuine feedback on their performance and in turn set challenges and goals for themselves that further their learning.

A person who is performance goal oriented is motivated by their own achievements and sets new goals that are likely to result in further personal reward. They only seek and respond to positive feedback. They are only receptive to positive strokes. For them performance leads to performance.

Learning goal orientation is positively related to self-efficacy; self-efficacy is a person's belief in their ability to succeed. Self-efficacy determines how a person approaches objectives. Someone with high self-efficacy believes that they can perform well, and they are therefore likely to view challenges as something to be mastered rather than something to be avoided. So, someone with a learning goal orientation is also likely to be someone who grasps new challenges as exciting opportunities for learning.

Performance goal orientation is found to be negatively related to self-efficacy. That is to say that someone who is performance goal oriented is not likely to have a strong belief in their ability to succeed. They are unlikely to see a new challenge as an opportunity to learn but rather as an opportunity for personal reward.

It's important to understand these two different orientations in people. Some people rise to challenges because they get some personal reward or gratification for achieving great things. Others rise to challenges because there is opportunity for learning and self-betterment. Managers need to have different strategies for dealing with these two different orientations and they need to understand the way feedback will be processed by people with either orientation. Understanding these two orientations is key when using performance appraisal as part of the process of identification of training and development needs.

The presence of two mindsets, and the differing objectives needed to motivate them, suggests a clear need to hire the right person for the job and to then use objectives in line with their orientation.

6.3.3   *About money and motivation*

The basic rule is that money (pay, bonuses and other economic benefits) is not a motivating force. Generally, the accepted wisdom is that money is a 'negative hygiene factor'. If the employee believes that there's not enough of it, or if the method by which it's awarded to employees and colleagues is deemed unfair, it quickly becomes a demotivator.

So, for the manager-employee relationship to work, and hence for the whole idea of objective setting and performance appraisal to work, the whole money environment in the firm must be fair and well-matched to the labour market. In many firms, the salary and benefits systems are broken, placing stress on other systems such as those under discussion here.

But for those who are achievement motivated, money may be seen as attractive because it allows them to buy the things that they value in life. As a result, and for those employees, money has the capacity to focus behaviour. Typically bonuses and commission target specific financial metrics such as sales value. Managers need to be careful that the focussing of one employee on a single metric does not preclude other desirable behaviours and thwart achievement of other objectives.

We discuss money further in Chapter 10.

Reflection 6-2: About your people and their orientation

Thinking about each person in your firm, identify whether you consider
them achievement oriented or personal growth oriented.
Consider then the sorts of objectives that you might set for
each person considering their mindset.

6.4   Setting objectives

Over the past fifty years or so, significant research has been published into objectives in a wide range of disciplines such as management, sport, medicine, and criminal justice. This research has concluded that there is a relationship between goal setting and performance. As a result, it's generally accepted that goal setting is effective in maintaining and improving performance.

So, it works. But how should managers use it?

6.4.1 *About objectives and people*

We saw, above, that objectives have a place in motivation because they assist in identifying what the employee must focus on.

Objectives have a place in leadership too. They give the manager a reason for talking to and wanting to influence the employee. We discussed in Chapter 2 that managers and employees need to be engaged in initiatives. Objectives are initiatives.

Objectives demand persistence by defining the duration for which assignment of personal resources are necessary. A project starts when the objective is formed and accepted and ends when the objective is complete.

And objectives illuminate starkly the distance at any one time between the agreed result and the achievements so far. That gap energises the employee.

This all assumes that the objectives are specific to each employee. They must be of appropriate difficulty – easy objectives don't motivate, and near-impossible objectives demoralise. If the employee is a poor performer, setting objectives in the hope that they will suddenly excel will fail. The reasons for the poor performance must first be understood and other interventions used. Objectives fundamentally demand that the employee has the required competencies and behaviours.

The employee, in accepting the objectives, must be familiar with what's to be done. Where tasks are routine, the objectives must be clear, specific, and achievable. On the other hand, when the tasks are complex, specific objectives likely narrow the focus unnecessarily.

6.4.2 *Role of objectives in business*

The idea is simple enough. At the firm level, the manager, often in conjunction with the Board, determines what the firm should achieve in the coming few years. Here are some examples of corporate objectives.

- Using skills and market position in the fine dining sector, develop into the Italian restaurants market, achieving 10% market share in the region within three years.
- Using the parent company's patents in mathematical modelling, develop a series of PC-based modelling tools for the engineering consulting market.
- Closing the smaller cafes and consolidating staff in the restaurants in the main towns in the region to fight off competition and sustain our current 40% market share in the family restaurant segment.

Each is some departure from the firm's current position. Each is specific. Each employee has a contribution to make and it's just a question of how this contribution is defined.

A turnover objective of say £2.5m for invoicing in a company of 25 people means £100k per person. That doesn't mean that everyone is responsible for turnover directly, just that in each sector a metric translated to 'per person' is easily benchmarked with other firms of differing size and differing turnover.

A turnover of £2.5m for a firm with a sales staff of five means £500k per head. Whilst some may be senior and some junior, the objectives need to balance out to give the top line figure: £2.5m. Likewise a turnover of £2.5m at a sales success rate of 30% means quotes to the tune of £8.3m. If each job is typically worth £20k, this means over 400 individual quotes. If each customer typically asks for two quotes per year, this means around 200 customers. Given 200 customers asking for quotes, and a conversion of one hundred possible clients to one actual client (say) this means that marketing must reach 20,000 people with a possible need for the firm's services. It's a cascade from potential customers to hard orders described by the sales funnel model in Figure 6-3. This shows how the three departments of marketing, sales and operations are linked though departmental objectives.

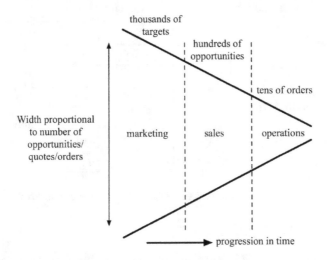

Figure 6-3: Sales funnel model

Whatever the actual figures, this shows that a high-level objective yields individual department objectives and ultimately individual personal objectives. Each objective needs the manager to then say how it will be achieved – and this then loops back to strategy. The 'how' says how the high-level objectives will be met. The turnover objective of £2.5m in this example will need five sales staff (say). But if there are only three today, this then needs a strategy that will recruit two new heads in time to be effective to assure the objective met. And it needs a marketing strategy that will generate enough leads for the two new heads to develop an effective pipeline. And so on.

Objectives make the strategy real and achievable.

6.4.3   *Setting organisational objectives*

In 1996, Kaplan and Norton described what they termed a 'balanced scorecard' for the expression of strategy. An example balanced scorecard is shown in Figure 6-4.

The idea of the balanced scorecard is to expand strategic thinking and execution away from just turnover and profit to finance, process, customers, and employees. The thinking is that the four cover all dimensions in a typical firm.

Some may argue that there's a level above the balanced scorecard covering corporate values. There's also been some discussion about the need to express strategy simply as, *"Because A has a problem with B, we reckon if we do C to D, we'll get E"*. The point really is that however strategy is stated at the level of the firm, it can be broken down to show the contribution of each person, and that's what we're interested in here.

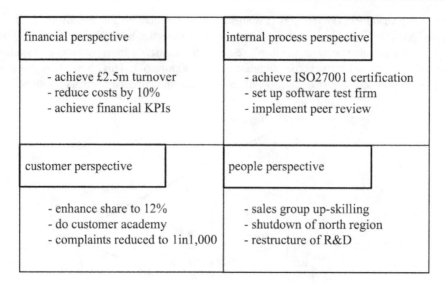

Figure 6-4: The balanced scorecard at the level of the firm

6.4.4 *Setting group objectives*

The cascade from firm to employee transits all groups or divisions: the sales group, the R&D group, the finance group. Clearly objectives can be set at all levels.

In so doing, we move from the psychological, in-person, mechanisms about objectives, to the social, group mechanisms. We discuss group dynamics in Chapter 5.

Interdependent objectives can contribute to the performance overall, giving the group a shared purpose and a reason to discuss progress. We would argue, however, that most firms function with cooperative employees as group members rather than through highly integrated and cohered teams. Employees cooperate. They need personal objectives, and they can then cooperate with one another to achieve those.

Interdependent objectives are difficult to set up and manage and are too easily decimated by the unhelpful group processes that are quite normal in firms.

6.4.5 *Setting personal objectives*

So how does a manager go about setting objectives? We've argued that objectives should be developed from the firm's overall strategy.

There are two 'inefficiencies' in this perfect process.

Firstly, not all employee objectives will be achieved. If all employees are competent and motivated, a manager might optimistically expect that their employees will achieve 70% of all objectives. The manager's analysis will need to accommodate this risk and mitigate it by setting objectives whose outcomes overlap – though clearly, conflicting objectives must be avoided. Of course, in this state, if all objectives are achieved, the firm will over-achieve, but no-one will be unhappy at that.

And secondly, there may be good reason to set objectives for personal growth, that don't stem directly from the corporate picture.

But those aside, the corporate balanced scorecard can then be developed to yield individual balanced scorecards for each employee. Forcing the balanced scorecard structure might seem overly rigid, but like all tools, it should be used and moulded to the manager's needs. The key benefit is simply that it encourages everyone to develop balanced objectives, accepting a financial, process, customer, and people aspect to every employee's work life.

Finally, there's an argument that when employee job tasks are complex, very specific objectives should be avoided because they focus too narrowly on a few obvious outcomes at the possible exclusion of others with higher contribution. In the end, it's for the manager and the employee to agree what objectives are the most useful.

6.4.6   *Involving employees in setting objectives*

There's a debate in organisational psychology circles about just how the objectives should come to be introduced to the employee. Should the employee, for example, on knowing what's needed in their job, propose objectives. Taken to the limit, should they be invited to set their own objectives? The argument here is that it will be so much easier to gain commitment to self-set objectives. Or should the manager set the objectives, following the logic that we describe, and 'tell and sell' those to the employee?

Clearly with self-set objectives, the management overhead to educate the employee is huge. And for most employees, it is simply not needed. Asking the employee to set their own objectives, or to propose objectives, given the organisational need, is a misguided romantic notion.

In fact, research suggests that manager-set objectives are significantly more potent. As a process, this sits better with most managers. Provided that the dyadic relationship between manager and employee is sound, the employee will be happy to commit to objectives that the manager and firm need. After all, that's something they can give as part of the manager-employee exchange process.

But beware. Exchange is two-way. Managers will need to reciprocate in due course.

6.5   Defining performance

Outside of working with objectives, performance is hugely difficult to measure. Take our waiter (in 5.2.6). What metrics might we use to judge their performance? Is the sales value per week per waiter useful? Or are responses in a customer questionnaire helpful? Or is the number of tips given by customers a better measure? For a waiter, much depends on the tables to which they are assigned. And of course, there's the even more complex need for the waiters to support and cover for one another. How on earth do we judge all that?

Performance is probably the most important, and yet most difficult, word in the manager's dictionary. So, when a manager is considering implementing performance appraisal, they must think carefully.

6.5.1   *Performance dependencies*

However we judge it, a jobholder's performance is always dependent on many facets of the job. All jobs are a combination of human competence and technology function. Productivity can often be enhanced by giving the jobholder improved tools. And productivity can be enhanced by improving personal competencies and behaviours.

Jobholders' work will also be dependent on other group members. No-one works in isolation. From a customer's perspective, a waiter's performance will depend on the performance of the chef. An operative in a car manufacturing plant will depend on the robots and on the programming of those robots by production engineers. And a software developer will depend heavily on colleagues who have determined the system architecture and design.

We discuss below how performance assessment might be done. Managers should ensure that anyone assessing others understands the complexity of the assessment task and the determination of the root cause of performance.

6.5.2   Performance in an evolving environment

And finally, we should remember that firms change year by year. Pressures on and in the firm are different, new contracts are won, new technology is implemented, and staff come and go. Dependencies change. Managers will be keen to compare this year's performance with last for each employee to see trends and corroborate beliefs.

Firms' environments change and comparison of employees' year on year performance is difficult and error prone.

6.6   Appraising performance

6.6.1   The use of rating

In rating an employee's performance, managers must be clear about the use to which those ratings are to be put.

There are two obvious options for use: first, for development and second, for what some academics term 'administration' – this second reason is to set pay, plan succession, and make promotions.

Our opinions are clear, and we'll elaborate further below - any system used for such emotive purposes as development and administration that involve employees, managers and colleagues will inevitably be open to distortion and bias and managers should tread carefully.

6.6.2   Rating performance

Performance can often be split in two: task performance and contextual performance. Task performance is, as it implies, how well someone performs the tangible aspects of the job. In a hotel it would be a waiter's performance in delivering the right food to the right table at the right time. Contextual performance, on the other hand, is the way in which the delivery is made - for example, did the waiter smile and, as a result, how did the customer feel. The idea of splitting performance in two is shown in Figure 6-5.

The basic idea that performance comes from behaviour, and that performance goes on to realise outcomes, has been common throughout this book as a central model. The variables from previous diagrams have now been split in Figure 6-5.

Contextual performance is significant because it often determines whether the customer will visit the hotel again. Contextual performance is a major contributor to competitive advantage. It is also a measure of employee extra-to-role behaviours.

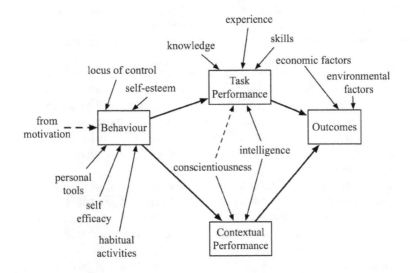

Figure 6-5: Task and contextual performance and their moderators

Contextual performance is seldom written in the job description, but it would likely be at the forefront of everyone's mind when recruiting a new member of staff. The willingness on the part of an employee to offer extra-to-role behaviour comes substantially from their personality and motivation (remembering that motivation depends on how well their manager taps their intrinsic and extrinsic motives). Figure 6-5 shows that contextual performance is influenced by intelligence and specifically what is termed an individual's emotional intelligence. Emotional intelligence is part innate and part learned.

High performance is therefore as much about positive behaviours (and the presence of extra-to-role behaviours) as it is about tangible positive outputs. Ratings of performance must cover both forms.

6.6.3   *Doing rating*

Human judgement is hugely subjective. It's very difficult for a manager to avoid giving an opinion about a subordinate's performance without that opinion being open to question.

Humans making judgements about others in a social environment such as a firm will inevitably be subject to bias and political influence. Research shows that if a manager likes the subordinate, a more favourable assessment will result. Research also shows that the opinion of a peer about another's performance is influenced by what reward the assessing peer might subsequently get because of their judgement. We might say that these failings or imperfections are just human nature.

There are five possible rater groups: self, boss(es), subordinates, peers, and customers/ suppliers. Many large firms favour use of all five and use technology to capture these opinions. Managers in smaller firms are likely only to consider their own rating, whilst perhaps polling others for anecdotal and unstructured views.

One of the main aims of having so many raters, giving so many different points of view, is to increase the appraisee's self-awareness. Self-awareness can be defined as the degree of agreement between the appraisee's self-assessment of their performance and the way that their performance is viewed by the other rater groups.

There are four primary measures of quality in performance appraisal.

- Reliability: the extent to which a measure is free from error with temporal stability and internal consistency. Temporal stability is the idea that if a rating is given at one point in time, the same rating score will be given again by the same rater a few months later. In other words, it's the requirement that the rating is not influenced by immediate events but is a balanced view. Internal consistency is the idea that raters will consistently apply the same criteria across all appraisees.
- Convergent validity: that there is agreement in the views of all raters, for example between self and supervisor ratings and between self and peer ratings.
- Bias: differences between ratings or evaluations because of belief or another factor. The example mentioned above is leniency. If a manager likes a subordinate, they are likely to give a more lenient rating.
- Predictive validity: the degree to which measurement of past performance is a means of predicting future performance rather than simply recording history. This is of particular interest in succession planning and in determining training and development needs.

So to summarise, in implementing performance appraisal, managers will want to know that ratings:

- were reliable (and not influenced by the moment or given using varying criteria)
- were convergent (tending to a single rating),
- were not subject to undue bias, and
- were useful in predicting future performance.

These requirements are tough to achieve and may explain why there is little consistency in opinion about how performance appraisal should be done. Some believe that using all five rater groups better meets the requirement while others consider that there are so many errors introduced in multi-rater systems that the old-fashioned manager-employee appraisal still has greatest merit.

6.6.4   Multi-rater systems

So, let's assume that the manager is giving an opinion on the employee's performance. This is the reference case against which all other possibilities are evaluated.

Researchers have found that allowing employees to participate in their own appraisal may make them more aware of and committed to performance goals. There is therefore a significant argument in favour of self-appraisal. Individuals are, however, more lenient in their opinion than others, although this leniency diminishes with self-appraisal training.

Subordinates may also appraise. Subordinate ratings may also be somewhat lenient since they may feel they have to live with the fallout of their opinions in months to come.

Peers, those of a similar grade in the firm, may also be asked for a view. Peers tend to pay more attention to the degree to which the appraisee helps them achieve their objectives rather than perhaps focusing on the appraisee's own outputs. Peers may therefore measure organisational citizenship behaviours more often than others.

And finally, customers and suppliers could be asked for an opinion. In some senses the customers' view is the real view that matters to the firm because it is an assessment of the firm's competitive advantage.

How then does one proceed? Each appraiser group has some bias. Some will be more lenient than others and some will be more politically influenced than others. Some, such as the manager (or managers, in a matrix structure), will focus on task performance whereas others will be more interested in how the appraisee helped them achieve their goals.

One could simply take an average of all the ratings. One could also plot the ratings and seek a median. Note that plotting the ratings can result in a complex, perhaps multi-modal, distribution being realised rather than something where a single central tendency is obvious. The fact that the frequency distribution of ratings might be complex shows one of the failings of taking a simple average – the single result can mask a host of issues with one or more rater group. This issue of how to process the ratings from multiple sources is one of the key problems with 360-degree or 'multisource, multi-rater' appraisal systems. Just because there are now many judgements does not make the final rating awarded any less subjective and introduces potential for huge error, with one group or other skewing results.

6.7 Appraisal and personal development

Typically, managers, in conducting appraisals, aim to review existing employee objectives, discuss obstacles that prevented those objectives being met, give and discuss the all-important performance rating, and then discuss forward-looking topics such as the employee's need for training and development, their prospects for promotion and their long-term potential.

As we've discussed, the objective-setting and review elements can give huge benefit, but both are complex. Probably the most easily won benefits in running a performance appraisal scheme is when its primary purpose is appraisee personal development. Here the manager can gain enhanced competencies and behaviours and enhanced commitment and, if other necessary conditions are met, enhanced engagement with the job. But there is one huge caveat – the right person must be in the right job.

6.7.1 *The right person in the right job*

We've illustrated a comprehensive model of employee performance in Chapter 5. This illustrates that performance depends on the one hand on the job and the environment of the job and on the other, the personal characteristics of the job holder.

In discussing the prospect of developing the person, we are suggesting a planned change to those personal characteristics. And as we see from the model, there's significant scope to effect improvement. We discuss how this might be done more fully in Chapter 8.

All personal development depends fundamentally on the foundations upon which the employee is to build. For every competency and every behaviour there are prerequisites. Let's consider those prerequisites for a salesperson.

Firstly, they need to be numerate, able to add, subtract, multiply, and divide to manage pricing and margins. If they don't have this foundation, no amount of development will bring the employee to be able to sell. So those prerequisites centre in turn on core competencies and core behaviours.

Secondly, they need to want to meet people and interact with them. This comes from their personality. If the salesperson is not somewhat extroversive, they'll naturally find the people side of selling difficult. And they need the right level of intelligence. Bright people learn easier.

The manager may believe that they can develop the job holder by using the performance appraisal system – but they will fail if they don't have the right person in the job.

Reflection 6-3: The right person in the right job

Considering the diagram in Figure 6-5 that illustrates the various antecedents and moderators of performance, and thinking about each of your employees and the jobs they do, do you have the right person in the right job? And therefore, now think through how the process of objective setting and performance appraisal might proceed with each. What might you do to ensure that all proceeds well?

6.8   Setting objectives and doing performance appraisal

Doing objective setting and objectives management, and performance appraisal and development management is no small undertaking for a manager. As we show in Figure 6-6 it comprises four phases and there are five key milestones at which certain documents must be in place before proceeding. These documents are shown as boxes with wavy bottoms and document title within. Manager and employee action at the mile post (MP) is shown in speech bubbles. Manager status is noted at the foot of the mile post.

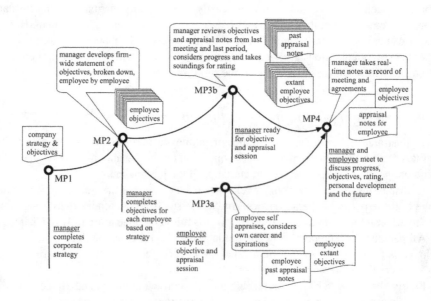

Figure 6-6: Objective setting and performance appraisal summarised

We recommend that the manager develops their own documentation that meets the needs of the firm. Picking up off-the-shelf forms is wrong. That adopts a process and documents that someone else thinks are important and, whatever the content, those forms are unlikely to suit you, your firm, and your employees.

We have not suggested a timescale for the round. This depends entirely on the firm's needs. At the longest, the full cycle should be run annually. However, priorities often change within the year, requiring re-setting of objectives, and in any case, the manager must manage employee progress week by week.

The whole process is, however, a sizeable task and any thought of running the cycle in less than, say, three months is probably unrealistic. It's possible that the objective setting phases might be completed every six months with the manager and each employee sitting down in an appraisal meeting every three months. Informal catch-up meetings might then be held monthly or even fortnightly.

Objective setting and performance management meetings are like quality audits – easy to put off, but eventually they catch up with you. Putting them off risks destroying any benefits thus far realised. Managers should get used to those meetings as an integral part of their management life.

6.8.1   *Objectives and appraisal meetings*

Of prime importance are the feelings, attitudes, and beliefs that the manager wants the employee to leave the meeting with. We would suggest that the employee should leave smiling rather than spitting.

There are established, proven tools for giving feedback to staff. It's essential that all managers are trained in their use. And there are established methods for having difficult discussions with staff to reach a positive outcome. Managers must be familiar with these too.

The meeting must therefore be planned. If there is to be a difficult discussion, that had best be done in the middle of the meeting. There's then time to congratulate and build on all the positives at the beginning and recover the meeting and leave on a positive note at the end.

Adequate time must be allowed for all eventualities. If the manager cuts the meeting short in response to other priorities, this signals a lack of commitment to the process and will counter any good work done.

We recommend that managers allow two hours for an appraisal meeting. The manager should not schedule any other commitments within one hour of the planned meeting close to allow for overrun. In any case, managers will soon learn how much time is needed for objective setting and performance appraisal meetings in their firm.

More frequent but less formal review meetings should be scheduled too, but these will take much less time.

Objective setting and performance appraisal meetings are fundamentally meetings between equals. This places a big responsibility on the manager to avoid a 'tell and sell'. Objectives and criticism will be accepted if due time is given for discussion. The manager must also be prepared to change their mind – this builds trust in the process. The manager's approach should be one of coach, as the facilitator of understanding. They are in charge, but it does not do to impress this on the employee. We discuss the advantages of adopting a non-directive leadership style in Chapter 2.

6.8.2 *Process pitfalls*

Firstly, managers have, in the past, been overly inclined to sign up to the process of performance appraisal in the belief that process alone will yield due benefit. They believed that simply collating and giving multi-rater feedback, was enough to cause performance change. It wasn't. The result has been a host of books saying that performance appraisal is a terrible technique, only for the authors of those books to advocate implementation of performance appraisal by another name.

Dogmatically following process in search of benefit has led to development of a host of smartphone and computer apps for 360-degree feedback, as if collecting and giving feedback were all managers need do.

In general, research does not support the assertion that the receipt of feedback alone, and specifically feedback from multiple sources, will motivate individuals to improve their performance.

Similarly, goals alone are not enough. It's a three-part system involving setting, reviewing, and improving through development.

Secondly, we note that managers must decide why they want to implement objective setting and performance appraisal. As we noted earlier, there are two established reasons – typically known as administration and development.

Administration links objective setting and appraisal to pay, promotion and succession. Development links the process to business planning, motivation, and progress. They're not mutually exclusive, but managers must take care in biasing the objective setting and performance appraisal to money. Remember, money does not motivate, and can encourage all the wrong behaviours. Taken to the limit, a company system oriented to raw achievement, with a focus on financial rewards, will likely result in a cadre of narcissistic employees high in the need for personal or P-power. Such firms are characterized by tears, fears, and high staff turnover.

Thirdly, running an objective setting and performance appraisal system as we describe it here takes manager competence and the right manager behaviours. Unless managers have been trained, it's unlikely that they will have those from the outset. Manager development is essential to excel in objective setting and performance appraisal.

There are many necessary competencies and behaviours, mostly common with those needed to be a good manager. For a list, we'd refer readers to the 23 competencies and behaviours outlined by Richard Boyatzis in his book, *The Competent Manager* and these are summarised below.

- Efficiency orientation: interest in continually doing things better, innovating, improving.
- Proactivity: disposition towards doing, acting, rather than waiting to be told by others.
- Diagnostic use of concepts: seeking patterns, frameworks, and concepts in activities.
- Concern with impact: an interest in using power over followers to make things happen.
- Self-confidence: confident in the knowledge that actions will lead to success.
- Use of oral presentations: organising thought into valid argument.
- Logical thought: ability to present events and activities in a rational causal sequence.

- Conceptualisation: the ability to recognise patterns and develop them into themes.
- Use of socialised power: inclination to build alliances, networks, coalitions, or teams.
- Positive regard: ability to believe in others, causing others to feel valued.
- Managing group processes: stimulating others to work together effectively as a group.
- Accurate self-assessment: having a realistic or grounded view of yourself.
- Developing others: competent at helping subordinates, acting as mentor and coach.
- Use of unilateral power: stimulating subordinates to go along directions desired.
- Spontaneity: expressing self freely and easily, acting emotionally, expressing concern.
- Self-control: inhibiting personal needs and desires in favour of organisational needs.
- Perceptual objectivity: able to be objective, not limited by personal bias or prejudice.
- Stamina and adaptivity: able to sustain long hours of work, adapting to change.
- Concern with close relationships: able to build close working relationships.
- Relevant knowledge/knowledge used: establish frameworks for specialised knowledge.
- Function/product/technology: using facts of the business, products, and technologies.
- Recognition versus utility: able to determine what needs to be known and used.
- Memory: the accurate, appropriate remembering and recall of information and activities.

A scan of these 23 shows that all the essential competencies of a manager are brought to bear during appraisal. At its heart, the appraisal process seeks efficiency – improvement in both employee and firm. Setting objectives demands use of concepts – both manager and employee must be able to imagine what's needed to grow. And logical thought will help turn those concepts into a logical sequence of achievements that will overall meet the goal.

Of all those, though, the single most important, along with various associated behaviours, is the ability, and desire, to make good use of evidence. Objective setting is about achieving results. And whether those results will have been achieved, when it comes to performance appraisal, will depend on evidence. It's not about opinion based on a few events that the manager can recall occurring recently. Performance appraisal requires the manager to take good notes continuously and to use those in objective discussion. Many inexperienced managers fail here and risk destroying the integrity of the system.

6.8.3   *Power in performance appraisal*

Managers should be aware that as soon as people come together in a social environment such as the firm, there will be political activities throughout, with individuals trying to influence others towards their way of thinking. The performance appraisal has, as its outcome, both benefits and rewards, and dis-benefits and sanctions, for all participants. The result is that both managers and employees will work the system to achieve what is best for them.

Commonly, power is the mechanism by which a manager effects behaviour changes in an employee. Power is also the mechanism by which the employee influences the manager to ensure a good rating, a pay rise and favourable future work. Both manager and subordinate hold some power but often one will have the upper hand. Power can therefore be unilateral or bilateral, imbalanced, or balanced.

Unless controlled, both parties will use their power to distort the performance appraisal outcomes in their favour.

Power comes from several sources.

- Authority: the manager is the boss and hence holds legitimate power through appointment. The manager is also the one to grant meaningful reward, like a pay rise.
- Social class: one party is from a higher class than the other and hence is seen as holding power.
- Charisma: the employee is in awe of the manager and would follow them anywhere. Charismatic managers influence because employees want to share in the limelight that goes with that charisma.
- Expertise: the manager is trained and is seen as having higher expertise. Or perhaps power in the reverse direction exists because the employee knows how to do the job while the manager doesn't.
- Persuasion: the manager is acknowledged as being better at using argument to persuade – or vice versa. Either party may be an accomplished arguer, making the other disinclined to enter the debate.
- Knowledge: one party is known to have greater knowledge about the job, the market, or the firm.
- Moral persuasion: drawing on moral argument, one party is acknowledged as able to persuade the other. This is not just restricted to charities and public services like teaching, though it's here where perhaps moral arguments for action pervade.
- Tradition: it's always been the case that one person holds power over the other.

Ultimately, the manager must act to move the performance appraisal from a 'tell-and-sell' meeting to a joint problem-solving activity where the aim is to develop the employee to improve competence and to encourage behaviour. That way the manager gets what they want and the employee progresses.

With that done, the performance appraisal moves from a polarised event, in which power determines outcomes, to a social exchange activity. In this, both parties desire something of the activity without necessarily expecting specific action in specific timescales. In this case, both want to progress. And in fact, this idea of exchange continues from performance appraisal to everyday management.

If both manager and employee are set to benefit and both believe that benefit is equitable, though not necessarily equal, both will come to the table with balanced power. Under such conditions, the performance appraisal stands to yield maximum perceived justice in the employee's mind with maximum benefit for all.

6.8.4   *Dos and don'ts of objectives*

As we indicate, there's a lot to think about to make objective setting and performance appraisal work as a management tool. Here are some dos and don'ts from our experience.

- Make the whole meeting, and the process at any point in time, personal to the employee. Don't treat it as a huge machine, calling out, metaphorically, 'next!'
- Keep the process and each meeting simple. Take and share handwritten notes. Keep a master file for each employee.
- Do allow employees to self-assess their achievements and performance and provide evidence in discussion. But remember that a manager-set goal has more potency.
- Do train yourself and all employees, such that you and they come to understand how objective setting and performance appraisal fits in the firm's overall activities.
- Be prepared to support development with appropriate funding. Don't go into a meeting knowing there's a need for development without the funds to make it happen.
- Your needs, the needs of the firm and the needs of each employee will change over the coming year. Be prepared to respond with additional meetings and be ready to re-set objectives.
- Remember that you are playing with the psychological contract – the understanding that your employees have about their relationship with you. Earn their trust always.
- Never force rankings or guide rater feedback. Don't seek to identify those at the bottom of the scale to dismiss or discipline. That's a failing on you.
- Think beforehand about how you want the person to leave the appraisal meeting - spitting or smiling. Having employees leave angry or aggrieved does nothing for future performance.
- Keep a sense of how the meetings and the process overall are going. Make changes to the process and how you conduct the meetings. Learn from each meeting.
- Collect feedback about each employee's performance over the year/period and make sure there's plenty evidence. Never open discussions with, "I think that you….". Always seek objectivity.
- Be open to change your opinion considering additional evidence but be forceful if you believe your evidence trumps this.
- Strive for procedural justice. Remember that employees talk, and each will have shared their experiences with colleagues. Treat all equitably.
- Focus more on the positives of employee achievements and performance than the negatives and take care not to be portrayed as the bearer of bad news. Don't just act as judge/critic.

6.8.5   *Evolving the process*

Objective setting and performance appraisal must be tuned to work for the manager, their firm, and the employees. So, every system is going to be unique.

No manager is going to get their objective setting and performance appraisal system right first time. So, the process will evolve. Of course, it's important to get started, but in some ways, where it starts is less important than asking the employees about how they feel about the process and reacting to their feedback. After all, if they are happy with the process, and feel that they will benefit from engaging with it, the system is likely to be fair and worthwhile.

If the manager is happy with the way the process runs, it's very likely that the system will benefit the firm. And if, for some reason, it doesn't, it must be changed. Running objective setting and performance appraisal is too costly to continue to run a broken system.

6.9   Chapter Summary

The idea behind objective setting and performance appraisal is simple enough, but the complexity comes in doing it. It's a narrow arête that defines success. And the 'drops' either side of the metaphorical ridge are steep – it's easy for managers to fall at various points along the way.

At the outset, managers will set high level objectives for the performance of the firm. Conceivably, if the manager doesn't ripple these objectives down to the employees, the high-level objectives won't be met. We illustrate how a firm aiming to turn over £2.5m might develop objectives for its staff.

This idea of rippling down objectives from the central corporate objectives has merit. But even with a high degree of objectivity and linking to the firm's fortunes, it's still difficult to set measurable objectives for all. We use the example of a waiter to discuss why this is. Ultimately managers need to set objectives in the tangible business metrics of performance, productivity, quality (and the minimising of wastage) and safety.

We illustrate how the accountabilities in an employee's job description should link to their objectives – the objectives make the job description accountabilities specific and current. This illustrates the key importance of a well-crafted job description setting out at a high level what the jobholder is to achieve.

Ultimately, we argue that objectives have a key role in making performance management central in launching initiatives. Initiatives and their associated objectives give managers reason to intervene day to day in the business lives of their people. Intervention enables leadership and ensures success in those initiatives. Management will fail without accountabilities, objectives, and initiatives.

Some academics argue that setting objectives stifles creativity and there is truth in this. Narrow objectives can be set where the desired outcomes are specific. But broad outcomes, like 'ensuring success', might be used in complex business scenarios with unclear end goals. Objectives for research scientists will look very different from those of a project engineer; the latter will likely be broad, whereas the former will concentrate on delivering contracted outcomes.

We don't subscribe, though, to the idea that objective setting is only useful for 'white collar' employees. We argue that it's wrong for professional and managerial types to have a monopoly on sitting with their manager to discuss performance. We argue that all the performance of all employees can benefit from goal theory.

In search of the practical, we advocate the use of a balanced scorecard to entice managers to spread attention across the four aspects of management: finance, process, customers, and employees. In the end, financial goals will be achieved by action in the other three quadrants.

Performance is a complex metric. We believe that splitting it into task performance and contextual performance helps understanding and the setting of meaningful and objective goals. Splitting also helps identify where personal development may be needed for goal satisfaction – many employees fail to master the softer skills of contextual performance and in that case, it's there where managers often must focus.

Turning to performance appraisal, we look at the various ways that appraisal might be done. We evaluate the use of multi-dimensional, multi-rater systems and highlight some of the issues and the dangers. In appraisal, it's very easy to catastrophically damage trust and the psychological contract, and hence who is invited to offer a rating on an employee should be decided with care.

Finally, we look at the skills needed by managers in objective setting and performance appraisal and draw on Boyatzis' 23 manager competencies. We argue that the manager must be multi-competent. They must be prepared to train for management and that will naturally cover the essential skills and knowledge of objective setting and performance appraisal.

We describe a paperwork trail and a timescale for the process of the appraisal 'round', suggesting that objective setting and performance might be run on a six-monthly cycle with interim review meetings every few weeks.

Finally, we discuss the detail of the objective setting and appraisal meetings. We highlight the critical question – how is it that the manager wants their employee to leave the meeting. And we suggest the dos and don'ts to help the manager stay on the ridge, with trust intact.

7

Managing Relations

Many managers might skip this chapter. They've not had to look closely at the employment relationship. They've managed their employees by sensitively exploiting the dyadic relationship. The relationship between themselves and each employee. And their efforts have worked - so far.

Others will need to continually refer to the contract of employment, the various policies, and procedures in the firm, and ultimately to the courts and tribunals. This latter group will have had to resort to formal process to ensure that employees behave, and that staff discipline is maintained.

For some, formal processes are a distraction representing a problem they don't have. For others, formal processes are essential. In the end, all managers need to understand the lawful redress available to them and how this should be applied. And certainly, all managers need to understand the responsibility that the employment contract places on both parties, both legally and morally, to sustain a harmonious workplace.

7.1   The employer-employee relationship

The employer-employee relationship begins with the employee entering an employment contract with the firm. That simple act is not simple at all.

7.1.1   *Economic and psychological relationships*

All lawyers will concur that agreements must, in the end, be interpreted and argued day by day by the parties when it comes to determination. English is just too vague a language, and there's neither the time nor the inclination to remove ambiguity.

In the case of employment contracts, the written terms cover the highlights, like the number hours to be worked and the rate of pay, but they leave significant detail to be defined in other support documents, and to be assumed in the minds of the manager and employee.

The employment contract is part-economic and part-psychological. The common model to describe this is the iceberg – a small visible island above the water representing the economic element and the huge, deep, submerged mass below the water representing the relationship in the minds of the employee and manager. This is shown in Figure 7-1.

We described in Chapter 1 how the supplier 'came indoors' to the entrepreneur's firm and agreed to come under the entrepreneur's direction in return for a wage. The supplier then becomes an employee under a contract of service to the firm. It's an economic arrangement.

The manager, as agent, can tell the employee what to do and when, though this authority comes with conditions.

The psychological element of the contract is more abstract. As tiny examples of the complexity of the psychological contract, the employee assumes that the manager will treat them fairly, take an interest in them as a person and give them interesting work. The psychological contract involves the building of trust. Trust is built slowly as the employee's assumptions are supported by the manager's actions. But it's destroyed in an instant when the manager, in the employee's mind, breaches the terms of this unwritten agreement, perhaps though perceived crass behaviour.

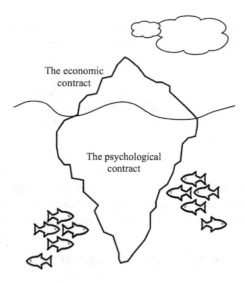

Figure 7-1: The iceberg metaphor for the manager-employee relationship

So, managers must implement robust, expressed, written economic contracts and must be mindful that this documentation relies on a strong psychological contract for real-world operation.

7.1.2 Understanding emotions and disputes

Since the days of the ancient philosophers, we humans have always been considered to have two parts to our being – a rational self that listens to reason and makes decisions slowly following cognitive thought, and an emotional self that reacts quickly on instinct.

Added to this, humans compete over resources. If we can be encouraged to think, we know it's better to cooperate. But all humans are wired to maximise the outcomes of any contest in their favour. We're also wired to defend from any invasion the resources that we do control. And of course, we're biased – we're right and everyone else is wrong.

Our actions in competitions are instinctive and fast, so it's easy therefore for conflict between two or more employees, or between employees and their manager, to flare over benign issues. Only our inhibition and self-control stemming from our upbringing, the norms of society, and an understanding of the consequences prevent all-out war! Those consequences are set out in the economic contract and its associated documents and supported by expectations in the psychological contract.

So, disputes are commonplace, and the manager must be ready to act to pre-empt and diffuse conflict.

7.1.3   *Acting to defuse conflict*

Managers are trying to navigate a minefield. They know what's written, but they know that there's a whole load more going on too in the various relationships.

And the manager is the only person who can act. The power vested in the manager by the firm places them right in the middle of the action. The manager understands the economic and psychological contracts as they are realised in each person. And the manager is close to the employees: remember that management is a contact sport. As a result, the manager can sense how each employee likely feels and can predict how their emotional selves are likely to react to day-to-day situations. They just need the tools and the inclination to engage to defuse conflict.

We described in Chapter 2 the difference between a leader and a manager. It's in interpersonal and behavioural issues that this difference becomes stark. Intervention may be irksome and unpleasant, but it's the manager's responsibility to act.

7.2   The central role of the manager

Action is a greyscale, and the manager must continually review the facts and decide the appropriate intervention. At one end of the scale, the manager will act lightly without reference to formal process. At the other end, they will need to apply the full power of formal investigation, analysis, and decision.

7.2.1   *Defining discipline and grievance*

In society, we decide what's acceptable behaviour, and what's not, by referencing accepted laws, norms, morals, and standards. The firm is a microcosm of society. And the firm merges those societal laws, norms, morals, and standards with elements of the contract of employment it has with its employees. This amalgam of expressed and implied terms becomes the firm's behavioural code.

Employee behaviour that, in the eyes of the manager, breaches this behavioural code is dealt with using the firm's disciplinary procedures. Colleague and manager behaviour that, in the eyes of the employee, breaches this behavioural code is dealt with using the firm's grievance procedures.

And there's then the special case where the employee fails to perform for reasons of poor capability, rather than poor behaviour. Capability is the product of employee competence and the function of the technology that they use. Some managers use their disciplinary procedures to correct capability gaps. This is wrong. There should be a separate capability or performance management procedure for use in improving capability and capability-related performance.

7.2.2   Discipline and grievance day to day

As an agent of the firm, the manager is empowered to act on disciplinary and grievance issues. And the employee agreed to adhere to the firm's behavioral code as soon as they signed the employment contract. So, all employees have agreed to accept the manager's intervention – trusting, of course, that the manager will play fair, behave honorably, and treat all employees equitably without fear or favour.

The manager therefore has the right to act, and the law will support them, if they act fairly, compassionately and with supporting evidence.

Legally, the manager acts with reasonable belief. They are not a police detective - there's no need for proof beyond reasonable doubt. And it's not a civil court – there's no need for proof on balance of probabilities. The manager must sense, investigate, intervene, judge, administer penalties (where relevant) and move on.

There's nothing here either that suggests formal action in all cases. Nothing ordinarily demands the calling of meetings, prescribed agendas, attendance of friends or representatives or the right of appeal against disliked sanctions.

Managers can, and indeed, must, act informally day by day on disciplinary and grievance issues but with the same general process as used when 'going formal'.

7.2.3   When relations turn sour

From time to time, informal disciplinary and grievance management processes will not be enough. It may be that the employee continues to transgress. It could be that the employee remains aggrieved. Escalation is needed in management intervention.

It's difficult for the manager to judge when this should happen and it's impossible for any external expert to say. Some managers are disinclined to act when they should. Some online support service companies advise that managers should 'have a word' – keep things informal - rather than flex their management muscles and wade in.

The reluctance of such service companies to advise moving to formal procedures is understandable. Risk to the firm rises when that happens, particularly when managers are inexperienced or ill-trained. Since such support service companies often also insure the firm against employee risk, it's not in their interests to recommend 'going formal'.

And at the other end of the action spectrum, some firms have little time for the informal, using their disciplinary and grievance procedures to manage every problem.

So, the manager senses performance and behaviour. From time to time, they sense issues, investigate, and act. That action must be proportionate. What is not proportionate, is for the manager to decide on summary dismissal. Due process is essential.

7.2.4   The manager as prime actor

It's for the manager – that is, the immediate line manager – to act. That manager expects to lead. They expect, through profits, bonus, or career advancement, to reap the benefits of their employees' efforts. They must not delegate upwards to have directors or even chairs of boards take responsibility. We defined management as taking responsibility for the actions of others who work for you and that applies without qualification.

Of course, if the manager is not trained or experienced in managing disciplinaries or grievances, they might want to get some support. That's different. Come what may, the manager must not shirk when things get tough. The manager must get trained.

7.2.5   *Understanding the perspectives of the parties*

In any disciplinary or grievance activity, there are many players.

The miscreant (in disciplinaries) or aggrieved employee (in grievances) is in the middle of it all. Whatever the reason they're there, they are looking for swift action, fair treatment, and maintenance of their personal integrity. They must come out of it having saved face. And their commitment, motivation and engagement must recover afterwards.

The manager just wants it all to go away. They have too many sleepless nights as it is! The manager is in the Board or senior management's spotlight. Their competence is being challenged and they want to come out of it all unscathed and be seen to be a good manager.

And the employee's colleagues are looking on with interest. What happens is a guide to how they'd fare if they were in the disciplinary or grievance frame.

And professional support, such as online support companies or lawyers, are treating the whole thing as a case. They are impartial and it should be kept that way. Their only role is to provide high quality advice.

Reflection 7-1: About formal and informal procedures

Think back over the years. Identify several instances of disciplinary and several of grievance. For each one, identify the turning points when informal became formal. What caused that change? Did you act too soon? Or drag your heels and delay? Could you have acted sooner or at a different time to better result? And ultimately, was there anything you could have done better?

7.3   Setting the employment foundation

7.3.1   *Legal basis of the relationship*

We noted that the employee agrees to serve the manager as agent of the firm, and to be under the manager's direction. If we translate this simple idea to an employee joining even a small to medium sized firm, it's easy to see that the employee is at a disadvantage. When compared to the financial, and likely intellectual, resources of the firm, the employee is relatively weak. The firm is powerful and unless regulated, will win every argument between it and its employee(s).

That idea of the powerless contracting with the powerful has spawned the raft of statutes governing the employment relationship. The State implements Acts to redress the balance.

There are three primary Acts or Statutes that govern the relationship, augmented by about 15 Statutory Instruments (Regulations and Orders), and five further Codes of Practice. In addition, there are about eleven European Union Directives and about three International Obligations – all taken into UK law. Readers should check the status of statutes since all are subject to change post-Brexit and at the whim of right-leaning government. The main Statutes at the time of writing are shown in Figure 7-2.

Statutes of the UK Parliament	Main rights acquired/transferred by the employee
Employment Rights Act 1996	To be told about the conditions of the employment. Not to suffer detriment in employment. To be clear about the conditions under which the employer may terminate the relationship. To expect the employer to treat the employee fairly.
Equality Act 2010	To not be discriminated against because of protected personal characteristics.
Copyright, Designs and Patents Act 1988	To automatically transfer rights in the work done to the employer.

Figure 7-2: Primary Statutes Applying to the Employment Relationship

We've included here the Copyright, Designs and Patents Act 1988 since the idea of transfer of rights from employee to employer is central to many activities today, such as software development, web design and product design. Without this, the absurd state would exist where the employee would retain the rights to work delivered by their employer to its clients and customers.

No such automatic transfer occurs concerning work done by suppliers – freelancers, sub-contractors, sole-traders, personal services companies, and the like.

Since the UK operates common law, part of English law that is derived from custom and judicial precedent rather than statutes, the legal elements of the economic contract will be modified by employment-related judicial decisions of courts and employment tribunals.

7.3.2 Economic and psychological contracts

The economic contract is defined by the statutes above and set out in documents that the employee receives from the manager. In simple terms, the economic contract can be summarised by the statement from the employee to the employer, "In return for a wage, I agree to come under your direction under the following expressed terms…". Then, of course, there's the reciprocal statement by the employer about pay in return for work done.

The psychological contract is similarly defined. There's just more of it, everything's implied and it takes a long time to put in place.

The economic contract is, at its simplest, defined by twenty clauses defined in a Written Statement of Employment Particulars. These clauses define headline information and more on what's required is set out on the UK Government website. As one might imagine, the Written Statement of Employment Particulars is a 'bare bones' legal affair and managers should strive to improve on this. Two sides of A4 are unlikely to create the necessary warm feeling as an employee reads a job offer.

7.3.3 Role of the staff handbook

Many firms issue a staff handbook – a document of around 30 pages. This document aims to put flesh on the bones of the economic contract. It aims to provide a compendium of information that surrounds and makes real the economic contract.

Most human resources practitioners go to great pains to avoid the staff handbook being considered legally binding and hence instrumental in defining the legal elements of the economic contract. They strive to avoid having the staff handbook appear to elaborate the twenty clauses of the Written Statement of Employment Particulars. Care is needed here when drafting beyond simply labelling the staff handbook 'non-contractual'.

A clause or contract that is 'contractual' must be adhered to, otherwise the defaulting party would be in breach of the contract. And something contractual can't be changed without agreement.

Since the staff handbook goes a significant way to define the culture and the relationship between managers and staff, it has a particularly important role in differentiating the firm from others and hence attracting key talent during recruitment.

7.3.4   *Role of policies and procedures*

Policies and procedures illustrate how the firm will enact discipline and ensure fairness. Typically, the policies and procedures for a small firm occupy around 70 pages as an annex to the staff handbook. They define how managers and employees should act in certain circumstances. Again, generally, these policies and procedures should be 'non-contractual'.

There are typically 20 policies and procedures necessary to ensure correct functioning of a small firm, spanning anything from use of information technology systems to capability management. Whilst basic disciplinary and grievance procedures are well defined in the ACAS Code of Practice 1: Disciplinary and Grievance Procedures (Revised 2015), we consider that all firms should have their own policies and procedures, compliant with those from ACAS, but tailored to the firm's local context. ACAS, the Advisory, Conciliation and Arbitration Service, is the UK's independent statutory Government-sponsored employment-related advice and guidance body.

7.3.5   *Changing the foundations*

The economic contract can be changed by the manager. Change is a simple enough process requiring the manager to explain the changes to the employee(s) and consult with them (abiding by appropriate timescales) – asking them for opinion and considering and genuinely taking account of that opinion.

Changes to the economic contract are then confirmed by modifying and re-issuing the Written Statement of Employment Particulars or employment contact and other papers containing the expressed terms. Of course, change to the economic contract affects the implied terms of the psychological contract too, often negatively. Do not unilaterally change the terms and conditions of employment. This constitutes a breach of contract.

7.4   **Managing discipline and performance**

Firms take disciplinary action when an employee does something that is considered to constitute unacceptable behaviour. All managers should have rules in place to assist them and their colleagues in dealing with wayward employees. The rules also let employees know what is, and is not, acceptable behaviour.

In dealing with discipline of employees, the most important thing is that all managers must follow their own firm's documented disciplinary process.

7.4.1   *Won't do versus can't do*

Discipline and performance improvement are very different concepts, albeit linked.

Discipline is about correcting wayward behaviour – the 'won't do' case – where the employee breaches the firm's behavioural code. Performance improvement, on the other hand, is about changing the task-related and general competencies and behaviours exhibited by an employee to have their performance return to that acceptable to the manager – the 'can't do' case.

Firms should have a separate process that provides a more positive way of managing the poor performance of an employee. Whilst the disciplinary process can be used, lack of ability to perform (through lack of competency or task-related behaviour) is different to wilfully undertaking unacceptable behaviour. Use of a disciplinary process for performance improvement sends negative messages to the employee at a time when positive, encouraging messages are needed.

So, always keep a clear distinction between 'won't do' and 'can't do', both in management tone and procedures used.

We combine them here to avoid duplication because the procedures in the two cases are functionally identical.

7.4.2   *The behaviour expected*

We need, here, to distinguish between task-related behaviours such as pro-activity and tenacity, and social behaviours such as aggressiveness and rudeness. Task-related behaviours are influenced by the employee's personality and motivation. Assuming that the employee is not naturally badly behaved, behaviours like aggressiveness and rudeness and transgressions like theft stem from emotional reactions to work circumstances.

Our focus here is on those social behaviours. This is the 'won't do' case we discussed above.

There's no absolute need for employees to like their colleagues and managers. But they are expected to cooperate with them. Unfortunately, humans, as social beings, do need to also like those they cooperate with. Liking is the foundation of trust and respect. Trust and respect are then reinforced by action. Bad behaviour often follows some event that challenged trust and respect.

The manager must intervene to return the 'won't do' behaviour to a 'will do' attitude. They may also need to correct whatever caused the relapse. Examples of anti-social behaviour should be listed in the disciplinary procedures both as a warning to employees and as guidance to managers.

7.4.3   *The capability expected*

We describe elsewhere that capability is a combination of human competencies and behaviours and technology function. If performance was once adequate, and is now not, managers should investigate the root cause.

The capability required, and hence the competencies and task-related behaviours, should be set out in the employee's job description (see Chapter 6) and in agreed objectives.

Failure to meet the accountabilities and responsibilities of the job description or to achieve the objectives may occur because the employee did not have the necessary competencies and task-related behaviours. Of course, logically, this should have been determined when hiring the employee for that job; at performance appraisal and objective setting; and generally, when managing the person day to day. With apparent competency gaps, support could have been given earlier.

But now, assuming that poor competency is the root cause, the manager's task is to launch the performance improvement procedure to effect change, recover performance and achieve agreed objectives.

7.4.4   *Formal and informal management*

There are two clearly distinct ways of proceeding: informally and formally. Informal proceedings are the normal management actions where manager and employee sit down together to discuss issues about behaviour and performance. Formal proceedings are announced as such, are minuted and follow a prescribed agenda. It is always best to try to resolve issues informally if possible.

The ACAS code, lumping performance and bad behaviour together, states that the employer and employee should try to resolve disciplinary issues in the workplace as soon as possible. Often, ACAS suggests, issues can be resolved through informal workplace mediation.

So, how does the firm use informal, and then formal proceedings?

In the work situation the manager has the right to have one-to-one informal discussions with any member of their team at any time on any subject. It is quite appropriate to have informal discussions to explain that behaviour is unacceptable and that it must improve. Clear guidelines can be laid down and the employee advised that if the inappropriate behaviour continues then formal action may have to take place.

In many cases informal discussions will solve the problem as the employee becomes aware that their behaviour is inappropriate and is being checked.

Formal proceedings are a different kettle of fish!! Formal proceedings involve letters and other formal communications, meetings, and investigations. Managers must never invite an employee to a meeting saying it is 'formal' unless they have followed their published formal process.

Formal meetings must be planned and a letter must be sent inviting the employee to the meeting. Employees must be advised what the meeting is about and any documents which are going to be used in the meeting must be shared in advance. The employee should be given the right to have a companion in the meeting to support them.

We consider that a letter (delivered by first class post) or an email are good ways of inviting an employee to a meeting. There must be a good chance that the employee receives it and that they acknowledge its importance. Never use text messaging or social media to make the invitation.

7.4.5   *Using the various policies and procedures*

As we note, small to medium sized firms need around 20 policies and procedures to effectively manage most eventualities.

When drafting the policies and procedures, managers should refer to the relevant Acts, Regulations and Codes of Practice. All internal documents must a) be drafted for the firm and relevant for the firm's environment and b) be in line with those Acts, Regulations and Codes of Practice.

Policies and procedures should be minimalist but complete. Managers should avoid creating a cupboard full of files that no-one understands or reads. Techniques such as diagramming should be used to reduce the burden of complex English. These are working documents and are best drafted by managers, or consultants who have been managers, rather than lawyers. Simple, clear English is essential.

All employees should be familiar with the policies and procedures and have unfettered access to them. Managers should understand their contents and be able to apply them whenever needed.

7.4.6 Role of investigations

All managers must establish the facts before any disciplinary or performance improvement intervention. Unfortunately, 'fact' is a difficult concept when dealing with employees and hence somewhat elusive. If the manager had to establish the fact of every matter, they would be for ever investigating and would never take any action.

But managers must investigate. That investigation may simply be a review of their own notes about the situation and employees, or it might be a more formal investigation carried out by an impartial investigating officer such as a colleague manager or an external consultant.

Formal investigations are done by an investigating officer who is given a brief – generally an outline of a claim of a breach of the firm's behaviour code. The investigating officer then interviews those associated with the event, reads email and other communication and metaphorically 'turns stones' to discover what happened. Investigations into complex issues may involve many interviews and hundreds or even thousands of pages of communications read. The resulting data may be so large that techniques like thematic analysis may be necessary to reduce the data, without loss of meaning and strength, to something succinct that can be understood by the manager.

The result of an investigation is a report setting out what, according to those close to events, happened. As we note above, the manager is bound to make decisions using reasonable belief. If the manager reads the investigation report and, using reasonable belief, comes to conclude that the events portrayed occurred, and that some transgression likely occurred, then they are justified in acting.

7.4.7 Disciplinary and performance processes

The processes are simple enough. The manager reads the investigation report and determines if there is a case to answer – if the employee likely breached the disciplinary code or if their performance was indeed below that expected.

Generally, there are three levels of severity of the transgression or poor performance. Each includes examples of the events that might trigger the process. At the lower level, it might be, for example, that the employee has shouted and cursed at a colleague. The middle tier may describe reckless use of the firm's property. At the top level it might include the inability to carry out duties through intoxication.

Each level has with it a likely penalty. For lower-level transgressions, the penalty will be a verbal warning. The mid-tier may attract a written warning. And the upper tier, with the most serious categories, may attract a final written warning or even dismissal.

If there is a case to answer, the employee must be asked to attend a meeting with the manager. If the meeting is formal, the employee may have a colleague or trades union officer present at the meeting as a friend. The friend is not entitled to respond for the employee but can ask clarifying questions and may also address the meeting. Typically, disciplinary or performance improvement meetings last around an hour.

Someone should attend to take notes. Those notes should be typed up afterwards and shared with the employee as a record of the meeting. We suggest that such meetings should not be recorded – recording illustrates low trust, just when employee and manager need to trust one another.

Disciplinary and performance improvement meetings must be called correctly. Failure to call the meeting with adequate notice and due formality may result in the process being deemed automatically fair. For more on this, refer to ACAS guidelines.

Likewise, if the meeting could hand down a sanction of dismissal, this possibility must be stated in the letter inviting the employee to the meeting. Failure to cite this precludes this outcome.

7.4.8   *Making decisions and handing down sanctions*

On reading the investigation report, and on hearing what the employee has to say, the manager, as chair of the meeting, must determine if the assertion that the employee has misbehaved is supported. And if related to performance, the manager must determine if the employee's performance has indeed fallen below that expected.

Reasonable belief, the basis of decision-making in disciplinary and performance management, employs the idea that, given the same data, most reasonable people would reach the same conclusion. And it's not to say that the manager is right in this decision, since 'right' is an even more difficult concept. They may be mistaken, but they believed that the decision that they arrived at was appropriate in the circumstances and proportionate, and that's what's important.

When considering information from investigations and from the meeting, the manager must give enough time to reach reasonable belief about the assertion. Where necessary, the manager can call for further investigation and can adjourn to seek further information.

The meeting can be adjourned for a few hours for the manager to think and consider what they have heard, or even adjourned and a date set to reconvene to give the judgement. In any case, the decision should not be delayed unduly.

The decision and sanction should be given in person by the manager and then supported immediately afterwards in writing. Social media or texting should never be used.

7.4.9   *Escalation in disciplinary management*

Typically, the procedures embrace the idea that an employee who continually transgresses or whose work is repeatedly of a poor performance standard can face increasingly tough sanctions to effect corrective action.

On handing down a sanction and discovering repeated issues, the manager can move from verbal warning to written warning to final written warning or dismissal. Sufficient time is needed to allow for improvement. The meeting schedule discussed above is then implemented again for each level of escalation.

In the end though, dismissal can occur, with only a few weeks between investigation and sanction. This can be shortened for employees with under two years' service.

7.4.10   The appeals process

All disciplinary and performance approval procedures must allow the employee to appeal the decision. The letter setting out the decision should say to whom the appeal is to be made.

The appeals process follows the same process as the initial meeting but is chaired and heard by someone other than the manager involved in the initial meetings. It hears the employee's reason for the appeal and considers any new information that has come to light. An appeal meeting can lead to the original decision being quashed, upheld or the sanction decreased or increased.

7.5   Managing grievances

Grievances are treated functionally like disciplinaries, with investigation, meeting, decision, and appeal. The possible end state includes the risk of the employee taking a tribunal claim. The same end state is possible with disciplinaries.

7.5.1   Why grievances arise

There are perhaps two reasons why grievances arise. The first is simply that one employee finds that something that another employee or manager says or does is not to their liking. The grievance procedure is their method of recourse – their way of complaining in the hope that something can change, and they can return to a previously acceptable state. The second is where the employee is about to be disciplined or to be investigated for poor performance. In this latter case the grievance is a form of retaliation. It's a blocking tactic.

When used as a block, the disciplinary or performance management process should be halted, and the grievance dealt with first. The decision from the grievance may then influence the disciplinary or performance management outcome.

7.5.2   Basic grievance process

In essence, the process for grievances is the same as that for disciplinary and performance improvement. The firm's grievance procedure should set out this procedure and say to whom the complaint should be made.

Once a complaint is made, the manager must launch an investigation which will lead to a report. The manager is then bound to allow the employee to elaborate on their grievance at a grievance meeting. Considering the information presented in the report and elaborated on in the meeting, the manager must determine if they support the employee's grievance or not.

7.5.3   The role of investigations

The investigation process is identical to that above in the discussion about disciplinary and performance improvement cases. Again, it's essential that an impartial investigating officer be appointed. The investigating officer conducts the investigation using the employee's claim as a guide. The investigating officer should not be the person hearing the case.

7.5.4   Grievance meetings

There is quite an issue about who chairs grievance meetings. Generally, grievances are either directly or indirectly about the employee's manager. This means that it would be inappropriate for that manager to be involved in the investigation or hear the case. In large firms, this is easily avoided – another impartial manager can hear the grievance. In smaller firms, a non-executive director or an external consultant may need to be drafted in.

7.5.5   Making decisions and appeals

The decision made is based on reasonable belief. Again, it's not expected that the chair of the grievance meeting is legally qualified. They must consider all the information and decide if they agree with the employee's claim.

The range of outcomes from a grievance meeting is wider than that for disciplinary or performance improvement meetings, extending to the launch of disciplinary procedures against staff and managers, instigation of training, redeployment, and requests to change the firm's methods.

If the employee's grievance is not assuaged, and they are still aggrieved, they can appeal the decision of the meeting. The appeal process is identical to that for disciplinaries and performance improvement.

Ultimately, if unsatisfied with the outcome, the employee can take their case to an Employment Tribunal.

7.5.6   When grievance leads to tribunal

An Employment Tribunal is the place where an employee goes to seek a decision on something that aggrieves them.

A tribunal is chaired by a legally qualified Tribunal Judge. Often tribunals sit with specialist, non-legal, members. An employment tribunal may include members who are able to take both the employer and manager perspective. Tribunal judges and members listen to the evidence and question both the employee and the manager to clarify and gain further information.

Tribunals will expect the employee to have exhausted the firm's grievance procedure through initial meeting, decision and appeal before the case moves to tribunal.

7.6   Managing bullying and harassment

In the workplace, the manager should deal with allegations of bullying and harassment.

7.6.1   Definitions of bullying and harassment

The Equality Act 2010 defines harassment as unwanted conduct related to a relevant protected characteristic, which has the purpose or effect of violating another person's dignity, or creating an intimidating, hostile, degrading, humiliating or offensive environment for that individual.

The protected characteristics are age, disability, gender reassignment, race, religion or belief, sex, and sexual orientation.

For harassment to be deemed to have taken place the alleged behaviour must have had either purpose or effect.

Harassment is also defined in law in the Protection from Harassment Act 1997. This Act suggests that harassment is when someone behaves in a way that makes another person feel distressed, humiliated, or threatened.

We consider that the legal definition of harassment is too clinical, too one-sided, asking primarily if the conduct, so defined, happened. With the legal definition, we consider that an unfair decision could result – particularly where events took place, but where those events had little or no effect on the victim. The psychological definition, on the other hand, requires that there is both event and arousal of sensibilities – asking 'did it happen, and did it matter' - and this two-part definition provides a much more robust criterion for managers. This definition allows small action to have a large effect, and significant action to have little effect.

Bullying is the use of superior power in one person to intimidate or harass another person, often to cause the bullied to do something for the bully. That power may come from physical, mental, or social differences or from relative positions within the firm. And it may involve protected personal characteristics such as sex, and sexual orientation.

Bullying can exist between two employees or between manager and employee. Generally, in the latter case, the manager is the bully. Groups of employees, as bullies, can also gang up on one or more other employees.

Bullies use threats, abuse, and aggression to dominate their victims. In effect, bullying is the repeated use of harassment over time. Bullying must not be tolerated by managers.

7.6.2   How attitudes have changed

The recent spate of high-profile sexual harassment cases has brought changing attitudes over time into stark relief.

In the 1960s, it was tacitly accepted by most women that to get established in a career, some tolerance of harassment by male colleagues and managers was normal. In those days, the events occurred, but because they were considered accepted, it took something significant before a complaint would be upheld. As a result, men enjoyed free rein in what would today be considered harassment.

7.6.3   Using relevant procedures

An anti-bullying and harassment policy should be in place. This explains to managers and employees what kind of actions constitute bullying and harassment, listing some of the more common forms. The procedure should have an informal and a formal stage, and both should be documented. It's important to make the process as painless as possible for the person who feels they have been harassed or bullied. It's also important to protect the identity of the alleged harasser.

The informal stage involves the person raising the issue with a senior colleague of their choosing. This person will then provide support to the individual. The informal process may involve the complainant telling the harasser how they feel either verbally or in writing. If the action doesn't stop, or the harassment is more serious, the formal process may be invoked.

It's the formal stage that triggers a full investigation, formal meetings and other action as discussed below.

When deciding whether a person has been bullied or harassed the manager hearing the case must decide if the action was intentional, and they must also consider if the complainant is overly sensitive and has taken unreasonable offence at a comment which may not actually constitute harassment. Whilst unusual, it has been known for employees to allege bullying and harassment when none has taken place. Such cases may then result in the complainant being disciplined.

7.6.4   Investigating bullying and harassment

It's not easy for someone to complain about harassment at work. It's even more difficult if the harassment is sexual. When someone makes a complaint, it must be investigated as quickly and as discreetly as possible. In many situations, it is likely that the person making the allegations will need to be separated from the alleged harasser. This may mean temporary redeployment of one of the parties, or suspension of the alleged harasser. Note that any suspension must be made with full pay and benefits – it is not a sanction.

The investigation must be thorough with information gathered from the complainant in a sensitive manner. It will be difficult for them to share what happened, but all the facts must be gathered for a fair decision to be made. Evidence gathered may include written documents, emails, and other media. Investigations follow the same format as discussed above. It remains, without saying, that they must be kept as confidential as possible and only shared with those who need to know.

7.6.5   Endemic cultures of bullying

Bullying and harassment takes many forms. Jibes, snide comments, exclusion, sexual innuendo, threatening behaviour, and physical and mental abuse are some common forms. Bullying and harassment is never acceptable. As mentioned, earlier attitudes have changed, but colleagues will still overstep the mark and abuse others - sometimes knowingly, other times by accident. Neither is acceptable.

As discussed above, the Equality Act 2010 and the Protection for Harassment Act 1997 provide protection to employees. So too does the Health and Safety at Work Act 1974. This places an onus of common law duty on the employer to ensure that the implied contractual term of trust and confidence is not breached. It's important to follow up all comments where someone suggests harassment or bullying has taken place.

7.7   The role of mediation

7.7.1   Defining mediation

Mediation is a voluntary process designed to resolve a dispute between two people. It usually involves an independent and impartial third-party to facilitate discussions. It's a tool open to managers when dealing with employees who are unable to resolve issues in the workplace.

7.7.2   The role of the manager

The manager is the best person to resolve workplace conflict if the two parties are unable to resolve the issue themselves. As discussed elsewhere in this book, the manager should be continually sensing what is going on with their employees. It should be apparent when employees are not getting on as well as they should. Behaviour will likely change, subtly at first, and then more overtly. This is when the manager should step in: a quiet word to ask if there are any issues; a watchful eye to ensure that the situation does not escalate. Hands-on managers can often diffuse situations quickly. As noted elsewhere – management is a contact sport!

Where minor issues are left to fester, they become bigger issues. Before too long a grievance has been raised and the situation takes far longer to resolve.

7.7.3   Selecting mediators

An impartial mediator works with the two parties to facilitate discussions. It's important that the mediator can be objective. They mustn't judge who is 'right' or 'wrong'. Their role is to facilitate discussions and develop a way forward.

Managers are free to manage and free therefore to select their own mediators. There is no qualification to be a mediator, unlike when mediation is used under the auspices of ACAS.

Often, it's best to have an external mediator, such as a consultant, to facilitate the discussions. The mediator will have confidential discussions with the two parties and must keep these discussions confidential. Any notes made about the meetings must only be shared with the relevant parties. They must not be disclosed to managers, or other employees, either verbally or in writing.

It is, however, acceptable to document the signed outcome agreement by both parties and place this on record.

7.7.4   The process of mediation

Mediation is a methodology for dealing with conflict of two parties within the workplace. There are several stages to mediation, and they follow a logical process as presented below.

- Setting the scene.
- Understanding the issues.
- Exploring the issues.
- Developing an agreement.
- Closing the process.

The agreement is generally best set out in a document. It can be a paragraph that says how the parties will work together and behave toward one another in the future, or it can be something more elaborate.

7.7.5   If mediation fails

Managers should have enough knowledge of their teams to recognise when there are issues. Informal discussions at an early stage are the best way to deal with conflict in the workplace. If mediation fails, or if a manager fails to act, the situation can quickly escalate.

Once people become entrenched in their analysis of the conflict, they are less likely to be amenable to mediation discussions. 'Digging in' and not being prepared to listen to the other person's viewpoint means that mediation will not work. Without the ability to have meaningful two-way dialogue, either face-to-face, or through an intermediary, there is no chance of gaining agreement between the parties. Employees and their manager are left with a single option: to raise a grievance or resort to the disciplinary procedure. Such an outcome will damage morale and commitment.

Where employees have issues that remain unresolved, their final option is to go to tribunal.

7.8   Practical disciplinary and grievance tools

7.8.1   *Suspension*

Sometimes the alleged actions of the employee may be so severe that suspension from work may be appropriate to allow an investigation to be undertaken. Suspension does not imply guilt and there must be no supposition of guilt at this stage. It should be used only in exceptional circumstances, for example, in suspected fraud, theft, severe intoxication, accusation of any form of racial or sexual harassment, and where criminal proceedings may follow.

Suspension would normally only be considered for allegations which fall within the category of gross misconduct.

Any period of suspension should be as short as possible and must be paid time off. All benefits remain in place too. Whilst paying wages during investigation may rile managers, it is what must happen. The suspension is not a disciplinary sanction. If payment or any other benefits are withheld, then disciplinary action has been taken before an investigation and formal meeting. This would likely be considered automatically unfair by a tribunal.

The firm must continue to communicate effectively with the accused employee during the period of suspension. Whilst the accused employee must be advised as to why they are being suspended, there is no need to divulge findings. Findings should be divulged in the invitation to the formal meeting that follows the investigation.

7.8.2   *Investigations*

According to ACAS the investigation step is not always needed. We caution that it is always good practice to go through the process of investigation even if the evidence against the employee is, on the face of it, compelling.

There are occasions where it will be appropriate for an informal investigation meeting to be held with the employee suspected of the inappropriate action. It is important to remember that this is an information gathering step and not a meeting which will result in disciplinary action or an accusation of guilt. This point must be made and recorded in the meeting minutes.

The investigation stage may also require information to be gathered from witnesses in a series of witness statements. Witness statements must be shared with the accused employee. The statements should be signed as a record of the facts based on what each witness believes to be true. The information in the statements will be used in the disciplinary meeting to suggest questions to elicit further information and will be used to inform a decision.

Sometimes the people giving information in witness statements will not wish to be identified because they feel there will be reprisals. Where it is deemed necessary, witness statements can be given anonymously. This must only be done as a last resort and only with good reason.

If an investigation meeting (as distinct from a disciplinary or performance improvement meeting) is to be held with the employee, they should be given adequate notice and time to prepare. It should be stressed in the invitation that this is an informal meeting to gather facts and that no decision will be made following the investigation meeting. There is no statutory right to have a companion at an investigation meeting. Whether or not someone is allowed to accompany the employee will depend on the firm's procedure.

7.8.3   *Processes in context*

Mangers should not consider the disciplinary or performance improvement meeting the end of the matter. As we noted, disciplinary and grievance processes can end up linked.

A disciplinary process is like a game and game theory applies. In game theory, the parties (manager and employee) 'play', basing their own actions on their prediction of the actions of the other. It is essential that the manager considers the various outcomes at each step and the actions that the accused employee might take. Take the following example.

- Round 1: employee is alleged to be under the influence of drugs at work and is to be disciplined. Employee is suspended pending investigation. Disciplinary meeting hands down a sanction of 'final written warning'. This is upheld at appeal.
- Round 2: employee responds with claim of breach of trust and confidence and instructs a solicitor to go for a case of constructive dismissal. Firm responds with 'we look forward to your return to work', since of course the sanction was only a final written warning and not dismissal.
- Round 3: employee goes off sick with work-related stress. Three months' absence follows with copious doctor's notes in support. The firm invokes independent medical review. The review supports the firm, suggesting that the employee's absence is unfounded.
- Round 4: employee claims her stress condition is covered by the Equality Act 2010. The employee's solicitor sets out a large financial settlement that his client would find acceptable in return for a Settlement Agreement. The firm maintains 'we look forward to your return to work' and holds its nerve.
- Round 5: employee and her solicitor realise futility and settle for contractual notice and a modest pay-off in return for a Settlement Agreement. Game over. Employee leaves.

Whilst this might appear a little extreme, it is a true case and shows where a simple disciplinary can end up. It is impossible to tell how disciplinaries might develop. In many cases, the employee returns to work normally and the issue is forgotten, and the transgression never repeated. In others the employee leaves voluntarily. But in many others the bitterness continues and one disciplinary spawns another.

7.8.4 *Practical sanctions*

Ultimately, assuming the employee is believed to be guilty of the alleged offence, the manager will issue some form of sanction to effect corrective action or to dismiss the employee from the firm.

The levels of permissible sanction will be determined by the firm's own procedures, or ACAS guidelines if no written procedure is in place. The following shows typical sanctions as the severity of transgression increases.

- Informal meetings to set objectives and resolve issues - no sanction permissible;
- Formal meeting – sanction of first written warning with objectives;
- Formal meeting – sanction of final written warning with objectives;
- Formal meeting – sanction of dismissal.

Sometimes verbal warnings are also given but this is just another form of written warning (since it must be advised to the employee in writing). It is often placed in order of severity below first written warning, effectively adding another step into the whole disciplinary process.

There is no requirement to work up through the levels, starting with informal, then first written, final written and then dismissal (unless the firm's procedure states otherwise). If the severity of the offence merits a sanction of dismissal, then the firm can move straight to that level. And the idea behind giving warnings is that if offences are repeated within a defined time, the process continues to the next level, with the employee moving ever closer to dismissal as a final sanction.

We urge all firms caution here. It is essential that firm's procedure is followed, and that the procedure spells out the way in which the offences, levels and sanctions will be used.

There is a range of sanctions that an Employment Tribunal would consider appropriate for a given offence. For example, whilst dismissal may be possible for the offence of being under the influence of drink or drugs at work, the tribunal may take a dim view if the firm moves straight to this sanction for a first offence, unless there is adequate justification. Simply, it does not do for managers to be heavy-handed.

Other sanctions are possible such as job change, reduction in pay and reduction in job responsibilities. Care is needed to ensure proportionality and that the firm has the ability within the contract of employment with the employee to take such action.

7.9 What to expect from a tribunal

7.9.1 *Early conciliation*

Employees make tribunal claims when they feel aggrieved about some aspect of their employment. Claims can be made within three months of the incident or the date of leaving employment.

Early conciliation describes attempts to resolve the dispute before it enters the tribunal system. An ACAS appointed conciliator will work with both parties to try to agree a settlement. This process is much quicker and cheaper than an employment tribunal. It also requires less management time and preparation than a tribunal.

7.9.2   *The tribunal process*

Unless an employee opts to use early conciliation, the first that an employer knows about a tribunal claim is when an ET1 arrives in the post. This is the document that the employee completes, making their claim to the tribunal. The manager responds with form ET3, putting the firm's case.

An ACAS conciliation officer will then attempt to mediate a settlement before the case goes to tribunal. If no agreement to settle can be reached, the case proceeds.

7.9.3   *Attempts to resolve before the tribunal decision*

It's possible to agree a settlement any time up to the point that the Tribunal Panel retires to determine their decision.

Settling does not admit any liability.

7.9.4   *Completing documents for the tribunal hearing*

It's important to provide as much information as possible in the ET3. The English ET3 (and the ET1) can be found on the government website. Evidence must be gathered and presented in a manner that allows the tribunal panel to clearly see the facts from the employer's viewpoint.

If the case is not settled by conciliation, then a document set will need to be developed for the tribunal. The 'bundle', as the document set is known, will need to be exchanged with the claimant ahead of the tribunal, at a date ordered by the tribunal. Likewise, the claimant must share their bundle with the employer. These are the documents that will be relied on in the tribunal hearing. Care must be given to the documents that you want to use in the bundle. They must be relevant and serve a purpose.

Often the bundle of documents can run to over 100 pages. The firm will need to provide several hardcopies of the bundle for the tribunal hearing.

7.9.5   *Judicial review*

All those giving evidence in the hearing will be required, as in any court, to swear that they are telling the truth before they give evidence and answer questions. The chair will ask questions as may other members of the panel. The claimant, or their representative, will also ask questions of the witnesses.

Once the case has been presented by both the claimant and the respondent, the panel will retire to determine their decision. Sometimes the panel's decision is given at the hearing, but generally it is advised by post after the hearing. In more complex cases the decision can take a few weeks.

7.9.6   *Preparing managers*

The employment tribunal is a legal process.

It's important that managers giving evidence understand what to expect. Each witness statement must stand up to the scrutiny of the claimant's representative – often a barrister. It's their job to question the statements made, the evidence and documents presented.

Without preparation, managers will be overwhelmed by the questioning that they get from the claimant's representative. We recommend that all those attending an employment tribunal on behalf of the firm are appropriately trained.

7.9.7 *Appointing counsel*

Whilst a manager can represent the firm in a tribunal claim, they are likely to face the legal representative for the claimant. It's unusual to find a claimant representing themselves. Solicitors, barristers and in particular employment lawyers are used to dealing with legal points of employment law. It's important to acknowledge this and consider appointing someone with experience to act as the firm's representative in the tribunal.

7.9.8 *Possible outcomes*

There are two outcomes. You win, or you lose.

As an employer, if you win, you will not be awarded any compensation. However, you can ask for costs to be awarded if the claimant has been vexatious in their claim.

If you lose, you may have to give the person their job back or pay compensation, pay witness expenses, and pay damages or loss of earnings. You will also be liable for the claimant's costs.

Where the employer disagrees with the outcome it is possible to appeal the decision. There needs to be a good reason for the appeal.

7.9.9 *Ranges of settlements*

If the claim against the employer is for discrimination, there is no limit to the amount of compensation that the tribunal can levy. In calculating an award, the tribunal will consider the financial loss of the employee resulting from the employer's action. This includes salary, pension, and other benefits. It may also include an amount for injury to feelings.

At the time of writing in October 2022, the maximum compensation award for unfair dismissal is a year's gross pay, capped at £93,878. Breach of contract claims are capped at £25,000.

If the tribunal determines that the employer is guilty of 'one or more aggravating features' they many also be required to pay a fine of up to 50% of the award, to a maximum of £5,000. This penalty is paid to the Secretary of State, not the claimant.

7.10 Chapter Summary

In this chapter on employing and managing people we centre on what's traditionally, in larger firms and governmental organisations, called 'HR'. Most employees have a poor view of HR, because it centres on corrective action of one sort or another. In so doing, it pitches the manager against the employee. Instead of cooperating in search of joint success, it portrays the employee as the bad guy – someone to be controlled and put back in their box.

But in the end, the employee has voluntarily 'come indoors' under a contract of service in return for a wage. The manager must work to ensure that the arrangement is successful for both. Ultimately, if that arrangement fails, the manager must act. The chapter outlines how.

We have described the nature of the employer-employee relationship, and from that, the manager-employee relationship. We illustrate that the relationship is described by two contracts. The first is an expressed contract of employment that is described part in statute and part in a written agreement. The second is unwritten. This second agreement exists in the minds of manager and employee. And, using the iceberg metaphor, we illustrate that this psychological contract is a whole lot more significant than the written and statutory economic contract.

The psychological contract relies on trust between the manager and employee – the very thing that the procedures and activities in the rest of the chapter challenge.

We highlight that the employee exists in a social entity – the firm. While the employees don't have to like one another or their manager, each employee must cooperate with their colleagues to do the manager's bidding. Each employee is under the direction of the manager. And various pressures stress those within-firm relationships. Problems that we see in society like bullying and harassment are often replicated in the firm. As a result, there must be some 'rule of law', some behavioural code in the firm and some process to allow manager and employee ultimate redress.

It's the manager's job to informally intervene to relieve stress in relationships. We describe that for many managers, this is the extent of their corrective activities. But from time to time the pressure is too great. Relationships break down and the manager must up the ante – they must invoke formal procedures in performance management, discipline, and grievance. We also describe that for other managers, this is the norm. Their lives revolve around running performance, disciplinary and grievance meetings, and that's sad.

Ultimately, all managers must at least understand the performance, disciplinary and grievance procedures. As a result, we describe the complete pathway from informal intervention through the escalation to formal procedures, and ultimately to legal redress at an Employment Tribunal.

If we do nothing else in this chapter, we hope that we convince readers of the benefits of putting in effort to manage informally. The content here is necessary, but managers should focus their attention on the other chapters of this book!

8
Developing People

8.1 The logic of staff development

8.1.1 *Development decisions*

Two questions define staff development. What is it that an employee presently knows, understands, and can do? And what is it that they need to know, understand and be able to do, to satisfactorily achieve the outcomes that their manager wants?

No employee has perfect capability. The difference between the manager's idea of perfect capability and the employee's real capability represents the development gap. For some employees, the shift needed will be considerable. For others, less so. And all other things being equal, the bigger the gap, the stronger the argument for development investment.

What's needed and how it's to be achieved, differs across jobs.

The 2017 London Grenfell Tower disaster, and the subsequent public enquiry, illustrated one shocking aspect of development – that in the case of firefighters and fire officers, their lack of training in some standard operating procedures precluded possible life-saving decisions and actions. The fire safety advice to residents in the blazing building to 'stay put' was rooted in national policy. Overriding that policy on-scene would have required commanders to have been trained in alternatives and for firefighters to have been trained in guiding casualties out of high-rise infernos. The commanders were not trained in alternatives and firefighters were not trained in evacuation and hence the 'stay put' policy with which they were familiar was sustained despite mounting real-time pressure to change. Real-time situation and problem analyses and evaluation of alternatives was not an option. Firefighters and commanders reported that they could only do what they'd been trained in.

Other highly regulated and controlled professions are similar. An electrician has little control over how they will implement solutions. Component parts are type tested as compliant with various standards and only approved components can be sold and used. What's done is substantially dictated in the Wiring Regulations from the IET, first published in 1882 and currently in its 18th Edition. And in England, Part P to the Building Regulations demands that work is tested, certificated, and registered. There's little scope in the electrician's job for deviation from those norms and operating procedures.

In both those cases above, what a jobholder needs to know and understand and what they must be able to do to achieve what the manager wants is clearly defined. If the employee can't achieve the standard of competencies and behaviours needed, they can't achieve the required performance and outcomes.

The job of manager is, on the other hand, neither regulated nor normalised. Anyone can be a manager and what a manager needs to know, understand and be able to do is negotiated between the manager and their firm. Likewise, a consultant advising government on wireless systems and how the wireless spectrum might be managed is free to use whatever analysis and reporting tools they are familiar with. They are free to use whatever analysis and reporting tools they feel are appropriate to support their arguments. What's used is between the consultant and their client and hence the client evaluates the consultant's competencies and behaviours when selecting who does the work.

In these latter two cases, if the employee can't achieve the standard needed, outcomes will be achieved, but to a lower level. Perhaps the manager's firm will make less profit. Perhaps the consultant's government client will gain less contribution to the nation's GDP from the wireless spectrum.

What a jobholder must know, understand and be able to do depends on the job. In regulated jobs, much is dictated and there's little incentive to excel – to exceed the standard. The measure of capability is compliance. In non-regulated jobs, nothing's set, and excellence is a variable.

Most jobs lie somewhere between these two extremes – norms do apply but there's scope for freedom. In many cases it's that freedom that creates opportunity for competitive advantage for the firm. Managers therefore have considerable choice about where on the capabilities continuum they want their employees to lie.

8.1.2   *Capability and required outcomes*

A firm's capability depends on the aggregation of all employee capabilities. Employee capability depends on the technology the employee is using and the competencies and behaviours they apply during its use.

This leads to the balance between human competence and technology function that we discussed in Chapter 4. The manager therefore has a choice – improve the technology that the employee is using, holding their competencies and behaviours fixed, or leave the technology as-is and improve their competencies and behaviours. And sometimes, of course, managers elect to do both to grow.

In this chapter, we're focussing on competencies and behaviours. Competencies and behaviours are the focus of all development. Behaviours are things people routinely do; like being pro-active, not waiting to be told to do things; or being punctual, attending everything on-time. These are not to be confused with behaviour resulting from motivation that we discuss in other chapters.

An employee has a competency if they possess the wherewithal to achieve something. Competency is the product of skills and knowledge. An employee only has a competency if they possess some skill and have some knowledge – neither can be zero. Skills also include understanding of a subject – not just knowing but being able to apply knowledge.

So, the net conclusion is that a competency is described by the ability of an employee to understand, know and be able to do. And all competencies assume that the employee will make use of some defined technologies.

8.1.3   *Can't do versus won't do*

We noted elsewhere that there are behaviours resulting from motivation and behaviours existing as part of the employee's personal characteristics.

We need to be very clear about the difference between the two – since that difference will drive different management action. If an employee 'won't do' because they are for some reason not motivated, it's for the manager to find the reason for the lack of motivation and effect some management intervention. This might involve adjusting the employee's job, taking some leadership action, or attending to the culture in the employee environment.

If, on the other hand, an employee can't do because they lack the skills and knowledge, self-efficacy, or habitual activities, it's time to develop the person by effecting corrective action. In this latter case, the manager needs to move them from 'can't do' to 'can do' by development.

8.1.4   *Business case for developing employees*

The benefits of developing employees must exceed the costs. It's that simple.

But of course, what we put in the cost and benefit sides of the equation depend on the firm's situation. Benefits are often easily quantified using the firm's key performance indicators like increased turnover. When considering costs, the manager needs to count lost opportunity – for example, the opportunity cost of not developing a salesperson to close deals is counted in fewer deals closed and lower turnover.

There are four big reasons why firms might want to develop – beyond the simple plugging of gaps in skills and knowledge.

8.1.4.1   *Developing to stand still*
The environment within and around all firms is constantly changing. Clients and customers change their needs, competitors rise and fall, government interferes in industries, suppliers change their offers and employees come and go. People development is one of many tactics that managers have in their repertoire to keep the firm functioning. It's not about development to improve. It's about development to stand still.

8.1.4.2   *Developing to grow*
Shareholders are motivated to risk their financial capital in the hope of returns later when they sell the firm. That means that most managers are expected to grow their firm.

Growth means increased capability. Even if growth comes from more of the same, it's rare for a firm to do that with the same employees with the same competencies, unless technology makes up the difference. Development aims to grow employees to grow the firm.

8.1.4.3   *Developing as an employee benefit*
Employees expect to be invested in. It's one of the arms of the psychological contract and it's particularly strong with Generation Y employees. So, development is in effect part of employee total reward. The size of this benefit depends on the competitive pressures felt by the firm in the labour market when it tries to recruit specific skills and knowledge. Development is therefore an employee benefit.

8.1.4.4   *Developing to exploit opportunity*
Paraphrasing Louis Pasteur, the famous scientist, "Opportunity favours the prepared mind", and in business, opportunity favours the prepared firm. Many managers recognise

that they need to be prepared, but as the hyenas in Disney's The Lion King famously quipped, "For what?" And there lies the issue.

Development to be able to exploit future unknown opportunities requires managers to develop a favoured future possible scenario and determine the competencies and behaviours needed in that. The scenario may not be the one that plays out, but the firm will certainly be better prepared for the future than if it did nothing.

8.1.5   Development benefits

Competencies are the skills and knowledge that allow employees to understand, know and do useful things. Behaviours are the employee's habitual and normally available activities that aid those competencies. Given those definitions, the benefits are the business outcomes when those competencies and behaviours are available to the firm over the state when they are not.

Of course, for outcomes, those competencies and behaviours must be converted to performance – but that's another story, and we discussed that in Chapter 5.

8.2   The language of development

8.2.1   Development driving performance improvement

In Chapter 5 we illustrated the flow that exists in every employee from job to performance and on to personal outcomes. The diagram from this discussion is repeated here in Figure 8-1 for convenience.

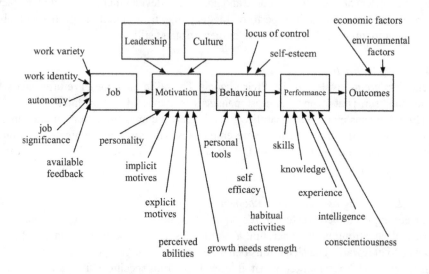

Figure 8-1: The flow from job to performance and outcomes

Under the headline of 'development', the manager has ability to change an employee's explicit motives, perceived abilities, personal tools, self-efficacy, habitual activities, skills, knowledge, experience and locus of control. Positive changes in any of these variables positively influence the conversion of motivation to outcomes. These and other variables are defined below.

8.2.2   *Performance*

Performance is one of the most difficult variables to define. It requires reference to two key documents: the job description (which defines what's wanted from the job and how the job contributes to the firm's strategy), and the objectives that have been agreed between employee and manager from time to time.

The job description must define the key responsibilities or accountabilities of the job. As we note in Chapter 6, these must be defined in the form, 'do something, to something, to achieve a result'. The result defines the outcome. What's to be done defines the required performance. What's to be done is then made specific and current by agreed objectives.

8.2.3   *Excellence*

Typically, the definition of performance centres on compliance: the jobholder meets the required outcomes by realising the required performance. There is no scope under this definition for the jobholder to exceed expectation. If the objective was to build the bridge, and the jobholder built the bridge, then the jobholder has performed and achieved the agreed outcomes.

But so often, objectives are defined in terms of other variables like time and budget. Achieving objectives in less than the allocated time and budget, for example, is greatly beneficial for the firm. Exceeding expectations repeatedly suggests that the jobholder is capable of excellence.

Managers need to decide how they will define performance – is it sufficient to meet requirements or do managers strive for excellence in all. Significant development and manager energy is needed for employees to rise to excellence.

8.2.4   *Competency*

We defined competency above as the ability of an employee to understand, know and be able to do. And all competency assumes that the employee will make use of some defined technology. We noted that competency is the product of skills and knowledge.

In academia, there is some debate about whether competency is an expression of the possible or a statement of the actual. We define competency as an expression of the possible. It becomes actual if the employee is motivated, and if their motivation is allowed to cause the necessary behaviour when moderated by leadership and culture.

8.2.5   *Behaviour*

Behaviour is in two parts: activity resulting from the employee's motivation, and activity which the employee routinely demonstrates. The latter is a personal characteristic and can be developed. Because some behaviours, as personal characteristics, are dependent on personality, implicit motives, and intelligence, they are more difficult to change than others. Some are also encouraged or constrained by the culture of the environment in which the employee works. Pro-activity, for example, can easily be supressed by crass management.

8.2.6 *Experience*

Experience is useful in encouraging the development of an employee's perceived abilities and self-efficacy. Both stem from the employee knowing that they have what it takes to perform. That confidence suggests to them that repeating behaviours will again lead to performance. Both set up a reinforcing loop: the more experience, the greater the confidence.

Confidence through experience helps overcome the emotional fear of failure that commonly blocks employee action.

8.2.7 *Intervention*

We have a strong dislike of the term 'training'. It has connotations of the traditional lecture where a subject matter expert imparts knowledge. Typically, training has very low efficiency.

Intervention, on the other hand, describes all possible efforts by the manager to effect development – including training, but extending to tools such as job change, coaching and simulated work.

It is for the manager to select the right intervention to cause the required development.

8.2.8 *Training transfer*

Despite our dislike of 'training', the norm in academia is to measure the effectiveness and efficiency of development using the metric 'training transfer'. Literally, this is the quantity of knowledge and skills imparted (by way of the intervention) compared with the quantity later effectively applied on the job. Traditional classroom training effectiveness can be as low as 12%.

8.3 The competencies and behaviours needed

8.3.1 *Using strategy as driver*

Arguably all development should flow from strategy. A simple but useful form of strategy expression cited earlier is the form, *'Because A has a problem with B, we reckon that if we do C to D, we'll achieve outcome E'*. The idea of doing C to D to produce the outcome E parallels the job description accountability form of 'doing something, to something, to achieve a result'.

But what if the firm can't 'do C'? What if its salespeople can't write bids to convince clients in a new market segment to buy? What if their installation technicians can't install the newly developed software?

Strategy depends on capability. If capability is lacking, strategy will not be achieved, and development must be invoked. Strategy requires capability. Capability requires skills and knowledge. Skills and knowledge gaps potentially demand development.

8.3.2   *Constructing jobs from the concept model*

Capability in each of the many functions can be modelled using the concept modelling technique outlined in Chapter 1. Take the example where the firm needs capability in product development and has set the strategy to develop a new software product. The firm will either have the capability to do this, or it won't. If it hasn't, the manager faces a decision: to make or buy. The manager must develop the capability by implementing new technology and associated competencies and behaviours or go into the market to buy this capability from a supplier. If the manager decides to 'make', this demands that one or more jobs are identified to realise this capability. Existing jobholders may have to be developed and new employees hired.

Concept modelling, exploring the various concepts that are to make the firm work, is a powerful way of linking strategy to jobs and from jobs to job accountabilities and on to competencies and behaviours.

8.3.3   *Institutional and organisational standards*

We noted above that many jobs are regulated. This gives rise to standards for competencies and behaviours demanded by institutions external to the firm (such as the IET). Likewise, standards develop across the labour market and ad hoc definitions for jobs such as 'software developer' result. With those come norms of competencies and behaviours. And to compare jobs internally, groups of managers within the firm come to agree internal standards.

There are many examples of external standards. There are membership qualifications of professional institutions such as the Institute of Chartered Accountants in England and Wales, the Institution of Mechanical Engineers, or the BMA (the British Medical Association). And there are norms like the NOS – the National Occupational Standards. The NOS was developed by two quasi-governmental bodies to specify a set of UK standards of competencies and behaviours that employees are expected to have in many common jobs. Jobs defined include, for example, care workers, sports coaches, and probation officers.

In Figure 8-2 there are some examples of competencies and behaviours in one National Occupational Standard for marketing in a logistics firm. In this example, the accountability of "Carry out market analysis and research to develop new markets in logistics operations", there are 34 competencies and behaviours needed. Considering that each person likely has five accountabilities, this leads to something like 100 competencies and behaviours per person, allowing for some overlap.

You must be able to:	Define and agree the marketing objectives of the logistics organisation to develop sales and distribution to new UK and international markets.
	Carry out research and analysis of the new markets identified as being available to the organisation and quantify the size of the opportunity.
	Evaluate the market potential for the organisation within identified markets, given the logistics resource.
You need to know and understand:	The indicators of market potential to be considered including geographic characteristics, economic, cultural and technological factors.
	Different ways of entering markets, and the implications and risk for commitment to a particular market.
	The potential for control and profitability, including exporting, importing, joint ventures and direct investment.

Figure 8-2: Example competencies and behaviours

8.3.4   *Determining what development is needed*

There are two approaches to determining needs for competencies and behaviours. Firstly, there are needs in pursuit of norms and externally determined performance such as those set for jobs in the fire service and for electricians. Secondly, there are needs set by the firm's strategy. What's needed is usually a mix of the two.

8.3.5   *Standardised method for determining need*

Whether competencies and behaviours are to be set locally or adopted through norms is not material. What matters is that there is a process by which it's done. Managers need a list of competencies and behaviours and a note against each about the degree to which they must be held by each jobholder.

Some years ago, Dave Bartram, then of the SHL Group, standardised the competencies needed in a firm into eight: he postulated that whilst one might be able to state a hundred or more, these could be boiled down to a small number. He defined those Great 8 competencies and we set those out in Figure 8-3 below. Each competency is scored on a scale of 1 to 10 with 1 at the centre of the figure scoring low and 10 at the outer ring scoring high.

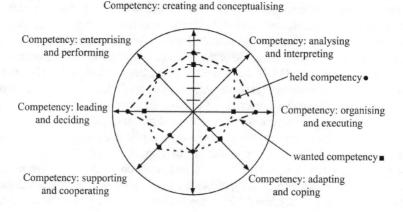

Figure 8-3: Bartram's Great 8 competencies

Assessment of the competencies held by each employee (the held competency) versus those needed by the job (the wanted competency) gives the competency development gap. A difference indicates that the manager might need to act.

8.3.6   *Defining the necessary mastery*

Knowledge and skill can be held at various levels. Someone early in their career will need help to build a client presentation, for example. They will be a trainee. Someone who has undertaken training and has significant experience will be more of an expert.

This idea that the same competency is held at different levels links well to the position of candidates in the labour market, to the salary and benefits expected by a suitable jobholder, and ultimately to age and experience. It also links to the idea of career and progression. Everyone starts as a trainee and develops.

We recommend use of the following four levels for each competency:

- Trainee: A Trainee has sufficient foundation skills, knowledge and understanding to allow them to contribute to the activity, though their work will be closely supervised.
- Supervised Practitioner: A Supervised Practitioner has sufficient skill, knowledge and understanding to be able to work without placing an excessive burden on the Practitioner or Expert supervising their work.
- Practitioner: A Practitioner has sufficient skill, knowledge and understanding to be able to take responsibility for deliverables. They will be able to work without the need for detailed supervision.
- Expert: An Expert will understand why things are done in particular ways. They will lead others in the development of methods. They will have sufficient technical and managerial skills to take responsibility for the performance of a capability.

In any firm, and for any competency, we might expect that about 60% of the workforce will be Supervised Practitioners. They will be led day to day by Practitioners (25% of the workforce). To keep a good flow of new employees, some 10% will be trainees. And all will be led overall by Experts (5% of the workforce). Each will hold their portfolio of competencies at different levels. Supervised Practitioners will be Experts in one or two competencies and even Experts will be Trainees in some competencies.

The numbers of Trainees, Supervised Practitioners, Practitioners and Experts in a firm will depend a lot on the nature of its market, the technology used and the way the managers and employees are organised.

8.4   Matching the needs of career and job

8.4.1   *The notion of employee careers*

All staff have a career: a sequence of employment-related experiences enjoyed over a working life of about 40-50 years. Both employee and manager hope that, at least for the employee's present tenure, they can work together for mutual benefit. The extant manager is therefore taking a relatively small part in the employee's career.

Employees seek a sense of meaningfulness that comes from employment. That employment must interest them, and they must be competent in it. And whether managers participate actively or not, employees will develop their careers. The only issue for managers is how best to intervene in employees' careers for optimum mutual benefit.

8.4.2   *Today's careers*

In the 70s and 80s, and even into the 90s, many employees joined a firm following education or foundation training and expected to stay with that firm for their working lives. With the loosening of the labour market after the Thatcher years, the jobs available changed. Today, very roughly, a quarter of the working population work for large firms, a quarter work for the Government (in central or local government or in a quango or government supplier), a quarter work for small to medium sized enterprises, and a quarter work for themselves as employees in their own firm supplying services to others.

It's now not uncommon for someone to start their career with a large firm, be made redundant and 'go contracting' and then end with several medium-term stints with small firms. Any mix, of any term, including complete changes from engineer to teacher or from banker to software developer are quite normal. This unsettled career pattern is termed Protean – after Proteus, the Greek god of the sea and of change.

8.4.3   Conflict between needs and wants

Government statistics suggest that as few as 30% of staff in UK organisations are happy with the opportunities available with their employer for career and progression. Given that employee commitment depends for a large part on employees feeling that they have a future with the firm, this suggests that most employees are uncommitted.

Whilst commitment can be built in many ways, the core reason for this poor state perhaps has its roots in UK shareholders' short-term expectations. After all, why would you invest in staff and put effort into their careers if you expected the firm's owners to sell up in a couple of years?

This low staff commitment is further exacerbated by the fact that suppliers (often termed contractors, freelancers, or associates) today fill many jobs, including management roles. Relying on suppliers can only be a costly and short-term fix but it fits well with the shareholder short-term view. It fits with the present-day disinclination to invest in people.

8.4.4   So, who develops the people?

Managers' disinclination to invest in people comes also from a popular myth circulating in the press that employee tenure is dropping – that there's increased inclination to voluntarily seek new employment after a couple of years with a firm. Then, if employees are not intent on staying, why would managers want to develop them?

The claim that tenure is dropping is just not true. Despite the protean nature of careers, recent reports suggest that in the UK, the average employee tenure with any one employer is just over eight years. The figure has been substantially static for the past 20 years and there is no real downward trend.

Tenure does vary with age but even millennials' average tenure is around six years. Some 60% will likely stay longer. Employees are most likely to leave if they are not developed. Development therefore makes sense to all.

As a manager, your attitude to development must depend on the nature of your business, the value you place in your staff and their uniqueness, and not on myth. Your attitude must depend on the contribution of different staff types to your competitive advantage.

8.4.5   Attitude by worker type

Different types of workers have differing value to the firm. The four types – knowledge workers, foot-soldiers, specialists, and contractors/suppliers – are characterised by their value to the firm and their uniqueness in the labour market. This is summarised in Figure 8-4 below. Your approach as manager should depend on this or some other reasoned characterisation.

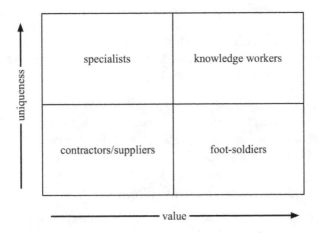

Figure 8-4: Characterising employees by value and uniqueness

Firstly, if you employ what's termed 'knowledge workers' you'll want to bring them close to you, give them varied work and show them a perceived career path. They're both highly valued and unique in the labour market. Those staff are your algorithm developers, research chemists and design engineers who give the organisation the bulk of its competitive advantage through unique methods and other intellectual property. They are people who have specialist skills and knowledge, and you will use them to secure your future.

For those knowledge workers, you'll want to give them ever increasing work scope and complexity. Your role in managing them is simple. You'll want to intensify their knowledge, grow their skills, and encourage them to gain greater experience of all aspects of your firm. They need comprehensive development plans, career coaching and perhaps funded academic studies. You'll want to invest, and they'll expect that.

Secondly, if you employ staff that are not unique in the employment market but are key to your future – or at least key now – you'll want to build a sound relationship. These are your foot soldiers – your bookkeepers, claims handlers and mechanics.

The relationship with foot soldiers must be good for both parties. That doesn't mean investing in their future but investing to exploit them – and they you. They'll want deepened and broadened experience in your firm in readiness for their next job. Your role is to understand their needs and make opportunities for both parties for as long as they are with you.

Thirdly, there's a group of non-permanent staff that are unique in the labour market but are not key to your future. They are perhaps in peripheral specialist roles like legal counsel, market sector advisers and subject matter experts. You need their skills and knowledge for what they are today, and you need to build an alliance with them.

This group will likely be part-time and employed by or contracting to others too. They don't expect you to invest in them – they'll do that themselves. They need to know the high value you place in them, and that the relationship will endure. Your role is to pay them well and allow them to expand their contribution.

And fourthly, if you employ contractors/suppliers or agency workers, you will engage them for the skills and knowledge they bring. You shouldn't expect to invest and will simply terminate one supplier and hire another if their skills and knowledge fall short. This extends to anyone who provides their services through an intermediary, even if that intermediary is their own firm. It includes osteopaths, personal trainers, IT technicians and software coders.

Your role is to pay them well such that they can take time off to maintain their continuous personal development. Because they will not be growing with your firm and their tenure will be more volatile, you must control, standardise, and secure their work through dictated methods.

Finally, you will of course need to bring all skills and knowledge of all employees and workers in line with the technology that they use. You have no option in that – failure to train on company processes and tools will degrade quality and productivity regardless of employee or worker classification.

8.4.6   *Supporting career changes within the firm*

There's a general belief that employees must move up to make progress. But in an SME, that's rarely possible. Modern SMEs have quite flat structures and opportunities to move 'up' are few.

As a result, it's often assumed that ambitious employees in SMEs must leave their present firm to advance.

Often managers don't accept that employees have transferrable skills – and that employees can develop to take on new roles. There's an assumption, for example, that if the business needs a salesperson, an engineer could never do that successfully. Or there's the assumption that someone from the shop floor just hasn't got what it takes to succeed in accounts. These assumptions are flawed. Skills are often transferrable, and staff can be developed.

Progress must also be re-defined on a personal level. It's the taking on of greater responsibility, making greater contribution to the business and gaining greater personal achievement. Some commentators also say that it's generally 'moving closer to the business', signified by inward movement on a circular spiral model. Key staff on which the business depends are conceptually at the centre of the spiral.

With that re-definition, development, to move employees ever closer to the firm, makes sense to all.

Reflection 8-1: About your attitude to staff development

Using a matrix of the form shown in Figure 8-4, think about each of the people that work for you - employees, contractors/suppliers, and specialist suppliers. Characterise each and place them in the appropriate box. Think through our suggestion for your attitude towards each. Is this appropriate, and how might you change this model and the boxes in which each now sits? And therefore, what will your attitude be to development of each person? What development action will you take?

8.5   The development process

8.5.1   *Progress from need to satisfaction*

The question is always, "how". How does a manager realise that they have a need for development, coming from organisational strategy? How does the manager lay development plans? How does the manager do it - what practical steps does the manager take? How long will development take? And ultimately, how successful will it all be in realising the outcomes wanted?

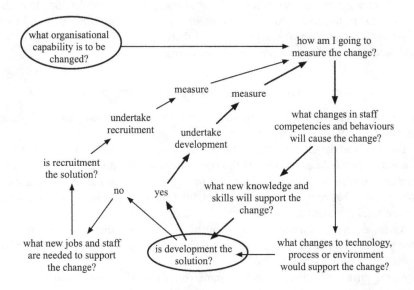

Figure 8-5: Managerial thought process of development

In Figure 8-5, we illustrate the thought process needed.

Ultimately, strategy requires some performance change. Strategy is always the starting point. The key question is whether the desired strategy can be achieved by development of existing staff or whether new staff must be hired. Either way, new competencies and behaviours are needed. And both routes may involve using new technology or somehow with people and technology organised in a different way.

Whether, ultimately, the planned changes will lead to success will depend on how the manager engages with the process. The manager must define in detail what's needed and assess the chance of success, given the investment and existing capability. There's clearly a risk of failure – but given a requirement to change, doing nothing is not an option.

8.5.2   *Building personal competency frameworks*

A personal competency framework requires the manager to develop a small number of principle accountabilities for the job holder's job description. Usually, five or six accountabilities is sufficient.

The manager must then ask for each accountability, "What competencies (and behaviours) are essential for each of my job holders to succeed in their job". We discuss in other chapters how objectives, developed from time to time, modify the job description accountabilities. Objectives provide specifics and must also be considered since it will often be the objectives that require additional competencies and behaviours over and above those tested for when the job holder was hired.

Figure 8-3 illustrates the idea of competencies wanted and competencies held. The difference between the two should then be discussed with the job holder and a plan implemented to develop the job holder to bridge the gaps.

If there are few competencies and behaviours, a radial model like that shown in Figure 8-3 can be used. Otherwise, a tabular form, perhaps using MS Excel will be needed. The personal competency framework should then be owned by the employee and they should build and own the resulting development plan.

8.5.3   Building organisation-wide competency frameworks

Building an organisation-wide competency framework satisfies the manager's need to set out in one place all the intended changes.

The aim is to develop a statement of the competencies and behaviours needed by the firm against those held at present. At the corporate level, the number at each level in each competency can be stated. In essence, the manager is stating that if that number of job holders possess that competency at that level, the firm will meet its corporate objectives. If not, there's development to be done.

Again, a gap indicates a development need – it's just that this time, there will be several people with the same gap. Figure 8-6 shows the sort of form the organisation-wide competency framework might take.

An organisation-wide competency framework for a 50-person organisation developed as part of a consulting project had 72 rows describing 18 discrete competencies, each held by various job holders at one of four levels. Each competency statement was rich and contained around five sub-competencies. Each differed and described specific abilities according to the level.

Title	Competency	Source of requirement	Level	Number needed at level	Number at level	Gap	Names, job titles and planned development
	Ability to...	Policy... Strategy...	Expert				
			Practitioner				

Figure 8-6: Example organisation-wide competency framework

In an organisation with many different complex roles, there may be many more competencies than in the above example. At the corporate level, however, numbers would be less than those at the personal level. Keeping an overview perspective avoids complicating the task.

8.5.4 *The continuum of development*

Development is continuous. The process demands that the manager assesses current capability, projects the capability required in the future and determines necessary interventions. We discussed the application of the feedback control loop in other chapters, and this is used continually to ask, "are we there yet?" Once competencies and behaviours meet those considered necessary just now, the process begins again with revised strategy as the firm grows.

8.6   The concept of talent management

The approaches so far illustrate who and what to develop. The approaches so far have been at the granular level of competencies – held now and needed for the future. Talent management is an approach to development that looks at employees as a block, suggesting which groups, characterised in a particular way, might be invested in, according to their potential.

8.6.1 *Who and what is talent?*

Many firms operate multi-tier development schemes, and indeed we discuss this in Section 8.4.5. It makes sense to target development funds to where they will have greatest effect. Within this context, 'talent' is everyone – but not everyone gets the same opportunities. Opportunity is job and person specific.

Some define talent management as, "Ensuring that the firm has the right person (with the right competencies and behaviours) in the right job, always". This is a very good high-level guiding definition. 'Always' gives a time dimension that engages with the idea that everything in the firm is changing. It conjures ideas about dynamic management of staff competencies, creating and filling vacancies like electrons jumping from hole to hole like a current flowing along a conductor. With this definition, everyone in the firm is 'talent'. Holes are continually being created and filled.

Ultimately, it's for the manager to determine their approach and to elect where to put development resources.

The following model describes a way of thinking about the dynamic nature of talent management.

8.6.2 *The talent management process*

The essence of talent management is pigeon-holing employees in categories according to their competencies and their resulting performance. The combination is useful because it deals with the problem that some employees may have high competencies but, because of low motivation, may be exhibit low performance. The model in Figure 8-7 shows the four possibilities.

The percentages in each category are those generally found. Some 60% of the workforce might be considered 'talent' with high performance and low, but adequate, competencies.

Those considered 'talent' are conceivably open to development to 'top talent', though as we noted earlier, this group might also be thought of as foot soldiers, and as a result all will be valued for their current skills and knowledge with only a few developed further.

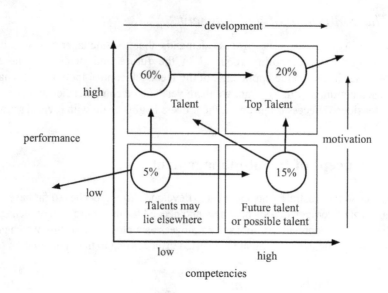

Figure 8-7: The four-box model of talent management

Those in top talent are most vulnerable to quitting, and as such must have the greatest investment to convince them of the benefits of long tenure. It will take management action (as opposed to development) to cause those who might be 'future talent' to recognise their opportunities. And those whose 'talents may lie elsewhere' might indeed be encouraged to quit – or be motivated to perform or be developed.

To work the model, the manager must assess each employee's competencies and their performance.

8.6.3   *Centralised talent management*

Talent management relies on data being available on each employee's competencies and performance. This places in sharp focus the performance appraisal system, objective setting, and day-to-day objectives management processes.

Of course, any one manager may not have oversight of everyone. As a result, many talent management systems are managed centrally and are combined with succession planning. In this case, a committee of managers might meet every six months or so to discuss the overall achievement of the competency framework and development plans and to discuss who is in the various talent categories.

Given a dynamic business environment, employees are identified by this committee for development and job change. Talent management and succession planning committees are the drivers of change. Generally, such systems work well, but committees do run the risk of nepotism. If all employees are to be treated fairly, committee members must be objective and non-parochial, always acting in the firm's best interests.

If talent management is defined as 'having the right person in the right job, always', talent must be managed. Talent management, as an overarching topic, embraces the shaping of the staff body in response to the long-term strategy of the firm.

Reflection 8-2: About your talent management

Considering the people in your firm, pigeon-hole each person into the four boxes – top-talent, talent, future talent, talents lie elsewhere. Are you happy with this classification? What percentage of the workforce are in each box?

How can you apply the thinking of motivation and development to move employees from one box to another? And how do you think employees will react?

8.7 Practical development interventions

In choosing an intervention, the manager must believe that it will cause the required behaviour or competency change. The intervention must be right, given the personal characteristics of the employee, and given their preferred learning method. People learn in different ways: by rote, socially, by trial and error, by rehearsal and practice, through understanding, by exercising models, or by following someone's example.

The following gives an overview of seven clearly distinct intervention types.

8.7.1 *Self-directed learning*

In many high-cognition, high-innovation, knowledge-oriented jobs, the job holders will effectively teach themselves what's needed. Indeed, often in those cases, there are few others in the world who could instruct them – and those are in competitor firms.

Those employees focussing on self-directed learning need to learn how to learn. Once that's done, they need to be tasked through the job description and objectives to seek out and read, discuss with peers, and use their new knowledge.

In this case, learning is facilitated by funding knowledge resources such as journals and academic papers. Learning is then enabled by allowing time to read and to discuss the learning with others as it progresses.

8.7.2 *Effective instruction*

Where employees must apply knowledge and understanding, there can often be no better way than to combine rehearsal and practice with instruction from a subject matter expert.

Take learning to solder electronic components in a circuit board. The principles can be taught in a classroom – about the temperature of solder, the tinning process, the purpose of flux and the need to have the solder flow. Then most people will need to be shown – to have effective instruction by a subject matter expert. The instructor would perhaps show how to tell if the joints are sound, and what to look for in a bad joint. In the end though, the only way to find out if your joints are of good quality is to do it – again and again – and to have your joints tested for their mechanical strength and electrical conductance until every joint is perfect.

Typically, effective instruction is done in a special school that mixes tuition and experience.

8.7.3 Computer-based training

There's an understandable belief that computers are the future in development. In part, it's true. They have their place because they offer techniques not available in other tools. Since a lecture can be built as a video and watched, computers can replace the subject matter expert and lecturer. Of course, there's no ability to ask questions, but when lectures are given in real-time as webinars, students can message the tutor and answers can be delivered to all.

Since the computer lecture can be interrupted and resumed at any time, various activities can be interleaved with the lecture delivery to test understanding. Answers can be scored, and the lecture dynamically adjusted to the student's abilities.

The teaching of facts can also be mixed with evaluation and analysis of information. This extension is common in university tuition. Assessments can be run by completing reading and interactive tests, and assignments can be set and dispatched for external marking.

And since computer-based applications can be run and re-run, activities can be repeated for little cost until the competency is mastered.

8.7.4 Simulated work

The advent of the computer, combined with innovation in mechanical devices such as motors and servos has given rise to the development of simulators.

The most common simulator is the flight simulator, where a would-be pilot sits in a chair within a synthetic cockpit in front of synthetic instruments and controls. The whole simulator moves and responds to the environment much like its real counterpart and the student can take off, fly, and land by doing what they will need to do in real life.

Simulators come into their own to develop employee skills, particularly where the business environment is hostile and where a mistake during training could have a fatal outcome. The list of applications includes mines clearance, tank entry, building evacuation, combat flying and keyhole surgery.

8.7.5 Traditional classroom training

Traditional classroom training – sitting in a class with others with the same learning need, listening to a teacher or lecturer – constitutes perhaps the largest part of the training industry. During classroom training, the students will be asked to reflect on what's said, on exercises they do and on the discussions that they've had with others.

The learning is primarily to enable understanding. The tutor has greater understanding and is tasked with transferring this understanding to the students.

Derogatorily, classroom teaching is all-too-often derided as 'death by PowerPoint', as the lecturer puts up slides one after the other. It's no surprise that this form of development has a low training transfer.

8.7.6 One-on-one interventions

Simply, one person can influence the way another behaves. Managers can coach and mentor their employees.

In coaching, the coachee has all the necessary task-related skills and knowledge, but somehow the context-related competencies and behaviours are lacking – the employee should be able to do but can't. The coach is not a subject matter expert and contributes nothing to the employee's skills and knowledge. Coaching can change the employee's belief in themselves. The result can be a change in performance, using the skills and knowledge and overcoming blockage.

In mentoring, the mentee does not have the skills and knowledge and the manager as mentor imparts this in one-to-one sessions, while also discussing experiences and reflections. Mentoring is particularly relevant in management development where the mentor is a peer with whom to discuss possible management interventions and resulting outcomes. The mentee then makes decisions on what action to take.

8.7.7   Evolved opportunities

Managers can learn to manage in their own firm, but often, being seconded to another has a much greater effect. Working in a new, unfamiliar environment, the manager's senses are attuned, and emotions are more intense. This idea of taking on other experiences is well established. This often extends to the outdoors, undertaking activities in the mountains and on the sea and to secondments to other departments and group firms.

The idea is also linked with other development opportunities. If succession planning demands that an employee gets marketing experience, what better way than to have them spend time in a marketing group or have them take responsibility for marketing in a smaller firm.

8.8   Getting good at development

The whole point about development is to improve the competencies and behaviours within the firm, given the firm's technology, organisation, and environment. The premise is that if employees are not developed, the firm will not achieve its strategy. The premise is also that if the manager is not intent on developing their staff, they will have to take other action, such as investing in technology or buying in new competencies.

8.8.1   Overarching approach and method

Getting good at development involves embracing the various processes. First the manager must determine the competencies and behaviours held by each person today. Then they must determine from the strategy, the competencies and behaviours needed tomorrow. The difference is the gap and that's the motivation for development action.

Success in development is then about selecting the right form of development for the person and required outcomes. Part of this decision process is the selection of an intervention in line with its position on a hierarchy of expectation taken from Benjamin Bloom's taxonomy of skills shown in Figure 8-8.

This is simply understood. If an intervention centres on teaching understanding, it shouldn't be used to expect a change in the employee's competencies and behaviours in evaluation. Evaluating is significantly above understanding in the hierarchy and such an intervention would fail to make the change.

The higher up the hierarchy, the more energy it takes to successfully make competency and behaviour changes. Each competency and behaviour requirement and the intended development tool should lie at the same level. A requirement for analysis should be matched by a tool that centres on teaching analysis. And it may also be that the employee will need to be developed in remembering, understanding, and applying before making the jump to conquer analysis. If the foundation is missing, the high-level intervention will fail.

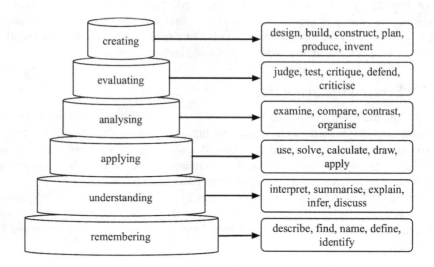

Figure 8-8: Hierarchy of expectation

8.8.2 *Measuring successful development*

Measuring success is nebulous. Ultimately all that matters is whether the required competencies and behaviours are achieved and hence if the employee exhibits the required new capability.

Most development is measured using what's derogatorily termed 'happy sheets' centring on the degree to which the employee enjoyed the intervention – on what they thought at the end of the intervention. The assertion is that if they enjoyed it, it is likely to have been successful in changing competencies and behaviours. That assertion is flawed.

A significantly better approach is shown in Figure 8-9 which shows four areas of inquiry.

The poorest method of judging success comes from sensing the reaction of the employee to the intervention. Judging reaction is easy. It's better, though, to assess what new skills and knowledge are now employed in the work. But it's not very effective since new skills and knowledge may be held but not applied. What matters is if the new skills and knowledge stimulate improved behaviour. For that, the manager must engage with the employee's work. That's good, of course, but ultimately what really matters is what changes there are to business outcomes. And that may take time to realise.

impact on business outcomes	ask: what measurable organisational impacts are evident as a result of the intervention
apparent behaviour change	ask: to what extent have the employees changed their behaviour in the workplace as a result of the intervention
learning achieved	ask: to what extent have the skills and knowledge changed as a result of the intervention
reaction of employee	ask: to what extent did the employees find the intervention useful

(left axis, bottom-to-top: increasing benefit to the business → ; increased effort needed to judge →)

Figure 8-9: Ways of assessing the benefit of interventions

At the bottom of the table, the measure is close to the employee – but poor in judging development success. At the top of the table, the measure is far from the employee (and now confused with other variables) – but change to business outcomes is exactly what the manager needs.

Judging development success is not easy but it's something the manager must engage with if return on investment is to be argued.

8.8.3 *Optimising training transfer*

We noted above that the metric used to assess the utility of an intervention is its training transfer. Fundamentally, all development must transfer experiences during the intervention to action in the workplace.

There is a universal approach that is considered essential for all interventions. This considers that each intervention should have three steps.

First, the employee should understand why they are engaging with the intervention. They should know the intention, and buy in to that, committing to give their best efforts and dedication. This can be done often with a little pre-intervention work to start them thinking about the subject and what they themselves hope to get out of the intervention. Many employees turn up on the first day of a course without any understanding of why they are there. If this is the case, the intervention is almost certainly doomed.

Second, the intervention itself should be well designed and targeted at the intended outcome. We discussed this at length above.

Third, the employee should have ample opportunity to use the new competencies and behaviours in the workplace. Many employees return to their day-job following an intervention buzzing with new ideas, only to be told that that's not the way things are done, and that they should return to the old ways.

You want them to be different on their return. Don't stop them being different. Rejoice and make the workplace ready for them!

8.9   Chapter Summary

Employees are described by a raft of characteristics, central in which are their competencies and behaviours. Employees can have all the personality, motivation, leadership, and culture to do a job that excites them, but without the competencies and behaviours necessary for performance, they will fail to deliver the expected outcomes.

Candidates for jobs come with some competencies and behaviours. Sometimes those are enough. And sometimes the firm has already changed, or wants to change in the future, to require different competencies and behaviours. Where change is needed, managers are likely to need to develop their staff.

All too often, managers send employees on courses. Courses are the universal intervention on which a huge industry has been built, and yet they are seldom the best. There are many types of intervention and it's critical that the manager (and employee) select well.

Selection should be done by knowing the change in competencies and behaviours needed. Identification of the change required should come from the firm's strategy.

There is a structure to defining competencies and behaviours. They are tangible things – measurable and describable. They can be categorised, and we define four levels at which each can be held: trainee, supervised practitioner, practitioner, and expert. The fact that they are measurable, and that each employee can hold each at a rising mastery until becoming an expert gives the idea that competency and behaviour development can be planned and managed.

We invite managers to adopt an attitude towards development. If the business does not need the manager to develop their staff, then that's fine, though if that's the case we'd suggest that perhaps the manager has not really understood the firm in its environment. Even static firms with 'as now' strategies must develop employees since the environment around the firm is changing. Such firms must develop to stand still.

In developing their attitude, we challenge managers to think about who, if anyone, in the firm gets the lion's share of the development budget – and how that budget is apportioned. It's sensible to put the money where there will be maximum return, and yet it can be a source of great inequity, fostering feelings that the manager is being unfair. Feelings of injustice heighten intention to quit amongst employees.

Given that managers are going to develop staff, we suggest several practical development management tools – the personal competency framework, the corporate competency framework, and the process of talent management. It's for the manager to determine what they will use and how, but it's essential to use something to manage the complicated data and process of development.

We amplify the requirement to take care in selecting the right tool for the right job. We illustrate this in several ways. We have given a description of the various tool types - seven in all - and there may be more as intervention technology improves. We use Bloom's Taxonomy to show graphically that the effect wanted, and the tool selected must match.

And finally, we comment on how a manager might assess the effectiveness of a development intervention. Assessing effectiveness is difficult.

Overall, employee development is a complex business, but there's no point in doing it if you, as manager, are going to disobey some of the fundamentals. If employees don't know why they are being developed, and are not committed to that development, and if upon their return to work, everything is to be as it was, you will fail to gain the performance change and fail to get the new business outcomes that you'd hoped for.

9
Managing Wellbeing

In 2013, General Sir Nick Houghton said something poignant in an interview with Caroline Wyatt, then the BBC's defence correspondent. His comment summed up 'wellbeing' and its place in the management of people. All managers should ponder on his words.

He was questioned about the morale of the British Army considering the pressures upon it because of reduced Regular numbers, increasing Reservist numbers and reduced budgets. He was commenting about how he looks at morale – a proxy for wellbeing. He commented: "*It's not about individual happiness. I couldn't say that everyone in the British Army is happy on a given day. But it's about the ability to... (perform)... in times of pressure. And if anything has demonstrated the resilience of the ... the British armed forces, it's the last couple of years and the fact that they continue to perform.*"

General Houghton was quite right. Happiness depends on many things. Events in employees' private lives impact their day-to-day happiness at work. And minute-by-minute customer, peer, and manager interactions and minute-by-minute successes and difficulties have a bearing too. But if the employee is doing a job they like, if they have the right competencies and behaviours to do that job well, and have positive attitudes and beliefs towards the firm, then they will have the resilience to perform and will enjoy high wellbeing. They will have high wellbeing despite the pressures – and, for the armed forces, despite the threats to their lives.

9.1   Wellbeing

Wellbeing, from a work perspective, is partly about how content employees feel in their job and partly about how much meaning and purpose the job gives them. If wellbeing is low, motivation is also difficult and other management interventions will have reduced effect. To understand why, we need to deepen our understanding of the complex interrelations between wellbeing and work.

9.1.1   Defining wellbeing

Wellbeing is perhaps best defined by its more easily characterised undesirable state – low wellbeing.

When someone has low wellbeing, they are suffering some unmitigated malady or maladies that prevent them from performing their work duties.

Those maladies can either be physiological or psychological, and there is significant spill-over between the two. Physiological maladies might curtail the employee's mobility, incapacitate them, and confine them to their home. Psychological maladies might include depression, stress, and panic attacks. Often psychological maladies generate crippling thoughts, fears, and attitudes and often this, in turn, spills over to cause physiological effects such as heightened blood pressure and poor kidney function.

Employees benefitting from high wellbeing have neither physiological nor psychological maladies that prevent them from performing – or, significantly, the maladies that they do have are mitigated in some way to reduce their debilitating effects. Sometimes poor wellbeing is caused by the work itself. And, in turn, sometimes the work itself may bring mitigation, reducing the effect of maladies.

Most people enjoy a wellbeing that lies somewhere between the two extremes of high and low – and they cope with maladies to sustain performance.

9.1.2   *Why people work*

At the deepest psychological level, people strive for meaning in their lives. Work contributes hugely to that meaning. The effects of loss of meaning are easily observed in someone who is made redundant and who fails to get a job. Many report hopelessness and some consider suicide.

Work, with its timelines and objectives out into the future, also gives a sense of purpose, of contributing to family and society, even if the employee has no financial stake in the firm.

There is no issue therefore: for high wellbeing, humans need to work.

Meaning and purpose, though, are on a greyscale. There's low meaning and low purpose on the left and high meaning and high purpose on the right. And all shades between. And work and the conditions associated with it must be of quality to promote both high meaning and high purpose. So, humans must be employed but that employment must be of quality to promote high wellbeing.

9.1.3   *Basic human needs and the link to wellbeing*

To get an initial feel for the interaction between work and employee wellbeing, we can look at needs theories and see what happens when needs are not satisfied. One idea in needs theories has it that employees need the ability to exist well – to earn an income and as a result, to be able to keep their families in reasonable comfort.

This existence recognises the instrumentality of money and the need to earn to pay bills. Research universally suggests that whilst money doesn't motivate, a reliable, reasonable income supports wellbeing.

Likewise, nobody wants to live their lives in isolation. Affiliation with colleagues supports wellbeing. Jobs must be designed to maximise human contact, even where those jobs are displaced from the firm's headquarters and conducted in virtual space and time. And whilst not everyone has high growth needs strength, everyone needs to feel that they are getting a share of the opportunities. Managers must care about their employees' growth.

As a foundation for high wellbeing, managers must secure existence, affiliation, and growth for all.

9.1.4   *Role of the manager in wellbeing*

Many managers expect employees to report for work well. That's not unreasonable and there is an onus on each employee to eat well, not drink too much alcohol or take drugs, get sleep, and take exercise. There's an onus on them to take time to relax. But many managers assume that work has no bearing on wellbeing and therefore they assume that they have no role to play. That assumption is misplaced.

Spill-over happens. Problems at home spill over to degrade feelings of positive wellbeing, to the point where those problems preclude work performance. And of course, issues at work that degrade wellbeing affect home life – to the point where marriages break down, debts rise, and homes are re-possessed. Whilst managers can't be marriage or debt counsellors, they do need to be mindful and aware of employee behaviour and be prepared to act to assist employee recovery and enhanced resilience – for the firm's good, if nothing else.

Unfortunately, many managers practice ambivalence at worst and containment at best. Neither is useful. Managers must intervene to achieve high employee wellbeing.

9.1.5   *Resilience and coping*

Employees experience many events and environments at home and at work. Each is a challenge to their wellbeing. Some will boost wellbeing. Others will degrade wellbeing. But avoiding events and environments altogether is impossible so employees must work through issues.

Academics talk of a set point – a state of wellbeing that is normal for each person. It's a point - high or low - that a person's wellbeing returns to if all pressures are off. Given this, two issues come to the fore – how can an employee's set point be increased, and how can the manager ensure that the employee's everyday wellbeing rarely dips below this. As General Houghton noted, everyone has bad days, but the set point must be high enough and the events and environment must be such that wellbeing rarely degrades to prevent performance.

This gives rise to the idea of coping. Often stressors can't be removed – stressors are, for example, pervasive in a busy hospital accident and emergency department – but the doctors and nurses working there, cope. Their normal state of wellbeing is high enough. They continue to perform - even when faced with the worst human tragedy – because purpose and meaning are high.

Employees build coping by building resilience to challenging events and environments. Employees experience psychological wellbeing and physiological wellbeing. Psychological resilience (enabling psychological wellbeing) comes from their psychological capital – from their self-efficacy, their belief that they can perform. And from experiences in their lives that give them hope for the future. Physiological wellbeing (and hence physiological resilience) comes from physical capital like good food, plenty of sleep and exercise.

The manager's task is to build resilience such that all their employees cope.

9.2   Poor wellbeing

Work can act to enhance each employee's wellbeing, or it can degrade it. Which it does depends on the person, the job they do and how they're treated by their manager.

9.2.1   *Genetics, childhood, and wellbeing*

As we discussed above, some people have a naturally high state of wellbeing while, for others, it's lower. And some people react more vigorously to events and the environment than others, and as a result, their wellbeing is more volatile.

The way that people react to events and their environment depends significantly on their unique personal characteristics. Those personal characteristics comprise, for example, intelligence, personality, and preferences. We discuss personal characteristics more completely in Chapter 3.

Intelligence helps people learn and make sense of events and the environment.

Research over the past 50 years or so has established the Big 5 personality traits as the normal personality definition. As discussed in 3.4.2, each personality descriptor has a greyscale between the two extremes. The Big 5 personality traits are shown again in Figure 9-1.

Personal preferences are built over the years. Preferences describe just that – what a person would prefer to do, like arts or investigative jobs. Together with intelligence and personality, they reflect a person's fit with a particular job. There is no right or wrong set of personal characteristics. Certain jobs benefit from certain characteristics: a salesperson should, for example, likely tend toward 'extroversive' and a research scientist should likely tend toward 'curious'.

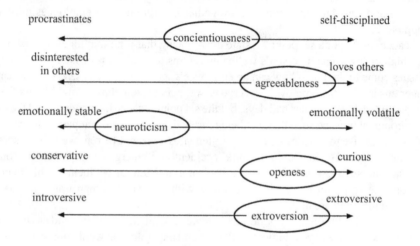

Figure 9-1: The Big 5 personality scales

About half of a person's intelligence and personality is determined by genetics – those elements of the characteristics are inherited. The other half is determined by childhood and upbringing. The result is that in adults those characteristics are substantially fixed.

For a large part, how someone reacts to events and to their environment depends on their personal characteristics – we might say that how they react depends on who they are.

A person's set point for wellbeing and how their wellbeing changes with events and environment is therefore significantly determined by each employee's personal characteristics.

9.2.2   Events, environment, and wellbeing

The requirement to fit the employee with their job (and perhaps too, the converse) demands that they are selected for that job. Achieving wellbeing and resilience starts at recruitment and selection.

But jobs change, employees are promoted, offered new jobs, and asked to work in new environments. That person-environment fit changes and to recover resilience requires that the manager and employee keep job change under review.

So, how someone reacts to events and their environment depends significantly on who they are. But their reaction also depends on other higher-level personal characteristics such as personal efficacy, locus of control and self-esteem. Reaction depends on many of the same factors affecting performance and personal outcomes that we discussed in Chapter 5. Someone, whose personal characteristics (of intelligence, personality, and preferences); who is a good fit for a job; and who performs well, is off to a good start when assessing wellbeing resilience. But employees don't exist in a bubble.

Management action creates events and the environment. The employee just reacts to what they experience.

There are several key workplace factors that create pressure for the employee and to which they will react.

As we said earlier, affiliation is a key human need. If relationships with their managers and colleagues are damaged, the employee will react. Since relationships are fundamental, even for those who enjoy working alone, poor relationships will degrade psychological wellbeing. Employees who have no ability to control the work they do and when they do it will experience the feeling of working in a 'rat run'. Lack of control and autonomy will degrade psychological wellbeing.

Excessive workload may cause pressure, but whilst it's often assumed to be a cause of poor wellbeing, we have seen that resilience and coping allows pressured employees to enjoy high wellbeing despite high workload. As we'll see later when discussing stress, it's all down to the temporal nature of the work and the ability to rest.

So, work events and the work environment influence wellbeing. How they do this, depends on the employee.

9.2.3   Job conditions

In discussing wellbeing, authors, academics, and policymakers are often overly eager to consider psychological wellbeing while forgetting physiological wellbeing. Physical events and environment impact significantly for many employees. And all should remember the spill over that occurs between physical and psychological events and environment.

Take employees digging holes for new telecommunications services and how problems with the work environment escalated. The employees fell victim to repetitive strain injury and large numbers fell sick. After some months of wide-spread, long-term absences, the employer realised that it was in its interests to have quality work done by employees enjoying high wellbeing. It launched a study, identified the issues, and offered the employees physiotherapy and physical training to counter the strain – in other words, to build their resilience.

Whilst an extreme case, this illustrates the importance of always considering both physiological and psychological wellbeing. It illustrates the need to consider the physical environment of the job.

9.2.4   Job security and change

We saw earlier that existence is a fundamental human need – employees must know that they can fund themselves and their family. And considering the psychological contract that describes all the unwritten expectations of both employee and employer, employees expect to be employed for the foreseeable future.

Any risk to continued employment challenges their psychological wellbeing.

In today's fluid economic environment, we see significant change. Firms downsize, merge, are taken over and collapse completely. The threat to job security is now almost always present, even for those employed by local and central government. The result for many is a continually challenged set point, weakened resilience, and reduced ability to cope.

9.3   Measuring wellbeing

Above, we said that wellbeing had two aspects – psychological wellbeing and physiological wellbeing. We also suggested a state of high or positive wellbeing and the opposite – a state of low or negative wellbeing. Each employee's wellbeing can be located on two lines as shown in Figure 9-2. The sliders (circles) can be moved to reflect a relative position.

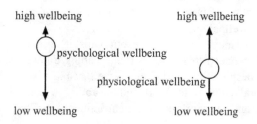

Figure 9-2: Describing an employee's wellbeing

There are two obvious approaches to assessing the wellbeing of employees in a firm. First, we can observe them. Second, we can ask them how they feel. Both are likely to be biased.

Manager observation is limited by the available time for interaction. Observation also requires that the manager is mindful enough to see effects that might allow assessment. Wellbeing is an in-person phenomenon. It's not written as a score on the employee's forehead.

Self-assessment often involves asking the employee to complete a multi-choice questionnaire. Self-assessment is biased by the interpretations that employees put on questions like '*Have you been constantly irritable, or have you easily become angry with colleagues over the past few months*', and the interpretations that managers apply. Such questions from self-assessment questionnaires are tempered by spill over from the home environment and interaction between psychological and physiological wellbeing. They're tempered too by how the employee feels when they answer the questions.

Despite this subjectivity, observation and self-assessment give the manager a starting point and the ability to compare individual employees and departments.

To objectivise wellbeing, we can also add a reference. We can go back to the factors that influence employee performance and personal outcomes. If the employee once performed in their job and now doesn't, and all other variables are as they were, this may suggest that degraded wellbeing is affecting employee motivation.

9.3.1   Hedonic wellbeing

Psychological wellbeing can be further broken down into hedonic and eudaimonic wellbeing.

Hedonism argues that pleasure and happiness are the aim of human life. Hedonic wellbeing suggests that wellbeing is about how happy employees feel and how frequently and intensely they experience positive emotions. This sits well with self-assessment questionnaires that ask about feeling and with polite manager questions asking, '*How are you today?*'

The assumption here is that if an employee reports that they feel well, their wellbeing is high.

Whilst we might criticise the simplicity of hedonic wellbeing, it perhaps avoids the need to consider psychological and physiological wellbeing separately. A positive response to hedonic questions is likely to indicate that the employee is both psychologically and physiologically well – or at least coping.

9.3.2   Eudaimonic wellbeing

The word 'eudaimonic' derives from two Greek words *eu*, meaning 'good', and *daimon*, meaning 'spirit'. Eudaimonic wellbeing stems from the antecedents of high motivating potential in a job – autonomy, work variety and work identity – but it extends to satisfaction of needs of the jobholder and specifically the need for personal growth.

Eudaimonic wellbeing is built by deriving high purpose and meaning in work achievements. It occurs when employees complete complex and difficult projects and tasks. They enjoy a mastery over the work and perhaps work closely with colleagues, satisfying their affiliation needs. Eudaimonic wellbeing theory has much in common with motivation theory – and perhaps with engagement or 'super-motivation' discussed in Chapter 5.

This type of psychological wellbeing links to personality and attitudes. There are those people who get their kicks by following extrinsic motives. They seek to enjoy hedonic wellbeing brought about by pleasure. And typically, they seek task performance in pursuit of hard reward such as money, for money allows purchase of further pleasure. Conversely, there are those who seek personal growth – everything they do is to achieve, learn and pursue intrinsic motives. Hedonic wellbeing has no place in this category. Such people will endure hedonic hardship to pursue their idea of happiness.

9.3.3   Using a scorecard to manage wellbeing

Kaplan and Norton's balanced scorecard designed for expression of strategy (6.4.3) can be used as a dashboard to manage wellbeing. An example is shown in Figure 9-3.

The scorecard has four topics – organisation-wide financial issues reflecting wellbeing, internal processes (in pursuit of good wellbeing), wellbeing issues experienced by customers and people initiatives targeted at securing good wellbeing. The scorecard should be updated as wellbeing and associated interventions and initiatives change.

financial perspective
  - staff turnover
  - agency staff
  - financial KPIs
	internal process perspective
	  - staff survey results
	  - high quality appraisals

customer perspective
  - customer satisfaction
  - quality measures
  - complaints
	people perspective
	  - innovations
	  - feedback from training

Figure 9-3: Example wellbeing scorecard

Reflection 9-1: About wellbeing

Draw two vertical lines for each of your staff. Mark the left as psychological wellbeing and the right as physiological wellbeing. Mark the tops as high and the bottoms as low. Where on each line does each person ordinarily sit? Is this their set point? How does their wellbeing move considering work events and environmental changes?

9.4   Stress

Under the syndrome we call 'stress', an employee finds themselves exhibiting either psychological effects (thoughts and beliefs that cause undesirable behaviours in the person) or physiological effects (physical conditions that debilitate the person) because of one or more stressors. Stressors are things like high workload or high responsibility. Stress is normal. Everyone is stressed. It's just that in many cases, the stressors are balanced by beneficial characteristics of the person and the job, thereby allowing each person to cope.

In a person in whom stress manifests psychologically or physiologically, there is an imbalance. Their coping strategies are not strong enough to balance the strain. This imbalance may be extreme for a short while or may be moderate but sustained over a long time.

When things come to a head, it's normally because something has happened. The person was coping but now they are not. It could be that a team member has left, and everyone is having to pick up the slack. It could be that a new system has been installed without training.

That gives a clue about the approach to stress management. Managers must act to regain the balance – to recover a state of coping. The only issue then is, by doing what?

9.4.1   *Workloads, pressures and performance*

Not all strain is harmful. One research thread suggests that in fact, all employees need a modicum of pressure to perform at their peak. The graph in Figure 9-4 gives the idea.

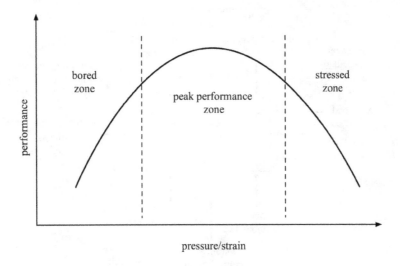

Figure 9-4: The peak performance zone

The concept is that everyone needs just enough pressure. Too little and the employee switches off. Too much, and they are stressed. The difficulty with this simplistic approach to work life is that the manager must simply control the pressure. The single big pressure is workload. This ignores concepts like coping and resilience. For many, they can't reduce workload.

This idea of workload control is used by general medical practitioners in treating stress – they sign the employee off sick for four weeks, thereby removing the work-related strain but the stress re-occurs on their return to work and the cycle repeats.

9.4.2   HSE model of management effectiveness

In trying to advise managers, the UK's Health and Safety Executive (HSE) has a neat framework comprising a set of stress Management Standards. Each gives a centre for analysis and action. Each suggests cause and solution. These Management Standards reflect all current research on the stressors that contribute to strain (and ultimately stress) and the positive aspects of jobs that reduce the effect of those stressors. The problem is that the HSE approach assumes that the manager is the only entity that must act to recover the balance in the employee. Both manager and employee must be prepared to work at a solution. The HSE model is shown in Figure 9-5.

The essence of the HSE model is that, given stressors like workload, management expectations and responsibility, psychological and/or physiological stress results. This is exacerbated by poor management intervention in each of the management 'standards'. If for example, the manager does not support the employee, stress is heightened. On the other hand, if the employee enjoys good manager support, stress will be reduced.

The six management standards are therefore moderators of the relationship between stressors and stress outcomes. The management standards are demands, control, support, relationships, role, and change.

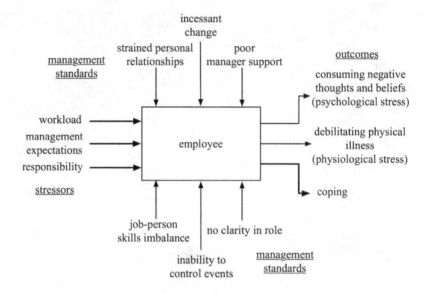

Figure 9-5: The HSE management standards model

9.4.3 *Practical action to manage stress*

Like many management activities, management of stress demands that the manager assesses the stress that results in staff from the various stressors. The HSE model also includes a 35-question inventory in which each of the six management standards featured have between three and nine questions.

Managers have two approaches. First, the questionnaire can be given to each employee to be completed. Anonymous response allows the quality of operation of the management standards to be compared across groups of employees. Second, the questionnaire can be used to talk through the management standards with individuals. Either way, the manager can talk about stress and the effectiveness of their management. Clearly this second approach needs a very open manager who is prepared to listen, even if the story is critical of them.

Reflection 9-2: About stress

Search the Internet for the HSE management standards indicator tool (see https://timelesstime.co.uk/knowledgebase/practical-use-of-the-hse-management-standards-indicator-tool). Consider each of your employees in turn. Complete one questionnaire for each employee. Amalgamate the responses. Is stress high or low? As a manager, how successful are you at managing your employees' stress?

9.5 Burnout

9.5.1 *When the machine crashes*

We've seen in Chapter 5 that employees bind themselves to a firm through commitment. If conditions are right, commitment evolves to motivation. Under certain other conditions, motivation deepens to become super-motivation or engagement.

Engagement is described by special behaviours like immersion in the work, losing all track of time and heightened vigour. It's enabled and fuelled by feedback from the work done through personal development to tap intrinsic motives with increased learning, and to tap extrinsic motives with achievement.

Conceivably, one could continue to grow engagement with personal growth and achievement, and with that, realise ever-increasing performance. So, is there no end to this apparent perpetual 'machine'?

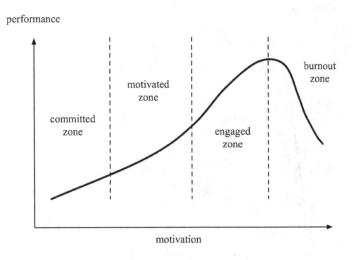

Figure 9-6: Conceptual model of motivation and burnout

Continuing the metaphor, employee performance can indeed continually increase until their machine runs out of resources. Performance can enhance through engagement in line with demands until physical, mental, and emotional resources are depleted.

So, while several conditions must cohere, engagement can lead to burnout. The situation is shown conceptually in Figure 9-6.

9.5.2 *Front line versus defence*

Suggestion as to how to avoid burnout comes from many studies in the military.

When on the offensive, a soldier's performance is high because the normal operating approach is to attack, capture ground, and then rest up, awaiting reinforcements. Conversely, various studies have shown that troops defending positions from incessant bombardment suffer burnout more commonly because the stressors are unrelenting.

Motivation is often described as the assignment of personal resources to a task. So, there's little argument that motivation, and super-motivation, with appropriate assignment of resources, is useful. But by assigning all their resources to a task for a prolonged period, an employee will eventually suffer burnout.

Engagement is good, but burnout must be avoided by ensuring that there is adequate downtime to replenish personal resources – whether through alternative leisure pursuits or just good quality rest. Rest and recuperation are essential to pull the employee back to the engagement zone.

9.6   Absence

9.6.1   *The nature of absence*

Illness is part of the human condition. Managers and colleagues would universally prefer that an employee has a few days off to recuperate and recover instead of continuing to attend work when sick.

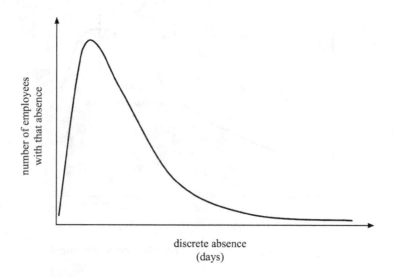

Figure 9-7: Typical absence profile for a firm

Descriptive statistics define employee absence behaviour. A small number of employees will have no, or a very few, days off; a large number will have around 5 days a year off; and a few will have several weeks off. Even fewer will be off long-term for many months. This is shown graphically in Figure 9-7.

The total number of days lost is the area under the curve. Managers budget for this loss of a few percent and sustain operations, despite the loss, using various tactics. The most common tactic is to simply overstaff slightly, such that colleagues can stand in to cover.

Not all sickness absence is genuine. There are employees who go sick when in fact they are not. There are employees who believe that it is their right to take time off sick.

There are those who see their doctor for the slightest malady and are signed off sick. And there are a vast majority who go absent as a last resort. It's for the manager to make sense of what they are being told and intervene in each case.

9.6.2 *Absence management approach*

When it comes to managing sickness absence, some managers adopt a pacifist attitude, ignoring the issue and accepting what they're told, while others come down hard, assuming that the employee is dishonest. A better approach is that of rationalist.

First, the manager must always endeavour to find out as much as possible about the employee's reason for absence. Second, if the cause is illness, the manager must research and learn about that illness. And third, the manager should already have notes on all previous absences by all staff and hence be able to investigate trends. Decision-making needs information.

Decision-making also needs policy and procedures. The employee-employer contract of employment and the company's employee handbook are all that's needed. The handbook should give sufficient process for all absence types. It's then a matter of following procedure.

Finally, whilst it doesn't do to always look within the firm for causes of employee absence, it is always worth questioning the data to determine if there's any link between the environment, the employee's colleagues and the work done and absences.

9.6.3 *Spotting trends*

Older readers will remember the song *I Don't Like Mondays* by Irish band The Boomtown Rats about the 1979 Cleveland Elementary School shooting in San Diego. The title came from the reason a sixteen-year-old gave for why she shot so many of her peers.

Unfortunately, some employees do live their lives with low wellbeing resilience and volatile private lives in which they don't look after themselves. The result is that they don't like Mondays, or Fridays or whatever. Whilst they'll not take to violence, they may go absent.

Managers must keep records of absences and keep notes of all discussions that they have with employees about absences. We recommend using a daybook – a hardback notebook – in which all discussions and relevant events are logged. When data is needed for decision-making and absence management, it's available.

Routine data gathering is most relevant when the work involves some departure from the norm – like night working, field work or virtual working, with a workforce shifted by geography and time. Managers should also watch for presenteeism – employees at work when they should be home, recuperating, and employees routinely working long hours, always there, aiming to be seen by managers as committed.

9.6.4 *Comparing absences*

In the 1980s, the Bradford University School of Management studied the subject and came up with a calculation that allowed comparison between many short absences and a few long periods of absence. The basis of the Bradford Factor is that frequent, short, unplanned absences are more disruptive and costlier to the firm than longer absences.

In the calculation, B, the Bradford Factor, is equal to S squared times D ($B=S^2xD$). S is the number of absences and D the total number of days of absence of the employee. All are measured over a rolling 52-week period. The Bradford Factor is a relative measure allowing absence data to be compared across a workforce regardless of the frequency and number of days off.

9.6.5   *Practical absence management*

The manager's aim is simple – to have the employee back at work, enjoying good wellbeing. In information gathering, the manager may need to undertake investigations. To understand the malady, the manager may need to engage the services of an occupational health practitioner, particularly if the employee has a malady coming under the Equality Act 2010. In this latter case, the firm may have to adjust the employee's workplace to enable them to carry out their job.

Once back at work, all returning employees should have a back-to-work interview to discuss the absence. This meeting allows the manager to raise any irregularities associated with the absence and to understand if there are any actions that the firm should take to help improve wellbeing.

9.6.6   *Managing long term absence*

From time to time, one or two employees in a workforce of a hundred will go off long-term sick. Each absence must be managed. Often, they're not well enough to be in full time, every day, but they're nonetheless capable of contributing to the firm while they recover.

In such cases, managers should work with the sick employee on their return-to-work plan. Returning to the normal place of work is best, and a phased return should be developed where the employee comes back for a few hours, building to full time over say three or six months.

Whilst some employees 'swing the lead', most absences are for genuine illness. The manager must actively manage all cases without fear or favour.

9.7   Intoxicants

People drink, smoke, and take drugs. That's life. In moderation, most stimulants and intoxicants are fine, and hence are unlikely to ever influence an employee's attendance or abilities. But in a small number of cases, taking stimulants leads to problems.

9.7.1   *Tobacco*

Smoking tobacco is a known risk to health and hence a source of reduced wellbeing.

Smoking in the premises of a firm, it's vehicles and other enclosed shared space is illegal. Managers also have a duty of care to ensure that employees are protected from the effects of second-hand smoke or vapour. Smoking e-cigarettes or vaping is generally considered anti-social and not permitted in most firms. These and other rules are usually covered in a firm's smoking policy.

Some firms construct outside shelters for smokers. Others permit smoking at seldom-used entrances to buildings. Managers must carefully consider their attitude to smoking.

9.7.2   *Drugs or alcohol*

Broadly, managers should consider drugs or alcohol taken in the employee's own time as their private affair – unless, as a result, the employee's cognitive, emotional, or physical abilities are impaired, and their wellbeing degraded.

Managers should consider, universally, that the taking of drugs or alcohol while at work is against company policy and is, as a result, a disciplinary offence. To do anything else would suggest that drugs and alcohol are somehow different from other factors that degrade wellbeing.

As a result, it would be quite hypocritical of a manager to condone drugs or alcohol but act on high stress, poor health and safety or uncontrolled inherent danger in the job.

9.7.3   *Managing drugs or alcohol at work*

Employees who take drugs or alcohol while at work or attend work under the influence of drugs or alcohol need help. Drugs or alcohol are a serious threat to the employee's wellbeing.

Unfortunately, those consuming drugs or alcohol are generally devious and conceal their activities well. Discovering them and getting them to seek that help is hugely difficult. They rarely allow a manager to catch them in the act.

Often, it's a change in behaviour, or discovery of a peculiar behaviour that first alerts a manager. It might be going home at lunch time – every lunch time – or drinking from a lemonade bottle that makes no 'psshhhh' when the top is turned. Often, it's colleagues who notice and alert the manager.

For others, it's appearing on a conference call, sounding vague and 'out of it', not making coherent sense. Of course, in all cases, the perpetrator will vehemently deny taking drugs or alcohol and they know all too well that getting proof it is near-impossible. For successful management of drugs and alcohol, it's critical to collect data on instances.

Management of instances when employees have been taking drugs or alcohol at work, or just before work, centres on two keys principles: that the manager needs only 'reasonable belief' that the consumption took place to act, and that, like other behavioural issues, the manager must run the process with great care.

Reasonable belief is a legal term that places the burden of proof lower than 'beyond reasonable doubt' (the criminal law requirement for proof) and lower than 'on balance of probability' (the civil law requirement for proof).

And whilst the manager must have compassion, they must stick to the script. Those surreptitiously taking drugs or alcohol will mount an aggressive campaign that will test the best manager.

9.8   Benefits as mitigations

Employee benefits have a place in employee reward to keep the firm's rewards package competitive. In many labour markets, things like bonuses and healthcare are expected.

But managers also need to consider benefits for their benefit to the firm. From a business perspective, costly benefits must be balanced by adequate return. Benefits must also be applied equitably (but not necessarily equally) across the workforce.

9.8.1   *Wellbeing-related benefits*

Wellbeing-related benefits fall into two camps: preventative benefits and corrective benefits.

The list of preventative benefits is long. Some, such as the Cycle to Work Scheme, are supported by the Government and qualify for tax relief. Ultimately the aim is that the firm gives or pays for something and in return employee wellbeing rises. It's a question of choosing benefits that link to wellbeing and that do indeed reduce sickness absence.

Corrective benefits are basically insurances that accelerate treatment for the employee and possibly their family. The most common is private medical insurance. Also popular, income protection (IP) insurance acts to reduce the stresses on the employee and their family that come from long-term sickness. By reducing stress, IP insurance also accelerates return to work.

9.8.2   *Commitment-building benefits*

We note in various chapters that once the employee is committed, all other management action becomes possible. Without commitment, the manager-employee relationship is basic and economic. Commitment-building benefits are designed to engender the feeling that the employee wants to work in the firm.

Many commitment-building benefits can be granted as part of the exchange. Flexitime, home working, compressed working week, annualised hours, term-time working, reduced hours, job share and career breaks are popular. Some also directly benefit wellbeing by reducing stress on the employee and their family.

9.8.3   *Engagement-building benefits*

We note in Chapter 5 that engagement or super-motivation occurs when the employee works well, succeeds, and taps their extrinsic motives. And they engage in learning and tap their intrinsic motives. These work in a positive spiral to further spur motivation and performance.

Managers can intervene in each employee's working life to fuel engagement. The most obvious benefit is the granting of paid learning opportunities. Whilst technical training is useful in building skills and knowledge, engagement is encouraged though advanced learning. Such opportunities will be unique to each individual and might include funding to join industry peers in standards-making, secondment to exciting new groups, leadership of ground-breaking projects and the taking of higher-level courses and research. Each must, of course, relate directly to the task the employee does.

Reflection 9-3: About benefits and wellbeing

Consider your existing employee benefits. Which has the greatest
benefit in bolstering employee wellbeing? What changes to your
benefits might you make considering the above?

9.9   Flexibility and the workhome

As we noted in 4.6, several modern trends, along with the upset of the Covid virus, have put pressure on firms to accept more flexibility in the way their employees work. Arguably, flexibility and working from home can enhance wellbeing. Where employees once worked a 40-hour week in a factory during daylight hours, many now work fewer hours, when they can, around other commitments and jobs, and often from home.

These changes are often accompanied by the parallel shift from employment to self-employment and we discuss this separately in Chapter 3. Throughout this book, we describe those who are self-employed as suppliers.

9.9.1   *History*

Working from home and working flexibly is nothing new. In the eighteenth century and before, almost everyone worked from home and worked around their families and spouses. Traditional single room 'longhouses' accommodated the family, multiple trades, and beasts such as cows and sheep.

Then the industrial revolutions of the nineteenth century attracted huge swathes of workers from poor conditions on the land, and other situations, to work as employees in factories. Towns and cities grew and with that growth, houses reverted to be places only to dwell.

Perhaps the greatest and final shift from houses in which work could be done to houses only for dwelling came after the World War II. The UK Government sponsored the building of New Towns and other regeneration. The dwellings built were purely for coming home to after a day's work and for bringing up families.

The shift was, of course, not total. A minority of workers remain today in dual-purpose houses. Tradesmen and women such as undertakers, publicans, and shopkeepers 'live above the shop'. Otherwise, most Britons live in a house specifically designed for the family that is spatially separated from work. Except for a few custom builds, no house is today designed for dual use.

This spatial separation demands that employees commute between work and home. Manufacturing and services are concentrated in towns and cities and employees live in the suburbs, progressively moving further and further away from their employers. Employees today typically spend an hour commuting to work in the morning, and an hour back in the evening. And others who relocate to the country in search of lower cost housing and a quieter life away from the busy cities commute for anything up to three hours in the morning and repeat that again at night.

9.9.2   *Pressures*

The Covid pandemic focused minds. The Government demanded that employees worked from home where possible. And employees themselves had time to reflect on their previous lives, the current state and what they wanted for the future. Many recognised the absurdity of commuting for hours.

Of course, not everyone could work from home. Lockdowns revealed previously hidden categories of essential employees. Many of those were suppliers and earned too little and got no social security support. As a result, they continued at work when they shouldn't and were exposed to the virus more than most. Times were tough for many.

The result was a rethink of what work was. No one moved from the fundamental that work gives meaning to life. It was just that huge numbers of people redefined what life was for them. Many enjoyed the new flexibility of working round the kids. Many revelled in having up to four hours a day more leisure time. Others on the front line fighting the pandemic realised how work grew to engulf them, to trash their wellbeing, and they collapsed or rebelled.

There have been movements for many years demanding flexible working, reduced hours, a four-day working week and other departures from the mainstream grind of work. As a result of Covid, there is now a possibility that those movements will grow and new 'normals' will emerge.

9.9.3 *Workhomes*

The Covid pandemic exposed how variable an experience working from home was.

On the one hand, some employees found working from home just ghastly. They worked in a rented a bedsit and spent their time with a laptop on their knee. Others perhaps found it quite tolerable. They bought drop-down desks that folded to return the bedroom to its domestic purpose after clocking-off time. Some employers recognised their responsibilities and delivered extra screens and tools to the home to replicate those in the workplace. Other employees just set up office in their spacious library or study and embraced the new relaxed regime.

Much also depended on where the employee lived. Those near the countryside or urban parks exploited the new daytime outdoor access.

Overall, though, the reports of loneliness spiralled. Traditional workplaces gave camaraderie. In 2020, singletons working in a bedsit, and even those in the heart of a family had a lonely time. Meetings focussed only on purpose and casual chit chat and gossip was lost.

Traditional workhomes enjoyed community. Spinners lived and worked in rows of houses with other spinners. They socialised together. Fishers fished together in fleets and their families joined together to gut and pack the fish at the quay head once the boats came in. Until the 1960s, work and home were frequently entwined. Subsequent years of government town planning policy has meant that, today, home working can suit some, but certainly does not suit all.

Managers need to consider what they and their employees want from flexibility and home working. There can be huge benefits for both parties, but flexibility and home working can fail too.

9.10 Health and safety

Many health and safety briefing papers from industry bodies, directors' clubs and professional institutions preach the importance of health and safety management in firms – but they rarely say how it should be done. Here we discuss the subject and give clear guidance about how to provide employees with a safe working environment.

9.10.1 *Risk in work activities*

Just driving to town or crossing the road carries with it a risk to a person's safety – there could be a collision in which the person may be injured or even die. The chance of occurrence of an injury and the likely severity of that injury are both low. For most people, days pass without event.

This relatively benign state from the private lives of citizens serves as a reference for health and safety at work assessment. People would normally expect a safe world and the risk to personal safety should not be heightened when they work.

And yet, employees do experience heightened risk. Lone care workers routinely visit the elderly at night, walking through poorly lit streets. Builders crawl on roofs to replace tiles. Electricians work on live circuits to replace fuses. And salespeople fly to distant cities to find their way around where they speak no local language. Employment often makes an untoward event more likely.

Various situations exacerbate the risks. Risk is heightened by the sheer size and specialised nature of plant and machinery with which employees work. And by working long hours, perhaps outside the 'normal' business day, employees get tired. Fatigue heightens the risk of an error or accident.

To return the risk to an acceptable state, managers and employees must take continuous programmed action.

On the one hand, the firm has a duty of care for the safety of its employees. On the other, each employee has a duty to report fit for work, behave appropriately, follow managers' instructions, and engage with managers in safety-enhancing activities. In the UK, the basis for the control of health and safety at work is the Health and Safety at Work Act 1974.

9.10.2 *Nature of accidents and incidents*

Since the introduction of the Health and Safety at Work Act, health and safety at work has improved hugely. Generally, workplaces are not bad places to work, and the employee is not generally going to have a serious injury. Nonetheless there is a greyscale of chance and severity. For the purposes of discussion, we will divide firms into two classes: on the one hand there's the office and on the other, the complex industrial firm. The latter covers any firm that is not near-risk free.

For near-risk free offices, provided that the manager buys modern office equipment and rents or buys modern premises, the firm's obligations under the Health and Safety at Work Act 1974 are easily discharged. A simple risk assessment can be complete on the Health and Safety Executive's web site. The highest risk activity is often lone working, and for most, this is mitigated by communicating with colleagues, implementing an action plan in the event of problem. On completing the ensuing actions, risk will be minimised, and health and safety controlled.

For the complex industrial firm, there's work to be done and more to be understood by managers.

Analysis of accidents tends to show that there's seldom a single cause. Take the West Japan Railway Company 2005 disaster. On the face of it, the driver powered the train too fast round a curve in the track. But investigation showed five independent causal factors, four of which were situational or cultural. Earlier in the day, the driver had overshot a platform by a few metres. The driver lied to a manager about the overshoot and the conductor supported him by fabricating facts. Both men knew that unless the overshoot was played down, the driver would face a humiliating experience at a corrective school – something management considered necessary to keep discipline.

Reporting the overshoot took time and as a result, the train was running late – exacerbating the likely punishment. As he speeded up to recover time, the driver was called on the radio by his controller demanding and explanation, but he ignored the calls, heightening his stress. The result was that a simple error of judgement grew to a disaster that killed 105 passengers and crew.

The point here is that it was not the excessive speed but the management practices and culture that caused the disaster.

In 2016, the London tram derailment killed seven and injured 62. As with the accident in Japan, there was one apparent cause, but 15 contributory factors and recommendations. Again, fear of management reprisals stopped employees from reporting previous near-misses from which safety lessons could have been learned.

Managers must look wide for threats.

9.10.3   Integrated management process

The essence of health and safety management is twofold: a) understand the risk your people are under on your behalf and b) implement controls to militate and mitigate those risks. In the complex industrial firm, health and safety must be managed by continuous action. A suitable process is shown in the flow chart in Figure 9-8. While the description that follows is for employees, it can also be expanded to cover third parties like customers and the public.

The start is for the manager to determine the firm's strategy. The manager, after all, determines the jobs that employees are to do in the firm, and the environment in which they work. We discuss how to define strategy in other chapters.

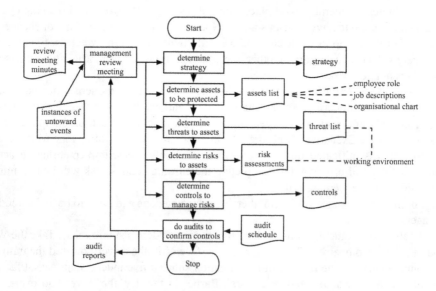

Figure 9-8: Integrated health and safety management process

The management review meeting works to ensure a safe working environment and ensures that the firm's responsibilities under the Act are discharged. The figure shows the classic risk-management flow from assets through to controls.

First, and given the strategy, the manager decides the people to be employed, their competencies and the technology they will use. Job descriptions describe the jobs they do and the way in which they are organised. Together that gives the asset list.

Next the manager must determine the threats to their assets – the employees - given those jobs and the working environment. Threats are accidents like a fall from height, being overcome by fumes in a tank or suffering an electric shock when working on live circuits. This gives a threat list specific to the jobs done and the environments worked.

Then the manager must assess each of the threats to determine the chance of occurrence and the severity of injury or degradation to wellbeing. There are various approaches to this but generally chance is determined as a percentage and the injury is scored numerically. A better, but perhaps more controversial outcome scoring method is the effect on turnover. At the lower end of the severity scale, the employee's effort could be lost for several weeks following an accident, with ensuing loss of revenue of perhaps £20k. At the upper end, a fall from height, for example, could trigger an HSE investigation, a fine and considerable loss of revenue through damage to reputation – perhaps amounting to a total loss of revenue of £500k.

Chance and severity are multiplied. A threshold score is decided upon. For scores above the threshold, controls are developed.

Finally, an audit activity is mounted to ensure that for every job and environment, controls are effective. The form and frequency of audit and the reviews of each activity will depend on the business and the threats. Review ensures minute-by-minute that controls have been implemented. Examples of review activity might include inspection of equipment by a colleague prior to use; stepping through a job with a colleague, describing to a colleague how controls will be implemented; or review of impending activities against a work sheet written by a subject matter expert in which controls have been embedded.

The written-up reviews are then audited from time to time to ensure that the controls are effective. Note that this is not a tick-box exercise – the reviewers and auditors must always assess the adequacy and effectiveness of the controls.

Instances of untoward events like accidents and near-misses are then reported to the management review meeting. As part of strategy, the manager sets the acceptable levels of chance and severity of untoward events and decides on the acceptable loss to the firm through accidents and reduction in wellbeing. Any untoward event would trigger an investigation into the adequacy and effectiveness of the controls. Where necessary, controls would be modified to drive down accidents and generally improve health and safety.

The above is a generic form. In many environments and for many job types, controls are prescribed in statute – for example in the Control of Substances Hazardous to Health Regulations 2002.

9.10.4 *Safe patterns of work*

Managers will write employment contracts that set out the number of hours to be worked per day and a pattern of workdays each week. The result is a working week of somewhere between 30 and 40 hours for someone considered to be working full time.

The present working week was set in the early 1900s when most people worked in a factory. Today, with teleworking and the 24-hour society, many people work in 'timeless time'. The boundary between work and private lives is now not so clear. Many work on-call. Some work part of the week working from home, part from client sites and only a short time hot-desking from the office. Couriers work the time needed to empty their van. Call-centre employees man telephones and screens in the evening and at night supporting foreign sales activities in shifted time zones. Simply, things have changed. Flexibility is essential for the firm to get the best use of its assets and to serve its customers.

Generally, fatigue increases with time worked and errors and accidents rise with fatigue. The average UK working week today is 37 hours worked over five days, typically starting in the morning, and ending late afternoon. There is no evidence that a shorter working week reduces fatigue. Studies have, however, confirmed that regularly working more than 48 hours a week can lead to chronic fatigue and is to be avoided. Long working hours have been linked to cardiovascular disease, non-insulin-dependent diabetes, risk of disability retirement and early mortality.

Regular breaks, an interesting job, reasonable workload, ability to manage the work, good colleague relationships and adequate resources all moderate fatigue.

Shift work has been the subject of many studies. Working shifts disrupts the natural circadian rhythm and degrades wellbeing and has been linked to musculoskeletal problems. There is evidence that if shift work is necessary, the best option is for three shifts of 12 hours with at least three days' rest before the next work period. Certainly, working split shifts (of morning and evening, for example around the rush hours) is to be avoided.

Overall, the simple guidance is for patterns of work that permit recuperation and sleep between periods of work. Employees must also take short breaks from work from time to time throughout the work period and in any case after six hours, in line with statute.

9.10.5 *Leading a safe working environment*

In the rail disasters discussed above, management culture influenced safety. Simply, in a different culture, where managers supported staff to encourage improvement, the accidents described might not have happened.

As we noted in Chapter 5, the manager influences a firm's culture and therefore the manager influences health and safety and employee wellbeing.

The manager must create a culture where mistakes, errors and near-misses can be discussed openly. There must be no fear on the part of employees that they will be blamed or punished. Employees and managers must learn what causes untoward events and how, in the future, those untoward events can be avoided.

In Chapter 2, we discussed leadership as a dyadic affair involving the manager as leader and the employee as follower. In health and safety, it is for the manager to build that dyadic relationship such that they can influence the employee to embrace behaviours that encourage good health and safety using the most appropriate approach and style.

Being practical, studies suggest that a transformational leadership approach is effective in inspiring followers towards safety goals. And transactional leadership works in persuading employees to follow procedures, emphasising adherence with safety rules. Managers must select their leadership approach with care.

9.11   Chapter Summary

Many commentators connect happiness with wellbeing. As a result, they exhort that managers must ensure that their employees are happy. That's rather a superficial approach.

Others connect absence of apparent illness or malady with wellbeing. As a result, they focus on physiological illness and suggest that managers encourage gym membership and other practical wellbeing-related benefits.

Both are wide of the mark. Wellbeing is a complex concept. A good way to understand it is to look at someone like Professor Stephen Hawking. Whilst we haven't discussed Stephen Hawking in the chapter, his case amplifies the concepts we discussed. Stephen Hawking was beset with almost total debilitation for most of his 76-year life, and yet arguably, he had high wellbeing. The reason is that despite his debilitating maladies, he had such a meaningful and fulfilled life. Despite not being able to walk or talk, he coped, and he performed. His professional career mitigated his physiological constraints. And despite his obvious poor physiological wellbeing, his psychological wellbeing seldom suffered – he avoided the detrimental two-way spill-over that often occurs between physiological and psychological illness.

Stephen Hawking's extreme situation helps managers understand wellbeing. It helps managers understand that the aim in managing wellbeing is to have the employee cope. Coping is achieved by the manager intervening, and we discuss how this might be done, both to avoid poor wellbeing and to manage poor wellbeing when it does occur.

The syndrome called stress occurs commonly today. Many managers and health professionals assume that stress is managed by the removal of stressors. And yet, in today's busy world, that's often impossible. Again, stress management is not about trying to remove the causes, but rather to build employee resilience, and to ensure that the manager takes all necessary action to enable coping.

We advocate the use of the UK Health and Safety Executive stress management model and its associated questionnaire. We can report good success in its use.

Psychological wellbeing – wellbeing of the mind - is the topic of the decade. If the press is to be believed, 'mental health problems' are ubiquitous. But all searches to define mental health as a single psychopathology will fail. There are simply too many discrete disorders and too much spill-over with physiopathology. Managers can't hope to become even a little informed in these huge subjects. In summary, we recommend managers practice awareness. And when issues arise, they must seek specialist help.

At the other end of the scale, many employees work so 'hard' that they burn out. We use a machine analogy to propose a model. Initially the employee is committed to the firm. They're then motivated to perform. And then they might enter the super-motivation or engagement zone. Many managers would rejoice when this occurs. But if the employee does not have the personal physiological and psychological resources to cope with this heightened work state, and they continue with increased motivation, their 'machine' will crash and burn. We advocate that managers should be mindful and help employees to be engaged with their job without risk of burnout. And we highlight the importance of rest and recuperation.

All managers must manage employee absence from work. Many do this badly, simply through lack of record-keeping – and by that we mean simple notes, rather than anything electronic. We also note that many managers decline to engage with absence, ignoring it until individual cases become problems. Managers must act early on absence.

In 2020 and 2021, the World was hit by the COVID virus. The result was the ubiquitous take up of home working. We note here that home working and its related concept, flexibility, can be of great benefit in achieving employee wellbeing. But we also note some of the issues and counsel managers to only introduce those ideas after considerable analysis and thought.

And finally, we discuss in brief the broad subject of health and safety. Most managers and their employees will work in safe environments, not unlike their own homes. Here, risk assessment is a bit of a joke, where inspectors chase benign trip hazards around desks and scald hazards in the kitchen.

For others, health and safety is a crucial business outcome. We highlight that in industrial environments, events typically align to cause catastrophe. Accidents occur when several discreet errors or faults aggregate. And most of these events are people related. In many cases, the accident has its roots in poor people-management – in psychological concepts like organisational culture, beliefs, and competencies.

Employee wellbeing is a huge topic. Managers must engage in it because it materially affects business outcomes.

10
Paying People

10.1 The idea of a wage

10.1.1 *A brief history of pay*

There are some brilliant rationales for how much an employee should be paid in economist Adam Smith's, "An Inquiry into the Nature and Causes of the Wealth of Nations", published in 1776. He says that:

"First, the wages of labour vary with the ease or hardship, the cleanliness or dirtiness, the honourableness or dishonourableness of the employment."

"Second, the wages of labour vary with the easiness and cheapness, or the difficulty and expense, of learning the business."

"Thirdly, the wages of labour in different occupations vary with the constancy or inconstancy of employment."

"Fourthly, the wages of labour vary according to the small or great trust which must be reposed in the workmen."

"Fifthly, the wages of labour in different employments vary according to the probability or improbability of success in them."

So, there you are: pay and benefits summed up in five statements and first proposed over 200 years ago. Smith goes on to give examples and rationale with remarkable parallels to jobs and professions today and their relative pay.

But things have moved on. Our liberal governments have seen fit to grant protection to employees to avoid the poverty that would have come with some employment in Smith's era. Hopefully future governments will retain these protections. And our markets and industries have changed. The independent physician has been replaced by a national health service. Our factories are staffed with robots and all firms rely heavily on technology, giving managers a choice of resource in which to invest.

Managers now pay employees a salary, and workers a wage. As a result, some are paid an annual return (divided by 12 and paid monthly) for their efforts while others are paid hourly or even by the gig. Here, we don't distinguish between the two, referring generally to the reward from involvement in a job as pay, unless we are specifically discussing an annual salary.

Our aim in writing this chapter is to set out the modern pay environment, capturing many aspects, in order that managers can understand and pay their people what's due, to benefit both parties to the employment contract.

10.1.2   Pay and contracts

The basis of pay is the employment contract, and we discussed this in Chapter 3.

We discussed in Chapter 1 how the employee surrenders some of their freedoms (as an independent entrepreneur or supplier) and agrees to come under the direction of the employer in return for a wage. It's an economic contract. And it's negotiated. Both parties can attempt to re-negotiate at any time, and both parties can, subject to conditions, end the contract. The firm is free to re-make the contract with a new employee and the departing employee can re-make the contract with a new employer.

In commercial contracts, we tend to talk of the consideration – the price that is paid in return for goods or services. In the employment contract, the employee agrees to come under a contract of service and the consideration is the wage. Wage is an old-fashioned word, and we tend today to talk of pay or salary.

10.1.3   Paying employees, workers and suppliers

In Chapter 1, we divided the people in a firm into three categories: employees, workers, and suppliers. Many managers confuse the three types when it comes to paying pay. That confusion can be costly and a mention about this confusion is essential.

A supplier is a firm, personal service company or sole trader (sometimes referred to as consultant, associate, or contractor) that is under a contract for the supply of services. They are not employees or workers. They do not get paid an amount each month in return for attendance and/or effort. They are asked to supply deliverables and invoice the firm upon delivery and acceptance of those services.

Employees are people who enter a contract of service with the firm. They get paid a salary or wage. Workers are people who enter a contract of service with someone – often an intermediary between them and the firm – and they get paid a wage. Generally, workers are hourly paid. The term 'worker' also covers those who are under a contract of service with the firm and are paid for their effort (rather than for their attendance).

Many managers enter a contract for the supply of services with, for example, a contractor, and then go on to pay them regularly at the end of each month for 37.5 hours of labour. The HMRC would regard them as employees and expect the firm to pay National Insurance Contributions on their wage. We cover the differences between employees, workers, and suppliers in other chapters.

This chapter covers pay for employees and workers, though care is needed when discussing workers, since the intermediary may also seek consideration for its services. This chapter is not about suppliers.

10.1.4   Concepts of fairness

Pay difference is an emotive subject. Employees think about the effort-reward relationship continually – the amount of effort that they put in and how much they get paid versus the effort and reward for a colleague. If they perceive that they put more effort in for the same reward as others who do the same work, they may feel that the pay system is unfair.

There are two parts to this feeling of fairness, this feeling of justice done, or not done. The first is the absolute comparison – distributive justice. Seeking distributive justice, each employee wants a fair slice of the reward 'pie'. The second is the way the pie is divided up by the manager - procedural justice. Seeking procedural justice, each employee wants to know that the manager uses a fair method of apportioning reward, and that this is related objectively to effort.

Of course, employees consider distributive and procedural justice from their perspective and with considerable ignorance and bias. But this does not stop them having an opinion.

10.1.5   *Who gets paid what and why*

The way things work out in many firms, employees can be grouped according to their significance. We introduced this concept in Chapter 8 where we invited managers to adopt an attitude towards the development of different groups. Here, in effect, we are suggesting that managers adopt an attitude to pay according to their contribution and value. And value also matches the market price (for labour) and hence how much the employee is paid. This is illustrated graphically in Figure 10-1.

Median pay is shown for each group by the dashed lines. We've assumed that pay for each group follows a normal distribution in each case, typified by the bell curves illustrating the spread of pay.

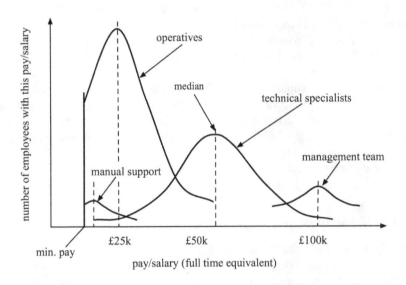

Figure 10-1: Pay of different employee groups

In this firm, conceptually, the bulk of the workforce are operatives of one sort or other, employed to deliver the service that the firm offers to its customers. The operative median pay is about £25k. The technical specialists group has a median of around £60k. The spread of this group is bigger and hence the curve is broader than that for the operatives, and there are fewer of them. This group might describe the marketers, software developers and product designers and their range of pay is from £25k to over £100k with the bulk paid between about £40k and £80k.

Above this group is the management team. As we've shown it, a few well paid technical specialists are paid above the lower-paid management team members. It's not untypical for the Managing Director to be paid, say, £130k, with perhaps the financial controller to be paid £90k with three or four others paid around the median of £100k.

We also show a small manual support group, perhaps comprising cleaners or gardeners. The bulk of these employees are paid just above the statutory minimum pay.

Any of these distributions could be skewed. In a more homogenous firm, one distribution might be adequate to describe pay across the firm. This picture has been built with several example 100-employee firms in mind, but the form applies to all SMEs, and indeed to all firms.

10.1.6   *Pay differences*

We saw in Figure 10-1, that pay in a firm tends to follow one or more frequency distributions, and to a rough approximation, pay in a firm follows the bell-shaped curve of the normal distribution. The middle value is the median and there's a spread of values about that median.

The spread is typically described by the standard deviation, a pay value either side of the median. About 68% of the population (of employees in that category in the firm) has pay that lies between the upper and lower standard deviation. The standard deviation of the technical specialists in our example is about £20k – the median is about £60k and 68% of the population lie between about £40k and £80k. The standard deviation is often used to describe pay differences within a population, such as for engineers within a firm.

Comparison of medians is typically used to compare pay between different populations. We can say, for example, that often women are paid a lower median pay for a given job than men – this is the well-publicised 'gender pay gap'. We can quantify this statement by saying that the difference in median pay between male and female engineers is, say, £6.8k, with women paid less than men. Likewise, we could state the difference in medians of the market rate for a software engineer when employed in Manchester or London – the median pay is likely higher in London and we discuss this later.

10.1.7   *The way people think about pay*

Universally, studies have shown that money, and hence pay, is not a motivator. There is no influence or causality or moderator or mediator involving pay which affects the relationship between the job a person does and their motivation. There is no relationship that links a pay rise to improved performance.

But pay still has a part to play in enabling and potentially thwarting a person's performance. Pay is considered instrumental in the relationship. If there is enough pay for the employee to keep themselves and their family in the style that they believe is their right, they will be content. The relationship between job and performance that we describe in other chapters is then valid. But if there is not enough pay, motivation will be sapped, and performance will suffer. Motivation is sapped through the feeling of injustice.

So, pay is a so-called 'negative hygiene factor'. Enough or too much does nothing and managers should focus their performance management efforts elsewhere. Too little saps motivation. Low pay acts negatively until, on increasing pay, some threshold of pay is reached, and the negative affect abates.

Pay is considered instrumental in life. It's not pay itself, but what pay enables, that matters. To a young person, it may be the flashy car that it allows them to buy, or the expensive holidays it allows them to go on with their mates. An employee in their thirties and forties may value pay to provide for their family. And an older employee may need less pay because they need less money – their values have shifted towards contribution to society over hedonistic personal enjoyment.

Pay also links to the employee's perceived position in society, created by what they can buy, and this creates a general feeling of wellbeing and pride.

Typically, an employee's pay rises with increased competence and confidence that comes from experience. The more an employee can earn for an employer through their increased competence and experience, the more they will likely be paid. In many people, there is therefore a link between career advancement and pay. This link is a long-term extrinsic motivator that drives their personal development. Others simply take the money and spend it without any great thought for the future.

10.2   Pay and the law

10.2.1   *Pay and contract terms and conditions*

The way a person is paid is determined in their contract of employment. Some people are paid an hourly wage whilst others are paid an annual salary. Whilst individuals can negotiate their own pay, it's important to ensure that the payment system doesn't lead to inadvertent discrimination, injustice, and lack of transparency.

Pay should be expressed in the terms and conditions of employment. The employee has a right to be paid for the work they do. And the employer has a right to expect the person to undertake the work for which they are being paid.

There are many terms used for the money paid to employees in exchange for the work that they do. Pay is often used to refer to those paid by the hour, whereas salary tends to suggest an annual figure that is paid in twelve equal parts.

There is no legal stipulation on the frequency of pay. In the past many people were paid weekly in cash. Most people now have their pay or salary paid directly into a personal bank or building society account. Many people are now paid monthly, easing the burden on firms of managing both weekly and monthly payrolls.

10.2.2   *Discrimination*

Discrimination can occur when managers pay part-time staff on a different rate to full time staff, or when jobs of equal value are paid different rates. The Equality Act 2010 stops employers blocking employees from discussing pay to check if there are any pay differences.

In the UK all employees, irrespective of gender, must be treated equally if their work is of a broadly similar nature (termed 'like work'). There are various ways of determining what is 'like' work. A robust job evaluation system and pay and benefits analysis will help. This is discussed fully in 10.5.

10.2.3 *Minimum wage*

Each April the National Minimum Wage (NMW) is set by the UK Government. The relevant hourly rate is dependent upon age and whether the person is an apprentice. It is an offence to pay below the minimum wage. Care must be taken to ensure that the NMW is not accidentally breached, for example where someone works additional hours but is not paid for them. These unpaid hours must be included when calculating the 'real' hourly rate.

A National Living Wage (NLW), as distinct from the above minimum wage (NMW), was introduced in 2016. Anyone aged 25 or older must be paid at least the NLW. This figure is also reviewed each April.

10.2.4 *Employee rights*

Employees have a right to have a payslip that details their pay before and after deductions such as tax. The reason for the deduction must be specified on the payslip. The payslip can be a printed document, or it can be an online document, and it must be provided on or before the date of the payment.

10.3 Statutory payments, deductions and tax

Employers are not allowed to make deductions from pay unless it is for a permitted reason. Tax and national insurance deductions and student loan deductions are allowed. Deductions can also be made based on court orders, under an Attachment of Earnings order.

Deductions can also be made when the employee specifically agrees, for example to repay a season ticket loan or for family health care cover.

If an overpayment of pay or expenses is made, then the overpayment can be deducted. It is always worth ensuring that the oversite of the employer does not cause hardship to employee when the repayment is made. This might mean making the deduction over several payment cycles.

10.3.1 *Social security*

The social tax in the UK is the National Insurance Contribution or NIC. Both employee and employer pay a contribution based on the earnings of the employee. The NI contributions allow the employee to draw state pension (at the relevant age) and access other benefits such as maternity allowance. For the tax year to April 2023, the employee normally pays contribution of 13.25% with a further 3.25% of earnings over £4,189 per month, and the employer pays 15.05%. These figures may go up or down in future tax years at the behest of the government in power. The employer withholds the employee's contribution and pays it to HMRC, the government tax agency.

10.3.2 *Income tax*

Income tax is paid by all employees when they reach the tax threshold(s). Each year the government determines what the personal allowance will be. This sets what tax payments are due. As with NI contributions the employer withholds the tax and pays it directly to HMRC.

10.3.3   *Pensions*

Since the Pensions Act 2008 came into force all employers must put eligible employees into a workplace pension scheme. Automatic enrolment is a legal requirement unless the employee opts out. The minimum contribution of both employee and employer has been increasing since 2008. From April 2019 the minimum contribution that the employer can make is 3%. The total minimum combined contribution to workplace pension schemes is 5%. As with other taxes, the employer is responsible for withholding the employee contribution and then paying both employer and employee contributions to the pension provider.

Employers need to be sure that when people become eligible for automatic enrolment, they are put into the pension scheme unless they opt out. Triggers for eligibility could include overtime payments pushing the level of pay above the earnings threshold. If a trigger applies, the employee must be automatically enrolled unless they opt-out.

10.3.4   *Benefits in kind*

A benefit in kind (BIK) is something provided by the employer that is not pay. Often referred to as 'perks' or 'fringe benefits' they include company cars, private medical insurance, and free gym membership.

Benefits may be provided free to the employee, but they must pay tax on the benefit. Employers are required to issue a P11D certificate to all employees receiving benefits. The information provided allows HMRC to calculate the amount of tax due from the employee. The personal allowance is then adjusted, and the employer advised of the tax code to be used for the tax year ahead.

10.3.5   *SMP, SAP, SPP and SSP*

Statutory Maternity Pay (SMP), Statutory Adoption Pay (SAP) and Statutory Paternity Pay (SPP) are all paid to eligible employees, as is Shared Parental Pay (ShPP). Eligibility depends on earnings and length of service.

Statutory Sick Pay (SSP) is paid to eligible employees when they are absent due to sickness. In 2014 the scheme enabling employers to reclaim SSP payments from the government was abolished. However, firms could be eligible for an employment allowance which reduces the Employers NI liability. SSP is a very low monetary allowance and is not enough for an employee to live on.

Employers need to understand when the relevant dates click in for the different types of pay and absence or leave.

10.4   Basics of pay systems

Pay management in a firm is aided by a policy, a structure, and a system. The policy states what the manager hopes to achieve in the pay system and outlines how pay will work in the firm. The structure is the relationship between pay and likely performance (or its antecedents of competencies and behaviours) and we illustrate how structures might be constructed. And the pay system is the complete set of tools that help the manager achieve fairness and we discuss those.

10.4.1   *Idea of a labour market*

Firms are in competition for the efforts of employees. Firms enter the labour market by advertising vacancies and compete in that market based on price. One firm will out-bid another and win an employee's service. In the end, the amount that firms are prepared to offer versus the amount that employees will accept stabilises around a 'market price' for an employee with a given set of competencies and behaviours. We then get the idea of a market median salary for, say, a software developer in London of £55k.

Scarcity of certain competencies and behaviours allows the employee to hold out for a higher salary.

The result is the classic economics supply and demand curves representing market (demand) and industry (supply).

Economics theory suggests that every employee is a rational being who is out to maximise their own gains. If this were so, no-one would work for a charity, no-one would do voluntary work and no-one would take an internship. Those and many other employment types pay much less than the market rate.

Instead, people are emotional, thinking beings who will strive to maximise their utility – a much broader aim that encompasses enjoyment, contribution to society and feelings of value. Employees also hedge. They engage in something with no pay or low pay today, in the hope of greater rewards sometime in the future.

The price is therefore much more complex than just the pay offered. It extends to non-financial benefits and even to the reputation of the employer – since even this has a future value on the employee's CV.

Market median pay, supply and demand, payment for rare skills and all the trappings of a labour market are important, but so too are many idiosyncratic factors. Managers must think beyond money in pay negotiations. Pay is a complex practical and psychological concept. Pay must engage with both human logic and emotion.

10.4.2   *Pay policy*

Pay policy is the stated way in which the firm will respond to the labour market and hire people it needs while paying them what it can afford.

It may state, for example, that the firm will pay median pay for all employees, gaining competitive advantage (and hence being able to attract top talent) by offering exciting work and excellent conditions and benefits. Or it could recognise scarcity in some skills and knowledge and state that it will use scarcity supplements to elevate pay to lie at the upper decile of that pay distribution.

The point is that pay policy should be quantified and used to guide offers made.

10.4.3   *Spot pay systems*

Arguably, the spot system is simply a reflection of the labour market for all the jobs in the firm and is not a system at all – it's simply a record of deals done to get employees to join and then a continuing record of in-firm pay negotiations.

If a manager searches for a new employee and makes a pay offer that's accepted, that gives one point on a spot system representing a price paid for those competencies and behaviours. If the manager repeats such deals 50 times, they build a range of pay from the most junior to the most senior. Each has a point of market equilibrium at that point in time and under those conditions. If a software developer comes on board for £55k, the salary for a developer is set at £55k for future deals until further deals provide further information about the market price.

Most SMEs in the UK run spot systems.

In principle, a spot system is a perfect reflection of the perfect market and hence should be a perfect system. And it takes no real effort. An example is shown in Figure 10-2.

But as modern economists concur, perfect markets don't exist, mainly because the manager does not have perfect knowledge about price. And the spot system is no exception.

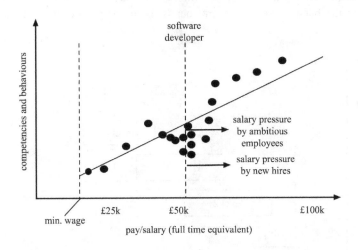

Figure 10-2: The spot salary system - salaries plotted against value

Firstly, the pay is often suggested by the recruitment agent doing the search. The agent sees a snapshot of the market and will not have an accurate price. The search fee is also a function of the first year's salary and hence it is in that agent's interest to talk up the salary and benefits. And decisions to join may be made based on non-financial criteria. The deal salary is therefore inherently errored.

Secondly, the competencies and behaviours of one software developer, for example, will be different from those of another. Even by benchmarking to a perfect market, there will be a range of salaries for any one job.

And thirdly, nothing's static within the firm. Each employee will be pitching to the manager for more pay. Each will be threatening to quit. The manager will be pressured to increase pay for ambitious employees, possibly while ignoring others less vocal.

Spot pay systems are not systems at all. But plotting salaries like this can be useful when combined with job ranking as a job evaluation system to find and correct irregularities and reason an offered pay.

10.4.4 *Banded pay systems*

Most pay systems with associated structure are banded systems (Figure 10-3). Job size is represented firstly by several bands rising from the lowest to highest and secondly by

progress along a band. Conceptually, someone could enter the system at Level 1, progress
through levels 2 to 4 and end their career as Managing Director at Level 5.

The narrower the band, the less scope each individual manager has for negotiating
pay. Conversely, if the band is wide, the manager can elect to place the employee at a point
in the band of their choosing. Wide band structures might have band widths that are 50% to
100% or more of band median.

Typically, points scoring evaluation systems determine which band the job falls
into, leaving the manager to propose the actual position in the band. Often bands link
to competencies and we discussed how development might be linked to categorisation
of trainee, supervised practitioner, practitioner, and expert. This categorisation might
apply within the band or across several bands as the employee grows their skills and
knowledge.

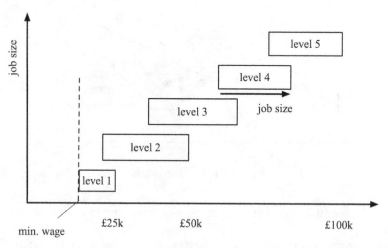

Figure 10-3: An example banded salary system

In pay structures in public services, where unions demand that all employees doing a job
are paid the same, job evaluation leads to a pay spine system. An example is the higher
education pay structure where there are 51 separate spines or salary points grouped in lots
of five or six to give eight pay bands. Jobs are evaluated to lie on spine points and progress
is by promotion to a different job on a different spine point. This yields a very inflexible
system that most private sector managers would cringe at.

Wide band systems give flexibility and movement within the band, and hence pay is
under the manager's control.

An example of the likely pay distribution within a wide band is given in Figure 10-4.
Most employees will have a pay around the middle (in the Working Region). Those who
have been promoted incrementally to the top of the band (in the Expert region) may,
subject to conditions about competency, be ready for promotion to the next level or band.
Those just promoted from the level below will be in the Entry Region.

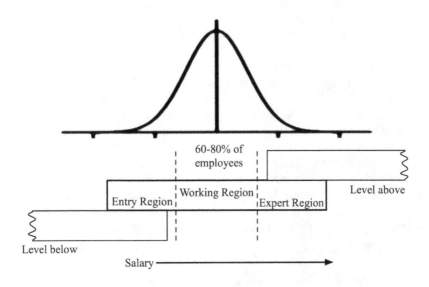

Figure 10-4: Typical pay distribution within a band

10.4.5 *Lifecycle of pay systems*

Pay systems have finite lives. Typically, they are developed considering the extant needs of the firm and they link to the labour market at a point in time. There are two aspects to system maintenance.

Firstly, the link between the labour market and the system must be re-set annually by benchmarking. This avoids the system drifting out of sync with the market (and its associated prices) from which the firm hires its new employees. Once adrift, the system will soon degrade as managers make more and more local corrections.

Secondly, the system should be assessed every few years for its continued ability to provide a fair means of managing pay, considering the changes in the firm and in the business environment. A good example is the introduction of a new route to the top technical levels in response to reduced numbers of manager opportunities as the firm re-structures to cut costs. Before the re-organisation, it may have been that the normal way to get more pay was to become a manager.

10.4.6 *Performance-based pay*

Typically, systems of pay assess the size of the job by the impact that it has on key competence-based performance measures. They assume that if someone has the required competence and behaviours, and that they are suitably motivated, they will yield the required performance and outcomes. Progression up the pay structure requires increases in competencies and behaviours commensurate with those of the level above.

But not all pay is determined in this way. Some managers consider that money is a motivator and pay directly for performance, attempting to by-pass all the complexities of organisational psychology. Pay for performance comes in many forms under the guise of bonus, commission or piece rate. Payment is conditional on some performance, defined from the outset by the manager.

Piece rate is simple enough. A Deliveroo worker, for example, is paid for every delivery made. If they make no deliveries, they get no pay, and if they manage to deliver twice as many as their colleague, they'll earn twice as much pay.

Commission is popular in sales where the salesperson earns a percentage of the sales value. Sometimes the firm is happy to be contractually bound to pay this commission come what may. In other instances, the link between performance and pay is less closely coupled. Here the firm may pay a bonus if the sales budget is achieved, but only also if the firm is profitable. The bonus may be structured more as a post hoc reward than an incentive.

Practical pay systems often comprise a competency-based core system to determine a base pay, topped up by a performance-based element of pay.

In our opinion performance-based pay systems don't work. All research suggests that they focus the employees on short term personal success and encourage all the wrong behaviours, particularly if the employee relies on the performance-based element for their livelihood.

10.4.7   *Giving employees a share*

We differentiate between individual performance-related pay and giving employees a share of the profits.

Individual performance-related pay (and even group performance-related pay) tends to reward individualistic, anti-social and damaging behaviour. On the other hand, tying reward to the success of the firm tends to foster the idea that 'we're all in this together' and hence encourages employees to work together, contributing to one-another's success.

Any performance related pay should be completely independent of the main pay system. The pay system should pay all employees a good wage for the job done. Other systems should add to this and be in all senses a 'bonus'. They should never be intended as an overt incentive but should strive to tap intrinsic motives like achievement and responsibility.

Reflection 10-1: About your salary policy, structure, and system

---

If you have a good, functioning pay system supported by a considered policy, think now about how it might be improved considering some of the principles we've discussed above.

If you have a spot system, or some other rather unstructured, chaotic system, how might you now implement some of the guidance given here?

10.5   Sizing jobs and setting pay

Logically, a job has a value to the firm. If the manager can exploit one job to give greater returns than another, the job giving the greater returns should be rewarded correspondingly.

We can therefore say that, in terms of returns to the business, some jobs are bigger than others.

Job evaluation is the sizing of each job in readiness for setting pay in line with that size.

10.5.1 *What gives a job a value?*

Simply, a job is of greater value if it earns more for the firm or has greater leverage in aiding the firm in meeting its strategic aims. A junior telecom engineer who is given small projects earns little for the firm. A principal engineer who works with clients' engineers to deliver hugely important solutions worth millions of Pounds earns a lot for the firm.

As Adam Smith suggested, a job holder with scarce skills and knowledge can negotiate a higher pay, particularly where those skills and knowledge enable other work. And likewise, when a jobholder takes many years to reach mastery, they can argue that their pay should recompense that training.

Generally, too, jobs that are more complex, more difficult to do or are generally in nasty environments are not necessarily bigger but earn more points on the value scale since fewer employees can or are prepared to do them.

So, value is first about earnings potential, and second is about scarcity – rewarding the few people possessing the skills and knowledge, and inclined or able to do the job. If the job earns little for the firm, there's little argument to pay well. And if everyone had the skills and knowledge, competition between would-be jobholders would deflate the price.

10.5.2 *Formal job evaluation*

Job evaluation aims to makes sense of the spot salary system by ordering the jobs in order of value to the firm. We give five examples below of how this might be done.

10.5.2.1 *Job ranking*
Under job ranking, a committee, comprising managers who know the jobs, would sit together, and rank all the jobs in the firm. It's as simple as that. They would turn a random list of jobs into a rank with less valuable jobs needing commonly found skills and knowledge at the bottom and very valuable jobs demanding scarce skills and knowledge at the top. The order should then reflect the pay for each job.

Typically, the managing director would be at the top of the heap and an admin assistant would be at the bottom.

In effect, job ranking is something that a manager might do to a spot salary system to check its sense. If the spot salary system and the job ranking don't match, corrective action to pay may be needed.

10.5.2.2 *Pairwise comparison*
Job ranking is easy when there are less than ten jobs. When there are, say, 30 jobs, pairwise comparison gives a neat process for achieving the same aim. Under pairwise comparison, we create a matrix of jobs as shown in Figure 10-5. Again, a committee is generally used comprising managers who between them know all the jobs.

Each job is compared with every other job as a pair. If the Accounts Ledger Controller is considered by the committee to be a bigger job than the Bought Ledger Controller, it scores a '2'. If it is judged to be the same size, it scores a '1'. And if it is judged lesser, it scores a '0'. Obviously, the converse must apply and hence when compared the other way around, a '2' scores a '0', and when the same, both scores should be '1'.

When the scores are added up for each job, this gives a rank order. The salaries should therefore match that order. If not, corrective action may be needed.

	accounts ledger controller	bought ledger controller	computer operator	customer service agent	marketing assistant	receptionist	sales manager	secretary/ personal asst.	total score	rank order
accounts ledger controller		0	1	0	1	2	0	0	4	7
bought ledger controller	2		2	2	2	2	0	2	12	2
computer operator	1	0		1	1	2	0	0	5	6
customer service agent	2	0	1		2	1	0	1	7	3
marketing assistant	1	0	1	0		2	0	2	6	5
receptionist	0	0	0	1	0		0	0	1	8
sales manager	2	2	2	2	2	2		2	14	1
secretary/personal asst.	2	0	2	2	0	2	0		8	3

Figure 10-5: Pairwise comparison matrix

It might take a committee of six people eight hours of hard work to appraise 70 jobs in pairwise comparison. We believe that 70 is about the limit for this tool.

10.5.2.3   *Job classification*
If the firm is too large to make the above approaches viable, the ranking activity may be done on one department. That department can be used to set the structure for jobs company wide. Jobs in other departments can then be compared laterally with this reference set.

The Sales Manager job in Figure 10-5 might be considered the same size as a Product Manager in Marketing, a Test Systems Manager in Production, and a Product Owner in Software Development. There is therefore no need to complete a pairwise comparison considering these jobs in isolation.

Note that this method realises a rank order where jobs have the same score and hold the same relative position. Some jobs may attract a scarcity supplement, making the actual salary paid different.

10.5.2.4   *Rate factor*
Whilst ranking approaches may give a relative position and hence a relative pay, they do not tell a manager how much to pay an employee. The first of the 'factor methods' – the

rate factor method – allows the manager to read off a rate for each job. This is perhaps the first useful method where hiring is delegated, and managers need to quote pay without reference to others.

Here, several factors are agreed on as being universally desirable. In the example in Figure 10-6 four factors are shown: skills, effort, responsibility and working conditions. A range of monetary values for each would then be agreed by a panel of managers.

job	factors				hourly rate
	skill	effort	responsibility	working conditions	
admin assistant	£5.00	£2.00	£2.00	£2.00	£11.00
secretary	£5.50	£2.50	£3.50	£2.00	£13.50
supervisor	£8.00	£3.50	£5.00	£1.50	£18.00
manager	£11.00	£4.50	£7.00	£1.50	£24.00

Figure 10-6: Rate factor method of job evaluation

Then final pay is the sum of the monetary awards for each factor for each job. In the example, the Manager is paid £24.00 per hour whereas the Admin Assistant is paid £11.00.

10.5.2.5 *Points factor*
The rate factor system works, but it is perhaps inflexible. Each factor must be continually updated to account for changes in cost of living and market price. Points factor systems allow the manager to assemble polynomials with relevant factors for the firm and to determine pay using a single conversion once a total points score is available.

The essence of points factor methods is the development of the factors. The factors represent important aspects of each job in a firm. Each factor is assigned points for size. This is best understood by way of an example. Here's a polynomial with three factors.

$$\text{Wage (£)} = f(Pkh + Pps + Pa) \times k$$

In this case, the factors are know-how (kh), problem solving (ps) and accountability (a). Those factors are important to the firm and give each job a measure of size. Points for know-how (Pkh) might comprise points for technical knowledge, management breadth and interpersonal competence. Problem solving (Pps) might include points for working in a complex thinking environment and with difficult thinking challenges. And accountability

(Pa) might include scope of freedom to act, magnitude of allowable action and impact of that action.

The salary is arrived at by summing the points, multiplied by any constants (k). The equation gives a total point score. Referencing a lookup table that converts points to pay gives the final pay.

Some firms develop and maintain their own points factor job evaluation systems. Others subscribe to systems like the Hay (now Korn Ferry) system on which the above example is based. Established systems are generally tried and tested for various industries. Since such systems have access to a lot of data, the subscription generally also includes benchmarking with jobs across the labour market. The downside is that generally the manager must adopt the scheme in its entirety. There's little scope for simplification and customisation.

Systems of evaluation where jobs are classified and benchmarked in size across others in the firm leads to the notion of job families. A job family for engineers might comprise Junior Engineer, Engineer, Senior Engineer, and Principal Engineer. Each would have an escalating point score and hence salary. Each would be benchmarked (using their points score) to other families such as the accountants or the marketers.

10.5.3   *What makes a big job*

So, what gives a job its size, and hence, for a given firm, what determines pay for that job?

It's everything that you might think. In a for-profit firm it's responsibility for action across a large area, responsibility for the actions of many others, work in a complex environment, responsibility for high monetary value outcomes and the management of high risk. In a not-for-profit organisation, it might focus instead on key responsibilities that allow the charity or agency to achieve its aims. All managers will have their own ideas about what gives size.

10.6   Pay irregularities

10.6.1   *Pay by age and experience*

Logically, pay rises as the employee gains competencies, even if only where they repeat the job tasks. They will inevitably get better at the job and hence be of more value to the firm, and command more in the labour market. This means that pay will rise with tenure.

Employees also seek promotion and change jobs across their career.

Research shows that pay peaks for men when they're in their late 40s or early 50s and, corrected for inflation, typically doubles over the period from early 20s to the peak. After the peak, it declines to anything up to half across the period from peak to retirement.

The picture is similar for women, but the peak is much lower, at around 80% of the male peak, and the peak occurs earlier – typically when women are in their late 30s.

10.6.2   *Managing scarcity*

The pay systems and job evaluation that we describe above paints a picture that effectively 'points equal pay' and that pay is the same for similar responsibility whatever the employee's discipline. That's not the case in many industries.

British universities are churning out a glut of marketers, but not enough engineers, for example. Logically, for the same responsibility, both marketers and engineers would be paid the same. But because there is scarcity of engineers, they are often paid a scarcity supplement.

Scarcity supplements are a way of maintaining equity in the pay and job evaluation systems but responding separately to the need to be competitive in a market where demand exceeds supply.

A typical value for a scarcity supplement might be in the range 10% to 30% of median pay.

The great advantage of scarcity supplements is that they can be increased and decreased and even removed altogether if the labour market changes. Change can be managed without breaking the pay and job evaluation systems.

10.6.3   *Managing anomalies*

From time to time, employees will have to be paid outside the structure of the pay and job evaluation systems – thereby creating anomalies. This may be necessary to attract rare talent or simply because the firm bought another enterprise and the employees from that are transferred in at inflated salaries.

Generally, those paid above the in-house scales are 'red-circled' – they get no more increases until all others have risen over time to their level. Management of such anomalies is always difficult.

10.6.4   *Negotiating pay*

Pay is negotiated when a new employee is made an offer. It's negotiated again whenever an existing employee approaches their manager with a claim that their pay is out of kilter with the market.

If the manager is running a sensible salary policy, structure and system, the event of an employee wanting more is a problem. It suggests that the manager, by giving in and awarding an increase, must introduce an anomaly.

We consider that it is always better to continually review pay and to be sure that it is as competitive as the firm wants and can sustain. Then all claims can be confidently rebuffed.

10.6.5   *Bias and discrimination in pay*

It's illegal to pay men and women differently for the same work done. And it's illegal to discriminate in such a way against any group with protected characteristics. So, why is there is a gender pay gap, and indeed other pay gaps, between some groups and the norms for the firm?

In the case of gender, it's complex. Typically, women take time off to have children. On return to work, they also take the main role in child rearing and hence lose seniority and opportunity. Societal attitudes toward families and who does what in partnerships will have to change before the gender pay gap is eradicated.

Managers should, however, try hard to remove gender bias and bias against other people such as the disabled, ethnic minorities and older employees. A diverse workforce is rich in diverse thinking and should be encouraged.

10.6.6   Directors' pay

Directors may be advisors or employees. If they are advisors, they are typically under a director's service contract and are paid a negotiated fee for their attendance at Board meetings and the like. If they are employees, they should participate in the firm's job evaluation system and associated pay system.

Some firms, however, negotiate employee-directors' salaries and hence the salary system excludes them. This produces a two-tier company and introduces stresses. Managers should take care when determining directors' remuneration.

The press is full today of stories about director's pay. We consider that no director should be paid more than five times the median salary and no more than ten times the salary of the lowest paid employee.

10.6.7   Pay transparency

Employees talk to their colleagues about their pay. And it's never difficult to estimate what another person is paid. So, there is no such thing as total pay secrecy.

Managers should, however, never disclose information about the pay and conditions of individual employees. Making the pay structure and job evaluation system public is, however, very wise – it allows employees to see that there is a fair system used to determine pay and shows what each employee must do to advance.

10.6.8   Managing an international workforce

Designing pay systems to manage justice is difficult enough in the UK alone. International operations complicate things dramatically.

Employees are employed under the laws of the country in which the job is 'habitually done' – even if they work for a UK firm. Where the job is done is normally where the employee lives. So, they are paid under local laws. If they are living and working in France, the French codes and tax system apply. And that means that their salaries may also be governed by French statute and collective trades agreements.

It also means that they will benefit from insurances like unemployment insurance and health insurance that we in the UK consider a 'benefit'. In France, if someone is made redundant, they are paid about half their present salary by the government for a minimum of two years to help them find a new job.

Many countries also have hugely generous state pensions that click in early. By comparison, the UK Government pays a meagre £9.6k per annum from the age of 66. In line with the UK's government policy for the past decades, UK employees must use part of their salary to buy a private pension. Employees will naturally factor in this need when discussing pay.

There are many countries where normal financial conditions surrounding work are significantly better for the employee than in the UK.

Statutory 'benefits' must be funded by governments – and the social taxes paid by foreign employers to fund them are very high – in France, for example, social taxes on employers are around 70%. This compares with the UK's 15.05% Employers' National Insurance (2022/2023). Arguably, employees in any country get what their firms pay their government for. Comparison of salaries and 'benefits' worldwide is therefore complex.

In the UK, some employers provide additional benefits that might come close to those provided by governments and firms abroad, while others don't. Some UK employers elect instead to pay a high base salary from which employees can fund such benefits privately.

10.6.9   *Cost of living and corresponding salaries*

When comparing salaries, there are two additional elements that must be considered. First, countries have hugely different costs of living. As examples, Figure 10-7 shows the cost-of-living indices for six cities. The effective salary, converted to Pounds Sterling required to give the jobholder the same standard of living, is also shown in the right-hand column.

Country/city	Cost of living index	Relative salary (for a Lead Software Developer)
London (reference)	100%	£68,000
Manchester	88%	£60,000
Madrid	65%	£45,000
Alicante	50%	£35,000
Berlin	85%	£58,000
Milan	85%	£58,000

Figure 10-7: Relative salaries across Europe

London is the most expensive city in Europe in which to live and that's reflected in the highest market salary. In the list shown, Alicante is the least expensive.

This table illustrates that to create a given standard of living worldwide, salaries must be adjusted in line with cost of living. And as the indices for London and Manchester show, salaries across a country must likewise be adjusted. This alone causes huge issues for international pay systems. Someone earning £38k in Alicante will likely be very upset to learn about someone earning nearly double in London. They will likely not consider cost of living.

Second, salary depends on labour market supply and demand. If there is no demand for Software Developers in Cape Town, for example, but there are many leaving local universities such that supply exceeds demand, this will deflate the salary offered. It could be that in such a case, the equivalent market rate is, say, £20k. Again, the bad feeling that this may generate when someone in Cape Town learns about typical London salaries will likely be immense. Again, they will likely not consider rates for the job where they live.

And finally, people are somewhat mobile both within a country and internationally. Brexit has curtailed migration between the EU and UK, but it's still an issue across the EU27 and for high-skill employees who can meet visa rules. And of course, it's prevalent within countries. Employees will migrate to take advantage of higher pay elsewhere. It's relatively simple to move from Madrid to Alicante or from London to Manchester in search of more money. And with the rise in home working, someone can easily live in Manchester and benefit from a London salary.

So, to summarise, employees will need to be paid very different salaries across the World and even across countries. These salaries must reflect:

- The benefits that are provided to employees by governments because of social taxes paid by employers.
- The cost of living between cities in a country, and between countries.
- The market price (determined by the labour market) that must be paid locally by an employer to secure the services of an employee.

There are a variety of techniques that can be used to manage these differences. In all cases they need to be referenced to the core UK pay or salary system with its bands and points. They need also to make use of the job evaluation system to ensure that equivalent jobs are identified regardless of where in the world the job is done.

10.7   Company sick pay

A few mainly larger organisations pay what's termed Company Sick Pay (CSP). All managers should consider some form of CSP payment. Here we set out a possible structure.

10.7.1   *Background*

Many UK Government employees like nurses, police officers and teachers get full wages paid for anything up to a year of absence, so the Government, as an employer, pays its employees 'Company' Sick Pay.

Some firms have realised that to attract and retain key staff, they must do something similar. Some firms even create a two-tier workforce with key staff paid CSP while others (in the same firm) must rely on Statutory Sick Pay (SSP).

At the time of writing SSP is just under £100 a week for up to 28 weeks – a miserly level on which few can live. The UK SSP scheme compares badly with sick pay schemes paid by EU states. Many EU state schemes approach full wages paid for up to two years.

Whilst all managers in the UK might want to continue to pay full wages whenever an employee is off sick, only the Government and a few in the private sector can afford such generosity.

So, what are other managers to do?

The manager typically staffs their firm with the number of employees commensurate with the turnover. Generally, the manager will assume that a small number of staff will be off sick at any one time – and they will over-staff slightly to cope with the lost effort. The manager then budgets to make a profit at this staffing level.

The manager's typical starting position is that when an employee is off sick, the firm ceases payment of wages after a few days. The incremental cost to the firm of that sickness is therefore near zero and the situation is simply managed.

But that's not sustainable in an environment where the manager must strive hard to find, attract and retain good staff. Some compromise is needed to make the firm appear as a caring firm – one to which the employee will commit. Some scheme must be developed between the extremes of expecting employees to rely on SSP alone and paying full wages for ever.

10.7.2 *Typical absence curve*

To develop such a compromise, we first need to understand sickness patterns.

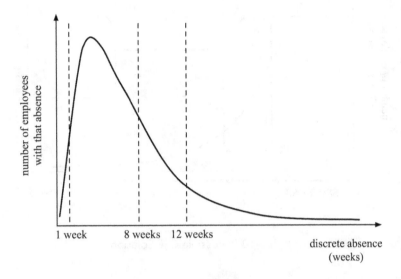

Figure 10-8: Typical Absence Curve

Typically, staff sickness days follows a skewed normal curve like the one shown in Figure 10-8. A small number of staff will go off for up to a week a year. The bulk of the employees will be off for no more than eight weeks a year. And a small but still significant number will be off for more time than that – between eight and twelve weeks. Finally, a very small number of staff (maybe up to one or two percent) will be off on long-term sick with absence spanning out into many months. The exact numbers will be unique to the firm, but most firms follow this trend.

If one accepts that most firms don't have the financial flexibility to pay CSP for periods of more than a few weeks, a CSP scheme must be developed considering both financial constraint and absence pattern.

Figure 10-9 shows one such solution. The firm implements a company sick pay scheme and pays full wages for a period from the start of sickness to, say, six to eight weeks out. Note that all CSP schemes must meet the minimum requirements of the employer's obligation to pay SSP. This is offset against the CSP scheme which can then be as generous as the company wishes.

At the six- or eight-week point, the CSP then deceases and the sick employee then enters a moratorium period when the firm drops the CSP to SSP levels. The employee must then rely on that and their own savings. They are advised about that on taking the job. Then to cover long-term sickness, the firm pays for Permanent Health Insurance (PHI), a form of income protection provided as a standard product by insurance companies.

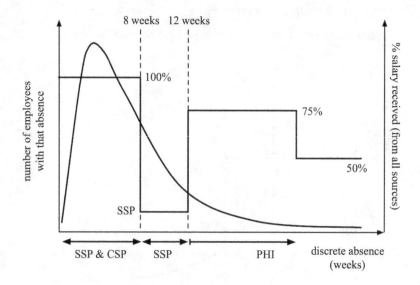

Figure 10-9: Possible CSP Solution

10.7.3 *About income protection insurance*

PHI is bought by the firm on behalf of all the employees and the costs are typically modest. There are various forms of cover demanding various moratorium periods and providing various options for amount and duration of cover. It would be for the firm to decide what it needs using the arguments above. As shown in Figure 10-9, one example of cover is to fund 75% of wages beginning at the end of three months and lasting one year. After that, the payments for someone suffering some life-changing malady or accident rendering them unable to work again would drop to say 50% of wages for life.

The big advantage of the firm paying for the insurance is that significantly better pay-out conditions can be secured by a firm insuring several employees over a single employee taking out PHI for themselves. A company scheme is viable – a personal insurance is less so.

Typically, employees are happy with this type of company scheme since it covers the two big worries that they have about falling sick.

First, they typically live by spending their wages each week or month, saving a little. Their first risk of falling into hardship is if they are off for several weeks. In the company scheme, the firm covers that risk and pays CSP.

Second, they worry about what will happen to their family if they contract some serious malady or accident that stops them working permanently. They know there's a low chance of that, but the effect is huge – severe hardship including perhaps loss of housing. In the company sick pay model, that's covered by the PHI.

They will of course have a lower-level worry about being off for longer than the period for which they have CSP cover – the eight-to-twelve-week period in the example. They will consider, however, that the chance of medium-term sickness is relatively low, and they'll accept this. They'll need a few thousand pounds in their bank to cover it.

This structure mirrors somewhat the 'benefits' of the French and Nordic systems where states pay sick pay, maintaining payments at liveable levels whenever a person is sick. It's a compromise. It makes the firm highly attractive as an employer to people in the 25-45 age range who value a caring firm to support their families. It means that no employee will be under financial hardship when it matters most. And all the employee's energy can be expended in getting well. But with the CSP (mirroring SSP in its later stages), personal savings and PHI, the firm doesn't carry all the costs.

The benefits to the firm of supporting employees when they are sick, with the aim of getting them back to work with minimum strain on their families, cannot be over-stated. Managers will also need to develop CSP policy for when employees have multiple periods off in any one year.

10.8   The benefit of benefits

Benefits are a strange notion. In the UK, we've grown accustomed to being paid a salary and then being given a string of other monetary and non-monetary goods and services like pensions, cars, and insurances. In many other countries, a good salary is paid, the firm is taxed, and such additions are provided by the government from those taxes.

The UK system of add-ons is as complex as it is strange. Some firms engage with add-ons. Others don't. But all firms must provide a certain bare-minimum set of entitlements. We discuss here benefits – goods and services above the statutory minimum.

10.8.1   *Why give benefits?*

There are two simple reasons why a manager might feel that they want to give benefits.

Firstly, they may have to. Competitors in the labour market may have made the decision to provide certain benefits. Any firm not providing equivalent benefits would not be attractive. There are many examples. Firms employing scientists and engineers may find themselves having to provide enhanced pensions, and funding and time off for higher degrees, and health insurance. Firms in London in certain industries may have to provide travel loans. And firms employing senior staff in the construction industry may have to provide a car and make it available for private use.

Firms can choose not to compete on benefits but instead provide an equivalent monetary amount to allow the benefit to be bought by the employee privately. This could work, though often a firm can use its buying power to buy better benefits for a lower price.

Secondly, they may realise that there's benefit in benefits. While employees may value benefits, so too should the manager. Private medical insurance avoids employees waiting in NHS queues. Sick pay and income protection build commitment. And personal development enables the manager to exploit employees' new skills and knowledge. Any benefit should be cash neutral – its cost is balanced completely by its contribution to the P&L.

The following are examples of common benefits.

10.8.1.1   *Removal expenses*
Payment of removal expenses is almost a given for new recruits with scarce skills and knowledge. These payments allow firms to hire employees who live outside the firm's catchment area and support them in moving house. Some relocation costs are exempt from reporting and paying tax and National Insurance.

10.8.1.2 *Cars and vans*

There was a day when a huge number of employees were given cars and free petrol for private use. Slowly over the years HMRC has made the tax regime less beneficial for the employee and now cars and petrol are taxed to make them unattractive for all but those who really need them.

Much more attractive today is the grant of a car allowance that enables the employee to procure a car and make it available when needed for work journeys.

10.8.1.3 *Private medical cover*

In today's National Health Service, it takes many weeks to receive treatment. This wait and associated suffering takes its toll on the employee, and on their family.

The result of illness is reduced performance. The provision of private medical insurance allows the employee to 'go private' and access a raft of private doctors and hospitals. The result is that the patient is seen quickly, absence from work is minimised and the debilitating effects of suffering avoided.

Many firms provide cover for just the employee, while others cover both employee and their family.

10.8.1.4 *Income protection and sickness*

There's nothing more worrying for an employee than not being able to meet mortgage payments and support their family if they are not able to work. The UK's National Insurance is a tax paid by employees and firms to funding state benefits for the employee in event of sickness. It is a contribution to costs, but for most employees, it is wholly inadequate.

We discussed above the notion of Company Sick Pay and how CSP benefits both employees and firm.

10.8.1.5 *Private pensions*

The UK Government mandates that firms pay a minimum of 3% (from April 2019) of each employee's salary into a government-approved pension scheme. The employee must add 5% to this to benefit from tax allowances and meet the minimum pension contribution level.

Most pensions advisors will concur that employees today will need to pay more than 25% of their salary into a private pension for their working life to come close to the recommended benefit of 70% of their income in retirement. This means that the Government's scheme is a bare-minimum and, we believe, is totally inadequate. Employees and firms must seek to encourage private pension schemes for all.

As we note, whether a firm engages with this idea depends on the competitive environment. Some will offer pensions close to the 25% recommendation where the employee pays, say, 8% and the firm tops up by a further 17%. Many will provide an inflated salary and tell employees to make their own arrangements. And many will do nothing (other than the statutory minimum).

10.8.1.6 *Other assorted benefits*

Simply, there are many other benefits from cut price cycle purchase though first-class travel to accounts and discount at staff shops or partner shops. Bizarrely, personal development is also seen by some firms as a benefit, and employees enter a learning agreement to pay back funding if they leave within a given time.

Today, there is much discussion about work-life balance, with employees able to work flexibly and with reduced hours (and perhaps correspondingly reduced pay). This too might be considered a 'benefit'. Whether such schemes are attractive will depend on the firm's attitude to wellbeing and its response to the competitive environment.

Reflection 10-2: About benefits

Considering the above discussion, and your existing benefits offered, do you think that your firm offers competitive benefits? Should you offer better benefits? And how might you use benefits to embrace work-life balance and employee wellbeing in the future?

10.9   Idea of total reward

Total reward emerged as an idea to highlight to employees that the benefit of working for a particular firm was not just counted in pay. As an argument, it aims to say, 'look, we provide a wide range of benefits' and emphasises that the total reward for an employee's efforts is extensive.

Such a notion is steeped in history. As an example, miners in the 19th century benefitted from pay, and free housing and coal. The value of free housing and coal then maybe exceeded pay.

10.9.1   *Concept of total reward*

Total reward includes all the things that an employee considers valuable. For example, feeling appreciated, opportunities for development, pay, and benefits. What the total reward looks like also depends on what the firm values. The total reward should help drive the business forward and provide competitive advantage. To do this it must be linked to the business strategy. Reward must benefit the business as well as benefiting the employees.

10.9.2   *Attempting links to motivation*

According to World at Work there are six elements that, when implemented effectively, can have a positive impact on motivation and retention: pay, benefits, work-life balance, recognition, performance management, and career development.

10.9.3   *Aligning reward to the business*

Each of the six elements of the total reward strategy is instrumental in attracting and retaining employees who perform effectively and contribute to the results and profitably of the business.

Having an effective reward strategy will ensure that the right people are in the right jobs. They will be rewarded appropriately for their efforts, and all other things being right, they will be motivated and engaged. When the total reward strategy works effectively it underpins the competitive advantage of the firm.

10.9.4 *Idiosyncratic employment deals*

Idiosyncratic deals or i-deals are special arrangements that an employee has with their manager. They are deals made that sit alongside the terms and conditions of employment. In many cases i-deals are contractual in the same way as the expressed and statutory terms and conditions.

Social exchange, discussed in Chapter 5 requires one person doing a favour for another. In this case the manager grants something that the employee sees as favourable. Maybe it's working from home every Friday or leaving early on Wednesday to run a Cub Pack. Commitment likely increases with the value of the i-deal agreement.

But beware, increased commitment from one employee could be offset by the negative effect this may have on the employee's colleagues. Also, take care that i-deals don't lead to inadvertent discrimination.

10.10   Chapter Summary

Pay is hugely important. But more so is how pay is determined for each employee.

The employee agrees to work under the direction of the entrepreneur (the owner of the firm, represented by their agent, the manager) in return for a regular wage. But how much wage? It was easy when the employee was an independent supplier – then the payment was an exchange in return for deliverables and was set by the market rate. But now, how is the wage determined?

This leads us to a long list of criteria that influence pay. The result is that, across society, people are paid anything from pay that keeps them in poverty to pay that keeps them in luxury. And managers must position their firm, and the jobs that their people do, somewhere on this greyscale. The pay will substantially be determined by how much the firm can afford, itself determined by the market in which the firm trades. But there's more.

Both the economic contract and the psychological contract demand that the system of pay is fair. This requires that both procedural justice and distributive justice is done – that the process of setting pay is fair, and employees feel that the amount that they get is fair, considering their effort expended on behalf of the firm. All systems of pay – formal and ad hoc – are continually evaluated by employees for fairness.

There is considerable science in pay systems. First, there is the idea of a market – that each employee has a market value – a pay that they would be offered by a new employer if they quit right now. To balance the market rate and what the firm wants to pay, the manager determines a pay policy – how they intend to manage pay, considering the constraints of market and firm. This leads to two criteria of pay – pay for competence and pay for performance. Both link to the profits available to the firm through competence and performance as a result of employing the employee.

The desire for procedural justice and distributive justice has led academics and firms to develop reasoned pay structures. The rationale is that if fairness is designed into the system through a structure, justice will follow. This does rather assume that the manager follows a policy, and that this policy embraces justice too.

Once a system (comprising a structure controlled by a policy) is in place, all that's then needed is some objective way of sizing jobs so that the manager can position all their jobs in the firm in the structure and literally read off the pay due. And there you have job evaluation.

All job evaluation methods are relative. Jobs are placed in rank order. We highlight four approaches. Simple ranking and pairwise comparison are useful methods for small firms. The rate factor and points factor methods are probably best for firms with the effort available to set up such complexity. Of course, like most complex systems, once the effort has been put in up front, the complete pay system and its associated job evaluation method are simple to operate. Ultimately, the points factor method is the fairest approach allowing good transparency in method.

Of course, not all jobs fit with such rational methods. In the end, the manager will have to pay someone with significant bargaining power a significantly different wage. Directors' jobs are often outwith the pay structure and job evaluation system. The pay for those jobs is often determined by negotiation.

And for those jobs requiring scarce skills and knowledge, some adjustment is needed to meet the market price. To negotiate all such jobs will quickly see the pay system destroyed. These jobs are often paid a scarcity supplement that can be adjusted and removed as the labour market changes for those scarcities.

In the end, if benchmarking is used to relate pay to the labour market and if a robust pay structure with an appropriate job evaluation method is used, pay will cease to be a big issue for managers.

Managers might then look to the concept of total reward – the combination of all financial and all non-financial rewards – to remunerate employees. Total reward aims to highlight to employees just how good it is to work for the firm.

11
Making Change

11.1 Introducing change

Organisations, comprising people and technology, exist to achieve desirable outcomes for their stakeholders. Outcomes at the personal level aggregate to the corporate to realise high-level metrics like turnover and profit. But the way an organisation is configured, the skills and knowledge of its people and the technology that they use to achieve personal outcomes is not God-given. It's designed by someone who throughout this book we refer to as the manager.

Since the organisation is designed with specific skills and knowledge and technology, it can be re-designed by changing the skills and knowledge of the people and by changing the technology. It can also be re-designed by changing the way in which the people and technology interact. And it can be re-designed again and again until the manager considers that the extant configuration is achieving the outcome they want. The migration from one design to another is called change and it can be plotted against time.

Often the problem for the manager is that there are a huge number of variables in a firm's system. It's difficult therefore to see what change will realise a desired new outcome. Is it, for example, a new marketing campaign that's needed, or is it training in sales. Will a new complementary product bolster a tired portfolio, or is a new product range needed, requiring new developers to be hired? Or should the manager make the sales group redundant and train all the engineers to sell? As a result of this complexity, it's difficult to determine the change needed for desirable new outcomes. Nonetheless, and despite this complexity, it's the manager's job to determine what's to be done and hence to plan for change.

And the alternative? To leave all to chance – and that would be a dereliction of the manager's duty.

11.1.1 *Change as strategy*

In earlier chapters, we showed a simple form that can be used to state strategy: *Because A has a problem with B, we reckon if we do C to D, we'll get E.* C and D are what most people understand as 'strategy'. Strategy, and the idea of doing something to something, to C and D, is illustrated by the adage 'selling coals to Newcastle'. Since Newcastle-upon-Tyne was itself a major coal-mining centre, we would likely not get much result E, but the form is correct. In our tongue-in-cheek example, doing C to D requires a capability – mining coal, transporting it to Newcastle and selling it successfully to those who already have plenty. Capability comprises skills, knowledge, and technology.

But A and B are just as important. A defines the customers and B states the problem that they have. In doing C to D, the firm believes it can solve B in return for a price. And of course, many other firms believe the same or similar and offer competing goods and services to the same consumers, A.

Figure 11-1: "Cheshire puss! Would you tell me please..."

We mentioned that in running a firm, there are many variables. Outcome E will depend on the manager's interpretation of A and B and the capability C that they put in place. And D may change too as competitors pile into the market. All is flux.

Change, then, is about reacting to realise or sustain an outcome.

What's critical out of all this is that the manager knows the desired outcome E. The manager must know the outcome achieved today and the outcome sought tomorrow, each for given capability. The difference between the two will define the change required.

11.1.2   *Defining the required outcome*

One of the tales from Alice's Adventures in Wonderland by Lewis Carroll in 1865 describes strategy, or rather the inability to describe strategy, in a nutshell.

'Cheshire Puss,' said Alice, 'Would you tell me, please, which way I ought to go from here?' [Define C and D.] (Figure 11-1)

'That depends a good deal on where you want to get to,' said the Cat. [Define E.]

'I don't much care where—' said Alice. [Unable to define E.]

'Then it doesn't matter which way you go,' said the Cat. [Unable to advise on C and D.]

There's a bit more that follows in Carroll's literature, all suitably amusing to a would-be strategist. Alice is, of course, the manager and the Cat is a suitably wise consultant!

Defining the desired outcome E is tough for all managers. Take an example. A firm is doing OK, but the manager considers that one division is faring less well than others. The manager wants to close the weak division and make all employees redundant without any analysis or modelling. A logical strategic response to an obvious problem, you might say.

That response involves doing C to D and is at a relatively low level – a tactic, rather than a well-formed strategy. In strategy formation, E is the outcome wanted – perhaps to return the firm to desired turnover and profit. But closing the division is only one possible change of many in any recovery plan. Managers must define A, B, C, D and E together at the highest level and they must do so without causal assumption.

There are of course many reasons why a firm might want to make change. Change is not just the manager's reaction to poor business performance. Those reasons may, for example, be in pursuit of sustainability and increased productivity.

11.1.3   *Change as reaction to events*

It's noble to think that change is always driven by managers. Often, however, change becomes necessary because the environment in which the firm sits has changed suddenly and perhaps hugely. Change can be in pursuit of recovery.

Change in pursuit of recovery requires the manager to know two states. First, they must have known the strategy in place, and that was serving the firm well up to the point of impact of the new scenario. Second, they must know the reduced outcome now being realised. In effect, this is simply the above strategy case worked backwards. Outcome E was in line with plans, and suddenly now it's not. New actions, C, are needed to recover.

11.1.4   *Pressure for sustainability*

Sustainability is a big and complex topic that concerns long-term world prosperity. Writers like Tim Jackson and Steven Pinker have written copiously on this at the global level. For us at the level of the single enterprise, a sustainable firm is one that will be in business next year and in the years to come.

Sustainability in a firm demands that the manager considers the goals and strategic decisions over time – and not just now or in the immediate future.

Traditionally, UK managers and their boards have taken a very short-term view. Investors are well known for expecting a return each year, and exit and recovery of their original funds, plus some, within two or three years. Many commentators argue that this short-termism stifles investment and is the root cause of the UK's productivity crisis. This contrasts with the general approach of German investors who are renowned for keeping interest in firms for over 10 years. Sustainability requires a long-term attitude to investment and management.

When investigating issues and when planning change, managers must make decisions for today but, overall, they must have a long-term horizon. They are the custodians of the firm working to protect the organisation for future owners. And they must acknowledge that many outcomes take considerable time to realise.

11.1.5   *Role of productivity*

There's no issue – productivity is a big deal. French employees generate the same wealth for their firms as British employees, but they do so in a 32-hour week. British employees take 37.5 hours. British employees are not as productive.

Productivity – the ability to achieve the required outcomes using the given capability within a given time – is a key metric in competitive advantage. For a given industry, any firm able to do more with less is going to have lower costs when compared to its competitors. Having lower costs means that the firm could, at its choice, reduce the price, making its products more attractive and hence selling more. Alternatively, it could maintain the price and make more profit. Profit can then be retained and invested in capability improvement, in turn further improving productivity in a self-reinforcing cycle.

Productivity is frequently a desirable outcome from change. Managers often want to achieve greater productivity and launch change initiatives in pursuit of productivity goals.

Mathematically, productivity is given by $P = f(T \times C)$, where $C = (s \times k)$.

Increase in productivity (P) requires increased technology (T) and/or increased employee competencies (C) (and competencies are themselves skill (s), times knowledge (k)). Speculating on the difference between French and British firms, the French invest more than the British in technology and have more skilled and more knowledgeable employees. If the UK is to be competitive with France, we have some investment to make!

And finally, this equation is perhaps overly simplified. We shouldn't forget that there are several other variables that also influence productivity – like the quality of management itself.

11.1.6 *OD as the central change management tool*

Change involves having employees do the same things differently or having them do different things altogether.

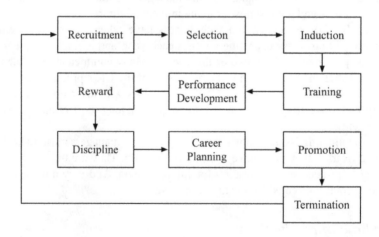

Figure 11-2: The HR system

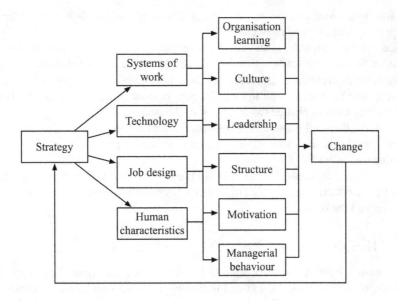

Figure 11-3: The OD system

A good example of doing the same things differently is to have employees improve their diligence to improve quality. Perhaps the manager has done some training in techniques.

An example of doing different things altogether is to have employees achieve the same outcomes using a new technology. With the new technology, the time taken is reduced, and with that, the cost per unit produced drops. This also includes doing completely different things because what was done before was not to the customers' liking and the firm now sells different goods and services in response. The outcome is the same but the route to the outcome is different.

There are two business systems at play here – the human resource management system (HR) and the organisational development system (OD). Each modifies the systems we previously discussed in Chapter 4.

The HR system assumes that, substantially, the firm is going to continue to do the same things. It does, to some extent, also cater for minor improvements as employees improve their performance though training. The OD system, on the other hand, assumes that everything that's done today may be changed in line with a changing strategy. The ideas of HR and OD are encapsulated in two diagrams – Figure 11-2 and Figure 11-3.

The HR system comprises all centres of management needed to sustain the status quo – (starting top left) hiring people against existing jobs, training and developing them to reach a defined performance, paying them and planning their career to eventually promote them to another existing job. If ultimately people leave (ending bottom right), the cycle starts again.

The OD system is the central system driving change. It requires strategy as its trigger. Strategy spawns the necessary processes/systems of work, technology, jobs, and human characteristics. These represent key areas in which managers will want to invest to effect change. We see, in this first column of centres of management, the balance between technology and human competencies discussed in earlier chapters. The balance point will depend also on the jobs and the way the jobs, technology and people work together in the various processes or systems of work.

Once set up, towards achieving the capability, the next column of centres of management follows: the way the firm learns, its culture, the competence of its leadership, its structure, the motivation of its people and the behaviour of its managers. This illustrates, for example, that there's no point in having a perfect front column if the culture is wrong. The culture may have to change too in pursuit of the strategy.

Ultimately, then, all those centres of management act together to give movement in outcomes. Each becomes a lens through which to look at the activities within the various systems that we outlined in Chapter 4.

The result, conceptually, is a matrix with the tangible systems of the firm on one axis modified by the effectiveness of the HR and OD systems (and their sub-systems/centres of management) on the other.

11.1.7 *Variables in change*

Now, change is a funny thing. You can't flick a switch. It's not digital. For every discrete combination of person, process, job and technology, the performance and output will be different. The result is a typical analogue outcome stemming from many combinations of variables. We illustrate this aggregation of many jobs towards one outcome in Figure 12-6.

In all cases, there's variance, and change must therefore be described stochastically (statistically, with several variables). Change must be described statistically when comparing people, groups and departments using the language of descriptive statistics – distribution (skew and kurtosis), central tendency (average, mean and mode) and spread (range, standard deviation, and variance). If those systems could be characterised mathematically, managers could perhaps use Monte-Carlo methods to randomly sample each variable and plot the outcomes to give a complete picture. This is the world of operations research, used to drive change in large organisations.

This idea of performance, and hence change, as an aggregation of stochastic processes is useful in setting expectations. The firm is a collective of people. Each uses technology in processes as part of a job and performance and output vary. Change initiatives should be planned with this stochastic concept in mind. Managers must talk routinely of distribution, central tendency and spread.

11.1.8 *Arguments against a planned approach*

Some commentators may argue that because there are so many variables, planning is futile.

As we commented above, not planning would be a dereliction of the manager's duty. The manager's job is to determine strategy. It follows that the manager will then need to determine what to change to achieve that strategy. Yes, it's complicated, but then that's what the manager signed up for.

We discuss below further ideas about change. In every case, change is not accidental – the manager must have an idea of what they want to achieve. We therefore don't subscribe to the idea of drift. We don't believe that management is a laissez faire activity. The link between change and strategy must be strong. And the manager must continually sense outcomes to feed into the change processes as a measure of change success. If one change is not working, another must be planned and implemented.

11.2 Understanding change

Change is complicated. Managers can choose to change any or all HR or OD sub-systems across part, or all, of the firm. Managers need to understand how change works before making plans and launching huge initiatives. We find that the following five ideas about change help that understanding.

11.2.1 *The concept of change*

Conceptually, change is simple enough. It's persuading people to do something different – either with the same technology or with new. It's taking some action such that the activities done tomorrow differ from those done today. It's changing the environment such that employees will change their performance. It's often described by defining the gap between today's outcomes and those wanted tomorrow. The gap can be analysed to yield the list of initiatives needed to cause the change to happen.

Change in firms has often been driven by a single force – a Machiavellian manager as dominant alpha who believes that dishonesty, deceit, deviousness and the 'killing of innocents' is perfectly acceptable in change. He (for it has mostly been men) believes that good ends justify bad means and dictates what is to be done.

Many of us have worked for such a person.

Over recent years, two forces have modified this norm causing a more considered style. Firstly, Generation Y entered the workplace. Those young people were simply not prepared to tolerate bad behaviour from their managers. They did, and still will, vote with their feet and leave if change and its drivers are not to their likening. Secondly, as women take management roles, a more feminine, nurturing, and collective approach is appearing. Women are no less forceful and driven, but their methods are perhaps less aggressive and directive.

The resulting consensual, participative management is more likely to persuade and hence is more likely to be effective.

However it's done, change is nuanced, affecting different people in different ways. And change is, as we discussed above, a stochastic process.

11.2.2 *A dynamic model of change*

Persuading people to change generally requires force or, more likely, multiple forces. Those forces are opinions held by individuals and groups both within the firm and outside in the wider environment of stakeholders. Even if there's a unified strategy, it will be interpreted by managers and those holding power in different ways. Forces modify proposals for change that are launched as interventions upon the company, its employees, processes, and technology.

The idea is not unlike Brownian motion where an electron (as metaphor for the original intervention) is launched into a cloud of randomly moving smoke particles (alternative opinions). The electron emerges sometime later with its location and direction somewhat modified.

In Figure 11-4 we see the original intention as vector 1 (point of departure) entering the cloud of opinion and exiting on a slightly modified trajectory illustrated by vector 6 (point of arrival). The strength of the vector (representing direction and strength of drive for change) will depend on the outcomes of the various interactions with countervailing proposals. The last interaction was from a significant player with a strong supporting proposal. Prior to this, and after several prevailing forces, the direction of travel was almost in reverse at vector 5. This interaction drove the result on a slightly modified trajectory from that desired illustrated by the angle W between original and new direction.

Mostly, however, there is no apparent final trajectory, agreed, written, and published. There's just an outcome that appears in the business results of turnover, profit, and other key metrics from which one might surmise the forces that caused it.

This conceptual model shows us that when an intervention for change is launched, it is modified by various opinions, beliefs, counter-implementation arguments, and scuppering tactics held by other managers, employees, and stakeholders. The change occurring is the resultant of all the various interactions encountered over time. The change that occurs is rarely exactly that intended.

Much of the manager's effort in achieving change is to minimise countervailing forces and to get 'everyone on side' so that generally the 'forces' support the desired change.

11.2.3   A static force-field model

The model below considers that the person is bumping into modifying proposals and opinion over time and space. At best, encounters will reinforce intention. At worst, they will oppose. It shows the resulting direction at any one time depending on the influence of a single interaction. Employees experience this phenomenon and realise their final opinion and attitude about the change following multiple interactions and meetings.

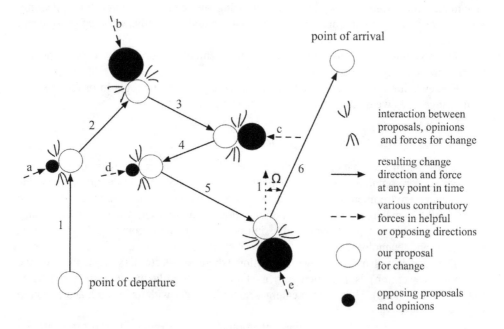

Figure 11-4: Dynamic model of change

In a single significant meeting at a single point in time and space, an employee might experience multiple proposals and opinions. At this single point in time and space, their thoughts will translate to action when the magnitude and direction of all forces combine to exceed opposing or restraining forces. Again, the manager's job in persuading others is to ensure that all significant voices are in line with what's wanted.

Change can be managed by using group meetings in which the manager communicates the need for change – a single significant interaction. Group discussion, and allowing group members to plan for the change, can then be used to generate a single useful direction to be achieved by all.

Clearly, though, this works until the employee meets others who were not in the meeting and the dynamic model applies again.

11.2.4   *Change is like the wind*

Change, or rather the net forces driving change in a firm, has been likened to the wind. It's a slightly fanciful metaphor, but perhaps useful in thinking about the big picture of change in the firm.

For many days in a year, there's very little wind – very little force for change – and hence the firm continues its course uninterrupted. Sometimes, there's a variable wind that rises in the morning and reduces later in the day. On a few days, there's a storm force, with chaos and damage everywhere.

Normally, in UK weather, there's a single prevailing wind from the south-west that is generally good, producing favourable outcomes. From time to time, external influences change and the wind blows an icy blast from the east – from Siberia – and freezes the country. And now and again we get light winds from the Sahara, dumping their film of dust on everything.

We could go on with this metaphor, but you get the drift. Wind is created by differing pressures in the atmosphere and, in this much, the wind metaphor is like the dynamic model. The drivers for change in a firm are likewise often manifold, coming from different positions, with differing beliefs and intentions. It's for manager to reduce the instances of storm and chaos, instead creating at any one time a single 'wind' for change from a consistent direction.

So, employees react daily to the forces of change. And like forecasting the weather, there are many variables to consider. The manager's task is to make sure that the prevailing wind will cause the change wanted.

But enough about models that try to give the idea of change in a complex firm with managers, employees, and other stakeholders. We need to return to the practical. We need to be able to determine what force to apply to what variable to effect the desired change.

11.2.5   *A systems model of change*

And so, to our fifth idea about change. The systems model of the firm is again useful. In Figure 11-5, inputs, enablers and constraints all change throughout the life of the firm, either under the manager's direction or because of external forces over which the firm has limited influence. And the manager likely wants to change the firm's master system – its capabilities and processes - in reaction to these forces to recover or improve outcomes.

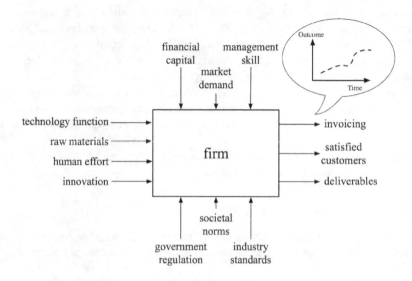

Figure 11-5: The firm as a system

This is a much more practical model than those conceptual ideas discussed above. It allows the manager to speculate on what to change as input, enabler, constraint, or capability (as human competence, technology function and system process) to effect change in outcome.

For full understanding, of course, all models must be considered together. The systems model suggests what to change. The HD and OD models suggest centres for management attention. And the dynamic and static models suggest what happens at a micro- or people-level.

This systems model, and modelling in general, will now be harnessed and improved as we go on to develop a more comprehensive discussion on change.

Reflection 11-1: About systems and forces in change

Model a change you made in your firm using the systems model described in Figure 11-5. What inputs, enablers, constraints, capability, and processes did you change? Now reflect on the dynamic and static models and their aggregation of forces metaphor. How did you harness the various forces to make the change?

11.3   Determining what to change

In managing change, the manager is responsible for deciding which interventions, applied to which variables, will produce the change needed. But first, the manager must know the state of the environment and the effect of that environment likely on future business. For this, the manager must be able to forecast.

11.3.1   *Forecasting with Delphi*

Under Greek mythology an oracle is a wise one who was consulted to forecast the future. One of the key oracles, Pythia, lived at Delphi. Delphi now gives its name to a method of forecasting.

The Delphi method of forecasting in business is a systematic method of arriving at a consensus about some future state or scenario. It can be applied to problems such as future market size and requirements, future technologies, and future societal attitudes.

Delphi has application when there is no single answer to a problem.

The Delphi method requires several forecasters to be selected for their insight into the subject. It's important that these forecasters are anonymous to the manager(s) and to one another. If their names are known, bias will be introduced and that will detrimentally affect the value of the outcome.

A consultant facilitates the set up and administration of communication with the oracles. The forecasting runs for two rounds. After each forecast by the oracles, the consultant amalgamates the responses to a single opinion, and this is used to again solicit another forecast.

The consultant may use a research question, questionnaires, or surveys to stimulate and guide the oracles.

After two rounds, the consultant consolidates the responses to a final statement. Delphi is a common method used by consultants. Consultants are used because they can run the process impartially.

11.3.2   *The role of modelling in change*

Modelling is an essential part of change. Somehow the manager must express in some tangible fashion the state of their firm today. And then they must set out how, using the same metrics, they want the firm to look tomorrow. Visualising that future state and the intervention needed to bring about the change can only be done using one or more models.

Models are views on current or future scenarios. When viewing a scene in real-life, the viewer can climb above and look down, or they can look from one side or the other. And developing the metaphor further, they can stand and view from a distance or come close to try to see every detail. They could even capture the scene at various times to see how the scene might evolve. And when it comes to capturing the scene, they may sketch an outline or go to molecular detail. The more views a viewer takes, the more they will understand the scene, until a point comes when taking another view adds little.

It's the same with organisational modelling. A single model, such as the system model shown in Figure 11-6 might explain a lot. Adding one or two more models, such as one capturing data flow and another capturing the state of various system outputs with time, might be all that's needed.

So, what models might a manager use?

The simplest ubiquitous model is, of course, the profit and loss account (P&L).

The P&L is an expression in financial terms of the business outcomes for a given strategy. It relates activities to turnover and profit. Many managers do produce a P&L at the end of each month though most of those see it as a report rather than the output of a model. Few use the P&L as a model of what might be, thereby exploring options. Many will use the P&L format in producing a budget for the coming year – and a budget is itself a simple model of a future desirable scenario.

The simple input-process-output model in Figure 11-5 can be 'overlaid' on the P&L – it's what causes the P&L. Stuff goes in, stuff comes out and satisfied customers pay their invoices. This can be expanded to cover all key variables and fits the argument that we're building here to model the firm.

System modelling (Figure 11-6) allows the firm to be represented first as a single system and then as several sub-systems, each doing something to contribute to the business outcomes and each enabling the desired change. Figure 11-6 shows a model of typical sub-systems. Here there are 11 sub-systems within an example firm. The Money sub-system might include, for example, the invoicing, credit control and banking processes.

The system boundary is shown. Where this boundary is drawn is up to the manager. It may be that the Governance sub-system is not within the manager's control, or it may be that the firm does not do Research in any form, relying on a group company or partner for this. Here, both Governance and Research would be beyond the boundary. In those cases, the corresponding sub-systems would be deleted from the overall model. Other forms of organisations will have very different sub-systems. As with all modelling, the model must be useful in perceiving the firm, the way it operates today and the proposed changes.

Each sub-system can itself be defined in ever more detail. The system model and the P&L can be combined, and budgets prepared for each sub-system. Some firms take this to the limit by having each system as a 'profit centre' – a mini-firm within a firm defining local turnover, costs, overheads, and profit. The firm is then described as several departmental P&Ls aggregating to a corporate P&L.

There are many other models both possible and useful.

The choice of models to be used is for the manager to select to fit the needs of their firm and the scenario or scenarios to be explored. Generally, we favour models from the Unified Modelling Language (UML) suite such as the use case model, the data flow model, and the workflow model. We're also fans of the IDEF suite of models. All can be found by searching the Web and many model templates are available for popular computer drawing applications. We also frequently use a form of systems modelling taken from the field of systems dynamics as illustrated in Chapter 1. Systems dynamics is particularly useful when working with concepts like reputation that have critical influence on outcomes and take time and effort to build, but perhaps don't appear in more practical models.

Each of the sub-systems in Figure 11-6 can be modelled statically using UML and each can be modelled dynamically using systems dynamics. As we labour here, the aim of all models is to show the detail of how the system or sub-system works now and how the manager intends it to work in the future.

Each model discussed so far can be built and then analysed with one or more perspectives. There are many perspectives. A good example may be culture – the departments, groups and people involved in the Research system may enjoy a common culture, and this may be very different from those in the finance department. The finance department is likely the player at the heart of the Money system. Change may involve only one system and only one perspective. Or, of course, it may involve many systems and many perspectives.

Some of the possible perspectives are shown in Figure 11-7.

Many management students will recognise the PESTLE acronym (Political, Economic, Sociological, Technological, Legal and Environmental) used to describe the external perspectives.

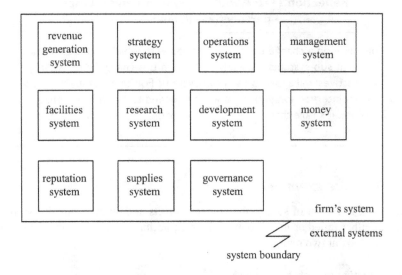

Figure 11-6: Systems model of a firm

As an example, in analysing the reputational system incorporating the firm's marketing tools, it's inevitable that the manager will initially focus on the finances – asking 'how much does it cost, and what budget do I have'. Any change in the reputation system will likely demand more investment, but equally it might be achieved cheaply by focussing on leadership. Looking externally, a change in the reputation system to enhance the firm's marketing might be proposed, but other analyses might suggest that the market simply would not respond regardless of how much funding is made available.

Modelling must be comprehensive enough to elaborate the scenario and explore the change while being simple enough for all stakeholders to understand. It's a matter of modelling at the right level of abstraction. Modelling in too much detail simply confuses those involved, but modelling too simplistically is useless, since it does not explore all the possible variables.

Possible internal perspectives	Possible external perspectives
Manpower	Political
Strategy	Economic (including markets)
Systems	Sociological
Competence	Technological
Leadership	Legal
Technology	Environmental
Politics	
Finance	
Culture	
Management	

Figure 11-7: Possible internal and external perspectives as foci for models

11.3.3   Change examples

Every manager has a list of successful change projects and an even bigger list of change projects that either failed or failed to meet their aspirations. But what sort of thing typifies change? Let's look at two real projects.

11.3.3.1   *Reacting to a changing market*

A consulting firm recognised that its market was changing. Its government clients were asking for ever bigger questions to be answered. Previously, those clients had their own engineering employees who would ask for small projects to answer parts of the big issues. Those employees would then aggregate all the various smaller projects, conduct their own analysis where relevant, and come to an overall conclusion about the big questions of the day. Our consulting firm competed well and won around 30% of the projects. It was a stable state for many years.

Over a period of a few years, government budgets were cut, and the clients' in-house engineers were made redundant. The clients still needed the big questions answering, of course. It was just that they had to go out to consulting firms with much larger, more complex, and much more cerebral questions – the whole question, rather than smaller parts.

And the consulting firm in question didn't have the quality of consultants or the embedded methods to be able to compete with larger consulting firms well used to responding to such big questions. As a result of a change in the clients, the market had shifted.

Change was needed in the consulting firm, or it would lose this market.

The solution adopted in the consulting firm was to develop its staff to match those of its bigger competitors. Now, it wasn't so much development as massive up-skilling. First the manager developed a statement of the capability necessary to adequately compete – to be able to answer those big questions. This was captured in a pan-organisation competency framework and a statement of the technology that consultants should use.

Then the manager developed a model of the capability available in the firm. This review revealed that the consulting firm had the tools, but its skills and knowledge were lacking. Of course, the manager knew this through his monitoring, but now he had it quantified. And no change can be planned without that quantification and associated costing.

You can imagine the result. Once the change needed was known, a change manager was hired. This person wasn't a god. She didn't magically make the change, but she allowed the manager of the consulting firm to get on with the day job – and indeed, to get on with his own development! The change manager effectively did the donkey work. She recorded what was needed and what was available. She met with each consultant and agreed their development.

And she monitored the whole activity until some point where she and the manager agreed that the firm was now up-skilled – that success had been achieved.

And of that success? Some consultants excelled. Others put in little effort despite the change manager's best efforts at persuasion. And that's the way things are in this sort of change. It's important then that the manager's expectations are realistic but still meet the need.

In this case, one year later the consulting firm won a huge contract to answer one of these huge questions – and had one of its bigger competitors as its sub-contractor. The project went on to be completed on time and to budget.

The change project had been a success. First, the manager modelled, capturing what was current and what was to be. He then identified the change needed. Then he implemented. And finally, he tested that the change had been embedded, though by winning the contract, the outcome was obvious.

11.3.3.2   *Implementing growth*
Growth is typically an intended outcome from change. In this example, a software tools firm was well established in the UK and the manager believed that the firm could grow by building presence in Norway and Germany.

Market research illustrated that there was scope for the firm in each of these countries. And each country allowed further access to others and on to the rest of Europe.

Now, the decision to invest in the territories was far from made. Each had to pass business plan scrutiny. And that needed modelling given several scenarios and assumptions. Each country operation had to be designed with the key requirement to build reputation to achieve turnover and return on the investment in setup.

The country operations were modelled using a conceptual model as we illustrate in Figure 11-8. Each country had specific needs for localisation of marketing, selling methods and product and this needed to be captured since each would have an added cost and a set of actions. The work was made easier since the firm had already won some business in each country.

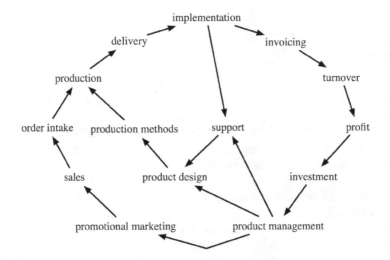

Figure 11-8: Example systems modelling of concepts

The mechanisms for how monies were to be handled were difficult and complex. The firm's management decided that they would set up branch offices in each country and employ locals in those branches. Employment itself was straightforward, but the money flows from the customers, through the branch, to the various governmental agencies for pensions, social taxes, income taxes and the likes and on to the employees as pay had to be modelled using a data flow method. And taxation was a particular headache. Data flow modelling showed the flows using various processes to and from various data (money) stores.

This money flow highlighted how easy it was to employ people in the UK, but how complex it was when working abroad. It also highlighted the changes needed in the UK headquarters to manage this money.

The outcome was that over a period of two years, the firm set up first one employee, then more staff in each country. Each branch enjoyed success and met management expectations, though the return on investment took longer than expected.

The change activity here was sizeable. The expansion followed some pilot success in selling directly from the UK. But managing business in-country, using a mix of in-country and UK-based production and supply services, led to significant complexity. And the money side of the venture was complex.

The overall change plan followed a conventional lifecycle for this sort of activity – investigation, pilot, first instance, adjustment, operation, growth, then repeat for the next country.

Reflection 11-3: On modelling change

Thinking about a significant change that you are familiar with, identify each of the phases of the change. For each, identify the discrete models that were developed to describe the venture. Say how each set of actions were arrived at from the models. How could the change have gone more smoothly with better modelling?

11.4   Issues in change

Change is complex. It is influenced by many variables, some able to be specified and hence controlled, and some not. The example in 11.3.3.1 illustrates that no matter how effective the planning, the intended outcomes may not be achieved, or not achieved in full. When it comes to changing people, not all will respond as planned. And not all those who are willing will achieve the new skills and knowledge required. What matters is that enough is achieved to give the momentum for progress.

Change involves people. What people think matters. People think about their position in the firm, and they develop attitudes and beliefs. Change is therefore psychological. Change can be achieved in part by changing the tools used. Change is therefore technological. And since people interact and develop those attitudes and beliefs through social contact, change is therefore both sociological and political.

Change defines the manager. It's what managers do – all day, every day. We discuss elsewhere that a manager is someone who accepts responsibility for change. In change, the manager is the person prepared to stake their future on this risky change venture. We've seen that there's no guarantee of success in change.

So, why is that, and what can go wrong?

11.4.1 *Overcoming inertia*

Newton's first law of motion tells us that an object at rest remains at rest, or if it is already in motion, remains in motion at a constant velocity unless acted on by an external force. It's also known as the law of inertia and strictly it applies to objects in a vacuum.

But Newton's law of inertia can also be usefully applied to change as a metaphor!

People are inherently conservative. They are inclined to prefer to do what they're doing today rather than change, even if this change might afford them benefit tomorrow. As the sociologist Thorstein Veblen remarked, "All change of habits of life, and of thought, is irksome". He also noted that the status quo is, "only to be overcome by stress of circumstances" – only to be overcome by force or deliberate activity of some sort.

Kurt Lewin, considered the founder of modern social psychology, captured this in his method for overcoming this inertia. He described the idea that the status quo must be 'unfrozen'. Something must be done to stop the present activity. Then, in a more fluid state, the people, processes, and technology can be changed. To complete the change, people, processes, and technology must be 're-frozen' into the new desired state through some equally deliberate event(s). Conceptually, if the re-freeze is ineffective, the people will revert to the pre-change state and the benefits of the change will be lost.

However it's put, the manager must do something positive and expend energy in events to overcome people-inertia. They must apply that external force. Change will not happen without effort. The size of the force and the amount of energy will depend on the firm, its people and the scale of the change needed.

Often change fails simply because no-one put in the necessary effort. It was all talk, and talk is no substitute for action.

11.4.2 *Winning the mandate for change*

The manager is expected to manage their firm. It's in the job description. Given that all is flux in a firm, managers are appointed as orchestrators of continuous change, continually intervening in search of optimal outcomes. And the manager is expected to balance costs and benefits and ensure that, however costs and benefits are measured, benefits exceed costs and there is a return on the investment expended in the change.

Managers must prepare cost-benefit analyses for all change. In the case of minor change within the manager's scope of authority, the manager needs only to convince themselves before getting started. Here, the manager need only rough out the plans themselves or with their local management team. But major change will need board or senior management authorisation and the preparation of formal cost-benefit analyses documentation. As with all initiatives in their firm, senior managers must be committed to the change and visually demonstrate their commitment through words and actions.

11.4.3 *Winning people over for change*

Any manager who sets about change without realising the importance of politics will fail. Employees and junior managers will act to defend the status quo and any fiefdom or turf that they presently command. Any manager playing political games risks the politics taking over and the change that they want becoming a side show. Considering this, the manager must take account of vested interests. Politics can't be ignored.

People with vested interests, attitudes, and beliefs must be persuaded to accept the manager's point of view. And this must be done with rational argument while minimising emotions. The energy needed for this should not be under-estimated.

Reflection 11-4: About issues in change

Think about a sizeable change with which you are familiar. What political activities would you engage in to help secure successful change? What vested interest would you need to manage and how?

11.5   The effect of time

11.5.1   *Effect of experience on outcomes*

In all systems there is a hysteresis. Upon some change in input, enabler, constraint, human competence, technology function or system process, we'll see a change in the output. But that change won't be immediate. In some cases, it will occur a few days later as the change tweaks something minor. In other more complex systems, it will occur in anything up to five years hence – and in some cases even longer.

A change in elements of the marketing mix (of product, distribution, promotion, price, and support), for example, could have an instant outcome where the firm sells direct to its customers. But where it sells through distributors, dealers, and retail outlets, for example, it will likely take many months to cause the intended change in customer behaviour.

In addition, change must be 'learned' by the firm. In some cases, a quick change to an algorithm in a technology-centric system might produce exactly the desired change soon after implementation. In other cases, the target output will be known but it will not be achieved immediately. Something lesser will be realised soon after initiation of the change activities but it will take time for the systems to react fully to reach the target. As the employees experience the change, they learn. As the technology experiences the change it too 'learns' as it is adjusted to optimise performance. This idea of learning by experiencing the change is described by a system's experience curve shown in Figure 11-9.

Many employees learn by repetition too, so it will take time for them to master new skills. New processes will take time to become error-free. Bugs will have to be found and corrected. Systems will need to use feedback to invoke multiple changes to eventually reach targets. And the independent variable is not just time. Volume matters too. Economies of scale typically improve purchase costs, but costs only reduce after increased volumes are bought.

All effects follow the general form of experience curves. Quite quickly or after a few runs of the systems, there will be a huge improvement, but it will take a longer time or production volume to achieve the target. The form, slopes and asymptote will depend on the nature of the system. In Figure 11-9, System B reacts quickly and eventually realises the target. System A is less responsive and never actually gets there.

Managers must be sensitive to experience curves and act when outcomes are slow to appear or are not achieved.

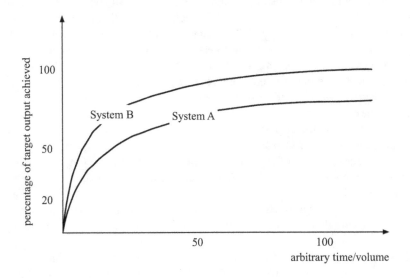

Figure 11-9: Experience curves

11.5.2   Trends in change

Our examples (in 11.3.3) describe bounded problems that suggested a defined set of initiatives in each case. Those initiatives were driven by a manager.

But there are changes going on in industries and markets that are nothing to do with the manager or the firm and will continue despite the manager and the firm. Some of those changes occur in society and business as the firm engages over several years with its environment. Those 'natural' trends can be exploited and used to realise positive change. There are many such trends identifiable. Four common trends are illustrated below.

The first trend is the application of the Ronald Coase's Theory of the Firm. At inception, a firm uses self-employed suppliers or agency-employed workers to grow. It has no funds for employees, and yet it has a marketable idea. Capability then grows using self-employed suppliers to match demand for the firm's goods and services. To reduce costs and increase flexibility, the manager progressively brings the capability 'indoors' and hires employees. The Theory of the Firm is a norm and features in most firm's growth stories. The mix of employees and self-employed suppliers or agency-supplied workers varies and changes in line with the firm's strategy.

The second trend is specialisation. As the firm grows, it's generally more cost effective to reduce the scope of the job each employee does. They specialise and become masters of a smaller competency set, requiring only a few skills and less knowledge. Firms specialise in search of lower costs and higher profit. Specialised firms are generally less adaptable and malleable than firms with generally skilled and knowledgeable employees. Low specialisation firms generally have messier processes. When markets change, managers must attend to technology, competencies, and processes. Change is not simply a case of re-skilling in a highly specialised firm. Managers must re-organise, embracing the whole OD scope.

The third trend is standardisation. Initially firms solve their customers' problems using all available technology and employee competencies. Inherently, there are many variables and irregularities and as a result the customers don't get a unified service. In search of higher quality and lower costs, managers seek to control what's done by dictating standard processes with resulting standard goods and services. Arguably standardised firms are less adaptable than those relying on employees to work independently to satisfy customers. But conversely, it's often easier to see the changes needed in a highly standardised environment.

The fourth trend is the displacement of employee competence by technology function. Colloquially, this is the moan from employees that "robots stole my job". As technology becomes more capable, it is often more cost-effective to buy a machine to do the job and make the human operative redundant. And when change is needed, it's simply a case of re-programming the machines. Historically this trend has caused the reduction in the demand for medium-skill jobs. Broadly, though, it is better to retain the employee, training them further, having them exploit the improved machine and improve overall competitive advantage for the firm.

Those trends go on around the firm, driving available staff and technology markets. For example, today, something like half of the UK's software developers choose to work as self-employed suppliers. Even if the firm wants to hire an employee, they may not be able to, or will have reduced choice. How the manager embraces those trends will depend on the firm's strategy and the surrounding environment.

11.5.3   *Forms of change plans*

Change takes time. It requires a plan that will set out when the various activities will be done. There are perhaps five distinct phases: exploration, planning, action, integration, and repetition. The first four steps describe how any project might be done. Adding repetition drives the firm and the outputs of its systems along the experience curve.

Not all changes are identifiable as major steps. Many changes are less distinct, and managers elect to make small, incremental step-changes or even continuously change as they evolve the systems towards the goal.

And others take a leaf from the world of software engineering and go 'agile'. The concept of 'agile' stems from the inability some years ago of the software industry to deliver complex projects on time and to budget while fixing function and quality. The leaders in the industry at the time argued that often when software was being designed, the end goal was unclear – and yet the developers were pressured to work within hard constraints.

Change stemming from an agile approach will be identifiable as a series of useable improved states of the firm on the way to a final broadly specified goal.

There are three basic requirements in effecting change – know your capability and results today, know what you want to achieve tomorrow, and plan to bridge the gap between the two.

This three-step process can be formal or informal. It can describe large or small changes. It can be set out in paper, or it can be retained in the manager's head. And its success measures can be specific or described in terms of broad wishes. Whatever the methods of change, it takes effort, and in all firms, this translates to money. In the end, all changes must be justified on the future P&L and balance sheet.

11.6   Practical change

Economists say that firms comprise people and capital. And hence change typically means developing or hiring more people, and using capital to buy more technology, to boost capability.

11.6.1   *Changing people*

There's the adage, 'If you can't change the people, change the people.'

People are defined by their intelligence, personality, preferences, competencies and behaviours, motives, needs, values, orientations, preferences, attitudes, and beliefs. Any change must therefore target one or more of those – but not all are under the manager's complete control.

Numerical and verbal reasoning (as components of a person's crystallised intelligence) can be developed. Likewise, a person's competencies and behaviours can be developed. We discussed in Chapter 8 how to make those changes. But abstract reasoning (as fluid intelligence) is innate – it can't be learned and hence can't be changed (though we discuss elsewhere alternative tactics for improvement).

Unfortunately too, an adult's personality is substantially fixed. The manager may be able to change the environment around the employee, and hence change various outcomes, but the manager can't change personality itself.

Preferences, needs, values and orientations are, of course, personal. It may indeed be possible to modify those and bring them in line with the firm's goals but it's for the employee to choose whether to cooperate. As we discuss in earlier chapters, it's more a case of selecting an employee for their congruence with the firm's values rather than trying to mould them after they join.

And an employee is motivated by the job that they do. Managers do have complete control over all jobs done and are free to design and re-design them at will. And motivation is moderated by leadership and the cultural environment in which the employee works. The manager has control over their leadership and can significantly influence the culture in the firm.

That leaves us with attitudes and beliefs. Attitudes and beliefs are in two parts – those associated with the firm and those in the employee's private life. Attitudes and beliefs towards the firm are the employee's reaction to manager interventions – and it's for the manager to design their interventions to have the right result. That result will include how it makes the employee feel – what their attitudes and beliefs will then be, following the intervention. But the other part of attitudes and beliefs is brought to the firm from the employee's family, upbringing, and out-of-work activities. Those are outside the manager's control.

So, all in all, managers have control of maybe half of the employee characteristics – they can change competencies and behaviours, and attitudes and beliefs, and motivation.

This idea of 'changing the person, or changing the person', is therefore true enough. Half of the characteristics can be changed through development and the other half can only be changed by dismissing the current employee and hiring someone new. That latter point might seem callous, but the manager must intervene to dismiss if the employee lacks the personal characteristics to perform in the changed firm. If the employee can't make the changes needed, the manager must consider hiring someone else.

11.6.2   *Change and contracts*

Change often involves asking an employee to do something different. Today, they are employed doing one thing. Tomorrow, you'd like them to do something else. Their employment today is on some premise: a job description, even if implied, and terms and conditions of employment, even if only in statute. And you want to change all, or parts, of those. Inevitably there are legal, economic, and psychological implications.

Typically, employment contracts include a clause that gives the employer the right to change the employee's contract and the job they do, but even with this right, change must be done in the correct way.

The essence of any change is consultation, taking due account of the employee's issues with the change. Sometimes in changing the work environment, the difference between the present employment contract and that needed to support the future employment post-change is too great. An example might be relocation of the job to another town or even country. Where the change between today and tomorrow is too great, the manager may need to consider dismissing the employee for reasons of redundancy – the job, as previously described, is no longer needed. Dismissal for reasons of redundancy must be handled correctly or the manager may find themselves at tribunal, facing a significant financial award against the firm.

Redundancy dismissal goes like this. The manager elects that the job done by the employee (legally, 'work of a particular kind') is no longer needed. A bigger job is required, and different skills and knowledge are needed from those held by the current jobholder(s). In this case the job is redundant. Redundancy occurs when employees are dismissed from their jobs for one or more reasons which are not directly related to their performance or behaviour in their present job. Of course, the reasons why redundancy is needed, and the business case for redundancy, must be sound and alternatives, such as employee development, must have been explored. Nonetheless, redundancy, as the manager strives to adjust their firm to the prevailing environment, is justified. And a new employee with differing personal characteristics can be hired – to a new and different job requiring the new competencies and behaviours.

Change can be forced through, but forcing employees to do different things, or to do things differently, is never a wise idea. Typically, when making changes to the scope, purpose, responsibilities, relationships and context of an employee's job, there's negotiation to be done. Job evaluation should be invoked to assess all jobs after the change and appropriate salary adjustments made.

Negative human reaction is generally softened with financial inducement.

Elsewhere, we cover the psychological contract – the unwritten agreement between manager and employee that substantially controls employee attitudes. There is huge scope during change to completely screw up the relationship between employee and manager – and conversely, there's huge scope to enhance it. How the employee feels and their level of trust in the manager depends much on how they are treated during the change. Communications, and specifically listening, is key.

Finally, a short note on change and the relationship with contractors and others on supplier contracts. Supplier contracts are generally easier to break and re-make than employment contracts, but managers will need to consider the impact of this on the business. Many suppliers are fundamental to the business and their continued support is important.

11.6.3   *Changing technology*

Ultimately, in launching a change initiative, the manager will seek change in their firm's capability and the way that capability is applied. As we keep repeating, capability is the product of technology function and human competencies and behaviours. We've discussed the option of changing the competencies and behaviours. The other possibility is changing the technology function, and indeed most changes may ultimately be a bit of both. We discuss this in Chapter 4.

Unfortunately, there are famous disasters where managers have sought to change technology. One of the most famous is the NHS NPfIT (National Programme for Information Technology). The system was supposed to improve NHS operation by joining up the various healthcare centres. It failed because the designers did not include the opinions and needs of the users in their designs and the users rejected the system once implemented. The final spend was something around £16bn and the system was scrapped – it was never introduced in its intended form.

Broadly, there are two approaches to changing technology.

First, if the new capability is known, the function needed is also known for given competencies. In this case, a specification can be written, and the new technology procured. This is the so called 'waterfall' approach.

Second, if the specification is not mature, but the need for technology change is strong, a project with a mixed lifecycle can be invoked. Parts that can be defined can be managed with a waterfall plan. Parts that can't, follow an iterative plan where an early-day solution is introduced to users for their comment. Those comments lead to a second phase development, and the deliverables from this replace the early-day solution, and so on until the users have what they need, or the budget is expended. This idea of iterative engineering of capability is referred to as 'agile' development.

But changing technology is not just about procurement. The UK Ministry of Defence has evolved an approach termed 'lines of development'. The MOD identifies that there are many lines or domains to be considered (including, as the MOD defines, 'training, equipment, personnel, information, doctrine and concepts, organisation, infrastructure, and logistics') when introducing new technology. Technology impacts all stakeholders and all parts of the organisation and not just those likely to use it. It's not just about buying a new computer and hoping all will be well when it's introduced. The NPfIT is a sad example of what goes wrong when the focus is on technology function alone.

Generally, when technology is to be changed, competencies and behaviours must change too. There are two elements necessary for the capability to be realised. First, there might need to be foundation development to enable the technology to be understood by the users. If the foundation personal characteristics are not in place, development associated specifically with the technology will fail. If the foundations (like the ability to reason or the ability to conduct research, for example) cannot be achieved, employees may have to be dismissed and new people hired. And second, there will be technology-specific personnel development needed to enable the users to build on their foundations with enhanced competencies and behaviours to realise the capability.

And finally, it's normal today for technology to embrace automation. Automation is where a process ordinarily done by humans is done by a computer embedded in a machine. It's also normal today to embrace artificial intelligence (AI). AI is where decisions made by humans are replaced by decisions made by a computer, making use of huge data sets.

We argue elsewhere that managers should embrace automation and AI but up-skill the people to gain hugely in competitive advantage. By embracing new technology, managers can re-design jobs to remove boredom and allow employees to make ever more complex calculations to aid decision making. In short, technology is nothing but good for employees, but its introduction must be planned.

11.7   The process of change

If you take nothing else from this chapter, it's that change takes energy. That energy needs to be expended first in determining the present state and second in defining the desired end state. Energy is then needed in setting out the plan for change. And of course, energy is needed to make the plan happen.

Change involves determining a model of what's to be done. We discussed various modelling types above. We identified that sometimes what's to be changed is obvious, but sometimes in messy systems with high human input, it's not. This difference gives rise to two approaches to getting started in change.

11.7.1   *Change in tangible systems*

Change becomes necessary because there's a problem to be corrected or an opportunity to be exploited and this involves doing something different from that done today. Often many sub-systems are involved and the path to the desired end state is unclear. A method is needed to explore options using rational methods.

The hard systems methodology assumes that one or more sub-systems are to be changed. The assumption is that once the problem or opportunity is elaborated, those sub-systems comprising people, technology and processes will be obvious.

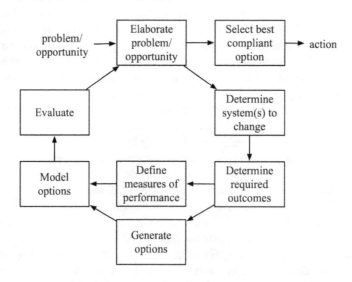

Figure 11-10: An integrated hard systems methodology

Once the systems affected are identified, the methods discussed in 11.3 are used to identify outcomes that would be acceptable and to explore options. Modelling using previously described modelling methods allows the best option to be selected and the change management plan implemented as action. The process is shown flowing clockwise in Figure 11-10.

11.7.2   Change in messy systems

In many instances, hard and soft mix to yield a mess. 'Hard' describes people, technology, and processes that we can discern separately, and we have discussed those variables at length here. But often there are too many of them. They merge with all the 'soft' stuff – the social, political, and psychological mechanisms – that are impossible to parse. Nothing provides an obvious route to modelling and conclusion.

Often too, it would take just too much time to model everything in the logical fashion that we suggest in 11.3. In this case we recommend use of the soft systems methodology shown diagrammatically in Figure 11-11.

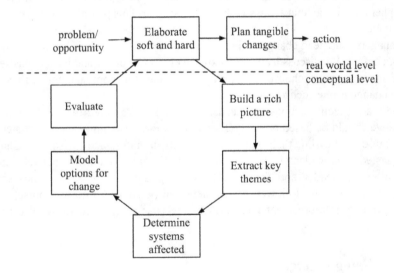

Figure 11-11: The soft-systems methodology for messy scenarios

The central tool in the soft systems methodology is the building of a rich picture. A rich picture acknowledges that things are messy, involving many disparate systems and many perspectives. To draw, or rather, construct, a rich picture, you need to go back to your childhood. Get some magazines out and use scraps of meaningful images and glue to build a single image that captures as much as possible of the problem or opportunity and its context. A rich picture can include symbols, words, sketches, pictures, arrows and more. It's for the manager to determine what is and is not a rich picture, so long as it has meaning for those who need to interpret it.

Once developed, the rich picture can be analysed to yield a few key themes. A theme is a common idea around which topics coalesce. It's a way of analysing to return to the approaches suggested earlier in this chapter – it's a way of converting a huge number of soft topics into something 'hard' and tangible for further analysis. The aim is that those themes in the conceptual world translate to systems in the real world which will be the focus of change. In the end, systems must be identified to develop actions for change.

The soft systems methodology is useful because, in a messy situation, it acknowledges the messiness up front and adds two steps from the world of qualitative analysis theory – rich picture drawing and thematic analysis.

11.7.3   Leading change

There is nothing certain about change. But the manager hopes that, with appropriate planning, they will be able to emerge at the other end of change with a firm that's more effective than before. Arguably, the six Ps apply: 'perfect planning and preparation prevents poor performance'.

In the end, though, the manager must make choices without knowing the full consequences of their actions. The manager must take responsibility for the actions needed and hence for the outcomes – good or bad, favourable, or unfavourable. Philosophers would say that always with hope, goes fear. This pair of emotions sums up the manager's lot.

Managers must lead change and give employees hope that their lot too will be better after than before. We discuss leadership extensively in Chapter 2 and we emphasised there that the manager must choose the appropriate leadership approach for each situation. Leading change is one such situation.

There are specific actions that leaders must take. We noted the need for planning. Any change should be based on analysis and plans. Plans should generate a shared vision of the future – showing that 'hope' is not just an unfounded 'wish'. In Chapter 2, we suggested that leadership works through a dyadic relationship between manager and employee – leader and follower. Leadership during change demands excellent communications driving follower involvement and persuasion. And of course, once the change is made, reinforcement must cement the change in place to avoid drift to the old ways.

11.7.4   Using change agents

And now to an emotive subject. Many commentators suggest that managers are not the right people to lead change. They cite the many projects that end in disaster and suggest that change should be led by a professional 'change agent'. A quick Web search shows hundreds of jobs for 'change managers' and the like.

We believe that this is fundamentally flawed thinking. If leadership is dyadic, and the manager is leader and embraces their responsibility, it is wrong to introduce a third party into the relationship. No manager should sub-contract change of their firm.

That said, we acknowledge the sheer complexity and size of many changes, needing extensive plans to be executed. Just as a regimental Colonel relies heavily on their Adjutant, a Major and administrator, so the manager can make good use of an assistant to manage the change processes. After all, there's a 'day job' to be done and the manager must simultaneously drive change and sustain turnover and profit.

Reflection 11-5: About making change happen

Consider a change that you'd like to implement in your firm. Select either the hard systems methodology or the soft systems methodology and sketch out a plan for the change. Estimate the amount of your own time you'll need to make the change. Read 11.7.4 carefully. Would it be right to employ a change agent? If so, how would you manage the change with them?

11.8   Transfer as the ultimate change

Throughout *Because Your People Matter*, we have assumed that the firm's ownership is stable and that the owners are committed to the business. Ultimately, of course, all shareholders are investors. Investors put their money in, and they expect a return on that investment from time to time and on sale of their shares.

We must therefore include a brief discussion about what happens to the firm at some future end point – and as it faces the ultimate change, at least in the firm's present form. There are many final outcomes for firms and here we lump all together under the general action of transferring the business to new ownership.

Managers must begin thinking about the end game when, as entrepreneurs, they start the firm. And while not being consumed by it in subsequent years, they must think about the end game every hour thereafter to maximise the firm's value – however that is measured.

The manager's sole aim, as agent for the owners, is to guide the firm to achieve that end point. We don't suggest when that should be or what form it should take. It could be an asset sale, merger, or acquisition. That is for the owners. But we do suggest that the firm's value is all-important.

11.9   What gives a firm a value?

All firms seek value, however that's measured. It's the manager's job to grow that value. And firms are often transferred at some point when they achieve a particular value. That may be a financial value or measured using some other metric. Typically, the firm aims to make profit and hence value can be defined as the ability of the firm to make profits for a new owner in the same fashion as it did in the past. Put simply, value is vested in the markets in which the firm trades, the products it offers and the people that make it all happen. Each enables future profit for someone.

11.9.1   *Ability to sustain profits*

The problem often is that owners and prospective buyers assume that firms can go through a transfer without disruption. Buyer due diligence will attempt to describe the firm honestly, but many a buyer has found issues later. It's insufficient to measure the stability and good management of the firm by crude indices like how few employee disciplinaries and grievances are in train.

We hope that, in this book, we have shown how employees working in a social environment yield performance and ultimately personal outcomes. We have illustrated in Chapter 5 the variables on which this performance depends. It's not difficult therefore to see from our previous discussions that any downward change in those variables caused by poor communication, breach of trust or other crass management at the point of change will disrupt performance. Since individual performance leads to the firm's performance, any upset leading up to a transfer, during transfer or after transfer could be disastrous.

There can therefore be no assumption that profits (and hence value) will sustain. The manager must work particularly hard during transfer, sensing performance and launching interventions, just as we describe in Chapter 5.

Employees are all-too-often considered by accountants as human capital to be pushed around at will without loss, rather than human beings who will quit in an instant, decimating any value that accountants might calculate.

11.9.2   Capability

Value can be measured in several ways. Fundamentally it's the financial returns available from the firm's ability to do something, to meet some strategy and achieve some goals. What it achieves may be realised by directly exploiting present capability or it may be realised in some other adjunct capability, where the firm's technology function and employee competencies augment that of some other enterprise. Either way, it's capability that matters.

From this definition, there are two ways of valuing the capability: the enterprise value and the substitution value.

The firm's enterprise value is the value of the firm measured by the future profits it will make, often compared to some alternative investment such as the interest available from a bank for an equivalent deposit. To determine the enterprise value, the firm must be modelled as a going concern. The future business outcomes are normally then set out in its speculative post-transfer business plan.

The enterprise value also includes the incremental value that another firm might realise by adding its capability to that of the transferred firm.

The substitution value is more complex.

Perhaps the firm to be transferred can provide a capability that replaces a capability that another firm may presently be buying in. A good example is the purchase of a firm whose business it is to provide fixed telecommunications links to mobile operators. Those operators will perhaps presently be buying in those links from BT, the UK's main telecommunications provider. The substitution value is the cost reduction available to the mobile operator, by acquiring a links company, that will then be integrated within its own operation. The in-house links will be substituted for the BT links. This is an illustration of the mobile operator's 'make or buy decision'. It previously elected to 'buy' and now it's going to 'make' by acquiring a firm.

Substitution can also be applied to assets (and specifically to intellectual property). A purchase of patents may enable costly licensing or supply arrangements to be terminated. In this case, the value is measured by what the acquisition allows the manager to do.

11.9.3   Markets, products, and people

In other chapters we described the capability as the function available in the technology that the employees use in the firm, multiplied by the competencies that they have. For the purposes of valuation, capability must be expanded to also embrace the firm's ability to command its markets to allow it to deploy its capability (and hence sell its goods and services to clients in those markets).

Capability also describes the firm's products – or more broadly, its products and services. Products and services also embody the firm's know-how, and hence it's intellectual property. Products, services, know-how and intellectual property are important for both enterprise and substitution value. It's possible to run an enterprise with these assets (and to make additional profits) and it's possible to substitute those assets (and hence increase profits by increased sales or reduced costs).

The balance of those three – markets, products, and people – will vary. For some it will be a roughly equal split. In other instances, it will be primarily one or other. Ultimately, though, value comes from people – people as designers of product, people as developers of intellectual property and people who build success in markets.

11.10   Chapter Summary

This whole book is about change. It shouldn't need a separate section on the subject – and yet there are specific approaches, methods and tools for use when making change to a firm's capability that deserve mention.

As we highlight, the manager's job is change; change to stand still in a moving environment, change to grow and change to react to specific challenges. But change can also be unplanned. There are always those in all firms with 'agendas', even if only to greatly further their own careers.

There are several useful models that help understand individuals' roles in change. We note the dynamic model of change, where opinions and plans are modified with every interaction. We note the force-field model of change, where opinions and plans are changed through each employee simply being in the meeting or firm or environment. And we comment that change is like the wind, with opinions and plans modified by irregular forces. These are not practical models. But they help managers move from the local detail to think pan-firm, pan-scenario, or pan-environment. They help managers understand that their plans are subject to many reinforcing and countervailing pressures.

As positivists, we provide models that relate manager action with resulting business outcomes. We therefore focus on models where managers can plan action to effect change. We return therefore to the systems model of change to encourage managers to identify what inputs, controls, enablers, or process might be changed to effect beneficial outputs or outcomes.

Key in this positivist approach is the determination of what to change. We note that in determining this, there are many approaches – the manager could consider their firm's prevailing culture and elect that this might change, or they might focus on technology, having determined that other approaches on which to focus energy are less likely to achieve the desired outcomes.

Reality normally requires multiple actions across multiple systems.

When it comes to changing people, one of the most practical aspects is the change to the way employees work. Frequently this involves change to employment contracts. We highlight that this is simple enough, and emphasise that the mechanism is though consultation, though in the end, the manager can generally also enforce change.

Change in outcomes takes time. Change requires the manager to make change to several independent variables. Change in the associated dependent variables may happen in a few days, in a few months or in a few years. How the system reacts to change in input depends much on the experience curve for that firm.

In closing the discussion on change, we categorise change as hard and soft. Hard change is when the manager is dealing with singular or small numbers of definable systems. Here, the change can be modelled using the systems models that we present in other chapters. Soft change is when there are just so many variables, or it's impossible to identify distinct systems that might be focussed on. In the soft systems methodology, the manager accepts that the scenario is a mess – that there's just too much going on to see with any clarity what might be done.

The soft systems methodology uses two key tools – the drawing of a rich picture, and the development from that of several themes. Those themes can then be worked on using the hard systems approach. The soft systems approach is effectively a way of making sense of chaos.

We comment on the leadership of change and the use of change agents. This is more for completeness since other chapters adequately dealt with the manager's job and their leader role.

And finally, we consider what gives a firm its value in readiness for some end point such as sale, merger, or acquisition. We acknowledge the significance of the value in products, services, management decision-making and the firm's competitive position, but in the end it's the employees and their ability to sustain profits that determines the lion's share of the value. All managers had best remember that.

12

Becoming a Manager

The title here is deliberate. People <u>become</u> managers. It's an evolution. It's a journey. There's nothing quick about it. And arguably it never ends. No-one ever knows enough about management.

Management is a massive, multi-facetted domain. No one emerges, chrysalis-like, as a manager. Managers who take on management without preparation, or start firms and appoint themselves as managers, are what we term accidental managers. They're not ready for the responsibility. They don't have the skills and the knowledge and hence will likely blunder around for years, learning by failure. Success will be accidental and more to do with the environment than their own competencies. Accidental managers will likely leave a trail of destruction because of their arrogance and poor skills and knowledge.

In this chapter we discuss how managers evolve and become expert. We discuss how a management journey might be developed.

12.1 Starting from ignorance

This book is all about competence. We define competence as a parameter having a greyscale with an expert level at the upper end that in practice is never totally achieved. A working definition of 'manager' for this section is perhaps someone who has studied the science of management and has enough subsequent experience such that they are able to deal with most day-to-day management issues. They have enough competence in enough of the job to succeed. We'll see later that they are likely to be what we term a Practitioner.

Now, there are four states of competence, and incompetence, in any job.

- Unconscious incompetence
- Conscious incompetence
- Conscious competence
- Unconscious competence

Unconscious incompetence represents most people's state when setting out on their management journey. They don't know what they don't know. They are ignorant – and that's not an insult, just a statement of where they are at. As would-be managers, every management scenario is new to them. They have not studied the subject and hence have neither sufficient theory nor sufficient experience. They have no real clue what to do. And the fact that they don't know that they are in that state makes those individuals dangerous.

Conscious incompetence is an improvement on unconscious incompetence. At least the manager knows they are incompetent. That's an enlightenment. They will hopefully, on becoming aware that there's competence to be had, be motivated to accept training, and move to the next stage – conscious competence.

Competence is a grey scale. All managers should be on a journey and conscious competence is not an endpoint. The challenge is to have the person who is consciously competent accept that their competence is never complete.

And finally, there will be rare individuals who are competent without being aware. They're the non-manager who talks sense in a meeting. Or the junior supervisor who has greater competence than they realise as a result, perhaps, of management in other businesses or activities such as volunteering. It's for senior managers to identify those people and develop their careers accordingly to exploit the competence they do have.

In writing this book, we assume that all managers want to be good at their job – to be a good manager - to be competent. It would be absurd to consider otherwise. The battle then is with those who are ignorant. This chapter aims to illustrate what's involved in becoming a manager – a good manager. We aim to have all would-be managers start and sustain their journey toward expert. We hope ignorance is just a momentary state for all.

12.2   Becoming an expert

Before we can discuss what it's like being good at management, we need a clear expression of what management is. We need to know what you are to be good at.

We describe elsewhere that management is about exerting influence over all aspects of the firm. It's about intervention in the working lives of employees. That intervention might concern employee motivation, competencies, or technologies used. It might concern day to day activities or strategic decisions requiring capital purchase. It's where a manager wants to make a change, or some corrective action in the systems of the firm, to achieve some new state.

To be capable of intervening, the manager must be able to select a possible intervention from a library of options. The first requirement is to have that library, to know where to look, or to be capable of improvising. Academia and peer reviewed texts are rich in options and the manager must be able to select, remembering that many options are specific to case, needing adaptation to be applicable to their firm and present problem. The manager must be able to predict that the favoured intervention will be successful. To be able to make that prediction the manager must understand the core science behind the topic of management.

That science will likely embrace psychology, economics, and law. As an example, a manager may think that a pay rise will enhance employee commitment. In making such a claim, they must understand the psychology of pay including the psychology of distributive and procedural justice. And there's the economics of the firm's present and future financial position. Then there's the law of pay embracing equality, discrimination, and the obligations to report pay gaps between, for example, men and women. A simple thought like this to solve a commitment issue must never be a decision on a whim. Experience adds to understanding to allow the manager to have the confidence to make and document the intervention.

Roger Kneebone, in his book *Expert: understanding the path to mastery*, describes the final qualification for membership of the guild of experts – the ability to improvise. Improvisation is an important management capability.

Improvisation is unique to experts. Management is never deterministic. For every action, like a pay rise, there are many outcomes, some wanted and expected, and some not wanted and very unexpected. To elaborate the point, some management interventions could kill the firm. An expert manager will know how to set up the intervention and then monitor outcomes. If the outcomes emerging in the coming weeks and months are not those desired, the expert manager will know how to recover the position – and the necessary sensing, analysis and improvisation comes from deep understanding and experience.

So, what's involved in getting to expert?

In the model in Figure 12-1, we show two concepts. The first is Kneebone's ideas about the evolution from apprentice through journeyman to expert. This idea is about how the journey progresses (as labelled on the x-axis in the figure).

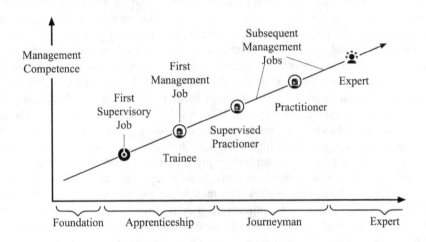

Figure 12-1: The route to expert

The second idea is that there are absolute levels, and we define four.

The ideas about journey and absolute levels are useful in understanding how a manager grows but each has different purposes. We discuss Roger Kneebone's idea first.

An apprentice has no opinion of their own about management – they simply don't have the knowledge or the skills. They identify with the desire to be a manager and are committed to the journey. They are at the conscious incompetence state discussed above. As we identify in Figure 12-1, the apprenticeship starts when someone in a discipline is to become a supervisor of others. They're not taking on a management job per se – it's more about helping others while reporting to a manager. And both manager and supervisor-cum-apprentice agree that the journey to manager should start – given appropriate foundation skills and knowledge.

Generally, an apprenticeship involves some academic study in management. It could be anything from reading quality texts to a formal course. The understanding acquired as apprentice is quite basic, but it's enough to progress to the next phase, the journeyman.

The journeyman phase is arguably the most important. In this, the would-be manager does time. The aim is for them to experience enough of the various interventions and outcomes to build skills, knowledge, and confidence in management. It ends when the would-be manager is getting more things right than wrong. Importantly, they become confident at analysing situations, researching options, intervening, and sensing outcomes as a complete process.

As Kneebone suggests, expert comes when the manager stops thinking about themselves and routinely thinks of others in their firm and beyond. At the expert stage, the manager realises that they are only an instrument – success for them comes when others succeed. That's a big awakening and fundamentally changes the manager's outlook and future potential.

12.3   Levels of manager competence

In the second idea, there are four levels of management – Trainee, Supervised Practitioner, Practitioner, and Expert. In some senses this matches Kneebone's three – apprentice, journeyman, and expert but it splits the journeyman phase in two.

Management is not a job with a single role or task. Each role or task requires several competencies. We discuss Boyatzis' 23 competencies of management in Chapter 6. The necessary competencies multiply if we add the requirement that all managers should also be competent in the business of the firm. It's easy to see therefore that it's likely impossible for all managers to be experts in every task. If we consider each stage of the four as a level reached rather than phases of a journey, we can then identify the various job tasks and allow a manager to be at one of the four levels in each. In this way, they can be an expert in some job tasks while a practitioner, supervised practitioner or even trainee in others.

Importantly, managers at supervised practitioner level for many competencies can employ the services of a mentor to work with them while still managing their fiefdom. It's just that to avoid conscious incompetence, they'll discuss their research, options, observations and intended interventions with another who themselves is expert. And as the would-be manager grows, they will move to practitioner, relying less on others.

This notion of four levels in each of many competencies allows a bespoke management development programme to be developed.

We go on now to discuss the detail of how to become a manager, and indeed how long it might take to reach those heady upper levels.

12.4   Defining management competence

There are two groups of competencies in which the manager needs to achieve a useful level: task competencies and contextual competencies. In the task competencies, the manager needs to learn to do. In the contextual competencies the manager needs to learn to interact with others. One is useless without the other. There's no benefit in developing a great business plan, but then failing to implement it. There's no benefit in developing a viable pay scheme and then failing to convince staff of its fairness. Contextual performance also includes learning how to function as part of a management team.

Let's look first at task competence.

Take a MD's job as an example. There are seven key accountabilities in this job centring on strategy; money; plans; products and deliverables; people; support to colleagues; and sales and marketing. In developing a person specification for our MD, we have developed 25 necessary competencies. These are shown below in the codex in Figure 12.2.

Broadly managers split their time worrying about making the best of the organisation as it is right now and making and implementing improvement plans.

The 25 headlines are broad. For example, 'Building reputation' covers everything associated with PR and promoting the firm. Likewise, 'Developing product' covers everything that might be needed to realise goods and services for sale or to be supplied as deliverables sometime in the future. And 'Managing risk' covers anything that might stop the firm trading. Each can be broken down further into many sub-competencies.

There's a huge amount to the MD's job.

Managers must also be competent in the domain in which the firm focusses. Consider a firm that focusses on telecoms regulation consulting. That's a hugely technical domain. The firm's consultants typically travel the world taking on projects for mobile phone operators and other wireless companies and for telecoms regulators. These projects embrace engineering, law, and economics. Telecoms regulators like the UK's Ofcom are arms of government. These consultants are almost exclusively graduate qualified, and most have second and third degrees and professional qualifications. It would be unimaginable for a manager of these consultants to be generalist. A generalist would simply not 'Understand the firm'.

Figure 12-2: Typical manager task competencies

The degree to which a manager must be a domain specialist depends a lot on how easy it is to learn the business. It will take many years to learn about telecoms regulation consulting, whereas it will take a lot less time to learn about a DIY store. The more time it takes to learn the business, the more likely it is that managers will require a background in the domain.

Let's now consider contextual competence.

Richard Boyatzis spent many years researching the necessary management competencies and developed a list of 23. We discuss these fully in Chapter 7. For now, it's enough to show these as a second codex overview.

Unsurprisingly, there's some crossover between the task and contextual competencies set out here.

Boyatzis, in his 23 manager competencies, calls for competence in 'relevant knowledge' and in 'function/product/technology'. These are both well covered in our discussion about domain competence. Technology also features highly in Figure 12-2 where we include the need for competence in 'Developing information systems' and in 'Developing business systems'. Systems in the modern world inevitably rely heavily on technology. And we specifically call for 'Exploiting technology' as an identifiable task competency. Technology features in everything the employees in the firm and the manager themselves will do in realising capability.

We have also added two modern contextual competencies that allow the manager to perform in the firm and its environment: 'Use of the social' and 'Exploiting digital'. Today's managers must understand that communications with employees is multi-facetted, and not restricted to downstream briefing from the manager. They must be able to exploit modern social communication. And in 'Exploiting digital', managers must have what are loosely defined as 'digital skills'; anything from being able to boot up a laptop and login to sites, to being able to draw diagrams, sending them off to colleagues to persuade them toward action.

Boyatzis proposed 23 competencies. We propose 25 and have added two that we consider fundamental. First, there's the ability to build processes and then trust that those processes will work and realise the required outcomes. Many managers today are weak in this – they want immediate results. Change takes time and needs the manager to stick to the plan. Second, there's the need to be able to tap the body of knowledge – to be able to research issues like the psychology of pay, or the legality of dismissal upon gross misconduct.

Finally, in describing the 25 contextual competencies in Figure 12-3, we propose that there are two groups – those personal to the manager such as 'Conceptualisation', and those more distal and projected by the manager, such as 'Use of oral presentations'.

So, in summary, managers need to know, understand and be able to do quite a lot! There are three main groups of competencies:

- Those associated directly with the manager's job – what we call task competencies;
- Those that allow the manager to function in their environment – the contextual competencies;
- And knowledge and understanding about the business – the domain competencies.

Task competencies are sometimes called 'hard skills'. Likewise contextual competencies are sometimes referred to as 'soft skills'.

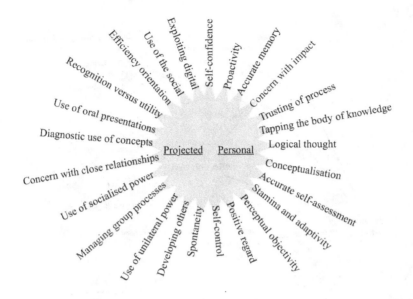

Figure 12-3: Manager contextual competencies

It's easy to see why we suggest that it is impossible for managers to be expert in every task and every competency. It's easy to see why managers must accept that they will be trainee in some, supervised practitioner in many, practitioner in others and expert in a few. And it's easy to recognise that management is a journey, growing competencies from apprentice through journeyman to expert. No manager has all the skills and knowledge from the outset, and no manager ever achieves expert in all.

12.5   Excelling at the little things

There's a raft of competencies that are common to task, context, and domain. We refer to them as the management primitives. A primitive is a basic building block of management, something that must be learned as an apprentice but improved and enhanced day by day. Primitives are amalgamated to give a standard operating form for all managers.

Some of these management primitives are shown in Figure 12-4.

Management primitives are best understood by example. Take the Office Efficiency group of primitives. All managers must become practitioners in the use of a spreadsheet for the manipulation of arrays of numbers. This will, for example, allow budgets to be prepared, pricing to be calculated for complicated jobs, and reports to be prepared for management colleagues. Spreadsheets also allow trendlines to be projected to speculate about the future. Spreadsheet competence starts at the beginning of the management journey and is never complete.

Again, in the Office Efficiency group, the daybook is a fundamental of management life. All managers must document every discussion they have with employees, suppliers, and management colleagues. It's not that the manager doubts the integrity of others. It's simply that there's so much going on in a manager's life that they must document for their own records and for future recall.

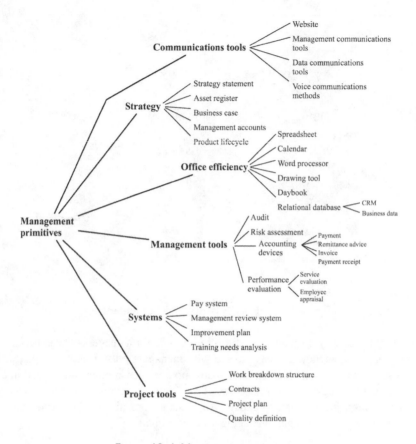

Figure 12-4: Management primitives

We won't discuss them all, but perhaps it's worth highlighting audit and work breakdown structure as two further examples.

Audit is a technique. It's the notion of knowing what was wanted and then assessing what's been achieved against that. Audit can be applied right across the firm from management projects to customer deliverables.

And the work breakdown structure (WBS) is a technique for describing a project of any sort. We show an example for a consulting project in Figure 4-4. It's a good idea to become competent in the use of a drawing tool to build the WBS.

The list in Figure 12-4 is not complete. Managers will need to build their own list and progressively improve their competence in each over the years. These primitives will be used again and again, week after week, year after year.

Finally, while still on management primitives, there are several normative management processes: processes that the manager must run, again and again, using the same approach. And these too might be considered primitive.

The following table shows five examples.

Process	Source(s) of normative method
Employee disciplinary	ACAS, the UK quasi-governmental body concerned with employment
Financial statements	The Institute of Chartered Accounts in England and Wales; Her Majesty's Revenue and Customs (HMRC).
Employee recruitment	The Recruitment and Employment Federation – though note that we discuss evidenced and deterministic methods in Chapter 3.
Analysis of business scenarios	The acronym, SWOTPESTL – considering strengths, weaknesses, opportunities, threats, and using political, economic, scientific, technological, and legal perspectives.
Product development	Logical approaches starting with stakeholder or customer needs, product specification and product or service implementation – followed by audit.

Figure 12-5: Normative Processes

These normative processes depend a lot on the business. There are a huge number of normative processes. Importantly, though, no manager would ever be expected to know the details of many of them. They would just need to know that they exist and how to use them to get further information. For example, ACAS has a lot to say about employment and managers would need to refer to the ACAS website many times in a year, querying several points of procedure and law.

Referring to the ideas of ignorance and competence, no manager should be ignorant about the presence of normative processes. No manager should blunder around, making up processes and documents. It should be routine for managers to query and investigate sources, then learn where relevant.

Reflection 12-1: Your primitives and normative methods

Identify the basic building blocks of management that you will need to use. Identify all the normative methods. Identify the level you need to be at. Identify the level you are at. What will you do to grow?

12.6   Scientific method as central competency

Scientists progress their research in many ways. One of the most common ways of scientific investigation requires a five-step progression. This method is one of the key normative processes common to all.

First, the manager develops the management question they have. An example might be, 'If I pay my people a bonus, will they work harder and more effectively'?

Second, the manager researches the topic and tries to find out what academics and other well-informed commentators have to say about the subject.

Third, they then develop their question into a hypothesis based on evidence from the research – for example, 'I believe that if I offer a 30% bonus, my people will work with sustained vigour'. There is evidence for this, though there is no evidence supporting increased vigour for lower percentage bonuses. Contrary to management myth, the bonus must be substantial.

Fourth, the manager then experiments with bonuses, perhaps offering a 5% bonus and looking at the outcome. If the outcome is not as expected and wanted, perhaps the bonus might be increased. From the research, we'd expect this experiment to fail until the bonus level reaches 30%!

And finally, given evidence and ongoing monitoring, the manager implements appropriate changes. Of course, if the hypothesis is not supported, the subject is binned – or perhaps the research question rephrased, and the activity repeated.

This example is well-documented and evidence from academic research in management is readily available. The scientific method of investigation can be used for all manner of issues. The central thread is a hypothesis supported or a hypothesis refuted by evidence, and progression based on that evidence.

12.7   The notion of performance in management

Performance of employees is relatively easily assessed and managed. If the employee is a salesperson, it's often about achieving a sales budget. If they're an installer or mechanic, it's about completing work in the forecasted time. And if it's a design engineer or other project-oriented employee, it's about delivering against time and budget.

But manager performance is much more complex. It's not simply about your efforts and outcomes as an individual. It's about the efforts and outcomes of the employees that you manage. As soon as you become a manager, it's no longer about you. It's about them.

This is an awakening for the Journeyman manager. Initially, the Journeyman revels in their promotion and responsibility. But it inevitably dawns on them that their success can only come about if the people working for them succeed as individuals and as a team. The manager's success depends on their ability to manage their people – with all that this entails.

We discuss the rule of eights in other chapters. In essence this suggests that a manager with eight direct reports must allot half their time to their people. The time available for other things diminishes with management responsibility. Managers who expect to still achieve as individuals soon realise that there is limited time for their own separate careers.

We discussed in Chapter 2 the two key models of management – the feed-forward and the feedback model. Both have manager performance at their heart. The manager has control over most of the variables influencing the activities – considering that they select the employees in the first place and can ultimately dismiss them.

We discussed in Chapter 5 dependencies on individual performance, and groupwork and how groups form and behave. In the feed-forward model, it's for the manager to set objectives for the group and then monitor performance to achieve outcomes. We illustrate this notion applied to groups in Figure 12-6. Outcomes are achieved through collective activities. Some activities can fall short – some of the group can have low motivation, behaviour or performance and the group will still perform through performance of others. It's for the manager to set the group up to succeed.

In Chapter 5, we applied the feedback model to individuals. In the case of a group, the performance will derive from the collective activities of all group members. The manager is of course interested in the group performance output and will use their own personal comparator to sense how that collective performance is working out. If intervention is needed to recover performance deficiencies, this might be applied individually, or it might be applied collectively to the group.

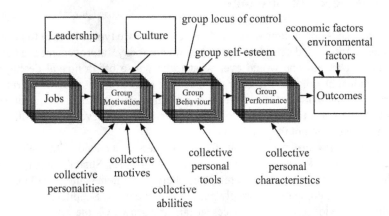

Figure 12-6: The feed-forward model applied to a group managed by a manager

In Chapter 1, we suggested that a manager is the person who accepts the responsibility for the outcomes required. The two figures here show how a manager takes this responsibility and makes change and intervenes to achieve outcomes.

By using these two models, nothing fazes a manager. Once the feedforward model is set up such that the outcomes should be achieved, and the feedback model is used to keep the outcomes on track. The manager is then in control. Provided that the system bandwidth is sufficient to cope with the adjustments needed, there is nothing that the manager can't achieve. The system bandwidth is all about the scope of change and of feedback-driven intervention. It's about how brave the manager is.

Of course, there will be mistakes. The manager will implement, for example, the wrong culture. Or they'll apply an inappropriate leadership approach. Or they'll hire people with the wrong personal characteristics. But they'll soon improve their knowledge and understanding, and their various competencies will grow. Over time and with experience, they'll develop from Supervised Practitioner thorough Practitioner to Expert.

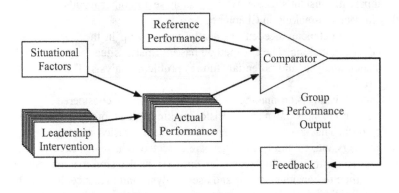

Figure 12-7: Feedback model applied to a group

12.8   The need for outcomes

Human existence is about improvement. As an example, we typically want to be safer than previous generations, and safer tomorrow than we are today. Improvement is a core part of the human psyche. No one would ever want to be worse off in mental health, physical health, emotional health, and the other parts of their person. And so it is in a firm. No firm ever starts up to fail. All want to grow, even if growth is defined more in terms of welfare of the members than profit to the shareholders. All want to grow, even if the profit motive is not the only driver and not the only outcome.

As a result, it's no surprise that all stakeholders associated with a firm focus on outcomes and that those outcomes carry improvement metrics. Shareholders typically want to see their financial stake provide a return on their investment – they would expect their stake to grow when compared to simply putting it in the bank. Suppliers would like to see their ability to provide goods and services sustain and grow over the years. And employees would like to know that they have a job on which they can base their families' future, allowing them improvement too.

The manager's lot is therefore all about outcomes. And it's no surprise therefore that all the models that we talk of in this book involve doing something, to something, to achieve a result. All the models focus on identifying the variables, making changes to these variables in the hope of an improved outcome, assessing the outcomes achieved, and then repeating this process fuelled by a general desire to improve.

Managers must therefore become outcomes oriented.

Critically therefore, managers must learn to identify the real outcomes needed and the variables that influence them. Part of being outcomes oriented is being able to identify the real goal or problem. We give a series of change models in Chapter 11, but it's worth just dwelling here on some key competencies: developing a disinclination to jump to conclusions (about what to do); the ability to gather and use information; and the ability to develop and trust improvement and solution processes.

Unfortunately, these competencies are unnatural. Humans jump to conclusions. Humans naturally make fast decisions with minimal information. Humans are also disinclined to dig deep to get information, preferring easily remembered simple models. And humans are inclined to be impatient and abandon plans in favour of something new that offers apparently instant success. We discuss these and other results of bias leading to irrationality in decision-making in Chapter 5.

The three competencies needed are neatly summed up in the Kepner-Tregoe (KT) approach to decision making. The KT method has four parts: situational analysis, problem analysis, decision analysis and potential (future) problem analysis. These are shown as a cycle in Figure 12-8.

In essence, this decision-making is slow, rational, and considered. We argue that managers must learn to slow down their decision-making and adopt rational approaches such as the KT approach. That takes practice – fast, bias-riddled decision-making often prevails in accidental managers and, culturally, managers are expected to have instant answers.

There's nothing, though, that precludes emotion in decision-making. Since the KT approach takes time to consider options and uses analysis and evidence, it does show what a pure rational decision might look like. But since it allows time, it enables the manager to slow down their emotional processing to think through emotions without the biases that blight knee-jerk gut decisions. Rational and emotional processing can exist side by side.

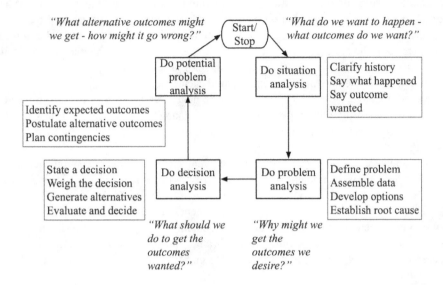

"What alternative outcomes might we get - how might it go wrong?"

Start/ Stop

"What do we want to happen - what outcomes do we want?"

Do potential problem analysis

Do situation analysis

Clarify history
Say what happened
Say outcome wanted

Identify expected outcomes
Postulate alternative outcomes
Plan contingencies

State a decision
Weigh the decision
Generate alternatives
Evaluate and decide

Do decision analysis

Do problem analysis

Define problem
Assemble data
Develop options
Establish root cause

"What should we do to get the outcomes wanted?"

"Why might we get the outcomes we desire?"

Figure 12-8: The Kepner-Tregoe approach to decision making

12.9   Getting the sense that you're an expert

We've already mentioned the idea that management is about realising that it's no longer about you; it's about them. It's about the people that work for you and their achievements and outcomes. If they succeed, you succeed.

It goes further than that though. As you grow as a manager and take on more responsibility until you are accountable for larger numbers of people, you gain a sense that you are responsible for a whole fiefdom. Ultimately an MD is responsible for the whole firm with its hundreds or even thousands of staff. So, success is not going to come from a single intervention or even tens of interventions. It's going to come from thousands of discrete interventions from hundreds or thousands of managers.

New or accidental managers become expert managers when they recognise and accept their fiefdom and everything that it covers.

Experts also develop a feel for the job. That's not to say that expert managers resort to gut feel and can abandon all that we discuss in this book. It's to recognise that an expert manager can, from their theoretical underpinning and extensive experience, sense what makes a viable intervention and what a likely outcome might be. It's rather like sensing how long a plank of wood is and then using a tape measure to confirm and get an accurate result.

But becoming an expert manager is not like becoming a virtuoso piano player. Nor is it like becoming a surgeon. Both those involve immediate or near-immediate outcomes. When a pianist plays brilliantly, they'll sense it. When a surgeon completes a complex procedure, they'll know. When an MD and their managers undertake numerous interventions to cause change, it may be months or years before the outcome is felt.

Management is a long game. Expert managers accept this.

No manager can experience everything that's needed to be expert. No manager can learn all the necessary theory. Expert managers have served enough time and learned enough theory to allow them to improvise interventions to every problem they might face. A good example might be building a unique salary policy and system to fit a unique company culture. The outcome might use some of the principles in Chapter 10, but it would be adapted to fit the specific local need. In another example where the manager is dealing with a very difficult employee, they might develop a unique approach to the meetings. They might adjust the meeting aims and method each time.

Expert managers also accept that they'll never really arrive. There's no end to management learning and experience. Expert managers will always question their decisions, discuss proposed interventions with peers and accept that they have no monopoly on what's best for their firm.

Management learning follows much of what's experienced by anyone learning a subject beyond basic competency – great progress will be reached until learning stalls. It may be that past dogma is found to have been recently debunked. Maslow's Hierarchy of Needs, for example, is a staple on many management courses today, but it was refuted and shown to be inaccurate many years ago. Management learning is full of re-learning as the science progresses. Managers must work through such new awareness to continually update theory and experience and move off the current plateau towards greater skills and knowledge.

Finally, experts must retain their expertise and grow further. As we note, management is a huge topic and no one every knows it all. There are several associations that can support management learning and to which managers should subscribe. The Chartered Management Institute is a practical association. The British Academy of Management is more academic but will take managers deeper and broader into the topic. Both, and others, have membership levels that calibrate members' experience and capability. And managers should subscribe to relevant management journals in line with their specialist interests, such as the Journal of Occupational and Organizational Psychology.

12.10   Working in a management team

Directors typically appoint one of their number to be Managing Director (MD) (or in American terms, Chief Executive Officer (CEO)). In the early days of a firm, the MD is often the sole manager. As the firm grows, the MD forms a management team. The core aim of that management team is to create competitive advantage for the firm.

Competitive advantage comes in the first instance from making the right decisions about which business to be in and what products and services to deliver. Michael Porter, in his seminal book from 1985, considers also that there are two types of competitive advantage: one coming from a more favourable cost position than competitors and one coming from a better ability to differentiate those products and services. Whatever the definition, competitive advantage is under manager control. Cost advantage leads to better profits, and differentiation leads to greater sales.

Management is a key capability for all who will lead and be entrepreneurs.

Management of a firm is a huge task. If there's only one manager, their competencies must likewise be huge. As soon as possible, the MD will aim to spread the load by appointing a diverse group to assist. As example of a management team is shown in Figure 12-9.

Unfortunately, this notion of spreading the load only goes so far. It's limited principally to domain knowledge. For example, rather than be expert in marketing, the MD will likely recruit a marketing specialist as Sales & Marketing Director. Likewise, the MD will rely on a Finance Director to advise and manage the money side of the operation.

Many management teams also include deep specialisations in domains like information systems and health and safety. Advisors in such specialist subjects can be part-time team members or even external consultants.

Each member will have their own repertoire of management primitives and normative processes essential for management within their domain.

So, the MD forms a management team, hiring domain experts – but those domain experts must themselves be managers on their own management journey. There's no escaping the need for all to have task and contextual competencies in management.

The management team's overall competence is hopefully greater than the sum of its parts.

The competitive advantage that comes from participation in a management team requires several competencies not yet discussed, and a few personality traits too on which there will be new demands. Members of all domains must be able to practice listening – to one another. They must be able to challenge one another. And that will require traits of assertiveness, extroversion, and agreeableness.

Individual members of the management team will bring differing experiences. Those experiences will bring complementary confidence to the decisions made. Members will be able to use one another as sounding boards for their own ideas, effectively using one another as mentors.

Figure 12-9: A typical management team

The management team is therefore an eclectic group, complementing and supplementing individual competencies. It will, however, inevitably comprise members whose individual competencies span Trainee, Supervised Practitioner, Practitioner and Expert in individual task, contextual and domain competencies. The aim of the

MD, when forming the group, is to ensure that the key competencies are well covered. If there are gaps, there must be personal improvement plans in place to bridge or new members hired.

12.11   Passing on your art

Frequently managers are appointed without the necessary competencies to manage. As the cynical adage has it, people are promoted to the level of their incompetence. The result is that any competent manager assembling a management team must expect to develop the managers working with them. Failure to develop those managers will ultimately result in a weak management team and a catalogue of errors as those newly promoted managers blunder around, learning by mistake.

Developing a management team is like developing any other group of employees. We discuss this fully in Chapter 9. The work starts with the building of a competency framework setting out the competencies and behaviours that the MD needs in the management team. The second step is to log the competencies and behaviours that the MD has currently in the team. That then exposes the weaknesses and shows the personal development needed in each manager.

The competencies needed are for a large part set out earlier in this chapter. Domain specific competencies must be added. And it's for the MD to determine priorities and mandates.

The MD has two principal opportunities to grow their people: when working one-to-one with them, and when working with them as a team in management meetings. Each event is a learning opportunity, but a balance must be struck between demanding compliance (with primitives, normative processes and other standard operating methods that would provide learning) and allowing free reign. It's a mentor-mentee relationship where the mentee retains responsibility for their function guided by the MD.

12.12   The Managing Director

So, who is this super-being? Who is the MD? What competencies do they need?

In the early days of all firms, their competencies must span all that we've discussed above. They likely won't be Expert in anything! But they will be Supervised Practitioner or Practitioner in most of the competencies we've listed. They'll be able to drive strategy and argue business cases and all the other task competencies. They'll be competent in oral presentation and in seeking efficiency and all the other contextual competencies. They'll have a good repertoire of management primitives and normative processes. They'll need competencies in all the domains of the firm. And most of all, they'll be able to build a team using the principles we've outlined here.

As the team forms, the MD will need to recall old competencies, like having a sense of what makes a good marketing plan, and they must learn new competencies centred around making the team function. Of course, they could re-ignite old flames – re-learn old competencies long since turned a bit rusty. But that's not needed now. There's a bigger job to be done and it's not now about the MD. It's about their management team. The key mantra for all managers is, "It's not about you. It's about them."

12.13   Author's stories

Both authors learned management and followed the sort of journey described above. It's useful to see how those journeys evolved and for readers to compare their journeys. It's not to say that those are the right sort of journeys. It's for the reader to determine what they need, in conjunction with their mentor and their manager.

12.13.1   *Sue Berry*

Sue's management journey started early. Elements of leadership were learned as a Brownie Sixer, a Patrol Leader in Guides and as a Young Leader in Ranger Guides. All involved grasping responsibility. Her first real exposure to management training was on an intensive residential programme to learn the science of non-directive leadership. Then, as a Venture Scout Leader, she used her learning to support young people in delivering their own adventure programmes. The management skills and techniques learned from The Scouts Wood Badge programme provided a superb foundation.

Sue trained as a teacher before moving into Human Resource Management. She taught sciences in a Secondary School at a time when there were too many teachers and subsequently re-trained in HR, starting her new career at the age of 22 as an HR Officer with Ciba Geigy. Right from the start of her HR career Sue managed departments of varying sizes across all HR functions. In Ciba, with HR, payroll, medical, and training teams to manage, she was soon on a corporate management training programme to augment completion of what was then the Institute of Personnel Management graduateship. Working alongside managers from all the Ciba divisions, she learned what it was to manage at both local and multi-national level, spanning subjects from strategy to budgeting and finance. All great grounding for all her future work.

Sue went on to head up HR provision in a wide variety of industry sectors – charity, manufacturing, not-for-profit and engineering. Her work has included supporting line managers both across the UK and worldwide.

TimelessTime as a consulting firm came about from a desire to have the flexibility to work with managers who believe that their people are important – that their people really do matter in achieving organisational goals. To ensure that she had the best possible skills and resources to support clients, she embarked on further education. Following on from her first degree and post-grad, Sue completed a master's in human resource management and then a BSc in Psychology, Economics and Politics. Aged 44 and following demonstration of relevant responsibility, she was elected a Chartered Fellow of the Chartered Institute of Personnel and Development.

Over the years Sue has striven to leave those with whom she works more knowledgeable than they were before. Now as a management consultant that knowledge and teaching is provided to clients.

As shown in this book, management is about a great many things. A good manager knows when to intervene, when to stand back, when to be supportive and when to 'lay down the law'. A good manager must understand the business they are in, the nuances of working with subordinates, colleagues, their own line manager, suppliers, and customers. There is a lot to learn. Sue firmly believes that her academic experience, her management training, and various supportive managers over the years have all played their part in her management journey.

12.13.2   *John Berry*

John would argue that his journey into management began at school and in Scouts. At aged 10 or 11 he was already 'leaning in' – taking on jobs at school where he was stretched. He became an enthusiastic Patrol Leader in Scouts and then a Venture Scout. In Venture Scouts he led many activities – big footpath walks, multi-pitch rock climbs and ham radio jamborees. As part of his Duke of Edinburgh's Award service he became an Assistant Scout Leader, giving back to younger kids.

This history has much in common with other successful managers. Managers typically start their management journey young, accepting responsibility for others. We discuss the question of whether managers are born or bred elsewhere, and we conclude that it's a bit of both. It's 'born' because managers have a natural leaning – a calling – to accept responsibility. And it's 'bred': because of that calling, they tend to volunteer and hence get identified and developed.

John joined the Marconi company and then Pye/Philips. In Philips, he was identified as a potential manager and given a first management opportunity to lead the Propagation Consulting Group at the age of 28. The instant he said 'yes', he was sent on a Diploma in Management Studies: a two-year course at the local technical college. There was no discussion. It was a condition of the appointment. That was the norm in those days. If anyone was offered a supervisor's or manager's job, they went on a CMS or DMS. John also studied at the Philips management school in the Netherlands with managers from the worldwide Philips organisation.

This trend of responsibility continued. John moved from electronics design through consulting to systems engineering, marketing, and product management. When he felt he didn't understand Europe adequately for his job, he completed a BA in European Studies. And when he felt he didn't understand software adequately, he completed an MBA with electives in technology management and software engineering. His story is generally one of an evolving understanding of, and skill in, the technics and contexts of management learned over a period of around 20 years. In parallel, he built a management portfolio that qualified him as a Chartered Manager and a Fellow of the Chartered Management Institution at the age of 45.

When he left Thales to start ATDI in 1996, he had many of the management competencies needed. As a result, he developed the firm to quickly turn over £2.5m with 25 engineers.

All management journeys differ. Some will be compressed, with 'expert' being achieved quite quickly. Others will be drawn out, perhaps mixing, as John did, a technical specialism like software engineering with management. Either way, the journey involves apprenticeship and journeyman phases to eventually become expert.

Reflection 12-2: Your management journey

Complete a personal audit of your competencies using the approaches discussed here. Position yourself as Trainee, Supervised Practitioner, Practitioner or Expert against each competency. Use our definitions of each from 8.3.6. Compare your competencies held with the competencies needed – develop your competence gap. What will your management development journey look like to bridge this gap? Repeat this for each of your management team.

12.14   Chapter Summary

We have assumed here that all managers – accidental or planned – want to be good managers. It would be strange to think otherwise. So, we've set out what's needed. We've approached this from the viewpoint of competence – asking what competencies and behaviours are needed for a manager to be good.

Importantly, we don't assume that all in the world is stable – that all that a manager need do is plan, learn the few competencies needed to execute the plan and success will come. Unfortunately, the world is not stable. Stuff happens daily to which all managers must react. Most firms will face existential threats every few years – and some more frequently. We assume that all managers must improvise and react to situations to maintain outcomes.

We recognise though that many, nay most, managers are untrained, and many of those will not embrace training and development to improve. That's sad, for it's difficult to see how any would-be manager could learn the necessary theory and gain the necessary experience to become good without some sort of formal development.

To help define what's meant by 'good', we've used first an idea from Roger Kneebone, author of *Expert: Understanding the Path to Mastery*. In his book he sets out three stages – Trainee, Journeyman and Expert. This usefully gives the idea of development as a journey. Kneebone doesn't give any idea of levels, so we introduce the idea of four levels – Trainee, Supervised Practitioner, Practitioner and Expert. This effectively splits his Journeyman in two. We use the four levels here and define them more fully in Chapter 9.

These levels are held in many task competencies – things like the ability to develop plans, and the ability to understand and manage risk. Some other commentators will talk of these task competencies as hard skills. These levels are also held in many contextual competencies. Contextual competencies allow the manager to relate to their people and function in their organisation. Some other commentators might refer to these as soft skills. It's often said that soft skills trump hard skills, but we would argue that all are equally necessary.

Importantly, we introduce the idea that managers will inevitably be Trainee, Supervised Practitioner, Practitioner or Expert in many competencies but certainly not Expert in all. This gives the notion of management development: targeting important competencies in which the manager has lower than necessary skills and knowledge.

Competence in hard and soft skills – task and contextual competencies – is not the only thing needed. We also highlight that in highly technical industries, managers must be steeped in the technologies of the business. We describe this as having domain knowledge. It's unlikely, for example, that a manager of teachers could be an accounts generalist. No amount of task and contextual competencies in an accounting practice could enable management in a school. Likewise, it's unlikely that a project manager could lead a software engineering firm. It might work out initially, but as the demands on the manager grow, the gaps in understanding would lead to ever-greater mistakes.

To complete the competency set, we also highlight the need for managers to learn what we term management primitives and associated normative processes. Management primitives are like the surgeon's procedures. Taking blood from a patient's vein is a routine that all medics must learn. For managers, it's the use of a spreadsheet, or the ability to complete a risk assessment. Managers must establish and grow their competence in necessary management primitives.

As we illustrate in other chapters, performance of groups of employees is an essential management outcome. Performance of others is the essence of management, and we amplify this. It's not about the manager – it's about their direct reports and all the people working in the business for whom the manager is responsible. We note that acceptance of this idea is one mark of Kneebone's Expert. It's an awakening, enabling further management growth.

We discuss when a manager becomes an expert. We argue that expert is achieved when the manager has amassed enough theory and understanding to be able to improvise solutions. Improvisation does not mean abandoning skills and knowledge, but rather it means using the substantial theory and understanding to build custom approaches, methods and processes tailored to the organisation and context.

So how long does it take to become an expert manager – someone who is Practitioner or Expert in many, if not most, of the necessary competencies? That's a difficult question to answer. It's context specific – specific to the person, their foundation training and experience, and to the nature of the business – but if we are pushed for an answer, we'd say that it's unlikely that anyone would achieve such competence with less than ten years of mixed study and experience.

One of the popular counters against any form of linear manager development is that business today requires agility. This, so the argument goes, precludes managers from knowing what competencies they need. As a result, personal qualities like emotional intelligence and business acumen, so the argument goes, must prevail. Such arguments suggest that since businesses must grasp opportunities as they emerge, there's no place for planning – and no place for management training. We disagree.

Louis Pasteur, the famous microbiologist, said that "chance (or opportunity) only favours the mind which is prepared." He was referring, in a speech, to the Danish physicist Oersted who was said to have accidentally discovered electro-magnetism. Pasteur noted that all scientists must be ready to use knowledge and experience to interpret new phenomena to further new science. In essence, he was saying there's nothing accidental or chance-based about opportunity. And so it is with management. Managers must be trained and ready to use their competencies, and to improvise new techniques and processes to exploit opportunities.

To conclude, we believe that management development is poor in the UK. There are many reasons why this state has come about: government policy promoting coaches as the panacea; the demise of large firms and their training programmes; media deification of the (untrained) entrepreneur; and a public despising of the manager class. But it doesn't have to be so. We outline here what's needed and the benefits to be gained.

Success as a manager requires candidates to learn the theory behind management science, and to do time through the Journeyman phase to become Supervised Practitioner or Practitioner in most management competencies. Then the real learning can begin, and the manager can cautiously acknowledge that they might be expert and have become a manager.

Bibliography

ACAS (2015) *Code of Practice on Disciplinary and Grievance Procedures, Code of Practice 1*, ACAS, TSO (The Stationery Office).

Alice speaks to the Cheshire Cat (from *Alice in Wonderland* by Lewis Carroll) at https://www.cs.cmu.edu/~rgs/alice-VI.html, accessed on 25th April 2022.

Bakker, A. B. & Leiter, M. P. eds. (2010) *Work Engagement: A Handbook of Essential Theory and Research.* Hove, East Sussex: Psychological Press.

Bandura, A. (1994) *Self-efficacy.* In V. S. Ramachaudran (Ed.), Encyclopedia of Human Behavior, Vol. 4, pp. 71-81. New York: Academic Press.

Bartram, D. (2005) *The Great Eight Competencies: A Criterion-Centric Approach to Validation,* Journal of Applied Psychology, Vol. 90, No. 6, pp. 1185–1203.

Blau, P. M. (2008) *Exchange and Power in Social Life.* London: Transaction Publishers.

Bloom, B.S., Engelhart, M.D., Furst, E.J., Hill, W.H., Krathwohl, D.R. (1956). *Taxonomy of educational objectives: The classification of educational goals.* Vol. Handbook I: Cognitive domain. New York: David McKay Company.

Boyatzis, R. E. (1982) *The Competent Manager: A Model for Effective Performance.* New York: John Wiley & Sons.

Brooks Jr, F.P. (1982) *The mythical man-month: Essays on Software Engineering.* Reprint with corrections ed. Reading, Massachusetts: Addison-Wesley Publishing.

Buchanan, D.A. & Huczynski, A.A. (2010) *Organisaitonal Behaviour.* 7th ed. Harlow: Pearson.

Burnes, B. (2004) *Kurt Lewin and the Planned Approach to Change: a Re-appraisal,* Journal of Management Studies 41:6, September.

Burnes, B. (2009) *Managing Change: A strategic approach to organisational dynamics.* 5th ed. Harlow: Pearson.

Checkland, P.B. (1981) *Systems Thinking, Systems Practice.* Chichester: John Wiley.

Chikudate, N. (2009) *If human errors are assumed as crimes in a safety culture: A lifeworld analysis of a rail crash,* Human Relations, Volume 62(9), pp. 1267–1287.

CIPD (2013) *Has job turnover slowed down,* Chartered Institute of Personnel and Development, Megatrends Report.

CIPD (2016) *Could do better? Assessing what works in performance management,* Chartered Institute of Personnel and Development, Research Report, December.

CIPD (2016) *Rapid evidence assessment of the research literature on the effect of performance appraisal on workplace performance*, Chartered Institute of Personnel and Development, Technical Report, December.

Coase, R.H. (1937) *The Nature of the Firm*, Econonmica, New Series, Vol. 4, No. 16, pp. 386-405.

Douglas, T. (1978) *Basic Groupwork.* London: Tavistock Publications.

Edwards, B.D., Bell, S.T, Arthur, W & Decuir, A.D. (2008) *Relationships Between Facets of Job Satisfaction and Task and Contextual Performance*, Applied Technology: An International Review, No. 57(3), pp. 441-465.

Federation of Communications Services, *Gerald David Award for Innovation in Business Radio* at https://www.fcs.org.uk/wp-content/uploads/2021/02/19-05-30-The-Gerald-David-OBE-Award-2019-Final-FORM.pdf, accessed on 18th October 2022.

Fletcher, C & Baldry, C (1999) *Multi-Source Feedback Systems: A Research Perspective*, International Review of Industrial and Organizational Psychology, Volume 14.

Forrester, J. W. (1961) *Industrial Dymanics.* 1990 reprint ed. Cambridge, MA: MIT Press.

Frijda, N.H. (2007) *The Laws of Emotion.* New York: Routledge.

Frischmann, B. & Selinger, E. (2018) *Re-engineering Humanity*, Cambridge, UK: Cambridge University Press.

Goldstein, I.L. & Ford, J.K. (2002) *Training in Organizations: Needs Assessment, Devleopment and Evaluation.* 4th ed. Belmont, CA: Wadworth.

Grässle, P., Baumann, H. & Baumann, P. (2005) *UML 2.0 in Action: A Project-Based Tutorial.* Birmingham: Packt Publishing.

Gunz, H. & Peiperl, M. (2007) *Handbook of Career Studies.* Los Angeles: Sage Publications.

Hackman, J. R. & Oldman, G. R. (1980) *Work Redesign.* Reading, Massachusetts: Addidon-Wesley Publishing.

Hackman, J.R. and Oldham, G.R. (1976) *Motivation through the design of work: test of a theory,* Organizational Behavior & Human Decision Processes Vol. 16, pp. 250-279.

Haidt, J. (2006) *The Happiness Hypothosis: Putting Ancient Wisdom and Philosophy to the Test of Modern Science.* London: Penguin.

Health and Safety Executive, *What are the Management Standards?*, at https://www.hse.gov.uk/stress/standards/ accessed on 18th October 2022.

Heslin, P.A., Carson, J.B. & VandeWalle, D. (2009) *Practical Applications of Goal-Setting Theory to Performance Management*, Performance Management, January.

Hofstede, G., Hofstede, G. J. & Minkov, M. (2010) *Cultures and Organizations: Software of the Mind.* New York: McGraw Hill.

Holland, J.L. (1997) *Making Vocational Choices: A Theory of Vocational Personalities and Work Environments*, 3rd Edition, Odessa: Psychological Assessment Resources.

Holliss, F. (2015) *Beyond Live/Work: the architecture of home-based work*. London: Routledge.

ILM (2011) *Great expectations: Managing Generation Y*, Institute of Leadership & Management and Ashridge Business School.

Jackson, M. (2013) *The Age of Stress: Science and the Search for Stability*. Oxford: Oxford University Press.

Jackson, R., Locke, M., Hogg, E. & Lynch, R. (2019) *The Complete Volunteer Management Handbook* (4th edn.). London: Directory for Social Change.

Johnson, G., Scholes, K. & Whittington, R. (2005) *Exploring Corporate Strategy*. 8th ed London: Prentice Hall International.

Jost, J.T. (2015) *Resistance to Social Change: a psychological perspective*, Social Research Vol. 82: No. 3.

Kanfer, R., Chen, G. & Pritchard, R.D. (2012) *Work Motivation: Past, Present and Future*. New York: Routledge.

Kaplan, R.S. & Norton, D.P. (2008) *The Execution Premium: Linking Strategy to Operations for Competitive Advantage*. Boston: Harvard Business Press.

Kehr, H.M. (2004) *Integrating Implicit Motives, Explicit Motives, and Perceived Abilities: the compensatory model of work motivation and volition*, Academy of Management Review, Vol. 29, No. 3, pp. 479-499.

Kellerman, B. (2012) *The End of Leadership*. New York: Harper Collins.

Kepner, C.H. & Tregoe, B.B. (1997) *The New Rational Manager: An Updated Edition for a New World*. Princeton, New Jersey: Princeton Research Press.

Khaneman, D. (2012) *Thinking Fast, Thinking Slow*. London: Penguin Books.

Kneebone, R. (2020) *Expert: understanding the path to mastery*. London: Penguin Books.

Knight, F.H. (2014) *Risk Uncertainty and Profit*, Mansfield Centre, CT: Martino Fine Books

Korn Ferry points factor work measurement at https://focus.kornferry.com/work-measurement-a-refresher/ accessed on 22nd October 2022.

Latham, G.P. & Locke, E.A. (1991) *Self-regulation through goal setting*, Organisational Behaviour and Human Decision Process, Vol. 2 (Part 2), pp. 212-248.

London Fire Brigade (2018) Witness statements to the Grenfell Inquiry from London Fire Brigade officers at https://www.grenfelltowerinquiry.org.uk/evidence accessed on 4th November 2018.

Machiavelli, N & Marriott. W.K. (2006) *The Prince*. Ann Arbor, MI: Borders Classics.

Mankin, N.G. & Taylor, M.P. (2006) *Economics*. London: Thomson.

McGuire, D & Hutchings, K (2006) *A Machiavellian analysis of organisational change*, Journal of Organisational Change Management, Vol 19, No 2, pp. 192-209.

MODUK - DEF STAN 00-250: PART 0 - Human Factors for Designers of Systems Part 0: Human Factors Integration (replaced by Def Stan 00-251) at https://www.gov.uk/guidance/uk-defence-standardization accessed on 4th November.

Morrell, M. & Capparell, S. (2001) *Shackleton's Way: Leadership Lessons from the Great Antarctic Explorer*, London: Nicholas Brearley Publishing.

Page Arnot, R. (1955) *A History of the Scottish Miners*, London: George Allen & Unwin.

Perkins, S.J & White, G (2009) *Employee reward: alternatives, consequences and contexts*, London: CIPD.

Peters, J.P. & Waterman, R.H. (1982) *In Search of Excellence: Lessons from America's Best-Run Companies*, New York: Harper & Row.

Pfeffer, J. (2015) *Leadership BS: Fixing Workplaces and Careers One Truth at a Time.* New York: Harper Collins.

Pink, D.H. (2011) *Drive: The Surprising Truth About What Motivates Us.* Edinburgh: Canongate.

Poole, J. (2014) *Textbook on Contract Law.* 12th ed. Oxford: Oxford University Press.

Porter, M. (2004) *Competitive Advantage: Creating and sustaining superior performance.* New York: Free Press.

Ramage, M. & Shipp, K. (2009) *Systems Thinkers.* London: Springer.

Ratner, P. (2019) *200 cognitive biases rule our everyday thinking.* Neuropsych, January 24th, 2019 at https://bigthink.com/neuropsych/cognitive-bias-codex/ accessed on 23rd May 2022.

Reilly, P. (2003) *The Link Between Pay and Performance.* London: The Institute for Employment Studies.

Reynolds, M. & Holwell, S. eds. (2010) *Systems Approaches to Managing Change: A Practical Guide.* London: Springer.

Rhodes, E. & Wield, D. (1998) *Implementing New Technologies: Innovation and the Management of Technology.* 2nd ed. Oxford: NCC Blackwell.

Robertson, I & Cooper, C. (2011) *Well-being: productivity and happiness at work.* Hampshire: Palgrave Macmillan.

Robertson, I. (2013) *The Winner Effect: The Science of Success and How to Use It.* London: Bloomsbury.

Rousseau, D.M. (1995) *Psychological Contracts in Organisations: Understanding Written and Unwritten Agreements.* London: Sage Publications.

Rousseau, D.M., Ho, V. & Greenberg, J. (2006) I-*Deals: Idiosyncratic Terms in Employment Relationships*, Academy of Management Review, Vol. 31, No. 4, pp. 977–994.

Rumelt, R.P. (2012) *Good Strategy Bad Strategy: The Difference and Why it Matters.* London: Profile Books.

Sartain, L & Schumann, N. (2006) *Brand from the inside: eight essentials to emotionally connect your employees to your business*. San Fransisco: Jossey-Bass.

Schmidt, F.L. & Hunter J. (2004) *General Mental Ability in the World of Work: Occupational Attainment,* Journal of Personality and Social Psychology 2004, Vol. 86, No. 1, pp. 62-173.

Scoular, A. (2001) *The Financial Times Guide to Business Coaching.* Harlow: Pearson.

Senior, B. (1997) *Organisational Change.* Harlow: Pearson.

Skills Development Scotland (2018) *What are national occupational standards?* At https://www.ukstandards.org.uk accessed on 4th November 2018.

Smith, A. (1993) *An Inquiry into the Nature and Causes of the Wealth of Nations.* Reissued 2008 ed. New York: Oxford University Press.

Smith, I. & Baker, A. (2010) *Smith & Wood's Employment Law.* 10th ed. Oxford: Oxford University Press.

The Cognitive Bias Codex - 180+ biases at https://commons.wikimedia.org/wiki/File:The_Cognitive_Bias_Codex_-_180%2B_biases,_designed_by_John_Manoogian_III_(jm3).png accessed on 23rd May 2022.

Tucker, P. & Folkard, S. (2012) *Working Time, Health and Safety: A Research Synthesis Paper*, Conditions of Work and Employment Series No. 31, International Labour Office, Geneva.

Various papers on motivation and retention at https://worldatwork.org/ accessed on 7th June 2022.

Waisfisz, B. (2015) *Constructing the Best Culture to Perform.* Helsinki: itim International.

Wedderburn, A.A.I. (1967) *Social Factors in Satisfaction with Swiftly Rotating Shifts*, Occupational Psychology, No. 41, pp. 85-107.

Wyatt, C. (2013) *Military faces huge challenges, new chief Houghton says*, BBC online at https://www.bbc.co.uk/news/uk-24605083, accessed on 22nd October 2022.

Yourdon, E. (1989) *Modern Strcutured Analysis.* Englewood Cliffs, New Jersey: Prentice-Hall International.

Yuki, G. (2010) *Leadership in Organizations.* 7th ed. New York: Pearson.

Index

A

Absence, 228
  management, 229, 230
  trends, 229, 230
  typical profile, 228
Abstract reasoning, 55, 68, 69, 73, 140,
  289
Accidental leaders, 56
Accidental managers, xxvi, 2, 32,
  299, 310, 311
Accountabilities
  CEO/MD, 97, 302
  defining, 62, 64
  individual, 42
Annualised hours, 103, 232
Appeals
  appealing the decision, 174, 182, 183,
    191
  process, 182
Apprenticeship schemes, 68
Artificial intelligence (AI), 99, 291
Attitudes and beliefs, 71, 126, 217, 284,
  286, 289
Audit, 78, 102, 114, 237, 306, 307, 316
Automation, 291

B

Back-to-work interview, 230
Bad behaviour, 178, 179, 275
Balanced scorecard, 15, 16, 18, 20, 155,
  156, 157, 168, 223
  individual, 157
Behaviours, 71, 197, 199
Behaviours (as a result of motivation), 39,
  127, 145, 179
Behaviours (as a result of personal
  characteristics), 6, 75

Beliefs, 71, 139
Benchmarking, 78, 249, 251, 256, 267
Benefits, 20
Benefits (hybrid working), 13
Benefits in kind, 247
Bias, xx, 139, 140, 141
  in appraisals, 160
  in selection, 75, 76, 77
Bias training, 140
Big 5 personality traits, 69, 70, 220
Board members, 10, 11
Board of Directors, 10, 92
Bradford factor, 229, 230
Branch office, 14
Brand building, 108
Bullying and harassment, 183,
  184, 185, 192
Bullying (culture of), 185
Burnout, 113, 129, 227, 228, 239
Business case, xx, 195, 290, 314
Business outcomes, 7, 35, 63, 126, 213,
  279
Business plan, 63, 164, 283, 296, 302
Business-to-business contract, 10, 14, 57

C

Capability, 51, 98, 100, 193, 270,
  272, 288, 300, 312
  existing, 205, 207, 296
  gaps, 173
  improvement, 6, 195, 272
  necessary, 178, 207, 282
  new, 212, 291
Capability (from skills and knowledge),
  198
Capability (from technology), 5, 98, 99
Capability model, 282
Career, 82, 83, 202, 203, 265

breaks, 232
path, 143, 201, 203, 300
progression, 122, 174, 201, 202, 245
protean, 103
Protean, 202
Casual labour, 60
Casual workers, 58, 60
Change, 269, 272, 293
    agile approach, 288
    change manager, 282, 283, 294
    change plan, 284, 288
    effect of experience, 286
    mandate, 285
    processes, 274, 294
    project, 283
    psychology of, 284
    success, 274
    trends in, 287
Changing people, 284, 297
Changing technology, 291
Chief Executive Officer, 3, 11, 312
Chronic fatigue, 238
Coaching, xxiv, 50, 134, 136, 198, 211,
    323
Coercion (in leadership), 31, 53, 55
Cognitive processes, 40, 69
Commission (in pay), 119, 153, 252
Commitment, xix, 72, 77, 82, 88,
    102, 123, 124, 125, 128, 138,
    144, 202
    affective commitment, 123, 144
    attachment needs, 124, 129
    continuance commitment, 123
    normative commitment, 123
Company culture, 274
Company Sick Pay, xx
Company structure, 29, 274
Company system, 93
Competencies, 6, 70, 99, 197, 199
Competency frameworks, 208, 314
    organisational, 206, 282
    personal, 205, 206, 214
Competency level
    definitions, 201
    expert, 70, 201
    of manger competence, 302
    practitioner, 70, 201

supervised practitioner, 70, 201
    trainee, 70, 201
Competent manager, 164, 314, 319
Competitive advantage, 63, 92, 100, 109,
    158, 203, 248, 272, 288, 312
Compressed working week, 232
Computer-mediated communications, 36,
    103, 105
Concept modelling, 29, 199
Confidence (experience), xxi, 83, 119, 198,
    301
Confidentiality, 106
Conscientiousness, 70, 74, 119
Contextual competencies, 313
Contextual performance, 158, 159, 168, 302
Contingent leadership, 44
Contract for services, 58, 87, 95, 242
Contracting out work, 95
Contract of employment, 14, 22, 58, 59,
    79, 87, 95, 124, 125, 171, 173, 189,
    192, 229, 242, 245, 290
    contract of service, 10, 95, 171, 191, 242
    types of, 57, 59, 103
Contract of sale, 90, 95, 114
Contractors, 10, 57, 58, 87, 202, 204, 290
Contracts, 37
Control, 61
Controls
    duck test, 61, 87
    health, safety and wellbeing, 236, 237
    risk management, 112, 113
Coping (wellbeing), 219, 221, 223, 224,
    239
Copyright, Designs and Patents Act 1988,
    ii, 176, 296
Covid pandemic, xix, 12, 56, 105, 115,
    233, 234
Crass management, 83, 113, 125, 172,
    198, 225, 296
Criminal records, 76
Criteria (in recruitment), 140
Cultural impact, 130
Cultural intelligence, 131
Culture, 45, 130, 131, 135, 138
Culture model, 130, 131
Customer satisfaction, 150

D

Decision making, 39
Decision making (ideal), 139
Decision making (rational), 141
Decision making (real), 139
Deductions, 60, 246
Defining performance, 157
Defining quality, 101
Defining wellbeing, 217
Delegating, 24, 92, 94
Demotivators, 126, 127
Descriptive statistics, 228, 274
Development intervention, 209, 214
Development investment, 193
Disciplinary, 178
Disciplinary decisions, 181, 183
Disciplinary procedure, 22, 173,
    178, 183, 187
Discipline (defining), 173
Discrimination, 139, 245, 266
Discrimination (gender), 143
Dismissal, 59, 174, 290
Dispersed firm, 12
Disputes, 172, 173
Distributive justice, 242, 266
Diversity, 75
Duty of care, 230, 235
Dyadic theory of leadership, 38
Dynamic model of change, 275, 276, 297

E

Earnings potential, 253
Earnings security, 20
Easy-going culture, 45
Economic contract, 172, 173, 176, 177,
    192, 242, 266
Effort-reward relationship, 242
Electronic communications, 12, 36, 51, 138
Emotional behaviour, 133
Emotional intelligence, 134, 159, 318
Emotions, 52, 129, 132, 133, 134, 145,
    172, 211, 223, 248, 286, 294, 310
Employee behaviour, 124, 129, 173, 219
Employee benefits, 58, 231, 232
    total reward, 66

Employee capabilities, 194
Employee development, 15, 215, 290
Employee needs, 124
Employee performance, 17, 118, 144, 147,
    149, 161, 222, 227
Employee rights, 246
Employee self-efficacy, 72
Employee tenure, xix, 83, 202, 208
Employee training, 23
Employer-employee relationship, 82, 171,
    192
Employment agencies, 60
Employment intermediary, 60
Employment relationship, 61, 62, 171, 175
Employment Rights Act 1996, 176
Employment status, 10, 57, 58, 59, 60,
    61, 91
Employment tribunal, 59, 61, 86, 142, 171,
    176, 183, 189, 190, 191
Employment tribunal claim, xx, 182, 189,
    190, 191
Employment tribunal (early conciliation),
    189
Employment tribunal (managers-evidence),
    190
Empowerment, 39
Engagement, 72, 82, 128, 150, 161, 175,
    227
Engagement-building benefits, 232
Enterprise value (at sale), 296
Entrepreneur, 2, 8, 28, 57, 90, 91, 92, 134,
    136, 171
Equality, 142
Equality Act 2010, 76, 142, 145, 176, 183,
    185, 188, 230, 245
Eudaimonic wellbeing, 223
Exceeding expectations, 197
Excellence, 28, 197
Experience curve, 286, 288, 298
Expert manager, 300, 311
Explicit motives, 43, 119, 127, 128,
    196
External locus of control, 119
External standards, 199
Extra-to-role behaviour, 158, 159
Extrinsic motives, 126, 127, 159, 223, 227,
    232

F

Fairness
  in pay and benefits, 242, 247
  in selection, 75
Fatigue, 235, 238
Fear of failure, 198
Feedback
  job characteristics, 35
  model, xxi, xxvi, 41, 117, 144, 151, 207,
    308, 309
  performance, 144
  recruitment and selection, 81
Feedback-driven management, 117
Feed-forward model, 308
Final written warning, 181, 188, 189
First written warning, 189
Flexibility, 103
Flexible working, xix, 59, 78, 104, 107,
  115, 233, 234
Forecasting, 277, 279
Foreign workers, xx, 14
Formal meetings and processes, 104, 171,
  173, 179, 184, 185
Formal procedures, 175
Freelance workers, 58, 60

G

Game theory, 188
Gender inequality, 143
Gender pay gap, 143, 145, 244, 257
General mental ability, 55, 73, 87, 119
Generation Y, 78, 195, 275, 321
  employees, 195
Gig-economy, 60
Goal illumination, 38, 39, 41, 56,
  152
Goods and services, 14, 28, 90, 91, 92, 98,
  102
Great 8 competencies, 200
Grievance, 173, 174, 182, 186
  meetings, 183
  procedure, 177, 182, 187, 319
Group behaviour norms, 137, 138
Group culture, 138
Group (formation of), 137
Group objectives, 156

Growth needs strength, 42, 71, 72, 82, 127,
  134, 218
Guiding principles (in strategy), 14, 16

H

Harassment, 183, 184, 185
Hard systems methodology, 292, 295
Headhunting, 67, 68, 87
Health and safety
  accidents, 150, 235, 237, 238
  incidents, 235
  loss of revenue, 237
  management of, 106, 234, 235, 236
  management process, 236
  obligations, 58, 105, 185, 235
Health screening, 76
Hedonic wellbeing, 223
High performance (in talent), 207
Home working, xix, 105, 106, 107, 232,
  233, 234, 240, 259
HSE model, 225, 226
Human characteristics, 6, 273
Human competence, 5, 17, 99, 100, 101,
  157, 194, 278, 286
Human resource management, 124, 272,
  315
Hysteresis (in change), 286

I

Identity (in job characteristics), 35, 121,
  122, 223
Idiosyncratic employment deals, 266
Implicit motives, 127, 128, 197
Impression management, 39
Improvement metrics, 310
Income tax, 246, 284
Independent medical review, 188
Inducting new staff, 81
Inflated salaries, 257
Influencing, 32, 34, 152
Influencing (followers), 31, 33, 38
Informal discussions and proceedings, 179
Informal procedures, 175
Informal workplace mediation, 179
Injustice, 82, 85, 86, 133, 214, 244, 245
Innovation, 4, 100, 109, 110, 131

Input-process-output model, 34, 280
Inspection of deliverables, 102
Instruction (to do work), 21, 209
Instrumentality of money, 218
Intelligence, 32, 55, 68, 69, 289
   crystallised intelligence, 68, 136, 289
   emotional intelligence, 134, 159, 318
   fluid intelligence, 289
   innate intelligence, 69
   tests, 73
Intention to quit (ITQ), 82
Interdependent objectives, 156
Intermediary (as employer), 10, 60, 187,
   204, 242
Internal and external perspectives (in
   modelling), 281
Internal (implicit) motives, 119
Internal locus of control, 119
International teams, 138
Internship, 83
Interviewing, 66, 73, 74, 76
Interview questions, 74
Intrinsic motives, 39, 42, 72, 126, 127, 223,
   227, 232, 252
Investigations, 141, 181, 182, 187
   formal investigations, 173, 180
   investigating officer, 180, 182
   investigation report, 180
Investors, 4, 5, 9, 271, 295

J

Job accountabilities, 199
Job change (disciplinary/capability
   sanctions), 189
Job characteristics, 118
   autonomy, 35, 118, 121, 122, 221, 223
   significance, 35
Job classification (in job evaluation),
   254
Job conditions, 221
Job crafting, 123
Job description, 61, 63, 64, 66, 97, 120,
   151, 168, 197, 206, 237, 290
Job design, 85, 121, 123, 129
Job evaluation, 253
Jobholder, 8, 70, 121, 199, 253

Job offers, 77
Job purpose, 64
Job ranking (in job evaluation), 253
Jobs, 62
Job satisfaction, 23, 114, 122, 123
Job scope, 64
Job security, 222
Job share, 232
Joint problem-solving (in appraisal),
   166

K

Knowledge workers, 202, 203

L

Labour market, 20, 248
Laissez-faire leadership, 46
Leader, 33
   leader personality, 54
   leader selection, 32
Leader-follower relationship, 33, 37, 45, 49
Leaderless leadership, 47
Leadership, 8, 31, 33, 119, 197, 289
   authentic leadership, 39
   democratic leadership, 48
   despotic leader, 31
   directive style, 8, 46
   distributed leadership, 47, 48
   dyadic leadership, xxv, 35, 40, 45, 49,
     50, 51, 53, 55, 138, 157, 171, 238, 294
   language of leadership, 33
   leadership approaches, 42, 45, 54, 55
   leadership context, 51
   leadership interventions, 32, 42
   non-directive leadership style, 8, 45, 46,
     47, 134, 163, 315
   vocabulary, 33
Leadership competence, 274
Leadership selection, 53
Leading change, 294
Learning goals, 152
Locus of control, 197, 221
Lone working, 235
Lost opportunity (developing employees),
   195
Low wellbeing, 217, 229

M

Make or buy decision, 92, 296
Management, 7
  action, 6, 16, 81, 124, 128, 130, 179,
    195, 208, 232
  board, 10
  culture, 238
  quality of, xxiii
  team, 302, 312, 313
Management learning, 312
Management primitives, 305
Management standards (HSE), 225, 226
Manager, 1, 11
Manager behaviour, 274
Manager competence, 164, 302
Manager development, 53, 134, 164, 318
Manager-employee relationship, 20, 153,
    172, 192, 232
Manager intervention, 138, 289
Manager selection, 134
Managing Director (MD), 314
Managing long term absence, 230
Managing scarcity, 256
Managing stress, 224
Managing wellbeing, 217
Manpower plan, 63, 64, 71
Market median salary, 248
Market price (in pay), 20, 90, 243, 248,
    249, 255, 260, 267
Matrix management, 50
Matrix structure, 161
McKinsey 7-S model, 27
Meaningfulness, 39, 43, 122, 201
Measuring performance, 150
Measuring successful development, 212
Median pay, 243, 244, 248, 257
Mediation, 185
Mentoring, xxiv, 50, 211
Method statement, 22
Mindfulness, 131, 134, 140
Minimum wage, 58, 60, 246
Modelling, xxvi
Modelling (change), 279, 281, 283, 284
Modelling sub-systems of a firm,
    280, 281
Motivating potential, 72, 126, 129, 223

Motivation, 8, 17, 34, 118, 119, 125, 151,
    194, 227
Motivational variables, 127
Motives and motivators, 126

N

National culture, 130
National Insurance Contribution (NIC),
    242, 246
National Living Wage, 246
National Minimum Wage, 246
National Occupational Standards, 199
Needs
  affiliation, 85, 107, 134, 137, 218, 221, 223
Needs theory, xxvi
Negative hygiene factor, 153
Negative hygiene factors, 85, 86, 244
Non-conformity, 101, 118
Numerical reasoning, 68, 69

O

Objectives, 120, 197, 206
Objective setting, 51, 147, 151, 154, 162,
    168, 206, 208
Occupational health practitioner, 230
Online recruitment, 67
Open culture, 45, 111
Operating procedures, 193
Operations, 89
Opportunity cost, 195
Organisational citizenship behaviours, 161
Organisational culture, 115, 131, 240
Organisational development, 99, 272
Organisation chart, 63, 64
Organisation structure, 49
Outcomes, xxi, 2, 25, 34, 120, 121, 196
Outcomes (collective performance), 308,
    310
Outcomes (required), 37, 46, 52, 70, 194,
    197, 211, 270, 272, 304
Overtime, 103

P

Pairwise comparison (in job evaluation),
    253, 254

Participation (in leadership), 39
Path-goal theory, 39
Patterns of work, 103
Pay, 10, 20, 241, 266
    annual, 241, 245
    commission, 252
    company sick pay, 261
    company Sick Pay, 260
    hourly wage, 245
    international pay, 258
    negotiating, 250, 257
    negotiation, 20
    pay and benefits, 252, 260, 262, 263
    pay differences, 244
    pay distribution, 248, 250, 251
    pay policy, 248
    pay structures, 250
    pay systems, 247
    performance related, 252, 266
Paying employees, 242
Pay systems
    banded pay, 250
Pay transparency, 258
Pensions, 20, 247, 264
    automatic enrolment, 247
People skills, 144
Perceived abilities, 127, 196, 198
Performance, xxi, 8, 17, 39, 196
Performance (achievement orientation),
    148, 152
Performance appraisal, 26, 147, 148, 158
    meetings, 149, 163, 167, 169
    performance appraisal system, 162, 164,
        167, 208
    ratings, 161, 164
Performance appraisal (quality), 160
Performance-based pay, 251
Performance dependencies, 118, 157
Performance goals, 152, 160
Performance (growth orientation), 148,
    152
Performance improvement, 148, 178
Performance indicators, 28, 34, 120, 150,
    195
Performance management, 104, 147, 148
Performance variance, 118
Personal achievement, 204

Personal characteristics, 32, 56, 99, 120,
    220
    pro-activity, 178, 198
Personal development, 79, 122, 140, 161
Personalised Power (P-power), 2, 135, 136,
    164
Personality, 32, 69, 70, 119
Personality inventory, 70
Personality profile, 54, 73
Personal outcomes, 36, 121, 196, 221, 222,
    269, 296
Personal service (test for), 61
Person-environment fit (P-E fit), 72, 124,
    129, 221
Person specification, 64, 65, 66, 67, 80, 87,
    151, 302
Physical capital, 219
Physiological maladies, 217
Physiological wellbeing, 219, 221, 222,
    223, 224, 239
Points factor (in job evaluation), 255
Policies and procedures, 22, 95, 96, 97,
    177, 179, 180
Power, 134, 166
Predictive validity (in selection), 66, 73,
    74, 75, 77, 87, 160
Pre-employment screening, 76
Preferences (in personal characteristics), 71
Prejudice, 142
Prejudice (in selection), 75
Presenteeism, 229
Principle accountabilities, 205
Private medical treatment, 20
Procedural justice, 125, 167, 243, 266, 300
Procedural leadership, 39, 43, 55
Process model, 97
Productivity, xxiii, 6, 150, 204
Productivity (role of), 271
Professional approach (leadership), 8, 38,
    39, 42, 43, 44, 50, 55
Profit, 6, 25, 34
    normal profit, 19
    profit and loss account, 62, 279
    profit motive, 19
    super-normal profit, 19, 28
Proof beyond reasonable doubt, 174
Proof of claims (in selection), 76

Proof on balance of probabilities, 174
Protected characteristics, 142, 184, 257
Psychological capital, 219
Psychological contract, xix, 79, 122, 172, 173, 176
Psychological maladies, 217, 218
Psychological need for power, 135
Psychological wellbeing, 219, 221, 222, 223, 224, 239
Psychometric testing, 32, 65, 66, 87
  15FQ+, 70
  16PF, 70
  NEO-PI, 70

Q

Quality, 6, 25, 34, 124, 150, 175, 204, 299
  assurance, 102
  costs, 150
  improvement, 101

R

Rate factor (in job evaluation), 255, 267
Rating performance, 158, 159, 160
Rational decision making, 310
R&D (research and development), 108, 110, 156
Reasonable belief (in decision making), 174, 180, 181, 183, 231
Recording (audio recording of meetings), 181
Recruiting volunteers, 83
Recruitment
  continuous recruitment, 80
Recruitment agencies, 66, 87
Recruitment and selection life cycle, 64, 65
Red-circling (in pay), 79
Reduced hours, 232, 234, 265
Reduction in pay (as sanction), 189
Redundancy, xix, xx, 25, 60, 125, 202, 218, 258, 269, 271, 282, 288, 290
Redundancy (business case), 290
Reference performance, 40, 41, 118
References, 76, 79
Regulated jobs, 194
Required performance, 51, 72, 126, 193, 197, 251

Resilience (in wellbeing), 217, 219, 221, 222, 225, 229, 239
Respect, 37, 55, 71, 78, 82, 83, 144, 178
Responsibilities, 26, 63, 97
Re-structure, 26, 251
Retaining volunteers, 85
Retention (staff), 81, 82
Rich picture, 293, 294, 298
Risk, 113, 235
  assessment, 113, 115, 235, 240, 317
  management, 112
Roadblock removal, 38, 56, 152
Role of the manager, 94

S

Safe patterns of work, 237
Safety, 7, 34, 150
Sales funnel model, 155
Scarcity, 256
  in job value, 253
  in labour market, 248
  scarcity supplement, 257
  supplement, 248, 254, 257, 267
Scientific method (in management), 53, 308
Search criteria, 64
Seasonal workers, 58
Selection, 73, 75, 76, 80
  assessment centres, 65
  testing, 75
Selection criteria, 64
Self control, 136, 165, 173
Self-directed learning, 209
Self-efficacy, 37, 152, 196
Self-employment, 57
Self-esteem, 119, 221
Setting objectives, 147, 153, 154, 157, 162
  organisational, 155
  personal, 156
Settlement agreement, xx, 188
Sexual harassment, 184, 187
Shareholders, 1, 5, 9
Shift work, 103, 238
Sickness absence, 228
Simulated work, 198
Skills, 70, 80, 194, 197

Skills and knowledge, xx, 195
Skills shortage, 80
Small to medium sized firm (SME), 2
Social class (in power), 166
Social exchange, 44, 166
Social exchange theory, 44, 124
Socialised power, 2, 135, 136, 145, 165
Social security, 234
Soft systems methodology, 293, 294, 295,
    298
Spatial nature of work, 104
Specialisation, 91, 287
Specification (of work), 22
Spill-over, 217, 219, 239
Staff development, 193, 204
Staff handbook, 79, 176, 177
Stakeholders, 1
Standardisation, 288
Standard operating procedure, 22, 193
Statement of work, 22
Static force-field model, 276
Statutory minimum pay, 244
Statutory payments, 246
    adoption, 247
    maternity, 247
    paternity, 247
    shared parental pay, 247
    sick pay, 247
Statutory Sick Pay (SSP), xx, 260
Strategy, 15, 112, 155, 198, 205, 223
Strategy (change), 269
Stress, 224
Stressors, 219, 224
Structured interviews, 74
Sub-contractors, 10, 57, 176
Subjective norms (in beliefs), 71
Subsistence needs, 124
Substitution value (at sale), 296, 297
Succession planning, 134, 160, 208,
    211
Super-motivation, 128, 129, 144, 223, 227,
    228, 232, 239
Supervisory board, 10
Supplier, 11
Supplier agreements, 90
Suppliers, 10, 20, 57, 87
Suspension, 185, 187

Sustainability, 111, 112, 271, 295
Systematising the firm, 93
System boundary, 94, 280
System (company), 17
Systems model, 278
Systems modelling, 17
    concept model, 18, 29, 63, 64, 114, 121,
        123, 199
    for change, 277
    simple system model, 94
    systems dynamics, 17, 29, 280
Systems of work, 273

T

Talent management, 207, 208
    process, 207
Task competencies, 313
Task performance, 158, 161, 168, 223
Taxonomy of skills, 211
Team building, 51, 102, 137
Teams, 33, 136
    self-managed, 48
    virtual teams, 51
Technical competence, 53
Technology, 4, 5, 36, 98, 99, 194
    function, 5, 17, 19, 70, 99, 100, 101, 113,
        115, 157, 178, 194, 278, 286, 288,
        291, 296
Temporal nature of work, 103
Terms and conditions of employment, 59,
        177, 245, 266, 290
Term-time working, 232
Thematic analysis, 180, 294
Theory of the firm, 90, 92, 287
Threats, 112, 237
    health and safety, 237
Threats (to the business), 113
Total reward, 265, 267
Touch points, 108, 109
Training, 20, 22, 96
    computer-based, 210
    effective instruction, 209
    evolved opportunities, 211
    one-on-one interventions, 210
    self-directed learning, 209
    simulated work, 210

traditional classroom, 198, 210
    training transfer, 213
Training transfer, 198
Transactional leadership, 40, 44, 56, 238
Transfer (of the firm), 295
Transformational leadership, 8, 40, 43, 55, 238
Trust, 24, 44, 52, 106, 125, 137, 138, 163, 172, 178, 188
Trust (during change), 290
Turnover, 6, 25, 28, 34

U

Understanding change, 275
Unified Modelling Language (UML), 280, 320
Unstructured interviews, 74

V

Valuation (on sale), 297
Values, 71
Verbal reasoning, 68, 69, 289
Verbal warning, 181, 189
Vetting, 76, 79
Volunteers, xxi

W

Walk through (work process), 102
Wellbeing, 217
    hedonic wellbeing, 223
    high wellbeing, 217, 218, 221, 239

impact of environment, 220
    intoxicants, 230
    measuring welbeing, 222
    negative impacts, 218, 221
    self-assessment, 222
Wellbeing-related benefits, 232
Why people work, 218
Witness statement, 188
Witness statements, 187, 321
Work breakdown structure (WBS), 95, 114, 306
Workers
    agency, 58, 204
Work experience, 83
Work groups, 127, 137, 144
Working conditions, 78, 144, 255
Work instruction, 21, 95
Work-life balance, 115, 122, 265
Workloads, 224
Work review
    manager, 104, 120, 151, 161
    peer review, 43, 102, 113, 300
    quality, 114, 237
Work sample tests, 65, 66, 74, 76, 77, 87
Written offer, 79
Written Statement of Employment
    Particulars, 176, 177
Written warning, 181, 189

Z

Zero defects (in quality), 101
Zero rejects (in quality), 102

CPSIA information can be obtained
at www.ICGtesting.com
Printed in the USA
BVHW021912160223
658686BV00010B/193